THE SILENT DICTATORSHIP

Martin Kitchen is Professor of History at
Simon Fraser University, Burnaby, B.C.,
Canada

KITCHEN, Martin. The silent dictatorship: the politics of the German high command under Hindenburg and Ludendorff, 1916–1918. Holmes & Meier, 1976. 301p bibl index 76-16055. 20.00 ISBN 0-8419-0277-1. C.I.P.

CHOICE　　*MAR. '77*
History, Geography &
Travel

Europe

Once one gets past the repellent physical appearance of this book (for $20.00, one expects justified margins), one comes up against an intellectual problem. Kitchen (Simon Fraser University), the author of two respectable studies of German military history, takes as his starting point the thesis of Marx, as modified by Engels, that the Bismarckian Reich was a "bonapartist" state. By extension, the Wilhelmian Reich that fought the 1914–18 war was also "bonapartist," without any redeeming democratic features; and the "pseudo-plebiscitary military dictatorship of the High Command" (Hindenburg-Ludendorff) was the logical conclusion of the "bonapartism" of the Bismarckian system and a way-station on the road to the demagogic, fascist dictatorship of Hitler. To reduce the complexities of history to such oversimplified terms seems a crime against the craft of the historian. As Kitchen, however, is a trained historian, has done a great deal of archival research (at least in the Reich archives), and has a thorough mastery of the published sources, the end product is not too bad. The Marxian

The Silent Dictatorship

The politics of the German High Command
under Hindenburg and Ludendorff, 1916-1918

MARTIN KITCHEN

HOLMES & MEIER PUBLISHERS, INC.
NEW YORK

First published in the United States in 1976
by Holmes & Meier Publishers, Inc.
101 Fifth Avenue
New York, New York 10003
Copyright © by Martin Kitchen 1976

Library of Congress Cataloging in Publication Data

Kitchen, Martin.
    The silent dictatorship.

    Bibliography: p.279
    Includes index.
    1. Germany – Politics and government – 1888-1918.
2. European War, 1914-1918 – Germany. 3. Hindenburg, Paul von,
Pres. Germany, 1847-1934. 4. Ludendorff, Erich, 1865-1937.
5. Germany. Heer. Oberkommando. I. Title.
DD228.8K5   1976   940.3'43   76-16055
ISBN 0-8419-0277-1

Printed in Great Britain

CONTENTS

To My Mother and Father

PREFACE

This book could not have been written without the generous and continued support of the Canada Council, for which I am most deeply grateful. I have also been greatly helped by the archivists of the *Politisches Archiv des Auswärtigen Amts,* Bonn; the *Deutsches Zentralarchiv,* Potsdam and Merseburg; the *Bundesarchiv,* Koblenz; the *Heeresarchiv* and the *Hauptstaatsarchiv,* Stuttgart; the *Staatsarchiv,* Ludwigsburg; the *Bundesarchiv Militärarchiv,* Freiburg; and the *Bayerisches Hauptstaatsarchiv.* Dr Wilhem Deist gave me much valuable help, and very kindly allowed me to see the unpublished manuscript of his excellent collection of documents on the domestic politics of the army in the war. Dr R.K. Debo and Dr L.E. Hill made some helpful criticisms and suggestions. The remaining faults are all my own. Laurence Olivier corrected many stylistic defects. The encouragement and assistance of Professor F.L. Carsten has been invaluable, and my debt to him is very great. Finally, my wife and children have had to put up with more than the usual discomforts of a scholar's family, and yet have been unfailingly cheerful and understanding. To them I owe a very special debt of gratitude.

INTRODUCTION

In the course of the First World War the structural weaknesses and contradictions within German society became increasingly acute under the strain of a war that affected all aspects of life. Just as the contradictions themselves had long been present, so the attempt to overcome them by means of a pseudo-plebiscitory military dictatorship of the High Command was the application of a form of rule that can be called characteristic of the Second Reich, even though in a drastic and critical situation it assumed a new and more radical form.[1]

The fundamental cause of these problems lay in the course of Germany's economic development. Industrialisation occured in Germany at a later date than in the other leading industrial states of the nineteenth century, and it was also more rapid and uneven. Social change and the growth of bourgeois liberalism lagged far behind the startling developments of industry. Concentration and monopolisation of industry was already far advanced before significant sectors of the economy had been fully industrialised. The result of this uneven development was the continuing existence of a large, though precarious class of petit-bourgeois artisans, a class that was constantly threatened with proletarianisation and loss of status, and which was therefore particularly susceptible to the anti-modernist and ultra-reactionary propaganda of anti-industrial conservatives. This petite-bourgeoisie could easily be mobilised by demagogic appeals for a struggle for God and King against a rapacious capitalism.[2]

At first it seemed that the conflict between the forces of production which were pressing forward, and the restorative social order that acted as a hindrance to further development, which had reached a political climax in the constitutional crisis of the early 1860s in Prussia, was solved by the *klein deutsche* solution of 1866. The victory over Austria effectively ended the constitutional crisis, gave Bismarck tremendous prestige and cemented Prussian domination in Germany and Junker domination in Prussia; but it soon became clear that Prussia had transferred its problems to Germany where they were to become even more intense. In the period of liberal free trade from 1866 to 1873, under the aegis of

Rudolph von Delbrück, the 'chief of general staff of the free traders', capital was released from the restraining influence of the state, and, given a further stimulus by the victory over France in 1870-71, further dramatic advances were made. The excitement and prosperity of the *Gründerjahre* helped to divert men's attention from the social question, and hence the effects of the great depression of 1873-96 were all the more acute.[3]

As a consequence of the depression the alliance of 1879 was formed under the shadow of protective tariffs: the alliance of 'rye and iron', of feudal estate and blast furnace, of the Junkers and industrial bourgeoisie. But the interests of these two groups were contradictory, and it was not long before it became apparent to the more far-sighted political scientists, among them Max Weber, that the economic forces that were unleashed by the unification of Germany under Prussia were likely to destroy the old and antiquated ruling class that was now no longer economically viable. The aristocracy, the officer corps and the bureaucracy could only preserve their predominance, in a period of rapid industrialisation and of universal suffrage, at the cost of creating further divisions and tensions within society, which were to prove increasingly difficult to master. Germany was thus plagued with divisions that could not be overcome without radical change and democratisation. There were the contradictions between Prussian hegemony and German federalism, between economic modernisation and constitutional reaction, between the bourgeois concept of legality and the demands of the military and bureaucratic elites, between agrarians and industrialists, and between bourgeoisie and proletariat, to name only the more obvious. These contradictions could only be papered over by frantic political juggling and the application of panaceas which in turn created further and more serious problems. The characteristic form of government in Germany from Bismarck to Hitler was thus bonapartism.[4]

It was Karl Marx who, in his brilliant essay 'The 18 Brumaire of Napoleon Bonaparte' gave classic expression to the theory of bonapartism. For Marx, bonapartism was a form of bourgeois rule in which the bourgeoisie felt unable to maintain its social position and had to relinquish political power to an independent executive authority. This form of rule was supported by peasants who upheld the bourgeois ideals of private property, but because they were not organised as a class were unable to enforce their class interests and therefore had to be represented. They thus looked up to authority to 'send them rain and sunshine from above'. Bonapartist government was further supported by the class of *declassés* whom Marx called *la bohème*. These were the rootless of all classes who lived in an ideological no-man's-land and who saw in the bonapartist state the possibility of finding a comfortable position within a grossly inflated bureaucracy. Here the petite-bourgeoisie, caught in the ideological crossfire of capital and labour, fearful of proletarianisation, yet hostile towards big capital, saw a gleam of hope. This alliance was held together by its own particular ideology. There was the resounding appeal to the glorious napoleonic tradition of nationalism, revolution and the victories of the army. Marx expanded his ideas on bonapartism in the 'Civil War in France' of 1871. In this essay he calls bonapartism 'imperialism', which he defines as 'the most prostitute and the ultimate form of state power which nascent middle class society had commenced to elaborate as a means of its own emancipation from feudalism, and which full-grown bourgeois society had finally transformed into a means for the enslavement of labour by capital'. The secret of this imperialism, or 'caesarism', was that it claimed to transcend the class divisions of society and act for the good of all. It claimed to rest on the support of the peasants, who were little concerned with the struggle between capital and labour; of the working class, who supported the destruction of parliamentarism which placed government in the hands of the propertied classes; of the bourgeoisie, because it guaranteed their economic position and relieved the threat of a democratic revolution; and finally it claimed to bring all these classes together in the pursuit of national glory. For Marx imperialism, or bonapartism, was the characteristic form of government when the bourgeoisie had lost or had not yet gained the ability to rule, and the working class had not yet developed enough to take its place.

Marx never applied his analysis of the class structure of the France of Napoleon III to the Germany of Bismarck, but his model is of considerable importance for the understanding of the Second Reich. It was Engels who saw the striking similarity between the two regimes. Writing to Marx in April 1866 he said that:

it is increasingly obvious that the bourgeoisie does not have what it takes to rule directly, and as there is not an oligarchy as there is in England which can take over the job of running the state and society, in return for generous payment, therefore a bonapartist semi-dictatorship is the normal form of rule; it looks after the great

material interests of the bourgeoisie, often against the will of the
bourgeoisie, but it does not allow them any part of government. On
the other hand this dictatorship is bound in turn to adopt the
material interests of the bourgeoisie, however reluctantly.[5]

Engels pointed to Bismarck's manipulative use of universal suffrage,
certainly in the tradition of Louis Napoleon, and described bonapartism
as the 'true religion of the modern bourgeoisie'.

Marx and Engels were by no means alone in thinking that the key to
Bismarck's policy, both foreign and domestic, lay in his attempt to
create, in Wilhelm Liebknecht's words, 'a princely insurance company
against democracy'. Jacob Burckhardt, for example, believed that
Bismarck's foreign policy was conducted in order to 'solve internal
difficulties', and that his wars were fought to counteract the pressures
of democracy and social change.[6] At the same time the true nature of
his rule was disguised to a considerable extent by the fact that he
appeared as the Kaiser's faithful servant and adviser, the protagonist of
conservative and traditional policy; but what often appears as
paradoxical in Bismarck's policies, the curious combination of the
conservative and the radical, was all part of his bonapartist approach.

The new tariffs of 1879 gave the industrialists and the agrarians the
protectionism they demanded, and the anti-socialist laws reinforced
their position against the demands of the working class. Repression
against the labour movement became all the more necessary for
Bismarck as the direct result of the protective tariffs was a worsening
of the condition of the working class. For Bismarck the anti-socialist
laws were a 'prophylactic institution' against danger from the left, and
it was in exactly the same sense that he instituted his social reforms,
which were the price he had to pay for overcoming the increased
tensions within Germany caused by his economic policy.[7] In his social
policy he freely admitted the influence of Napoleon III, for he admired
the skilful way in which Napoleon had taken the wind out of the left's
sails by rendering most Frenchmen dependent on the state, by making
France a nation of *rentiers.* For Bismarck, a state pension was an
excellent price for the ruling class to pay for social quiet, for he argued
that when a nice little pension was at stake few would risk revolutionary
violence against a benevolent state.

The combination of protective tariffs, repression of the labour
movement and social legislation proved inadequate as a means of
overcoming the intensified social divisions of Germany during the great
depression. More radical tricks were needed. Among such devices

Bismarck was perfectly prepared to use anti-semitism for his own political purposes.[8] Anti-semitism could play a useful role in a bonapartist state in that it could provide a scapegoat for social ills. Social aggressions could be diverted from their objective source and directed towards a group, in this case the Jews, that had nothing whatever to do with the objective cause of the aggressions. In Bismarck's Germany, the Jews played a particularly convenient role in that they could be identified to a certain extent with the 'spirit of capitalism', and could thus be used to mobilise and radicalise the discontented *declassés* against the modern age. By stimulating reactionary politics, anti-semitism could in turn discredit the bourgeois democracy of the industrial state. Anti-semitism furthermore was used to obfuscate class divisions. Race was intended to transcend class, and hatred of the Jews could be transformed into hatred of Bismarck's political opponents.

Bismarck never used anti-semitism as ruthlessly for his own political aims as it was later to be used in Germany, and he was in no sense a rabid anti-semite, knowing full well that radical anti-semitism could get out of hand and could present further problems to his regime, rather than help to strengthen the established order. He preferred to use foreign policy to reinforce his position at home. Just as in 1866 and 1870-71 he had used the crises with Austria and France to the advantage of his domestic policies, so with his imperialism and his manipulative use of foreign political crises, either real or deliberately fabricated, he was to attempt to buttress up the social *status quo* against the unrelenting forces of change.[9] The problems that beset such a policy were greater than ever. Foreign policy could be used to neutralise domestic political tensions, but there was an ever narrower field for manoeuvre. Bismarck's need to preserve the peace in Europe was such that there could be no repeat of the Schleswig-Holstein crisis, the Austro-Prussian war, or the Franco-Prussian war. At the same time the tensions at home that needed to find some outlet were to become ever more severe, particularly in the period of economic stagnation from 1882-86.

Bismarck's imperialism offered some relief to the economic and structural problems of the Reich. Foreign trade, state intervention in economic affairs and the beginnings of a formal empire offered some hope to the advanced capitalism of Germany that was caught in a cyclical depression. Imperialism also provided a useful means of disguising class divisions in a society that was becoming increasingly polarised as political reform became a pressing need. Imperialist enthusiasms, heightened by a crude anti-English nationalism, were the

effective ingredients of the political strategy of Bismarck and his
successors.[10] Social imperialism was thus part of an attempt to preserve
the social *status quo* at a time of rapid economic advance and social
change. As the need for fundamental change in the structure of German
society became more and more acute, so the attempts to divert this
political energy outside the Reich in the pursuit of imperialist goals
became all the more frantic.

If bonapartism in Germany was the result of an attempt to reconcile
economic modernisation and the preservation of the social *status quo,*
it was also constitutionally the only truly adequate form of government.
The pluralist society is the most effective form of bourgeois democracy
in that the opposition groups are effectively institutionalised and
integrated into the larger society. The opposition is loyal. This
characteristic form of government has little in common with the
constitutional practice of the Second Reich. By labelling the opposition
groups as 'enemies of the Reich', and by excluding them from effective
participation in political life, Bismarck blocked a significant social
safety valve and hampered the political and constitutional development
of Germany, so that it was soon to become hopelessly inadequate for
the needs of a modern industrial society. Germany was without
institutionalised means of integration, and with its anti-parliamentary
and conservative constitutional structure, integration had to be provided
by a figure who could inspire general approval and acclamation.
Constitutionally it was the Kaiser who was called upon to unite the
divergent elements of a socially and economically divided society and
because of his particular position he might be able to help the people
forget their differences and unite in a national group against enemies,
real or imaginary, at home and abroad. Here a bonapartist element was
immanent within the system, and William II's particular brand of
charismatic leadership and popular absolutism in the early years of his
reign was a perfectly adequate interpretation of his constitutional
function. Indeed during the war, when the Kaiser relinquished his
authority, the integrating role of the monarch was no longer in effect,
and the problems that this created for the conduct of the affairs of
state were considerable.[11]

Universal suffrage proved to be a useful implement of Bismarck's
bonapartist rule. By granting universal suffrage Bismarck had drawn the
sting from the liberals and had even gained the reputation in some
conservative circles of being a dangerous liberal himself. Universal
suffrage also gave the regime a pseudo-plebiscitary dimension that could
be used to maintain the *status quo.* But universal suffrage was not

without its obvious dangers when, as a result of a dramatic population change and increase, rapid urbanisation, and a significant growth of the wage earning class, the calculations on which it was based were proved false. Germany was no longer an agricultural country but an industrial state. Bismarck had enfranchised a conservative peasantry, and could therefore accept Lassalle's challenge to grant universal suffrage. Now universal suffrage was to become the weapon of an ever-increasing industrial proletariat led by a vigorous and well-organised political party. The 'red peril' was now both a useful myth and an alarming possibility. Bismarck and his successors had two answers to this problem — repression and the concentration of forces of the anti-socialist and anti-democratic parties: on the one hand the anti-socialist laws, the anti-subversion bill *(Umsturzvorlage)*, the penitentiary bill *(Zuchthausvorlage)*, the *Lex Arons* and the anti-socialist activities of the army; and on the other hand the concentration of the bourgeois parties, the compromise of political principles and interests in defence of the existing order, the policy of *Sammlungspolitik*.[12] The alliance of Junkers and industrialists supported by the small entrepreneurs and artisans was at best a marriage of convenience of the parties of order, but it could not overcome the often conflicting interests of the partners. By 1890 it was in ruins, was revived again under Miquel, but was further weakened with the collapse of the Bülow Block.

Sammlungspolitik, in spite of its ups and downs, and the fundamental contradictions on which it was based, was the characteristic political alliance of the era. Bonapartism, counter-revolution and *Sammlungspolitik*, aimed against England and Russia abroad and the proletariat at home, as Eckart Kehr argued, had to be constantly stimulated if it were not to fall apart. Prestige politics and social policy as insurance against social change were thus designed to hold this alliance together. As social stresses became greater, Bismarck's imperialist formula no longer seemed adequate. Something more drastic and dramatic was needed. 'World Politics', the bid for world power, was the new and more aggressive form of German imperialism.

The outward and visible expression of 'World Politics' was the fleet of Admiral Tirpitz, whose naval programme is a vivid expression of the politics of the ruling class of Wilhelmine Germany.[13] Tirpitz was determined that the fleet should be used to provide a 'great new national task which will bring economic gain and act as a powerful palliative against educated and uneducated social democrats'. In another passage Tirpitz wrote that the naval programme would place the 'social order in quarantine'. But his programme went further than a mere preservation of the social *status quo,* it was also politically reactionary. He attempted to revive Bismarck's recipe of an *Aeternat,* a perpetual naval bill that would obviate the need to secure Reichstag approval for the navy estimates, and thus severely limit the power of parliament. But Tirpitz's cure made the disease worse. The financial problems of the Reich dashed his *Aeternat* scheme and intensified the struggles between the opposition parties in the Reichstag and the proponents of a vast naval programme; and even more serious was the fact that however successful the fleet programme might be in achieving its domestic political aims, in foreign policy it was to exacerbate relations with England, provide evidence of the virulence of German imperialism and raise the possibility of a world war.

The mass support for the naval programme was provided by the Navy League *(Flottenverein)* which was but one of the many highly organised and effective interest groups of the post-Bismarckian period.[14] The interest groups were an alternative though often complementary means of circumventing the Reichstag and strengthening the bonapartist elements of the regime. They were a more strident and ultimately more dangerous form of political organisation. As Germany's wealth and population grew there was a vast increase in government funds, and as the bonapartist approach called for vigorous government intervention and social legislation it was caught in the unfortunate contradiction of thus strengthening to some degree the legislative body that it was attempting to weaken. The interest groups, organised on a mass scale, provided a form of anti-parliamentary pseudo-democratisation that seemed to offer a useful alternative to bourgeois democracy. The most significant of these groups politically was the Farmers' League *(Bund der Landwirte).* It was the first successfully organised mass organisation of this type. Its ideology was nationalistic, *völkisch,* social-darwinist, middle class and anti-semitic. Its political aims went far beyond the mere maintenance of agricultural interests, for its ultimate goal was a counter-revolution that would destroy industrial society. Its racism, anti-pluralism, cultural pessimism and its deliberate attempt to obfuscate class divisions gave to its ideology a distinct proto-fascist flavour. There is, moreover, a clear influence of such ideas on the thinking of the High Command (OHL), shown particularly in some of the more extreme memoranda of Colonel Bauer, which shows that the protagonists of total war, of the full exploitation of industrial technology could find an anti-industrial and anti-modernist ideology appealing, without stopping to consider the radical contradictions that such a combination of ideas involved.[15]

Just as bonapartism was incapable of resolving the social and political problems which it could merely obscure, so the interest groups proved to be an inadequate safeguard against the development of industrial society. The inability of the ruling class to stop the inevitable course of economic and social change, and the fact that their recipes often did little more than exacerbate the situation, gave them a sense of growing frustration. The fear of revolution at home, and a growing fatalism towards the inevitability of a European war, made many feel that a *coup d'état* from above was the only viable alternative to revolution from below.[16]

The idea of a *coup* was fraught with obvious dangers, the more so as those who had helped to intrigue against Bismarck feared that he might return as a '*coup d'état* chancellor', hardly an attractive prospect. A modified form of the *coup d'état,* which would have involved repressive legislation passed by the Reichstag, met with strong opposition and had to be abandoned. As the social democrats grew in strength it became obvious that the only viable Reichstag alignment would have to involve a break with the conservatives and a commitment to parliamentary reform − but such a policy would be considered capitulation, and Bethmann Hollweg was certainly not the man to engineer such a drastic political change. Frustration at the inability of bonapartism, *Sammlungspolitik* and the interest groups to provide viable solutions to the problems that beset an entrenched conservative order led to the characteristic politics of the Wilhelmine era − the politics of 'full steam ahead', the *Flucht nach vorn.* This was to give an even more aggressive accent to the necessary corollary of such radical conservative politics, the anti-English, anti-Russian and anti-proletarian thrust of imperial Germany. This in turn was to lead Germany into a war which was intended to strengthen the social *status quo,* but which Germany was objectively bound to lose.[17]

At first it seemed that the war was to achieve everything for which peacetime politics had striven so hard. The war seemed to provide a solution to the racial, class and economic problems of the Reich, and was an admirable substitute for the hopes and aspirations of those who thought in terms of a radical change in society. Many socialists had thought that governments would not go to war because they feared that it would lead to revolution. In fact the reverse was true. The declaration of a national defensive war, the end of party political strife in the *Burgfrieden,* and the war aims dangling like an enormous imperialist carrot in front of the noses of the German people, were all the natural consequences of these prewar developments. In August 1914 it seemed,

to use Toennies' terminology (which in turn was so much a product of
the age) that society *(Gesellschaft)* had become a community
(Gemeinschaft), thus reversing a trend which Toennies found distasteful
but inevitable in capitalist society. In spite of all divisions men were
united in a common purpose, and the field grey uniform seemed to
disguise class differences. This feeling was further heightened by the
initial successes of German arms, the speedy defeat of Belgium, the
march on Paris and the victory of Tannenberg in the east. The daring
war plan of Graf Schlieffen, a *va banque* strategy which was the military
expression of the politics of the age, seemed to be working its magic.
A dead man's dream of a gigantic Cannae seemed near to realisation.
But it soon became clear that the French could not be outflanked.
Errors of planning and execution and the shortage of men and materials
made it impossible for Schlieffen's plan to be realised, and in spite of
the extraordinary efforts of the German troops, it was the Germans who
were in danger of being outflanked by the French. At the Marne it was
the French, not the Germans who won a decisive battle. The Schlieffen
plan was in ruins. Both sides now tried to outflank the other in the
'dash for the sea', but neither side was successful. Germany had placed
all her hopes on a swift victory in the west as the only way out of her
precarious position. Now she was forced to fight a trench war and was
locked in a battle of materials in which she was almost certain to be
defeated. The situation was all the more serious in that the Austrian
offensive in the east had also proved a failure. Both the Serbians and
the Russians in Galicia had repulsed the Austrians and inflicted heavy
casualties, and there was soon a distinct possibility that the Carpathian
front would not hold.

Falkenhayn, who had hoped to break through at Ypres, and thus
escape from the *impasse* that some more far-sighted men realised would
result in the defeat of Germany, failed in his objective. The dreams of
world politics were dashed, and to add insult to injury, the Japanese
government declared war on 23 August and quickly seized Kiautschou
and the German possessions in the South Seas. Yet although the
frustration of the German war plan was an indication that the strategic
and operative aims of the army were out of all proportion to the
economic and human resources of the country, this fact only made the
ruling class more determined to fight until Germany had achieved an
indisputable position as a world power. They now found themselves in
the paradoxical position of demanding more excessive war aims as the
weakness of Germany became more obvious. Economic and military
shortcomings were thus used as evidence not that Germany should

attempt to negotiate a peace on the basis of the *status quo*, but that it should continue to fight so that her position would be impregnable in the next, and hopefully final battle for world power. Although many were aware of the precarious position of the Central Powers, the nationalists feared nothing more than a 'too hasty peace'. At the same time the parties of the *status quo* argued that the war would have to be fought to the bitter end for fear that the alternative would be social revolution. Victory would secure the social, political and economic domination of the 'national' parties. A peace that did not compensate for the sacrifices which had been made, it was argued, would cause such bitter resentment that it would spark off a revolution. Thus the war was continued for world power and the preservation of the *status quo*, but with totally inadequate means for the achievement of these aims. As the war continued the stresses and strains, which many had hoped the war would cure, were in fact intensified by the war itself; the means chosen to overcome them were incapable of providing a solution, and indeed further intensified them.

Moltke's successor as chief of general staff, Falkenhayn, no longer believed that the war could be won in a decisive battle, the more so after the appalling blood letting at Langemarck and the failure of the Ypres offensive. He now believed that the only hope lay in a strategy that would steadily weaken the enemy — *Ermattungsstrategie.* He hoped that a series of limited operations, aimed at tactical objectives, would gradually weaken the enemy and force the Entente to sue for peace. Falkenhayn felt, as had Schlieffen before him, that the decision would have to be sought in the west, but with a different strategy. Conversely Hindenburg and Ludendorff, flushed with their recent triumph, still believed in Schlieffen's concept of a battle of annihilation, but felt that it would have to be fought in their own theatre of war, in the east. Hindenburg and Ludendorff were however denied a repeat performance of the battle of Tannenberg, their initial and spectacular victory. The winter battle in Masuria, although it drove the Russians out of East Prussia, could not be followed up to gain the strategic objective of an encirclement of the Russian army. The Austrian operations in the Carpathians ground to a halt with heavy losses, but in April 1915 the German and Austro-Hungarian attack on the Russian lines at Gorlice was successful, and a breakthrough was achieved along thirty miles of the front. This was followed by further successes which resulted in the Central Powers occupying Warsaw and Brest Litovsk by August. But these successes in the east meant that there were inadequate reserves in the west where the German lines were constantly attacked, and the

operations at Arras, La Bassée, Artois and the Champagne could only be
halted by placing an almost intolerable strain on the German troops. The
pause in the fighting on the western front in the winter of 1915-16
came not a moment too soon.

There were thus two schools of strategic thinking which were in
increasing opposition to each other.[18] Hindenburg and Ludendorff still
believed in the possibility of a decisive battle that would win the war,
and thought in terms of a vast operation to outflank and encircle the
enemy. They were supported by the Austrian chief of staff, Conrad,
who constantly plagued Falkenhayn for reserves from the western
front so that he would be able to mount a large-scale offensive in
northern Italy that would force Italy out of the war, make possible a
massive joint attack on France that would lead to victory in the west,
and above all boost the morale of Austria-Hungary which was
threatening to fall apart under the stress of war. Falkenhayn still
believed that his strategy of slowly weakening the enemy offered the
only viable military solution. However much the Central Powers needed
a decisive victory, this could not be even operationally mounted
without building up sufficient reserves, and these reserves would have
to come in large part from the trenches of the western front.
Falkenhayn knew that he could not spare the men, and Hindenburg and
Ludendorff, when they were appointed to the supreme command, soon
realised that his judgement had been correct, even though they had
constantly and often viciously attacked him for failing to give them the
support which they felt they deserved.

If the strategy of the decisive battle was based on a serious
underestimation of the situation on the western front, and could
provide no satisfactory solution to the problem of defeating Britain and
France, the *Ermattungsstrategie* was based on equally fallacious
principles. In a war of attrition the Central Powers were bound to be
defeated, for they were unable to call upon the almost unlimited
reserves of men and material available to the Entente. The desperate
attempts to overcome the logic of this situation by unrestricted U-boat
warfare, by the Hindenburg Programme and the auxiliary labour law
were all inadequate.

In 1916 Falkenhayn tried to find a middle way. He did not believe
that it would be possible to force a breakthrough on the western front
as had been achieved in the east at Gorlice, but on the other hand he
wished to gain the initiative with a more active strategy. Convinced that
it was on the western front that the war would have to be won, he
decided on a massive attack on the fortress of Verdun. In order for his

plan to work he insisted that Verdun did not have to be taken, but rather that it should be constantly threatened, thus dragging more and more French reserves into the trap. The local army commanders, however, were determined to take the fortress. There was thus further confusion in a plan that was at best the result of desperation rather than clear and logical thinking, and which was highly ambiguous. Verdun soon threatened to become another Ypres, and Falkenhayn's reputation, which had never recovered from his set-backs in November 1914, suffered a further decline. The losses at Verdun on both sides were dreadful, the operation marking a new and ghastly phase in the history of warfare. The German high command refused to call off the offensive, fearful that an admission of failure after such a costly operation would have disastrous consequences. Although Verdun had strained the French army, and had called upon the last of the French reserves, the German army was in turn seriously weakened and was unable to exploit the advantages of this situation at any other point on the western front.[19]

The offensive against Verdun did much to upset the Entente's plans for an offensive in 1916, but while the attack on Verdun was still in progress the battle of the Somme began. Again the losses were appalling, the number of losses (killed and wounded) on both sides being about one and a quarter million, but the Entente was no more able to achieve its objectives than the Germans had been at Verdun. Although the line was held, the military position of Germany was now very serious. Verdun had failed, the battle of the Somme hung in the balance, and the successful use of tanks by the British army was a particular threat. In the east the Russians mounted the Brusilov offensive with considerable success. The Austrians lost 200,000 as prisoners, and had to evacuate Southern Galicia and the Bukovina. The Italians were also successful in their operations against the Austrians; in August Gorizia was taken by the Italians. Shortly afterwards Rumania declared war on the Central Powers. Such then was the military background of the appointment of Hindenburg and Ludendorff to the High Command on 29 August 1916.

The politics of the High Command under Hindenburg and Ludendorff must be seen against the background not only of the failure of the strategy of Moltke and Falkenhayn, but also in the wider perspective of the problems facing German society since Bismarck. They were called upon to engineer the decisive battle that Falkenhayn had failed to produce, and they were to restore unity to a badly divided nation. They were needed to deliver the decisive victory that would secure the achievement of the extensive war aims of the ruling class, and which it was hoped would cement the social *status quo*. The enormous popularity of Hindenburg, who had become a figure of almost mythical proportions, gave the supreme command a plebiscitary dimension which was to be exploited to the full by the military propagandists and chauvinist politicians. The country was to be united behind Hindenburg to achieve the 'Hindenburg Victory' which would provide a panacea to all Germany's problems.

No one was more fully aware than William II of the implications of Hindenburg and Ludendorff's appointment. He had failed to provide the leadership that was essential if there was to be administrative and political integration. In the 1890s William II had, to a certain extent, been the 'National Imperator', but in wartime the 'Supreme Warlord' was pushed into the background. William was aware of his shortcomings, but he did little more than write irascible and often foolish marginal notes on official papers, and indulge in periodic sabre rattling. He knew that Hindenburg and Ludendorff's appointment, accompanied by public clamourings on their behalf, was likely to have serious consequences for his constitutional position. Reluctantly conceding the public request for their appointment, William II knew that he was travelling further than he wished along the road to 'democracy', even if in practice that democracy was to be a form of military dictatorship. Bismarck had been careful to disguise the true nature of his bonapartist rule behind a discreet monarchical and traditional cover. Hindenburg and Ludendorff had few such scruples. Their 'state socialism' went far further than Bismarck's cynical manipulations of Lassallian ideas. Their ideology of the equality of field grey was far more extreme than Bismarck's appeals to the 'productive classes'. Their imperialist aims were far more extensive, just as the *Vaterlandspartei,* their main political support, was a radical version of *Sammlungspolitik.* The politics of the High Command under Hindenburg and Ludendorff were a militarised form of bonapartism. Their form of military dictatorship was as incapable of solving the problems of Germany at war, as was Bismarck's rule of solving the peacetime difficulties that beset an entrenched and outmoded social order. The intensification of those difficulties under the stress of the world war, and the violence of the remedies proposed by the High Command, only served to make the situation worse. The gulf that separated the excessive war aims from the possibility of achieving them could never be bridged, but those aims could also not be abandoned without changing the power constellation of the Reich. This interaction of social, political, economic and military forces makes the politics of the High Command under Hindenburg and Ludendorff unusually complex, but this complexity is an indication of the significance of the period for an understanding of the course of German history since Bismarck.

NOTES

1. As yet there has been no satisfactory study of the effects of the world war on German society. A. von Mendelssohn-Bartholdy, *The War and German Society*, New Haven 1937, offers some suggestions for lines of research. Jürgen Kocka, *Klassengesellschaft im Krieg 1914-1918*, Göttingen 1973, provides some useful material but gets tied up into some curious methodological knots. Marc Ferro, *The Great War 1914-1918*, London 1973, is a provocative essay.
2. See particularly: H. Böhme, *Deutschlands Weg zur Grossmacht*, Cologne 1966; H. Böhme, *Prolegomena zu einer Sozial — und Wirtschaftsgeschichte Deutschlands in 19. und 20. Jahrhundert*, Frankfurt 1968; P. Benaerts, *Les Origines de la grande industrie allemande*, Paris 1933; H. Bechtel, *Wirtschaftsgeschichte Deutschlands*, Munich 1956; K.E. Born, 'Der soziale und wirtschaftliche Strukturwandel Deutschlands am Ende des 19 Jahrhunderts', *Vierteljahrsschrift für Sozial — und Wirtschaftsgeschichte*, 50, 1963; A. Gerschenkron, *Bread and Democracy in Germany*, Berkeley 1943; G.W.F. Hallgarten, *Imperialismus vor 1914*, 2 Vols., Munich 1963; T.S. Hamerow, *Restoration, Revolution, Reaction. Economics and Politics in Germany*, Princeton 1958; W.G. Hoffmann, *Das Wachstum der deutschen Wirtschaft seit der Mitte des 19. Jahrhunderts*, Berlin 1965; W.G. Hoffmann, 'The Take-off in Germany', in *The Economics of Take-off into Sustained Growth*, ed. W.W. Rostow, London 1963; Hans Rosenberg, *Probleme der deutschen Sozialgeschichte*, Frankfurt 1969; W. Zorn, 'Wirtschafts — und Sozialgeschichtliche Zusammenhänge der deutschen Reichsgründungszeit 1850-1879', *Historische Zeitschrift*, Band 197, 1963; Wolfgang Sauer, 'Das Problem des deutschen Nationalstaates', *Politische Vierteljahrsschrift*, Band 3, 1962.
3. H. Rosenberg, *Grosse Depression der Bismarckzeit*, Berlin 1967; K.W. Hardach, *Die Bedeutung wirtschaftlicher Faktoren bei der Wiedereinführung der Eisen — und Getreidezölle in Deutschland*, Berlin 1967; also S.B. Saul, *The Myth of the Great Depression 1873-1896*, London 1969 with a useful bibliography.
4. E. Engelberg, 'Zur Entstehung und historischen Stellung des preussisch-deutschen Bonapartismus', in *Beiträge zum neuen Geschichtsbild*, hrg, F. Klein, J. Streisand, Berlin 1956; H. Gollwitzer, 'Der Cäsarismus Napoleons III im Widerall der öffentlichen Meinung Deutschlands', *Historische Zeitschrift*, Band 173, 1952; for a contrary but unconvincing view see: A. Rein, *Bonapartismus und Faschismus in der deutschen Geschichte*, Göttingen 1962; and A. Rein, *Die Revolution in der Politik Bismarcks*, Göttingen 1957. For the relationship between bonapartism and fascism see Martin Kitchen, 'August Thalheimer's Theory of Fascism', *Journal of the History of Ideas*, I, 1973.
5. Engels to Marx 13-4-1866, *Marx-Engels-Werke*, Vol. 31, p. 208.
6. Hans-Ulrich Wehler, *Bismarck und der Imperialismus*, Cologne 1969, p. 456.
7. See particularly H. Heffter, 'Bismarcks Sozialpolitik', *Archiv für Sozialgeschichte*, 3, 1963; W. Vogel, *Bismarcks Arbeiterversicherung*, Braunschweig 1951; A. Manes, 'Arbeiterversicherung in Deutschland', *Handwörterbuch der Staatswissenschaften*, Band I, 1903; H. Rothfels, 'Bismarck's Social Policy and

the Problem of State Socialism in Germany', *Sociological Review*, 30, 1938;
F. Lütge, 'Die Grundprinzipien der Bismarckschen Sozialpolitik', *Jahrbücher
für Nationalökonomie und Statistik*, 134, 1931; G. Adler, *Die imperialistische
Sozialpolitik*, Tübingen 1897.

8. See particularly P.W. Massing, *Rehearsal for Destruction*, in German as
Vorgeschichte des politischen Antisemitismus, Frankfurt 1959; Max
Horkheimer, 'Die Juden und Europa', *Zeitschrift für Sozialforschung*, Jahrgang
8, 1939, Heft 1 and 2; M. Nitzsche, *Die handelspolitische Reaktion in
Deutschland*, Stuttgart 1905; H.J. Puhle, *Agrarische Interessenpolitik und
preussischer Konservatismus im Wilhelminischen Reich*, Hanover 1966;
Rosenberg, *Grosse Depression*.

9. Wehler, *Bismarck und der Imperialismus* is an excellent modern study of the
problem of Bismarck's imperialism with a valuable bibliography. For a brief
account of his findings see Hans-Ulrich Wehler, 'Bismarck's Imperialism', *Past
and Present*, 1970.

10. Eckart Kehr, *Primat der Innenpolitik*, Hrsg. H.U. Wehler, Berlin 1965,
particularly the article 'Englandhass und Weltpolitik'; P.R. Anderson, *The
Background of Anti-English Feeling in Germany 1890-1902*, Washington 1939.

11. The latest study of the 'personal regiment' of William II is J.C.G. Röhl,
Germany without Bismarck, London 1967.

12. Dirk Stegmann, *Die Erben Bismarcks*, Köln 1970.

13. Eckart Kehr, *Schlachtflottenbau und Parteipolitik 1894-1901*, Berlin 1930;
Kehr, *Primat der Innenpolitik;* Volker R. Berghahn, *Der Tirpitz-Plan. Genesis
und Verfall einer innenpolitischen Krisenstrategie unter William II*, Düsseldorf
1971; Volker R. Berghahn, 'Zu den Zielen des deutschen Flottenbaus unter
Wilhelm II', *Historische Zeitschrift*, 210, 1970.

14. See particularly H.J. Puhle, *Agrarische Interessenpolitik;* Dirk Stegmann, *Die
Erben Bismarcks;* A. Kruck, *Geschichte des Alldeutschenverbandes 1890-1939*,
Wiesbaden 1954; Dieter Fricke, 'Der Reichsverband gegen die Sozialdemokratie',
Zeitschrift für Geschichtswissenschaft, Heft 7, 1959; K. Saul 'Der Deutsche
Kriegerbund. Zur Innenpolitischen Funktion eines nationalen Verbandes im
kaiserlichen Deutschland', *Militärgeschichtliche Mitteilungen*, Heft 2, 1969;
A. Galos, F.H. Gentzen, W. Jakobszyk, *Die Hakatisten. Der Deutsche
Ostmarckenverein 1894-1934*, Berlin 1966; H. Kaeble, *Industrielle
Interessenpolitik in der wilhelminischen Gesellschaft*, Berlin 1967; H. Nussbaum,
Unternehmer gegen Monopole, Berlin 1966; Leo Müffelmann, *Die
wirtschaftliche Verbände*, Leipzig 1912; M.S. Wertheimer, *The Pan-German
League 1890-1914*, New York 1924. As yet there is no detailed study of the
Navy League *(Flottenverein)*, Wilhelm Deist's forthcoming study of naval
propaganda will therefore fill a significant gap.

15. This same contradiction existed within nazi ideology, when anti-capitalist
ideology could be used for its demagogic effect but could not be allowed to
go too far. See R. Kühnl, *Die Nationalsozialistische Linke*, Meisenheim, 1966.

16. E. Zechlin, *Staatsstreichpläne Bismarcks und Wilhelms II 1890-1894*, Stuttgart
1929; J.C.G. Röhl, 'Staatsstreich oder Staatsstreichbereitschaft?', *Historische
Zeitschrift*, Band 209, 1969.

17. Fritz Fischer, *Krieg der Illusionen*, Düsseldorf 1969.

18. Karl Heinz Janssen, *Der Kanzler und der General*, Göttingen 1967; G. Ritter,
Staatskunst und Kriegshandwerk, Vol. 3, Munich 1964; *Deutschland im ersten
Weltkrieg*, Vol. 1, Berlin 1968.

19. Alistair Horn, *The Price of Glory, Verdun 1916*, London 1962; Hermann
Wendt, *Verdun 1916. Die Angriffe Falkenhayns im Maasgebiet mit Richtung
auf Verdun als strategisches Problem*, Berlin 1931; J. Pericard, *Verdun*, Paris
1933.

1 THE APPOINTMENT OF HINDENBURG AND LUDENDORFF

As the war entered its third year the military position of Germany was becoming increasingly critical. The massive offensive against Verdun on which the OHL had pinned such high hopes became a bloody and costly stalemate. The British offensive on the Somme placed the German forces on the western front in a precarious situation. In the east the Russian offensive under Brusilov was so successful that Austria-Hungary seemed to be on the verge of collapse. These military set-backs to the Central Powers on both the eastern and the western fronts encouraged those countries which were considering joining the war on the side of the Entente. Both Rumania and Italy had declared war, tempted by extravagant promises for a generous settlement when the fighting was over, and convinced that Germany was near collapse. Thus by the summer of 1916 the initiative was clearly in the hands of the Entente. German strategy had been based on an underestimation of the strength of the Entente, and an overestimation of the capacity of the Central Powers to provide men and munitions. An increasing number of people were beginning to feel, if only in brief moments of disquieting insight, that the impossible could happen, that Germany and her allies might be defeated and would have to negotiate a peace that would dash the imperialist dreams for a Europe dominated by Germany.

Austria-Hungary was in a parlous state. Shortages of food and munitions, the demoralisation of the army, the incompetence of much of the officer corps and the startling success of the Russian offensive all served to heighten the tensions and contradictions within the state that many had hoped the war would help to conceal. During the Brusilov offensive it was reported that Czech and Ruthenian soldiers deserted *en masse* to the enemy, the first ominous signs that national differences threatened the continuation of the Austrian war effort. The war minister Krobatin felt that the situation was so critical that a catastrophe was imminent.[1]

In Germany the euphoria and the exaggerated hopes of the early months of the war were giving way to widespread cynicism and to increasingly frequent outbreaks of hysteria. Under the strain of two years of war and the failures of 1916 the political truce of August 1914 was rapidly crumbling. There were the first political strikes, protests against the continuation of the war for what seemed to an ever larger number of people to be the selfish aims of a greedy clique, and against the shortages and privations which the government seemed either unable or unwilling to control. At the other end of the political spectrum the Pan Germans and the heavy industrialists were organising themselves to engineer the overthrow of the chief of the general staff and the chancellor, both of whom seemed to stand between them and the realisation of their ambitious annexationist dreams. Meanwhile the chancellor, Bethmann Hollweg, attempted with his 'politics of the diagonal' to steer a middle course and to achieve a liberal compromise, a policy which was doomed by its very nature to failure. He feared that the Pan Germans with their shrill demands ruined any chance for a separate peace with Russia, and he hoped that by playing down the issue of war aims he might be able to appease his critics on the left. Backed by the propaganda efforts of the German National Committee *(Deutsche Nationalausschuss)*, Bethmann Hollweg attempted, with singular lack of success, to achieve national unity and restore the *Burgfrieden*. These efforts were derided by the Independent Committee for a German Peace *(Unabhängige Ausschuss für einen deutschen Frieden)*, the organisation of the extreme annexationists lead by Dietrich Schäfer. Indeed the squabbles between the *Nationalausschuss* and the *Unabhängige Ausschuss* were symptomatic of the deep-seated divisions on tactical issues which were to become vital issues in German politics in the final two years of the war. In the summer of 1916 there was, however, a fundamental agreement between the two camps on one crucial question. For the realisation of the schemes of either party Germany would have to win a military victory, and without a change in the supreme command this was unlikely to be achieved. Agreement on this issue enabled Bethmann Hollweg to stay in power for one further year, but it meant that Falkenhayn could no longer remain as chief of the general staff. That he would be replaced by Hindenburg and Ludendorff, the victors of Tannenberg and popular idols, was almost a foregone conclusion. Their appointment, however, did not end the differences between the moderates and the extremists, but proved to be a decisive victory for the extremist faction within the ruling class with whom Ludendorff particularly had the closest associations.

The dismissal of Falkenhayn was thus caused by a many-sided attack, the result of some very curious alliances, and it was to backfire with disastrous effect on many of those who took part in the plotting. In this respect the affair was a dress rehearsal for the July crisis of 1917 which was to lead to the overthrow of Bethmann Hollweg.[2]

Falkenhayn had never been a popular figure. He had first become widely known when as war minister he had defended the excesses of the army in Alsace-Lorraine during the Zabern affair. His ferocious language in the Reichstag on this occasion had won him some sympathy in the army and the undying hatred of many parliamentarians, but even his admirers were put off by his coldness, sarcasm and snobbish aloofness.[3] Many senior officers regarded him as a pusher and a careerist, characteristics which were particularly repugnant to an officer corps that clung to its aristocratic image. He had in fact had a remarkably rapid career for a Prussian officer, becoming chief of general staff at the age of 52, a younger man than any of the army commanders and commanding generals. With his attack on Verdun a ghastly failure, which he obstinately refused to admit, and with the Russian breakthrough in the east coupled with the British attack on the Somme, Falkenhayn's position was indeed precarious. Unable to move troops to the east he enraged Hindenburg and Ludendorff who were convinced that he was determined to spoil their chances for another spectacular victory; the high hopes for the western front dashed, he was increasingly criticised by senior commanders. Prince Rupprecht of Bavaria had grave reservations about his capabilities since the days of Ypres. The war minister, Wild, whose attitude towards Falkenhayn was highly ambivalent, felt that he was fundamentally a 'weakling' *(Schlappschwanz)*.[4]

Many politicians had little love for Falkenhayn. Those on the left could not forget Zabern; the right resented his inability to create the military conditions for the realisation of their war aims programme. Many politicians were also suspicious of Falkenhayn's political ambitions, and rumours that he wished to become chancellor continued to circulate.[5] He treated the politicians with haughty disdain, refusing to keep them properly informed and constantly dabbling in political matters. It is one of the supreme ironies that many politicians, from Bethmann down, plotted to overthrow Falkenhayn so as to stop military interference with political matters, and to replace him by Hindenburg and Ludendorff whose political meddling was never surpassed, before or after, in the history of the German army.

Yet Falkenhayn was not without powerful friends, and the struggle for his dismissal was likely to be long and tough. Colonel Marschall of the military cabinet was a devoted friend to Falkenhayn and one of the few men who clearly saw the danger inherent in the appointment of Ludendorff — whose boundless ambition and pride would most likely lead him to continue to fight the war until Germany was ruined and exhausted.[6] His strongest support came from the Kaiser himself, who, in spite of nagging doubts and frustration, continued to support his chief of general staff until the very last moment. Falkenhayn was careful to cultivate good relations with William, always appearing as the humble servant of the 'Supreme Warlord', but never in fact allowing any interference in military affairs by the monarch. There was nothing in Falkenhayn of Hindenburg's deliberate acting up to public opinion which posed such a threat to the traditional position of the monarch with regard to the power of command. Whereas William never regarded Falkenhayn as a threat to his authority, he knew that such a threat emanated from Hindenburg and Ludendorff, and he clung to his chief of general staff knowing that the change would undermine his own position and introduce into the system an element of plebiscitary democracy that was abhorrent to him.

Bethmann Hollweg's motives for plotting the overthrow of Falkenhayn were complex. There had long been differences between the two. The chancellor resented Falkenhayn's interference in political affairs and had serious reservations about his military abilities. He had bitter clashes with Falkenhayn over the issue of submarine warfare and over the Balkans.[7] It has even been argued that Bethmann wished to get rid of Falkenhayn so as to make possible a peace of renunciation *(Verzichtfrieden)* under the leadership of the enormously popular and respected Hindenburg, but this is not convincing, even though he certainly considered this aspect of the question and had suggested that the German people under Hindenburg would accept 'any peace that bears his name'.[8]

The chancellor's main concern was for an eastern strategy that would force Russia to make a separate peace, and thus enable Germany to complete the victory in the west, using unrestricted submarine warfare if necessary.[9] For this policy Hindenburg and Ludendorff's strategy seemed ideal; Falkenhayn's had already proven bankrupt. Hindenburg and Ludendorff were the men of Tannenberg, Falkenhayn of Verdun. The tremendous reputation of Hindenburg would serve to paper over the divisions which were becoming all too apparent within German society, restore the *Burgfrieden,* placate the left and silence the chancellor's critics on the extreme right. With Hindenburg and Ludendorff the chancellor hoped to achieve the war aims which he had outlined as early as September 1914. He had no intention of hiding behind Hindenburg's back, abandoning his war aims programme and negotiating a peace on the basis of the *status quo.* At the same time Bethmann hoped that he would be able to use Hindenburg to convince the Pan Germans and the heavy industrialists of the wisdom of his more flexible attitude towards war aims.

Bethmann's calculations proved to be gravely mistaken. Ludendorff's political convictions, and his attitude to warfare placed him squarely in the camp of heavy industry. He had always called for close cooperation between the army and heavy industry, ideas which formed the basis of his notorious memorandum of 1912 calling for a drastic increase in the size of the army, and which had led to him being posted away from the general staff where his ideas were considered too radical. His vision of total warfare and total mobilisation was attractive to the heavy industrialists who not only stood to gain directly, but who also hoped that Ludendorff's energy would bring Germany the victory which alone would make possible the realisation of their ambitious war aims. Thus although Hindenburg and Ludendorff were men of the east, the ultra right hoped that they would overcome what they felt to be the suspicions and reservations of the chancellor and win a decisive victory in the west.[10] On Hindenburg and Ludendorff's appointment to the OHL, heavy industry was given direct access to the military leadership and thus the chancellor's opponents were greatly strengthened.[11] Bethmann's hopes that the appointment of Hindenburg and Ludendorff would scatter his opponents and restore political unity were soon to be shattered. The new OHL greatly strengthened the extremist faction and served to destroy the last remnants of the *Burgfrieden*.

The dangerous position of the Austrian army helped to undermine Falkenhayn's position. Valuable reserves had to be sent from the western front to the east, and Falkenhayn had to abandon his plans for a counteroffensive on the Somme. The Austrian general staff chief, Conrad, hoped to use these reserves in a grandiose outflanking movement which would destroy Brusilov's army, but the Russians simply changed the direction of their attack once they had been halted and inflicted severe damage on the point where the Austrian and German lines met. The Russian attack was finally halted, but only at tremendous cost of men and materials. Austria-Hungary was further demoralised, and it was only by sending German troops as 'corset stays' to the Austrian front that the situation could be saved.

The poor performance of the Austrian army in 1916 brought up the question of the command structure on the eastern front which was a particularly sensitive issue not only between the allies but also between the 'easterners' and the 'westerners' in the German army. Falkenhayn insisted that General von Seeckt should be appointed chief of staff to the Austrian Seventh Army if he were to send a German division to the

Macedonian front.[12] Conrad was unable to refuse this request, but he would not agree to a further demand that Von Mackensen be given temporary command over the front from the Pripet to the Rumanian frontier. Falkenhayn, by addressing his attention to the command structure in the east, was unwittingly strengthening the position of his great rivals Hindenburg and Ludendorff. Bethmann began to think in terms of giving Hindenburg command over all the German troops in the east, for at that time in spite of his imposing title of 'Supreme Commander East' he only commanded the northern sector. This would then make it all the easier to bring Hindenburg to the OHL.[13] Falkenhayn would not accept this suggestion, even though it would have been acceptable to the Austrians, and continued to press for the appointment of von Mackensen and von Seeckt as commanders of the Galician front, which in turn was unacceptable to the Austrians.[14]

Many influential voices spoke out in favour of Hindenburg's appointment to the supreme command in the east, and criticisms of Falkenhayn's intransigence became increasingly strident. The war minister, Wild, was convinced that if only Hindenburg and Ludendorff were given supreme command the defeat of the Russians would be a mere 'sleigh ride', and Falkenhayn's perverse refusal to listen to Wild's arguments was to force the war minister into the camp of the opposition.[15] The Kaiser's adjutant, von Plessen, tried to use his influence on the Supreme Warlord to secure the appointment of Hindenburg.[16] William II was somewhat more inclined to listen to criticisms of his chief of general staff as he had been complaining that he had been kept insufficiently informed of military operations, and had first heard of the use of gas at Verdun in the newspapers. Falkenhayn seemed to be losing his magic touch with the Kaiser.[17] Bethmann was also busy pressing for Hindenburg's appointment, arguing that the very name Hindenburg was 'the terror of our enemies' and that not to struggle for his appointment would be a denial of one's responsibilities towards 'God, Kaiser, King and *Volk*'.[18]

Those who hoped that the differences between the chancellor and the chief of the general staff could be ironed out and the question of military command settled without any major changes, among whom the military cabinet chief, Lyncker, was the most prominent, gradually realised that this was no longer possible. Falkenhayn had even gone so far as to accuse Bethmann of high treason and the betrayal of state secrets by shouting at the King of Bavaria, who was somewhat hard of hearing, so that a treacherous servant was able to pass on the plans of the attack on Verdun to the enemy.[19] It thus became increasingly clear

that a major confrontation was in the offing which would almost
certainly lead to significant changes in either the military or the civilian
leadership.

Meanwhile Ludendorff had gone into action. On 29 June he sent a
long diatribe against Falkenhayn to the undersecretary of state at the
foreign office, Zimmermann. With shaky handwriting and faulty
grammar, Ludendorff listed his criticisms of Falkenhayn's leadership.
He had failed to send troops to the eastern front which would have
ensured the capture of Riga in May. By delaying to send troops to the
Austrian front he had failed to avert the catastrophe that could have
been avoided if he had acted promptly. When he *had* acted he sent too
many troops thus ruining his chances for success at Verdun because of
the shortage of men, and acting too late to have much effect in the east.
Ludendorff insisted that Falkenhayn was incompetent, demanded to
know if the chancellor realised how serious the situation was and asked
rhetorically: 'Is there no one who can save us, will no one step forward
for what we have lived and fought for during the last two years: for the
greatness of the country?'[20]

Ludendorff's memorandum marks the beginning of an offensive by
members of the foreign office against Falkenhayn. Jagow, the secretary
of state, and Zimmermann worked in close cooperation with
Hindenburg and Ludendorff. Helfferich visited headquarters in Kowno
and kept in close contact with Berlin, acting as liaison and later as
a strong voice in favour of Hindenburg's appointment to supreme
command in the east. Admiral Müller supported the foreign office's
effort to convince Lyncker that Hindenburg would have to be
appointed, whatever Falkenhayn's objections, so that Germany's
flagging morale could be restored.[21]

Lyncker was now almost alone in his support for Falkenhayn, but
he gradually gave way to the arguments of those who thought that
Falkenhayn should relinquish command over the eastern front to
Hindenburg and Ludendorff. Lyncker then persuaded Falkenhayn that
his only course of action would be for him to take the initiative and
suggest the appointment of Hindenburg. Falkenhayn for all his serious
misgivings and reservations about Hindenburg and Ludendorff, realised
that there were no viable alternatives, knowing that the Austrians
would almost certainly object to such a proposal which went further
than the original suggestion for a unified command over the German
troops in the east.

Thus on 3 July 1916 Falkenhayn asked the Kaiser to appoint
Hindenburg, and echoed all the arguments that had been used by

Bethmann and Jagow. William II was furious, insisting that he was being asked to relinquish his royal prerogative in the face of demands of the public and of the politicians. He said that Hindenburg was the 'people's tribune' and that it was unheard of in the Prussian army that an appointment should be made partly through the pressure of public demand. Thus William with his concern to preserve the royal prerogative realised more clearly than others the pseudo-democratic and bonapartist elements in the struggle for the appointment of Hindenburg and Ludendorff, and it is extraordinary that those who were plotting to overthrow Falkenhayn did not even consider the predictable effects of such arguments on the Kaiser. Lyncker managed to save the situation by getting the Kaiser to agree that a request should be sent to the Austrians for the appointment of Hindenburg. The reply from Austrian headquarters in Teschen was prompt and curt. Lyncker was informed that such an appointment would be regarded by the Austrians as a grave insult. William flatly refused to bring the matter up directly with Austrian emperor, and when asked if he would agree to Hindenburg being made commander of all German troops in the east he replied that he had no intention of being deposed.[22] Having blocked the appointment of Hindenburg, at least for the time being, the Kaiser relapsed into a state of such deep depression that some people at headquarters began to have serious doubts about his mental stability.[23]

In addition to the intrigues of the chancellor, the foreign office and the military cabinet, there was now a new onslaught on Falkenhayn by the army commanders on the western front who severely criticised Falkenhayn for failing to foresee the extent of the British offensive on the Somme, and for acting ineffectively once it had begun. Men like General von Below and Crown Prince Rupprecht were outspoken in their criticisms of Falkenhayn, and Rupprecht even wrote to the chancellor saying that if Falkenhayn remained as chief of the general staff Germany would lose the war.[24] Von Below preferred to grumble behind Falkenhayn's back and lacked the courage to speak out openly to the Kaiser and Bethmann against him.[25] Some senior officers, even those who were critical of Falkenhayn, felt that the Crown Prince of Bavaria's actions were an unwarranted interference in the Kaiser's power of command and were sharply critical of his conduct.

Traditional respect for the Kaiser's power of command over the army combined with a lack of courage in speaking up against the chief of the general staff helped to stem the mounting tide of criticism. The German states were now pressing indirectly for the appointment of Hindenburg to the OHL, and the Württemberg minister president, von Weizsäcker, insisted that neither the Kaiser nor the Reich could tolerate a serious setback unless the 'genius and reputation of Hindenburg' was given full rein.[26] But although the anti-Falkenhayn faction had grown to such an extent that the chief of the general staff had almost no one who was willing to support him, the Kaiser still refused to consider his replacement, not so much because he had any great confidence in his ability, but rather because he was still reluctant to give way to pressure and thus relinquish any of his dwindling authority.

Bethmann Hollweg was given a further chance to strengthen Hindenburg's position in the middle of July when Conrad asked for German reserves so as to be able to mount a fresh offensive on the eastern front without which Rumania would almost certainly be tempted to declare war. Bethmann suggested that the Austrian request should be met, provided that Hindenburg was given command over all troops in the east as far south as Linsingen's army group. Bethmann felt that this was the maximum that would be acceptable to the Austrians, and Falkenhayn was prepared to agree to the suggestion. Falkenhayn's opponents hoped that perhaps by trying to ward off Hindenburg's excessive demands for supreme command over the entire eastern front he was in fact setting himself a trap that would lead to his own downfall.[27]

Primed with a set of exceedingly gloomy reports from the German foreign office on the situation in the Balkans and on Hungarian demands for a separate peace with the Entente the Kaiser demanded drastic action. On 18 July, when Conrad visited Berlin the Kaiser instructed Falkenhayn to request that Hindenburg be given supreme command over all the forces in the east. Conrad refused to accept this proposal, even though it was now acceptable to the Emperor Francis Joseph, Burian, the Hungarian minister president and the King of Bulgaria. Conrad's counterproposal which gave Hindenburg command over only part of Linsingen's army group was rejected by Falkenhayn on the grounds that there would then be no unified command at the critical point of the front to the west of Luck. Thus once again Falkenhayn triumphed against massive odds and Hindenburg's supporters had to accept the decision.[28]

With further defeats of the Austrian army, particularly in the critical sector near Luck, Bethmann renewed his demands for a change in the command structure in the east. Falkenhayn countered these requests with yet another compromise suggestion which had first been proposed by General Groener. Hindenburg should be appointed to command the Galician front, but he should be placed under the Austrian high command. Thus Hindenburg's legendary strategic genius could be put to the test without hurting the Austrians' *amour propre*. But this suggestion was promptly rejected by Bethmann and by Hindenburg as a 'half-measure'.[29]

Meanwhile the question of Hindenburg's appointment was becoming an important factor in Austrian internal politics. The Hungarian opposition leader, Andrássy, encouraged by the German ambassador in Vienna, Tschirschky, and with the support of the chief of the Austrian military cabinet, von Bolfras, suggested that the Austrian army be placed under Hindenburg's command, or else the war would be lost. Andrássy's intervention was most welcome to the foreign office in Berlin because he was known to favour the incorporation of Poland into the German Reich. The foreign office thus hoped that Hindenburg could be brought to the OHL via the Austrian command, and Andrássy could replace Burian as minister president whose demands for an Austro-Polish solution were frustrating German expansionist aims in the east. Andrássy was able to win considerable support for his initiatives on behalf of Hindenburg from those in Austria who wished to remove Conrad. The Austrian chief of general staff had been involved in a long and spectacular divorce case and had subsequently married a much younger woman whom he had taken with him to headquarters. There was much talk in Vienna of riotous champagne parties at headquarters with the glamorous society friends of Conrad von Hötzendorff's attractive new wife, and this served to make him even more unpopular in government circles. A somewhat sordid scandal campaign was mounted against him, and the standard quip in Vienna was: 'bella gerant alii, tu felix Hötzendorff nube'.[30]

It was finally decided that this vexed question of the command of the eastern front should be settled at a meeting at Pless where Hindenburg and Ludendorff, Conrad and the Archduke Frederick would be present. Bethmann also decided that he would attend the meeting, even though he had not been formally invited by the Kaiser.[31] The war minister, Wild, also managed to get an invitation to Pless from the Kaiser.[32] Falkenhayn and Conrad decided that they would go to Pless with an acceptable compromise already agreed upon, so that they would not get cornered by the politicians or by their opponents in the army. They agreed that Hindenburg should be given command over all Austrian forces between the Pripet and the Dniester. But as soon as they arrived at Pless Falkenhayn reverted to his old tactics of making demands which he knew would be rejected by the Austrians. Thus he insisted that Hindenburg should be given command over all forces from the Baltic to

Rumania, take orders from the OHL, and merely consult the Austrian High Command (AOK). Conrad rejected this proposal out of hand, and added that there was little point in tampering with the command structure when all was working so well.

The Pless meeting seemed to settle nothing. The Kaiser tried to calm his shattered nerves by playing *Skat* at the suggestion of his cabinet chief. To Admiral Müller he complained that he was being asked to square the circle, to which the Admiral rather feebly replied that at least the square was already a hexagon.[33] Falkenhayn, who was deeply insulted by the fact that the Kaiser had ordered him not to interrupt what Hindenburg had to say, was behaving in Wild's words like a 'sulky school girl'.[34] Complaining that he had toothache, Falkenhayn refused to attend the conference held on the evening of 27 July and thus virtually admitted that he had been defeated by Bethmann in the long struggle for the Kaiser's decisive support.[35]

The result of the negotiations with the Austrians was a compromise that certainly fell far short of the hopes of Hindenburg's supporters. At first it was agreed that Hindenburg should have supreme command over the entire German front in the east, and in addition the mixed German and Austrian army group Linsingen should be placed under his command. In other words the compromise solution proposed by Bethmann in mid-July and which had been acceptable to Falkenhayn was now official policy. On the following day the Austrians, encouraged by the fact that Ludendorff now seemed more willing to release some reserves, were prepared to make further concessions and to extend Hindenburg's command to include the second army of Böhm-Ermolli. Hindenburg was to remain formally under the OHL, but he was bound to consult the AOK on all matters concerning the forces south of the Pripet.[36]

Although there was some jubilation in the ranks of the Hindenburg supporters it was clear that the battle had yet to be won. But at least now it was clear that it was only a matter of time before there was a change in the OHL, so that even this thoroughly unsatisfactory compromise could be seen as a minor triumph. Falkenhayn for his part could take some satisfaction in the fact that it soon became apparent that the magic name of Hindenburg was not alone enough to secure the hard-pressed Austrian front. Hindenburg and Ludendorff demanded more men, but Falkenhayn pointed out that German forces on the Somme had held the line against a far more dangerous foe with remarkably few troops. He was perfectly correct to say that no further reserves could be spared without the virtual certainty of an allied breakthrough in the west. Hindenburg was not prepared to accept these arguments. After careful discussions between Major von Bockelberg from supreme command east and his cousin Major von dem Bussche at the OHL, Hindenburg decided to complain directly to the Kaiser about Falkenhayn's mishandling of the situation.[37] This move misfired, for Hindenburg's telegram of 10 August to the Kaiser demanding four or five divisions was deciphered by Falkenhayn's adjutant, and Falkenhayn was able to send one division to the east before the Kaiser even received the message.[38] The Russian offensive was stopped, so Hindenburg had no real cause to make further excessive demands for more troops, and the allied attack on the Somme finally ground to a halt. Rumania showed no great enthusiasm to enter the war, and Falkenhayn, although well aware that the danger from Hindenburg was far from over, could afford to devote his attention to the overall military situation and to ignore his rivals in the east for the time being.

Both the OHL and the AOK agreed that the weakest point now seemed to be the Italian front, and it was therefore decided that the Austrians should send one division from the eastern front to the Isonzo front, and that it should be replaced by a German division taken from Hindenburg's command. Hindenburg was incensed. He immediately sent an angry message to the Kaiser claiming that the eastern front could not be held if he lost this division.[39] This new attack on Falkenhayn occurred at the same time as the Kaiser was subjected to another plea from Bethmann Hollweg who insisted that the war could only be won in the east, that Austria had to be saved from collapse, and that the Verdun offensive would have to be halted, and a defensive strategy adopted in the west which would enable troops to be moved to the east where victory could be won under Hindenburg's leadership.[40] But in spite of this two-pronged attack the Kaiser continued to support Falkenhayn. In a rather terse reply to Hindenburg he argued, perfectly correctly, that German forces on the western front were stretched to the limit of their endurance, and that it was impossible to release any further reserves however desirable and necessary that might seem to the protagonists of the eastern strategy. Secondly Falkenhayn was being grossly maligned over the Verdun offensive. He had tried to step down the operation by only mounting small tactical offensives, but he had met with such united opposition to these suggestions from the army commanders, particularly from Crown Prince William, that the matter was left to the discretion of the commanders on the spot.[41]

The reaction to this reply from the Kaiser at supreme command east was one of frustration, bitterness and anger. At first Hindenburg, with his traditional respect for the monarchy and his reluctance to cajole the supreme warlord, prevaricated, prompting General Hoffmann to write scornfully: 'The fellow is a pathetic creature, this great commander and idol of the people.' Finally, after being pushed by his associates who had no inhibitions whatever about respect for the monarchy, he asked the Kaiser for an interview without Falkenhayn being present, so that he might list his grievances against the chief of the general staff. Once this unprecedented step had been taken Ludendorff and Hoffmann decided to force his hand. Ludendorff sent a note to headquarters at Pless saying that he might well be forced to resign, and Hoffmann indicated that he would do the same. Whereupon Hindenburg sent a telegram to Lyncker, the head of the military cabinet, saying that he assumed he no longer had the confidence of the Kaiser, and would feel obliged to resign if the Kaiser refused to grant him and Ludendorff a private audience.[42]

In the face of this extraordinary insubordination the Kaiser acted with skill and restraint. He gave lavish praise of Hindenburg's military abilities, but continued to support the chief of general staff.[43] Hindenburg replied with a particularly feeble report on the overall military situation, and an expression of regret that the Kaiser had not seen fit to grant him an audience.[44] There was no further talk of resignation.

Hindenburg's criticism of Falkenhayn's strategy was a poorly argued and unconvincing piece, and Bethmann Hollweg made little headway when he tried to use it as yet another weapon against the chief of general staff. Falkenhayn replied to his critics with a well-reasoned memorandum of 21 August in which he referred to his opponents as: 'Laymen, many of them in field grey and some in the highest ranks of the army.' He argued that to them warfare simply consisted in deciding where to hit the enemy, and then moving so many troops to that area that one had a marked superiority in men and materials. He suggested that such an attitude was almost criminally crude for it paid no regard to the immense complexity of modern warfare when Germany was fighting a war on many fronts against superior numbers. In the present situation it was not possible to move troops without endangering the point from which the troops had been taken. The strengthening of one part of the front meant the weakening of another, creating the very real risk of a breakthrough. Thus, for Falkenhayn, any talk of a 'decisive battle' in the west or in the east was merely idle chatter. If the Entente could be pushed back in the west there might possibly be a victory, but there could be no decisive victory against Russia. Although his attempts to justify the Verdun strategy are not particularly compelling, there is no doubt that the memorandum as a whole was very difficult to counter. It would have been madness to withdraw further divisions from the west when the battle of the Somme was still raging, even though the British offensive was now making no progress.[45]

The easterners replied to this justification with a memorandum written by the most extreme of Falkenhayn's opponents, Colonel Bauer of the OHL, which was given to Bethmann to give him general lines of criticism of Falkenhayn's leadership at a forthcoming meeting at Pless. Bauer listed Falkenhayn's failings under the general heading of 'hand to mouth strategy' that had brought Germany into a hopeless situation. Among Falkenhayn's countless mistakes, according to Bauer, the most glaring were his failure to work out a common strategy with Austria, complete strategic and tactical failure with the Verdun offensive, failure to adequately prepare for the offensive on the Somme, an underestimation of the strength of the Russian army, and failure to send adequate reserves to the eastern front. For Bauer there was only one way out of the mess that Falkenhayn had created, but even that seemed dubious. 'Perhaps a strong-minded man can save us, a man who can enflame the people, by the trust they have in him, and who knows how to make an audacious decision and carry it out.' Even this hope was qualified not only by the 'perhaps' but also by Bauer's statement that Germany could only hold out until the end of the year because she would no longer have either the men or the industrial capacity to meet the almost endless reserves upon which the Entente was able to draw. From Bauer's pessimistic report there was little that suggested that Germany might win the war within four months, even with Ludendorff, especially if Rumania entered the war which Bauer thought was highly probable.[46]

Bauer's role in the overthrow of Falkenhayn was critical. He was the most outspoken and ruthless critic of the chief of the general staff within the OHL, but he was also the most vigorous and ambitious, and in some senses the most brilliant officer at headquarters. He was a great admirer of Ludendorff, whom he resembled in many ways, except that Bauer had far stronger nerves and was even more ruthless. At this juncture he was in close contact with the chancellor, plotting with him to overthrow Falkenhayn, but he was soon to be calling for Bethmann's blood. Even more important were his close contacts with industry. Bauer was the spokesman of industry at the OHL and the key liaison officer between the big industrialists and the military. His memorandum, which was an extraordinary attack on a superior officer, was supported in essence by many leading industrialists. Rathenau had been an enthusiastic supporter of Ludendorff since late 1915 when he decided that he should replace Falkenhayn.[47] The shipping magnate, Ballin, wrote to Wolff-Metternich in July 1916: 'I have got nothing against Falkenhayn, he certainly has achieved a great deal, but he has had bad luck and luck is an ingredient of the success of a general ... "Let him go, he has no luck" said *der alte* Fritz to a brave officer who complained that the distinguished decoration that had been awarded to him by the king had been given by mistake to someone of the same name.'[48] Bauer was also in close contact with Duisberg and Krupp who were among the first visitors to the OHL when Hindenburg and Ludendorff were appointed. The precise extent of Bauer's relationships with the industrialists is unfortunately impossible to establish accurately. Bauer's papers were carefully examined for any compromising material by Richard Merton who destroyed any material which he felt should be handled discreetly. Enough remains, however, to establish beyond doubt the vital role played by Bauer in establishing the close links between big industry and the OHL which were characteristic of Hindenburg and Ludendorff's regime.

Bethmann received Bauer's memorandum, but as he was a comparatively junior officer no one seemed particularly impressed by his arguments. Furthermore as Bethmann had been unable to make much impression with Hindenburg's arguments, and as Falkenhayn's reply found wide support, he was reluctant to have another attempt at unseating the chief of general staff. Bethmann was in such a state of depression that he even suggested that Germany should make a peace on the basis of the *status quo,* with French Lorraine and upper Alsace to be exchanged for parts of Briey, which would give Germany a secure base for further expansion.[49] It is difficult to believe that Bethmann meant this remark seriously, and it must be attributed to his despondent mood. He had been unable to overthrow Falkenhayn, and was convinced by the arguments of Bauer and others that unless Hindenburg and Ludendorff were brought to the OHL the war would soon be lost. This, combined with his perpetual pessimism which was so maddening to the Pan Germans and the extreme annexationists, made him consider for the moment the idea of a negotiated peace. Yet there was nothing that indicated that this might be possible. Germany had failed at Verdun, and was still heavily engaged on the Somme. In the east there was the ever-present threat of the entry of Rumania into the war and the possibility of a collapse of Austria-Hungary. Germany was hardly in a position to dictate peace terms, however moderate. Bethmann admitted this at the meeting of the council of ministers on 19 August when he said: 'The prospects for peace are just as slim or even slimmer that they were before.'[50]

Thus although the intrigue against Falkenhayn continued there was now general agreement that little could be done, and many were now reluctant to speak out against a man who seemed destined to remain as chief of the general staff. Then, on the evening of 27 August, General Cramon telephoned the German headquarters that Rumania had declared war on Austria-Hungary. At first Falkenhayn refused to believe the report, partly because he thought it might be another attempt by the Austrians to get more German reserves, and partly because he did not want to believe the report. A rag-tag army of 30,000 men, mainly customs officers, poorly trained militia men and troops who were recovering from long spells at the front, faced a Rumanian army of 300,000 men. Although the Central Powers had intercepted telegrams between Bucharest and Paris and had minute details of Rumania's preparations for war, they had been singularly lax in their own preparations to meet this threat. If the Rumanian army had marched at once against Hungary, it would most probably have meant the end of the Habsburg monarchy.[51]

News that both Italy and Rumania had declared war on the Central Powers reached the Kaiser while he was playing his usual evening round of *Skat*. He immediately announced that Germany had lost the war, fighting would have to cease at once and Germany would have to sue for peace. The chief of the civil cabinet, Valentini, pointed out that peace would mean that Germany would lose Alsace-Lorraine, Belgium, occupied France, Heligoland and Germany's 'colonial possessions' in the east. He argued that it would be better to fight on to utter defeat than to accept such a peace. The alternatives were victory and the realisation of Germany's imperialist dreams, or defeat and utter ruin.[52] Although the names of Hindenburg and Ludendorff were not mentioned that evening, there must have been a tacit understanding that their hour had come, and that Falkenhayn was now doomed.

One by one the leading figures in the drama arrived in Pless for the kill. Bethmann was summoned by Valentini, even though the Kaiser had not been consulted.[53] The war minister, Wild, knew that if Falkenhayn was dismissed he would probably lose his job, so he tried to make himself as acceptable as possible to Hindenburg. In the end he fell between two stools, for he could neither enthusiastically support Falkenhayn about whom he had distinct reservations, nor could he wholeheartedly join Bauer in his onslaught on the chief of general staff.[54] Not to miss any of the excitement, the Empress also took a train to Pless.[55]

Shortly after Falkenhayn's daily audience with the Kaiser, Lyncker and Plessen went to see the Kaiser and spoke out against the chief of general staff. Their basic argument was that he no longer enjoyed the confidence of the army. The Kaiser burst into tears, insisted that he would have to discuss the matter with Wild, but agreed that Hindenburg should come to Pless to present his criticisms of Falkenhayn. This was practically a call for Falkenhayn's resignation, and when he was told by Lyncker of the Kaiser's decision he promptly offered his resignation. The Kaiser had already made up his mind that Falkenhayn should go, but he discussed the question in a brief interview with Wild out on the terrace. Wild continued to back both horses, speaking highly of Falkenhayn's talents, particularly of his skilful handling of Germany's allies, but once it was clear to him that the Kaiser had made up his mind to appoint Hindenburg and Ludendorff he supported the Kaiser's decision with the rather lame argument that if the Kaiser had more confidence in Hindenburg and Ludendorff than in Falkenhayn then a change was indeed necessary.[56]

NOTES

1. Fritz Klein (editor), *Deutschland im Ersten Weltkrieg,* 3 Vols., Berlin 1968-9, Vol. 2, p. 402.
2. Karl Heinz Janssen, 'Der Wechsel in der Obersten Heeresleitung 1916', *Vierteljahrshefte für Zeitgeschichte,* 7 Jahrgang 1959, Heft 4. Karl Heinz Janssen, *Der Kanzler und der General,* Berlin 1967. Gerhard Ritter, *Staatskunst und Kriegshandwerk,* Munich 1964, Vol. 3, Chapter 6.
3. For Falkenhayn's role in the Zabern affair see Martin Kitchen, *The German Officer Corps 1890-1914,* Oxford 1968, pp. 207-10, 217, 218.
4. Bundesarchiv Militärarchiv Freiburg, Nachlass Adolf Wild von Hohenborn N44/2, diary entry 2-5-16. See also Josef Graf Stürgkh, *Im deutschen Grossen Hauptquartier,* Leipzig 1921, p. 81.
5. Bundesarchiv Militärarchiv Freiburg, Nachlass Wild, N44/2, diary entry 9-3-16. Janssen, 'Der Wechsel der Obersten Heeresleitung', p. 339.
6. Ritter, *Staatskunst und Kriegshandwerk,* Vol. 3, p. 248. Janssen, *Der Kanzler und der General,* p. 215.
7. For further details see Janssen, *Der Kanzler und der General.*
8. Ritter, *Staatskunst und Kriegshandwerk,* Vol. 3, p. 227. Fritz Fischer, *Griff nach der Weltmacht,* Düsseldorf 1961, p. 307, attacks Janssen's argument in 'Der Wechsel der Obersten Heeresleitung', p. 65, that Bethmann hoped to use Hindenburg's prestige to enable him to negotiate a 'weak' peace. Janssen, *Der Kanzler und der General,* p. 243, replies to Fischer, but his argument is not particularly convincing, and does not address itself to Fischer's specific points about Bethmann's policy. For further discussion of this point see below, footnote 50.
9. *Deutschland im ersten Weltkrieg,* Vol. 2, p. 411.
10. Hellmuth Weber, *Ludendorff und die Monopole,* Berlin 1966, p. 41. The concept of 'total war' dates from 1935 when Ludendorff published his book *Der totale Krieg.*

11. Bundesarchiv Militärarchiv Freiburg, Nachlass Wild, N44/6, letter from Wild to Geheimrat Professor Zorn 1-1-17 in which he stressed the fact that heavy industry had direct access to the OHL and no longer bothered to consult the war ministry. Wild also pointed out that the new OHL was very sympathetic to the complaints and requests of heavy industry.
12. Janssen, *Der Kanzler und der General*, p. 213. Falkenhayn did not have a particularly high opinion of Seeckt. Bundesarchiv Militärarchiv Freiburg, Nachlass Wild N44/2, diary entry 29-6-1916, 'Falkenhayn does not have a very high opinion of Seeckt's ability. He is quite right.'
13. Rudolf von Valentini, *Kaiser und Kabinettschef*, Oldenbourg 1931, p. 230.
14. Politisches Archiv des auswärtigen Amts (PA) Bonn, Weltkrieg Geheim Band 30, Luckwald to chancellor 16-6-1916.
15. Bundesarchiv Militärarchiv Freiburg, Nachlass Wild N44/2, diary entry 22-6-1916.
16. Janssen, *Der Kaiser und der General*, p. 215.
17. Bundesarchiv Militärarchiv Freiburg, Nachlass Wild N44/2, diary entry 25-6-16.
18. Ritter, *Staatskunst und Kriegshandwerk*, Vol. 3, p. 227. Janssen, *Der Kaiser und der General*, p. 217.
19. Janssen, *Der Kaiser und der General*, p. 217. See also the papers of Treutler: Karl Heinz Janssen (editor), *Die graue Exzellenz − Zwischen Staatsrason und Vasallentreue*, Berlin 1971.
20. PA Bonn AA Weltkrieg Geheim, Band 30. The transcription in Janssen, *Der Kanzler und der General*, p. 292 contains a few minor errors.
21. Georg Alexander von Müller, *Regierte der Kaiser? Kriegstagebücher Aufzeichnungen und Briefe des Chefs des Marine Kabinetts Admiral Georg von Müller 1914-1918*, edited by Walter Görlitz, Göttingen 1959, diary entry 3-7-16. Karl Helfferich, *Der Weltkrieg*, Karlsruhe 1919, p. 191.
22. Müller diary 3-7-16; Janssen, *Der Kanzler und der General*, p.219. Treutler reported to the foreign office 5-7-16 that the chancellor was in favour of Hindenburg, as was the Kaiser, 'even though he was very reluctant'. PA Bonn AA Weltkrieg Geheim, Band 30.
23. Janssen, *Der Kanzler und der General*, p. 219.
24. Janssen, 'Der Wechsel in der Obersten Heeresleitung', p. 351; Valentini, *Kaiser und Kabinettschef*, p. 234.
25. Janssen, *Der Kanzler und der General*, p. 223.
26. Helfferich, *Der Weltkrieg*, p. 191.
27. Ritter, *Staatskunst und Kriegshandwerk*, Vol. 3, p. 237. Reichsarchiv, *Der Weltkrieg 1914-18*, Berlin 1929, Vol. 10, p. 526.
28. Janssen, *Der Kanzler und der General*, p. 226; Bayerisches Hauptstaatsarchiv Abteilung IV Kriegsarchiv M.Kr 1830, Berichte des Mil. Bevollmächt. i Gr. HQ 1916 111a XV 39.
29. Janssen, 'Der Wechsel in der Obersten Heeresleitung', p. 229; Ritter, *Staatskunst und Kriegshandwerk*, Vol. 3, p. 240; Janssen, *Der Kanzler und der General*, p. 229.
30. PA Bonn AA Oesterreich 95, Band 4.
31. Müller diary 23-7-16.
32. Janssen, *Der Kanzler und der General*, p. 232. Janssen tends to assume that Wild was more pro-Falkenhayn than he was in fact. There is sufficient evidence in Wild's diary to show that he had very mixed feelings about Falkenhayn. This is of course not to say that he was in favour of the appointment of Hindenburg.
33. Müller diary 26-7-16.
34. Bundesarchiv Militärarchiv Freiburg, Nachlass Wild N44/2, diary entry 26-7-16.
35. *Ibid.*, 27-7-16.
36. Janssen, *Der Kanzler und der General*, p. 237.
37. *Ibid.*, p. 240; *Der Weltkrieg 1914-1918*, Vol. 10, p. 553.
38. Andre Scherer and Jacques Grunewald, *L'Allemagne et les problemes de la paix pendant la premiere guerre mondiale*, Paris 1962, Vol. 1, number 305.
39. *Der Weltkrieg 1914-1918*, Vol. 10, p. 559.

40. Scherer Grunewald, *L'Allemagne et les problèmes de la paix*, Vol. 1, number 306; Müller diary 17-8-16.
41. Janssen, *Der Kanzler und der General*, p. 242.
42. *Ibid.*, p. 245.
43. *Der Weltkrieg 1914-1918*, Vol. 10, p. 636.
44. Janssen, *Der Kanzler und der General*, p. 246; Wilhelm Breucker, *Die Tragik Ludendorffs*, Stollhamm 1953, p. 41.
45. *Der Weltkrieg 1914-1918*, Vol. 10, p. 638.
46. Bundesarchiv Koblenz, Nachlass Bauer, number 2.
47. Harry Graf Kessler, *Walter Rathenau*, Wiesbaden 1962, p. 252.
48. Bundesarchiv Koblenz, Nachlass Bülow, Band 60.
49. Müller diary, 25-8-16.
50. Scherer Grundewald, *L'Allemagne et les problemes de la paix*, Vol. 1, number 311. Janssen, *Der Kanzler und der General*, p. 248, argues that Bethmann wished to remove Falkenhayn in order to negotiate a peace on the basis of the *status quo*. The evidence for this point of view is very sparse indeed, and the theory makes him appear even more politically naive than was the case. Significantly there is no mention at all in Bethmann's remarks to Müller of a settlement in the east. On 19 August Bethmann said that the aim of German policy in Poland was 'to create an autonomous Poland which must remain militarily and politically completely in German hands'. Scherer Grunewald, Vol. 1, p. 447.
51. Janssen, 'Der Wechsel in der Obersten Heeresleitung', p.369.
52. Müller diary, 27-8-16.
53. Valentini, *Kaiser und Kabinettschef*, p. 139.
54. Bundesarchiv Militärarchiv Freiburg, Nachlass Wild N44/4. Briefe an seine Frau. 'If it comes to a conflict they will get rid of Falkenhayn and myself to please Bethmann': 17-5-16.
55. Andreas Dorpalen, 'Empress Auguste Victoria and the Fall of the German Monarchy', *American Historical Review*, October 1952.
56. Janssen, *Der Kanzler und der General*, p. 251.

2 THE ORGANISATION OF THE HIGH COMMAND

The organisation which Hindenburg and Ludendorff were appointed to head, and which gave them the basis for their very considerable power, had been formed at the beginning of the war as a central body for the direction of military operations. Military headquarters, known as the *Grosse Hauptquartier,* was a very large and cumbersome organisation which needed no less than eleven railway trains to move it from one theatre of war to another. Within the *Grosse Hauptquartier* the High Command (*Oberste Heeresleitung,* or OHL) was the largest and most important formation. The OHL was headed by the Kaiser as 'supreme warlord', and by the chief of the Prussian general staff who, under the provisions of the imperial constitution and the imperial military law, gave the operational orders for the entire German army. The Prussian chief of general staff was given the new title of chief of general staff of the field army.[1]

During the initial stages of the war the chancellor and the secretary of state for foreign affairs were at headquarters, but they soon returned to Berlin where they remained for the duration of the war, making periodic visits to headquarters. The Kaiser remained at headquarters throughout the war, but in spite of the imposing title of supreme warlord he exercised very little control over military planning and decision making. Liaison between the OHL and the government in Berlin was maintained by representatives of the chancellor and the foreign office who were given a staff and a department within the OHL. Their important function of bridging the gap between the civilians and the military was to give them considerable political power.

The structural problems of the government of the Reich, which had become glaringly apparent during the Wilhelmine era, were further aggravated by the war. The relative weakness of the political leadership, and the strength of the military led to a serious imbalance, which could only be overcome if the Kaiser was prepared to play his constitutional role and overcome the differences between the two. If he was not prepared or not able to maintain the delicate balance between political and military considerations there were bound to be serious and harmful divisions within the leadership of the Reich and the authority of the monarchy would be significantly weakened. Without firm control from above which would unite all the departments of government in a common effort, the military was almost certain to become excessively powerful, and the administration would fall prey to the disease that afflicts so many bureaucratic structures, the petty rivalries between different departments for which the German word *Ressortpartikularismus* (departmental particularism) is so apt. William II's singular inactivity during the war was thus every bit as disastrous as would have been any attempt on his part actively to play the role of supreme warlord and use his power of command over the army to the full. In fact, William was manipulated and used by the conflicting factions to gain an 'order of the all-highest', and this sometimes gave him the illusion that he was indeed making important decisions. Periodic violent outbursts and heavily underlined marginal notes on important documents were however no substitute for government, and the inability of the Kaiser to perform the role that the constitution provided for him did much to undermine the institution of the monarchy. As the supreme warlord became little more than a symbolic figure, the OHL became exclusively identified with the generals and the Kaiser's true function as the real head of the OHL was forgotten. Thus Ludendorff was to make a clear distinction between the OHL and the Kaiser, a distinction which was constitutionally inadmissible and which justifiably enraged William II.[2]

As the Kaiser spent most of his time at headquarters, and was reluctant to play any significant role in the affairs of state, thinking of himself as a military man who shared the dislike and distrust of the soldiers for the civilians, the position of the OHL against the civilian government was greatly strengthened, and the already excessive power of the army was further increased. The chancellor, absent in Berlin and with only a small staff attached to headquarters, was in a distinctly disadvantageous position.[3] The soldiers found it very easy to feed the Kaiser's prejudices against the 'idiotic civilians', the 'inkpot diplomatists' and the 'demagogues' in the Reichstag, and regarded any attempt by the government to check the military as an unwarranted interference in technical matters in which they had no expertise and an attack on the Kaiser's power of command over the army. In this way, all the shortcomings of Germany's policies, all the setbacks at the front and all the shortages at home could, in the last resort, be blamed on the civilians. The ground for the 'stab in the back' *(Dolchstoss)* legend, which was to play such a powerful role in the right wing mythology of the Weimar republic, was thus being carefully prepared.

The question of the respective fields of competence of the chancellor and OHL was never satisfactorily settled, and the result was a constant running battle between the two. As Bethmann Hollweg correctly pointed out to Hindenburg there could be no question of a full and open discussion of the differences between the OHL and the chancellor, for this would only serve to weaken still further the position of the Kaiser – whose constitutional duty it was to ensure that the army and the civilians worked harmoniously together. An attempt was made during the chancellorship of Michaelis to overcome these structural difficulties by improving communications. Michaelis appointed a permanent representative of his office to headquarters, and the OHL sent an officer to the chancellery who reported daily back to the OHL. But it soon became obvious that the real problem was not one of lack of information, but was far more fundamental. As it was, these new appointees merely duplicated the work of the old liaison officers, so that the situation scarcely improved.[4]

Hindenburg and Ludendorff had no patience for all this talk about constitutional rights and correct procedure. They regarded themselves as standing outside the provisions of the constitution, and, in their more exalted moments, felt themselves as incorporating in some mysterious way the spirit of the German people. Hindenburg expressed this feeling very clearly in a letter addressed to the chancellor, Hertling. 'Because of our position, which has developed without our conscious efforts, we feel responsible to the German people, to history, and to our own consciences for the form of the peace settlement. This sense of responsibility cannot be taken away by any declaration.'[5] William II was thus perfectly correct to fear that the appointment of Hindenburg and Ludendorff with their massive popular support to the OHL was a challenge to the monarchical principle. It is remarkable that he was almost alone in realising this pseudo-democratic basis of their power.

The fundamental differences between the politicians and the military could not be swept aside by high-sounding appeals to principle and solidarity, and it is doubtful if anyone took them seriously. Successive chancellors were to complain that the OHL was meddling in politics, but without the support of the monarch, and without a forceful man as chancellor this was of little avail.[6] An unsatisfactory agreement was reached that the chancellor should be responsible for political decisions, but that the OHL was to advise him on a wide range of topics. If there was a deadlock then the Kaiser was to decide. In practice this meant that the OHL did not bear the responsibility for the decisions it made, and as the Kaiser was so much under the control of the military he nearly always decided in their favour.

It was not until the authority of the OHL had been seriously weakened by their appeal for an armistice, when the demigods of general staff began suddenly to look alarmingly mortal to all but the most incurable optimists and military fanatics that the chancellor, Prince Max of Baden, was able to launch a serious offensive against the political encroachments of the OHL. But this attack came too late to be of significant value, and the authority of the crown could not be restored at the last moment.[7] So close were the ties between the crown and the OHL that when the power of the latter began to wane the power of the crown was correspondingly reduced. In this way the OHL helped to destroy the monarchy in Germany as effectively as the most outspoken republican, and William II, by failing to play the role allotted to him and by siding with the military, was to dig the grave of the house of Hohenzollern. As a final irony it was the army, the 'pillar of the throne', that was to demand of the Kaiser that he should abdicate.

Within the *Grosse Hauptquartier* the general staff of the field army was the largest organisation.[8] The largest section was the operations section (Section I). It was responsible for strategic and tactical planning, for the movement of troops and for liaison with the Württemberg, Saxon and Bavarian armies. Chief of the section was Colonel Tappen, who was to be replaced by Colonel Wetzell as part of the reorganisation and extension of the section under Hindenburg and Ludendorff. The section was concerned with purely military matters, and thus played little or no part in politics.

The same cannot be said of Section II (Op. II) headed by the energetic heavy artillery specialist, Colonel Bauer, who was the most ambitious political officer at the OHL. His rise to prominence at headquarters was due to his effective deployment of artillery during the invasion of Belgium, and particularly the capture of Liège, the energy with which he dealt with the munitions shortage in the early weeks of the war, and later the detailed preparations for the Verdun offensive. Bauer was soon to establish close ties with leading politicians, the leaders of industry and with the Crown Prince. During the time that Falkenhayn was head of the general staff Bauer had shown a certain degree of restraint in his political ambitions, although he had played an important role in overthrowing Falkenhayn and securing the appointment of Hindenburg and Ludendorff. It was under the OHL that Bauer was to rise to real prominence, for he became the intimate advisor of Ludendorff and enjoyed the full support of Hindenburg. His section was to play a most important role in the militarisation and control of the German economy under the auxiliary labour law. He was a born intriguer and a man almost without principle or scruples. He helped to secure Ludendorff's ascendancy at the OHL, but as soon as

Ludendorff's star began to wane he plotted his downfall. As an expert on the war economy Bauer was to interfere directly in every aspect of politics, providing Hindenburg and Ludendorff with political programmes and attacks on individual politicians and civil servants which reflected his ultra-authoritarian, corporatist, racist and imperialist views. It was mainly through Bauer that the intimate links between the OHL and heavy industry and the OHL and the political ultras were forged. He was certainly more than a mindless puppet in the hands of these groups, but he always acted in their objective interests. More than any other officer at the OHL, Bauer acted independently, and certain of Ludendorff's support he worked towards his political aims which included a military dictatorship under Ludendorff, the exclusion of the Reichstag from active politics, and the total militarisation of the economy. But these fascist ambitions could not be realised under the prevailing conditions in Germany during the war.

Almost equal in importance to Bauer's Section II was Section IIIb which initially had been responsible for the collection of intelligence reports from abroad and for counterespionage at home. As the war progressed the section became increasingly concerned with political and economic analyses which were soon to become even more important than the more conventional forms of military intelligence. As the contradictions within German society became increasingly acute under the stress of war, the socialist and pacifist movements became more radical and had a wider appeal. The tendency was accelerated by the fact that the war aims of the Pan-Germans were so clearly out of all proportion to the situation of the armies at the front, and later, by the impact of the Russian revolution with its stirring appeal for peace without annexations. To counteract this trend Section IIIb played an increasingly important role in propaganda, and attempted to manipulate public opinion which seemed to be running against the ambitions of the OHL and their supporters in industry and on the political right. Censorship and propaganda soon came to be the most important activities of Section IIIb.

Another significant organisation within the OHL, and one which is frequently ignored, was the *Militärische Stelle des Auswärtigen Amts* (MAA).[9] This section was formed in July 1917 and was commanded by Colonel von Haeften. It was designed to give the OHL a decisive voice in propaganda abroad, which until then had been the exclusive preserve of the information section. Haeften proved to be a most adept empire builder, and within a very short space of time the MAA became the central organisation for the foreign policy of the OHL, a fact which was underlined when it was renamed the 'Foreign Section of the OHL' *(Ohla)* in July 1918. In October 1918, when the OHL was gradually losing much of its political influence, the war having been lost, the *Ohla* was reorganised under the direct control of the foreign office. Colonel Haeften not only created a very important position for himself in the field of foreign propaganda and policy formulation, he also played an important role in domestic politics by carefully editing army reports so that the true gravity of the situation on the western front was concealed. He also established 'Foreign Auxiliary Büros' in the occupied territories which sent reports back to the MAA, and thus formed an organisation independent from either the Foreign Office or the military attachés, directly controlled by the OHL and acting as its private foreign office.

The powerful position of the army throughout the war was due in part to the authority vested in it by invocation of the imperial law of the state of siege. During the Franco-Prussian war Bismarck had only used the law in certain areas, but from the very outset of the war in August 1914 the law was applied throughout the Reich.[10] The law on the state of siege, Article 68 of the constitution of the Reich, was based on the Prussian law on the state of siege of 4 June 1851. The law was therefore written with the memories of the 1848 revolution still very vivid, and was specifically designed to give the army considerable powers to deal with revolutionary unrest at home and threats from outside. It was therefore quite unsuitable and inappropriate for use in time of war and national emergency.

Article 68 stated that 'if the public safety of federal territory is endangered, the Kaiser may declare any part of the same to be in a state of war'. In that case the Prussian law of 4 June 1851 was to be applied. Interpretations of the state of siege law were many and varied, and the relative position of Article 68 and the Prussian law of 1851 was never satisfactorily settled. Further confusion was caused by the fact that there was no clear delineation between the concept of a 'state of war' and a 'state of siege'. This fact, coupled with the determination of the army to fight against social democracy, meant that it was generally assumed that Article 68 would be invoked in the event of war, and military planning was carried out on this assumption.[11]

The Prussian law on the state of siege gave executive power to the military commanders, and made them to a large extent independent of the civil government and the parliamentary bodies. The army willingly used this law as a weapon against its political opponents at home, and in doing so was acting in the tradition of the Wilhelmine army. For Bethmann Hollweg, with his woolly-headed notions of the 'parallelogram of forces' and the 'politics of the diagonal', such an attitude was a threat to the domestic peace of the country which he hoped to maintain. In July 1914 he therefore tried to persuade the Prussian war minister that the declaration of the state of siege could have 'disastrous consequences for the solidarity, depth and strength of patriotic feeling, and that any possible military advantages would not compensate for the harm that could be caused in the area of politics or ideals'.[12] The chancellor's attempt to avoid the inevitable political consequences of the declaration of the state of siege was swiftly countered by the military who argued that as the plans for mobilisation were based on the declaration of the state of siege, it would be impossible to change them at this late stage.

Section 5 of the law of the state of siege provided for the suspension of a number of important paragraphs in the constitution which guaranteed certain civil liberties. These included paragraphs 5 (personal freedom), 6 (freedom from unlawful search and seizure), 7 (guarantee of duly appointed judges and prohibition of all summary courts), 27 (freedom of speech and prohibition of censorship), 28 (punishment of misdemeanours by word, writing, printing or pictorial representation only by the provisions of the law), 29 (freedom of assembly), 30 (freedom of association), 36 (prohibition of the use of armed force to put down civil disorders and the execution of laws, except in cases and in ways covered by the law and at the request of the civil authorities). The right to suspend any or all of these paragraphs was vested in the Kaiser, but under the Kaiser's declaration of 31 July 1914 the right to decide which paragraphs were to be suspended was given to the military commanders. Thus the military commanders, the deputy commanding generals of the twenty-four army corps areas into which Germany was divided and the commanders of the fortresses, were given exceptional powers which were not restricted to purely military affairs, and they were given precedence over all civilian authorities, including the presidents of the Prussian provinces. The excessive powers given to the military commanders under the law on the state of siege were not seriously questioned until September 1918 by chancellor Hertling who asked the Kaiser to restrict their power, but this did not happen until the chancellorship of Prince Max of Baden.[13] Thus the law of the state of siege created a hopeless state of legal balkanisation throughout Germany, with different military commanders suspending different sections of the constitution. The civil liberties of Germany were now subject to the whim of the military authorities, and the power of the generals over the population seemed almost unlimited.

During the war some attempts were made to reform the law of the state of siege and correct some of the more glaring injustices which it created. In December 1915 the 'Lex Schiffer' changed paragraph 9b which stipulated that any activities that had been expressly banned by the military authorities would have to be punished by prison sentences. As the military authorities frequently issued bans that involved quite trivial matters this was clearly absurd and the 'Lex Schiffer' made provisions for fines up to 1,500 marks.[14] Criticism was mainly levelled at the chaotic legal situation in Germany, the autocratic behaviour of the commanding generals, and the fact that there was no appeal against the decisions of the army commanders except through the Kaiser as supreme warlord – a course of action which was hardly likely to seem particularly promising to an aggrieved citizen. A modest reform was made with the reorganisation of the Prussian war ministry in December 1916. The war minister was given the impressive title of 'supreme military commander' *(Obermilitärbefehlshaber)* and with it the power to coordinate the military commanders, but he was not given the power to command them and the orders which they gave could not be questioned. The war minister was empowered to hear complaints from individuals against specific instances of the application of the orders of the military commanders, but that was the extent of the reform. It was not until the last days of the war that the war minister was given the authority to issue orders to the military commanders, as part of the parliamentarisation of the Reich, thus bringing some order into a hopelessly confused and unjust situation.

One of the more grotesque provisions of the law of the state of siege was that the military commanders were given the right to expel anyone from their district or to imprison anyone, without having to state the charges against him or bringing him before any kind of court. The military commanders were thus given the right to lock up anyone they liked for as long as they pleased. The situation was improved a trifle by the 'Law of Preventative Custody' *(Schutzhaftgesetz)* of December 1916 which, with remarkable lack of precision, stated that an individual could only be arrested if he was deemed to represent a danger to the security of the Reich. The reasons for the arrest had to be given, and there was the possibility of appeal to the Reich military court. Prisoners also had to be brought before a judge within twenty-four hours of their arrest.[15]

Complaints against the implementation of the censorship, the restriction of freedom of association, and the censorship of private mail were voiced in the Reichstag, but little improvement was secured. An attack on the excessive powers of the commanding generals could all too easily be construed as an attack on the principle of military security. Attempts to define the notion of military security also proved fruitless, so the situation remained almost unchanged until the very last stages of the war.

The wide powers given to the military commanders under the law of the state of siege were the basis of the extensive political activity of the army in domestic politics.[16] Initially concerned with the organisation, administration and training of troops in the corps districts, they soon became involved with problems of the war wounded, prisoners of war and providing sufficient numbers of troops for the army. This led naturally to concern with broader economic questions, propaganda, censorship, control over the labour force and even over industrial plants. As the war progressed there was hardly an aspect of domestic politics that did not lie within the field of competence of the deputy commanding generals. Armed with Section 9b of the law of the state of siege they could act with dictatorial powers against which the people had no effective right of appeal. Their principal activity was directed towards the repression of the labour movement, the crushing of political dissent and the imposition of an ultra-conservative orthodoxy. This amounted to a continuation, but also to an intensification of the army's prewar political activities.

Relations between the deputy commanding generals and the civil authorities were never clearly defined and were open to a variety of different interpretations. There was no doubt that at least in Prussia the military authorities were supreme, and that the civil authorities were reduced to the rank of assistants and executors of army orders. Even in peacetime the commanding generals had taken precedence over the civil authorities. In the German states, however, the situation was greatly complicated by the fact that the commanding generals took their orders from the Kaiser alone in times of war and were thus not responsible to the civil authorities; this in turn was in direct conflict with the desire to preserve a modicum of state rights even in time of war. Württemberg managed to avoid some of the worst consequences of this conflict by combining the office of deputy commanding general and war minister. In Bavaria the law was somewhat different: the constitution remained in force except for the restriction of the freedom of the press. Although extensive powers were given to the military commanders, they were all within the framework of the Bavarian constitution. The Prussian government was left without any proper coordinating control over the military commanders, and all attempts to achieve a working arrangement between the civil and military authorities failed.

The chancellor had two possible channels open to him. He could either approach the individual commanding generals and try to persuade them to accept his point of view, or he could prevail upon the Kaiser to issue an order to them. But once again the Kaiser failed to fulfil the necessary function of coordinating the work of the military commanders, so that each commander was able to establish his own fiefdom which was virtually without any form of external control. The appointment of the war minister as supreme military commander did very little to rectify this situation, and it was not until October 1918 that the Reich government was given some power over the commanding generals.

During the war there was a certain tendency to strengthen the central government in Berlin, and this was coupled with a determination by the Reichstag to find redress for those who had been unjustly treated by the military. Both these factors tended to strengthen the position of the war minister, but his power was still very limited. Although two cabinet orders in 1916 obliged the military commanders to follow the recommendations of the war minister in certain instances, in practice they took very little notice of what the minister had to say.[17] The war minister's position was also strengthened with the creation of the *Kriegsamt,* the office for economic affairs, which subordinated the military commanders to a department of the war ministry in questions of economic policy. This centralising tendency was counteracted to a certain degree by the fact that the *Kriegsamt* under General Groener allowed a considerable degree of independence to its local branches, and also because the war ministry depended on the reports of the deputy commanding generals on economic conditions within the areas of their command. Thus, although there were factors which restricted to a degree the independence of the military commanders, in practice they were subjected to very little control or restraint.

The relations between the OHL and the military commanders were also never clarified. The enormous prestige of the OHL under Hindenburg and Ludendorff meant that the deputy commanding generals were particularly anxious to act in the spirit of the chief of the general staff, but Hindenburg never saw fit to address the military commanders as one body, and relations between the OHL and the commanders were never formalised. The influence of the OHL was felt indirectly, largely through the war ministry and the *Kriegsamt* in matters of economics, and through Section 111b in questions of censorship. The reorganisation of censorship in 1917 resulted in the military commanders following the political directive of the OHL much more closely, but even these changes did not result in a rigorous centralisation, and the military commanders retained a considerable degree of independence. Thus although the influence of the OHL over the military commanders was much stronger under Hindenburg and Ludendorff than it had been under Moltke or Falkenhayn, they were never reduced to mere executive organs of the general staff. On the other hand there was no attempt by the military commanders to frustrate the intentions of the OHL, and their independence from central control in no sense inhibited the power and authority of the general staff.

In the prewar years there had been frequent clashes between the war ministry and the general staff, and the ministry was determined to preserve its independence from their old rivals during the war. Hindenburg and Ludendorff, by engineering the dismissal of the war minister, Wild von Hohenborn, were able to assert their authority over the ministry and then secure the appointment of a subservient successor, von Stein, who was prepared to follow their lead, particularly in the vital matters of industry and labour. The reorganisation of official propaganda and the beginning of the 'patriotic instruction' programme in 1917 was a further step in the direction of establishing greater control over the war ministry by the general staff.[18]

Although the organisational structure of the German army during the war was confused, inefficient and lacking in effective coordination, it would be quite incorrect to assume that the system was paralysed by these obvious shortcomings. It was held together by the fact that there was general agreement about what was to be done, and differences, although often very important, were usually over matters of degree and expediency rather than over ends. There was agreement that the war was to be fought for the achievement of substantial war aims, and that at home the radical left and even the bourgeois democrats should be suppressed. They all knew what they were against, but there was nothing constructive in their programme. Reactionary politics of this nature at a time when profound changes were taking place in German society were bound to create great problems and cause a further polarisation of society. In the course of this process, the Reichstag was to emerge as a possible alternative to the quasi-plebiscitary dictatorship of the OHL, but the eventual victory of the parliamentary forces was the result of the defeat of the army at the front, and the blame for the humiliation of defeat was not to fall on the OHL, but on the Reichstag majority; the dangerous tensions within German society which the OHL had done so much to exacerbate could not be resolved, even in the moment of defeat.

The appointment of Hindenburg and Ludendorff to the OHL was part of an attempt to overcome the profound disorder within German society without resorting to the only measures that would have solved the situation, which would have included ending the war and effecting major social changes. If the war was to be won and the *status quo* preserved and strengthened then every effort would have to be directed towards mobilising the full resources of the country, maximising the output of war materials, increasing the manpower of the army and supressing unrest and criticism at home. Yet none of these aims could be achieved without further repression and militarisation of society, which in turn would inevitably intensify the very problems that the new OHL, with its almost mythical prestige, hoped to overcome. Thus one of the first concerns of the OHL was to control the press and to launch a massive propaganda campaign to achieve its aims.

Under both Moltke and Falkenhayn the OHL had only played a modest role in controlling the press and establishing guidelines for propaganda. The creation of a War Press Office *(Kriegspresseamt)* in October 1915 had given the OHL direct control over censorship. It had been sharply criticised by the press and by parliament, and was seen by the war ministry as another sinister move to strengthen the OHL at their expense. Faced with this criticism the *Kriegspresseamt* had shown a certain amount of restraint, but it soon became clear that Hindenburg and Ludendorff were determined to use it for the pursuit of their own political aims.[19] One of their first acts was to dismiss the head of the *Kriegspresseamt*, Deutelmoser, whom they considered to be too strong a supporter of Bethmann Hollweg and who had little sympathy for the OHL's criticisms of the chancellor's policies.[20] Once Deutelmoser was out of the way and replaced by the more compliant and ineffectual Major Stotten, Ludendorff lifted the censorship on the discussion of war aims, arguing that the promise of vast territorial gains would have a most welcome effect on morale.[21] Deutelmoser, who was now serving as press secretary to the foreign office, knew perfectly well that this move was designed to give perfect freedom to those who wished to attack the chancellor from the right, and with the support of Bethmann Hollweg he made some rather pathetic appeals for restraint and national unity which were simply ignored by Hindenburg and Ludendorff.[22]

Censorship of any sort was very unpopular, and the OHL was naturally anxious to rid itself of the odium of being the censor, while at the same time it was eager to retain full control over the press. Thus in December 1916 Ludendorff suggested that the press should be controlled by a central agency under the chancellor's control. This was rejected, largely at the prompting of Deutelmoser, for the chancellor knew full well that he would be blamed for all unpopular decisions, and the OHL would still be able to maintain ultimate control by insisting that 'purely military' questions were involved.[23]

Although Bethmann had avoided falling into this particular trap, he was still in a hopeless situation. As the press campaign against the chancellor grew increasingly violent, with the OHL heaping fuel on the fire, Bethmann had no means of redress. Hindenburg replied to his complaints by haughtily insisting that 'to my regret I am unable to offer censorship measures against purely political remarks, as political censorship is only justified when the interests of the military command have to be protected'. Such arguments were later to be used frequently by the OHL. If it was accused of being political it would insist that it was only interested in military matters, and if it was asked to curb its political activities it would blandly reply that politics was no concern of the High Command.[24] In this manner the OHL found an effective method for censoring political articles in the left wing press. The end of party struggles which had been proclaimed in the *Burgfrieden* was deemed a military necessity. Articles in the social democratic press which attacked the Pan Germans were seen as party polemics and a frontal assault on the *Burgfrieden*. Their censorship was thus a purely military matter.[25] Similarly censorship was also applied against any reports on food shortages, or of unrest caused by such shortages.[26] Attacks on shopkeepers and merchants as a class were also forbidden as spiteful attempts to destroy the *Burgfrieden* which was the basis of Germany's military strength.[27] Such an interpretation of censorship policies had little to do with military security and guarding against leaks of valuable information which was the original intent of the censorship. Under Hindenburg and Ludendorff censorship had become almost exclusively political, whatever the professions to the contrary; it was aimed at the destruction of the OHL's political opponents from the chancellor downwards, and at holding back the forces of social change. For these purposes censorship alone was clearly not enough, and the OHL was soon to launch a massive propaganda offensive to support their political aims.

The idea of the army as the 'school of the nation', playing an active propaganda role against liberalism, democracy and socialism had a long history.[28] Even though the experience of the past was far from satisfactory, as far as the army was concerned, it was agreed that every effort should be made to strengthen Germany's military power by crushing political dissent and strengthening the established order. It was never clear where patriotic propaganda ended and outright political repression began. The propaganda efforts of the army were yet another example of its active political role.

In the spring of 1917 the propaganda efforts of the army, which up till that time had been relatively modest, were placed under the direct control of the OHL. Major Nicolai, who had commanded Section 111b since the beginning of the war now headed an extensive propaganda apparatus which included the *Kriegspresseamt,* patriotic instruction, and the censorship and control of the press. In each army corps area a propaganda officer was appointed who was to be a specialist in his own particular area, and was to travel to Berlin frequently to be given instructions on how best to organise the propaganda in the corps area and to be armed with suitable materials for this purpose. But once again the relationships between Section 111b and the deputy commanding generals were never clearly established, and their work was further hampered by endless conflict between the military and the civilian censorship bodies.[29]

This decentralised organisation seemed to work quite well in arousing patriotic enthusiasm for the sixth war loan which was floated in March and April 1917. But in July 1917 Ludendorff took steps to ensure greater control by Section 111b of the OHL over the propaganda efforts of the military commanders.[30] This was part of an increased propaganda effort to counter the effects of the peace resolution of the Reichstag which had so incensed the OHL. Films, posters, newspapers and books were made freely available, lecture courses and sermons organised and cinemas and libraries used to support the propaganda campaign. Particular emphasis was to be placed on the origins of the war, an understanding of the economic consequences of defeat 'particularly for the German workers', Germany's successes to date, which would continue if arms and munitions were produced at an adequate rate, the need for authority and discipline, and for trust in the Kaiser and the military leadership. Once again the social-imperialist policies of the OHL were clearly evident. Defeat would bring chaos and ruin to a country already hard hit by the sacrifices of wartime. Prosperity and the solution to the deprivations and frustrations that were dividing the country would only come by a massive victory which would secure extensive war aims — the 'Hindenburg victory' which the OHL alone could bring. Such a victory would make democratic and socialist reforms unnecessary, and bring the peace, satisfaction and prosperity which the left promised but were unable to achieve.

As industrial profits swelled and the black market prospered an increasing number of people objected to the prolongation of a war which brought suffering to the masses and wealth to the few. Ludendorff thus denounced the 'gross egoism and selfish pursuit of profit and pleasure, the faint-heartedness, pessimism and neglect of duty' of an increasing number at home. This he blamed on the sinister activities of elements who wished to undermine and destroy the state, and who used the hardships and miseries of the time to pursue their own dangerous ends. Propaganda could help to counteract the weak-kneed and the feeble-hearted. Troops on leave would have to act as propagandists for victory and total war effort, and would be immune to pacifist and treacherous agitation.[31]

Such was the beginning of the programme of 'patriotic instruction' which was launched in the summer of 1917. Propaganda officers were appointed to each army corps, and were given the task of organising compulsory lectures twice a week. Strict instructions were given on how the lectures were to be conducted. The war was to be shown as the result of England's manipulation of 'French lust for revenge and Russian greed for land'. If the war were lost, Germany's economic base would be destroyed for at least the next hundred years. The troops were to be told that Germany's offers of peace were simply seen as signs of weakness, and the Entente had no desire whatever for peace. In this way it was hoped that the majority resolution of the Reichstag of 19 July 1917 for peace without forcible annexations which, in spite of its highly ambiguous wording, was likely to have an unfortunate effect on the morale of the troops, might be countered. It would have to be made quite plain that Germany had already won the war, and for those who doubted this, stirring accounts of the triumphs of the U-boats and glorious examples from the military history of Germany should be recounted. To keep the men on their toes a few lurid stories of atrocities committed against prisoners of war should be thrown in for good measure.[32]

These lectures were not only to be given to the troops. The army organised propaganda committees *(Aufklärungsausschüsse)* in each district *(Bezirk)*. Their work seldom rose above the usual level of chauvinist claptrap that characterised the propaganda efforts of most of the states engaged in the great war. The population was urged to 'Think German, speak German and write German and avoid anything foreign in speech and print'. In addition to this German equivalent of the British persecution of the Dachshund, German women were exhorted to be economical, not to hoard food, to use wild plants for salads, not to complain, and above all not to have sexual intercourse with prisoners of war. Walls have ears. Strikes do terrible damage. A 'feeble peace' would mean the economic destruction of Germany — only a 'Hindenburg victory' would save the country from being economically ruined and militarily defenceless.[33]

In his review of this propaganda campaign Ludendorff seemed to be quite satisfied, suggested only minor changes, and stressed the enormous importance of the propaganda effort. He did however suggest a wider discussion of war aims, and thus gave his sanction to endless tirades against a 'feeble' peace, the Reichstag resolution, and the policies of the government.[34] There is ample evidence, however, to suggest that Ludendorff's optimism was misplaced. Lectures on 'the use of the red berries of the asparagus plant and the fruit of the hawthorn as *ersatz* coffee', photographs of Hindenburg in various martial poses, and heavily slanted lectures such as 'what rights do the people have in democratic England, France and America?' were hardly likely to do much to raise morale and unify the country as it became increasingly rent apart by the effects of war on an antiquated and unjust social structure.[35] The patriotic instruction programme came under heavy attack in the Reichstag, and the social democrats' main speaker, Landsberg, came armed with impressive evidence that the army was indeed using the patriotic instruction periods for right wing extremist propaganda. The war minister was unable satisfactorily to counter these charges.[36] The war minister then sent an order to the military commanders saying that party politics should be avoided in the patriotic instruction periods and that restraint should be exercised in the discussion of peace proposals and war aims.[37] In practice the patriotic instruction was as politically biased as ever, and the fight against party politics was simply a fight against the left, the politics of the right seen as simple apolitical patriotism.

By the winter of 1917 it became clear that the programme was a failure. Its only successes were in pure entertainment, in the films and plays that were shown to exhausted troops behind the lines. Nicolai complained that there was too much 'art' in these films, and not enough propaganda.[38] But propaganda was by its very nature political, so that much effort was spent trying to find ways to prove that the discussion of economic and political matters was not in fact political. The result was a highly elastic concept of the political which could be used to exclude any controversial issues when ill-prepared propaganda officers faced difficult questions from the men, but could include propaganda on behalf of the political aims of the OHL.

With the wave of strikes in the early weeks of 1918 the main emphasis was on the danger of strikes which were seen as 'treason and fratricide'.[39] It soon proved impossible to talk about strikes without discussing the causes, both economic and political, of the strike movement. Most officers were quite incapable of differentiating between the revolutionary socialists of the left and the social democrats who were doing everything possible to stop the strike movement and had long since abandoned their Marxist principles. The struggle against the strikes soon degenerated into wild polemics against the social democrats and the unions, which showed no understanding of the true nature of the changes that had occurred within the labour movement. Many of the troops had considerable sympathy for the strikers, and the heavy-handed harangues of the propaganda officers only helped to strengthen this sense of solidarity.[40]

As the entertainment side of the programme was so successful it was decided to combine pleasure with propaganda. But this effort was not without problems. The 'Ring der Nibelungen', Kleist's 'Prinz von Homburg' and his 'Hermannsschlacht', Schiller's 'Wallenstein' and even surprisingly Lessing's 'Minna von Barnhelm' could all be presented as 'classic works of German militarism', but Goethe was highly suspect as a liberal, and had to be avoided as much as possible. German history, presented in a *völkisch* manner, 'is of an incredible greatness. Not even the most extraordinary imagination of a writer of extreme genius could think of anything greater.' This historical and literary survey was to stress 'a profound understanding of the spirit of technology which alone can save the German soul from mechanisation and Americanisation and from the workings of the gigantic machinery which threatens us by ourselves entering into the spirit of technology'.[41] This extraordinary mixture of halfbaked cultural pessimism, militarism and authoritarianism was typical of the OHL's thinking in the summer of 1918. The range of 'purely military questions' was ever increasing. By 1918 the OHL demanded the banning of the sale of contraceptives, a heavy tax on bachelors for failing in their 'natural duties' for which there was no excuse as there was an 'excess of German women', and further annexations to provide space and food for this increased population.[42]

In the final months of the war the propaganda effort was again stepped up. The main emphasis was now on trying to combat socialist ideas which were spreading among the civilian population, the army being regarded as still reliable. Frantic efforts were made to reorganise the whole system, and it was typical of the organisational fetishism of Hindenburg and Ludendorff that they believed that complex political issues could be settled if only the correct organisational framework could be developed. But these efforts met with no success, and finally at the end of November 1918 Erzberger took over control of all propaganda activities at home and abroad. Although he was restrained by the military, it was a major step forward towards civilian control over propaganda.[43] The change was welcomed by the military authorities and the right wing parties, for they could attack Erzberger for failing to provide adequate propaganda efforts against President Wilson, and use him as a convenient scapegoat for the failure of the army's own fruitless scheme of patriotic instruction.

Military censorship was repressive against the left wing press, although Hindenburg and Ludendorff frequently complained that the military commanders were too soft on the press, taking Frederick the Great's adage that the 'gazettes should not be inconvenienced' far too literally; but perhaps even more serious was the deliberately false information fed to the German public by the OHL's manipulation of the press. Stories of enemy atrocities, spies, agents and traitors were concocted to further mislead a public that had already suspended its normal critical faculties in time of war. Military setbacks and defeats were reported in the press in such a way that it seemed that nothing serious had happened. Shortages of men and munitions were hardly mentioned in the press, and even the food situation, a matter of grave and immediate concern to all Germans, was carefully disguised. The army also provided totally misleading figures of the wounded and killed.[44] The cumulative effect of this policy was the creation of those dangerous illusions that did so much to make it difficult or even impossible for the majority of Germans to deal with the harsh realities of a lost war.[45]

The OHL was thus never able to exert full control over the press or propaganda. The question of the relative importance and competence of the OHL, the commanding generals, the chancellery, the foreign office and the ministry of the interior was never settled. The endless discussions about the limitations of the concept of the 'purely military', and the strife between the civilian and the army authorities as to whether a particular problem was military or political made any consistent policy almost impossible. The centralisation of propaganda under Erzberger could thus be used as a vindication of the policies of the OHL which had constantly demanded that the civilians should be responsible for all unpopular measures, and the failures of the programme could be blamed on the civilians. The experience of Section 111b and the OHL in propaganda and censorship shows an absence of a structure of vertical forms of domination, a lack of norms and a degree of bureaucratic anarchy which seems to be a characteristic of totalitarian states and is so marked a contradiction of their avowed aim to offer decisive leadership.[46] Very much the same is true of Colonel Bauer's Section 11 which was largely responsible for the OHL's economic policy, to which we must now turn.

NOTES

1. For further material on the organisation of the OHL see Walter Hubatsch, 'Grosses Hauptquartier 1914-18', *Ostdeutsche Wissenschaft,* Vol. 5, 1959; Siegfried Schöne, *Von der Reichskanzlei zum Bundeskanzleramt,* Berlin 1968; Josef Stürgkh, *Im deutschen Grossen Hauptquartier,* Leipzig 1921; Otto von Moser, *Die obersten Gewalten im Weltkrieg,* Stuttgart 1931; Alfred Niemann, *Kaiser und Heer,* Berlin 1929; Hermann Cron, *Die Organisation des deutschen Heeres im Weltkriege,* Berlin 1923. The book by Wilhelm Crone, *Achtung! Hier Grosses Hauptquartier,* Lübeck 1934, has little more than anecdotal value. The best picture of life at headquarters is to be found in Admiral Müller's diaries.
2. Müller diary 8-1-1918. Schöne, *Von der Reichskanzlei zum Bundeskanzleramt,* p. 71. The prestige of the monarchy had declined so much that by April 1917 the military cabinet reported that it was receiving numerous letters asking that the Kaiser be requested to abdicate. Ludendorff was particularly anxious that these letters should not be published. Lersner to foreign office 29-4-1917, PA Bonn, AA Gr. HQ 28 Presse, Band 1.
3. This can be seen in numerical terms. In contrast to the large staff at headquarters the chancellery had a wartime increase of only five men, bringing the total up to a mere twenty-five. Schöne, *Von der Reichskanzlei zum Bundeskanzleramt,* p. 71.
4. See the useful introduction to the catalogue of the papers of the *Vertreter des Reichskanzlers bei der obersten Heeresleitung* in DZA Potsdam. Memorandum by Michaelis on reorganisation 18-8-1917 in PA Bonn, AA Deutschland 107, Band 1. Stein's appointment was partly intended to counter the OHL's scheme to attach Colonel Detlof von Winterfeldt, the former military attaché in Paris, to the chancellery as a liaison officer. The foreign office was deeply suspicious of this move. The OHL suggested von Stein, and intended all his reports to go directly to Winterfeldt. Thus the exchange was clearly to the advantage of the OHL. Both Lersner and Grünau were deeply concerned about this move and wished to warn the chancellor, but their messenger, Berckheim, fell ill with dysentery and was unable to go to Berlin. The exchange of letters in PA Bonn, Gr. HQ 237, Personalien Nr 25, Band 1. For Bethmann's attitude see PA Bonn, AA Deutschland 107, Band 1, Bethmann to Hindenburg 21-3-1917. Also Magnus Freiherr von Braun, *Von Ostpreussen bis Texas,* Stollhamm 1955, p. 139.
5. Hindenburg to Hertling 14-1-1918, DZA Potsdam, Reichskanzlei, Verkehr des Reichskanzlers mit den Gr. HQ 2403/6.
6. For a good example see: protocol of the meeting of the Prussian ministry of state 27-9-1918, Bundesarchiv Koblenz, Nachlass Heinrichs Nr. 28.
7. Prinz Max von Baden, 'Notiz für S.M. zur Besprechung mit OHL am

25-10-1918', DZA Potsdam, Reichskanzlei, Friedensverhandlungen 2447/2. Prince Max complained that the OHL had acted against the traditions of the Prussian army by securing the dismissal of Bethmann Hollweg and Valentini, and by demanding an armistice had undermined the morale of the army and encouraged the enemy.

8. For further details see Wilhelm Deist, *Militär und Innenpolitik im Weltkrieg 1914-1918*, Düsseldorf 1970, Vol. 1, p. lii; also Hubatsch, 'Grosses Hauptquartier', p. 430.

9. The best short account is Deist, *Militär und Innenpolitik*, Vol. 1, p. lvi.

10. There is an extensive literature on the legal questions of the law on the state of siege. The best account is H. Boldt, *Rechtsstaat und Ausnahmezustand*, Berlin 1967. See also Wilhelm Deist, 'Zur Institution des Militärbefehlhabers und Obermilitärbefehlhabers im Ersten Weltkrieg', *Jahrbuch für die Geschichte Mittel – und Ostdeutschlands*, Band 13/14, Berlin 1965. Johanna Schellenburg, 'Die Herausbildung der Militärdiktatur in den ersten Jahren des Krieges', in *Politik im Krieg 1914-1918*, Berlin 1964. I am indebted to Dr. Ekkehard Böhm for his very helpful comments on this difficult topic.

11. The various attempts of the army in the prewar period to use the law on the state of siege against strikers and political dissidents are described in Martin Kitchen, *The German Officer Corps 1890-1914*, particularly Chapters VII and VIII.

12. Johanna Schellenberg, 'Die Herausbildung der Militärdiktatur', p. 33.

13. See the meeting of the civil cabinet 28-9-1918, DZA Hist. Abt. Merseburg, Zivilkabinett 2-2-1 Nr 32411.

14. Reichsgesetzblatt, p. 813.

15. *Ibid.*, p. 1329.

16. The activities of the military commanders are outside the scope of this study. By far the best work to date is Wilhelm Deist, *Militär und Innenpolitik* which contains much valuable material on this topic.

17. DZA Potsdam, Reichsamt des Innern – Presse – 12273. The Württemberg, Saxon and Bavarian governments were very anxious that strengthening the Prussian war minister was the first step towards the creation of an imperial war ministry that would spell the end of any remaining independence of the non-Prussian states and armies. Heeresarchiv Stuttgart, Nachlass Marchtaler, Heft 24. For the reactions of the Bavarian military plenipotentiary see Bayerisches Hauptstaatsarchiv, Abteilung IV, Kriegsarchiv M.Kr. 1830, Berichte des Mil. Bevollmächt. i Gr. HQ 1916 IIIa XV 39.

18. Bundesarchiv Militärarchiv Freiburg, Nachlass Adolf Wild von Hohenborn N44/6, letter of Wild to Geheimrat Professor Zorn 1-1-1917 with his comments on the situation.

19. The most useful book on this subject, although it is very apologetic, is Nicolai, *Nachrichtendienst, Presse und Volkstimmung in Weltkrieg*. Kurt Koszyk, *Deutsche Pressepolitik im Ersten Weltkrieg*, Düsseldorf 1968 is rather disappointing. Deist, *Militär und Innenpolitik*, contains many valuable documents and editorial comments.

20. Heerasarchiv Stuttgart, Persönliche Angelegenheiten der Württembergischen Kriegsminister, Band 114. The Bavarian war ministry was anxious that there should not be a press campaign against Bethmann led by 'the well-educated civil servants, university professors, agrarians and heavy industrialists'. *Ibid.*, Nr 1081 Reichskanzler von Bethmann Hollweg, politische Umsturzversuche. Memorandum by Bavarian war minister 5-8-1916.

21. DZA Potsdam, Reichskanzlei: Presse 2438. Ludendorff to chancellor 8-11-1916.

22. Deist, *Militär und Innenpolitik*, p. 448.

23. DZA Potsdam, Reichskanzlei: Presse 2438 Ludendorff to chancellor 17-12-1916.

24. *Ibid.*, Hindenburg to chancellor 16-1-1917.
25. Heeresarchiv Stuttgart, Württ, Kriegsministerium Kriegsarchiv 1105 Zensurverstösse der Württ. Sozialdemokratischen Tageszeitung *Der Beobachter* während des Weltkriegs 1916/17.
26. Heeresarchiv Stuttgart Württ. Kriegsministerium Kriegsarchiv 1104 Zensurbestimmung der Presse Oct 1915 Juli 1918, 10-2-17. Also: Deist, *Militär und Innenpolitik*, Vol. 2, p. 668.
27. *Ibid.*, Vol. 1, p. 458.
28. Kitchen, *German Officer Corps 1900-1914*, Chapter VIII.
29. Walter Nicolai, *Nachrichtendienst, Presse und Volksstimmung im Weltkrieg*, Nicolai is a rather shadowy figure, and there are few references to him in the surviving papers and memoirs of the period. From the comments that have survived it would seem that he was not greatly loved at headquarters.
30. Ludendorff, *Urkunden der OHL*, p. 271.
31. *Ibid.*, p. 278.
32. Heeresarchiv Stuttgart, Württ. Kriegsministerium Kriegsarchiv 1084, Volksaufklärung während des Weltkrieges 1914/18. *Leitsätze für die Aufklärungstätigkeit unter der Truppen.*
33. *Ibid.*, for the papers of IV Armeekorps Magdeburg July 1917.
34. Ludendorff, *Urkunden der OHL*, p. 275. Heeresarchiv Stuttgart Kriegsministerium Abteilung für Allgemeine Armee – und für personliche Angelegenheiten 10001. DZA Potsdam, Reichskanzlei: Allgemeines 2398/11.
35. Heeresarchiv Stuttgart Württ. Kriegsministerium Kriegsarchiv 1084 Volksaufklärung während des Weltkriegs 1914/18. S.G.K. IV AK 28-9-17. In many instances officers were at a loss what to do during the instruction periods. One propaganda officer took his men to the local abattoir. The more usual approach was to deliver tirades against the wearing of ostentatious clothing and jewellery that would 'provoke the lower classes', and to issue calls for economy and hard work for the war effort.
36. The debates were held in the Reichstag on 6 and 9 October: see the *Stenographische Berichte.*
37. Heeresarchiv Stuttgart Württ. Kriegsministerium Kriegsarchiv 1084 Volksaufklärung wahrend des Weltkriegs 1914/18 IV AK 16-10-17.
38. Heeresarchiv Stuttgart Württ. Kriegsministerium 10001 Vaterländischer Unterricht.
39. *Ibid.*, Richtlinien für den vaterländischen Unterricht Stellv. Generalkommando XIX (2Ks) Armeekorps, Dresden 15-12-17.
40. Criticisms of the programme also came from officers connected with it. Deist, *Militär und Innenpolitik*, Vol. 2, p. 953, footnote 2.
41. Dr Ernst Horneffer, *Soldaten Erziehung. Eine Erganzung zum allgemeine Wehrpllicht*, Munich and Berlin, 1918. The book was officially approved by the OHL.
42. DZA Potsdam, Vetr. des RK bei der OHL 31. 'Denkschrift der OHL über die deutsche Volks und Wehrkraft'. The memorandum is almost certainly the work of Bauer.
43. Klaus Epstein, *Matthias Erzberger and the Dilemma of German Democracy* Princeton 1959, p. 263.
44. Koszyk, *Deutsche Pressepolitik im Ersten Weltkrieg*, p. 80. Fritz von Unruh, for example, was given the task of writing a propagandistic account of the attack on Verdun. The result was the book *Opfergang* which was cruelly realistic. Unruh was immediately sent to an assault battalion at the front, was then brought before a court martial and the book was banned. Fritz von Unruh, *Opfergang*, Frankfurt 1966 and the foreword by Kasimir Edschmid.

45. For an excellent discussion of some of these points see: Annelise Thimme, *Flucht in dem Mythos,* Göttingen 1969.
46. Franz Neumann, *Behmoth, The Structure and Practice of National Socialism,* New York 1963, for an analysis of this problem.

3 THE ECONOMIC POLICY OF THE HIGH COMMAND

With the failure of Falkenhayn's strategy at Verdun and the change in the OHL came a realisation that a radical increase in the production of war materials was needed for Germany to win the war and achieve her extensive war aims. This in turn was only possible if there was a massive intervention in the free workings of the economy so that it could be forced to work for the military machine. Until the summer of 1916 there had only been modest attempts to control the economy by channelling supplies of raw materials, foodstuffs and manpower so that the most effective use could be made of them for the war effort. Yet these measures, although they formed the basis of later and more extensive efforts, were still somewhat rudimentary, and private capitalism was allowed to continue almost unchecked.

There were a number of reasons why the government and the military were somewhat reluctant to interfere with the economy. In the initial stages, the war had been very successful for the Central Powers, and much of the strain on Germany's economy had been relieved by the exploitation of the occupied areas. There was concern among some industrialists that a controlled economy geared to war production would ruin certain sectors of industry and disrupt the structure of the German economy to an alarming degree. Many industrialists were slow to realise the fact that enormous profits could be made within a rigorously controlled economy, and therefore preferred to support the old *laissez-faire* system rather than risk an uncertain future. But the most important consideration of all was that the nature of the war had changed. An increasing emphasis was now placed on the production of war materials and on the use of more sophisticated technology. The 'battle of materials' was now to play a decisive role. Not only did the need for war materials, and particularly for ammunition, increase at a phenomenal rate, but also the demand for comparatively new equipment such as motor vehicles and airplanes which put a heavy burden on an economy that was not yet fully geared to war production. Meanwhile the economic superiority of the Entente became ever more apparent, and the need for a total mobilisation of the economy seemed to many to be of pressing importance.

By 1915 many industrialists agreed that some degree of state control over industry was necessary, and the idea of an 'economic general staff' was widely debated. But there was a fierce debate on whether the 'economic general staff' should be controlled by the civilians or by the military. By and large it was heavy industry which was most strongly in favour of close cooperation with the army, and the strongest spokesman for this view was Hugo Stinnes, who was in touch with Hindenburg and Ludendorff as early as 1915 pressing for controls which would favour heavy industry.[1]

Meanwhile at the OHL it was Colonel Bauer, head of Section 11, who was in close touch with industry and was calling for a more rigidly controlled economy. Bauer's efforts were constantly frustrated by Falkenhayn who had little patience with his grandiose schemes and ultra-political views; although he admired Bauer's undoubted organisational talent and limitless energy, he was determined to hold him in check. Bauer had served with Ludendorff in the general staff before the war, and both men were middle-class military technocrats who were keenly aware of the tremendous importance of industry in modern warfare, unlike many aristocratic officers who hankered after the good old days of the cavalry charge and the hand-loom. It is thus hardly surprising that Bauer, of all the officers at the OHL, was the most active in his support for the appointment of Hindenburg and Ludendorff.

Although the idea of a centralised military plan for an all out effort to increase industrial capacity had been at the back of people's minds for so long, the initial impetus came from heavy industry itself. On 23 August 1916 the *Verein Deutscher Eisenhüttenleute* submitted a memorandum to the government calling for a marked increase in production which would only be possible if there was a drastic reorganisation of the war ministry and procurement agencies. Bethmann Hollweg was handed the memorandum by his economic advisor, Helfferich, on 28 August when the chancellor travelled to headquarters to meet Hindenburg and Ludendorff. On his arrival he discovered that the new chief of general staff was fully aware of all the industrialists' concerns.[2] In the first few days at the OHL, Hindenburg and Ludendorff were constantly approached by industrialists asking for their support for measures to increase industrial production. Prominent among the supplicants were Krupp, Duisberg and Rathenau.[3]

Immediately on his appointment to the OHL, Hindenburg, prompted by Bauer, wrote to the war minister stressing the urgency of getting all available men to the front and of increasing industrial output so as to offset the enormous economic advantages of the Entente. Industry would have to become more productive, machines taking the place of men who could then be released to go to the front. The war wounded, prisoners of war, women and children would all have to be forced to work to take the places of those called to the front. Only highly qualified and skilled workers, whose expertise was essential for the war effort, should be excused from military service. An all out effort was needed to increase industrial production, which meant that those branches of industry which did not produce goods which were essential for the war effort would have to take second place, and if necessary go under. If industry was reorganised along these lines Hindenburg thought it reasonable to expect a one hundred per cent increase in the production of ammunition by the spring and a threefold increase in the production of artillery and machine guns.[4]

The implications of this programme were alarming. Increased production on this scale would only be possible if the exploitation of the natural resources of the occupied territories were increased. This in turn would be likely to strengthen demands for imperialist expansion. By increasing working hours, employing women and children, and by stepping up production at any cost, the exploitation of labour, which had already been markedly increased during the war, would be further intensified. The army was prepared to use its powers under the law on the state of siege to deal with any unrest occasioned by these measures, and to further restrict the free movement of labour. The plan would mark the triumph of heavy industry and a significant structural change within German industry. Finally, such coercive power in the hands of the OHL would further increase the tendency towards a militarisation of German society.

Further details for proposed legislation to increase war production were sent to the chancellor by Hindenburg on 13 September.[5] The measures he suggested included the reduction of the number of those exempted from military service, the raising of the military age limit to fifty, legislation to increase and control the work force regardless of the political effects of such a move, the movement of workers away from those sectors of industry which were not essential to the war effort, and the 'maximum exploitation' of all workers. All Germans should be subject to 'the time-honoured principle that he who does not work shall not eat'. Childless women 'who only cost the state money' should be forced to work, as should all women and children who had nothing to do, or who engaged in useless pursuits. All profiteers, pessimists and grumblers should be ruthlessly punished.

In a covering letter to the war minister that accompanied a copy of this memorandum, Hindenburg suggested the creation of a labour office *(Arbeitsamt)* which would be responsible for the entire population of Germany, including the prisoners of war. The labour office would be responsible for forcing all Germans to work, and no food would be allocated to those who did not work and who had no acceptable excuse for not working. All questions of wages would be settled by the labour office.[6]

These two documents mark a new and more drastic approach to the question of the mobilisation of the full war potential of the country. It amounted to a direct attack on the war ministry and the civil administration for failing to take steps necessary to maximise the war effort. The OHL rejected the old scheme of attempting a degree of cooperation between capital and labour and were proposing a militarisation of the economy, centralising control under Colonel Bauer's Section 11 and establishing the uncontested power of the monopolies which were pressing for vigorous control of the war economy.[7] The 'Hindenburg Programme' was thus a serious threat to the working class, a death sentence to those companies which were not considered essential to the war effort, and offered cold comfort to those who wanted to maintain competitive capitalism within a wartime economy.

For men like Bauer the aim of the programme was to achieve the dictatorial control of the OHL over 'all matters of war work, food and production of war materials'.[8] It is thus hardly surprising that the chancellor was concerned about the extension of the powers of the OHL and the further diminution of the authority of the civil government. His economic advisor, Helfferich, summed up his objections to the OHL's proposals in the phrase 'One can command an army, but not an economy.'[9] He wanted to ensure the maximum amount of competition and freedom within the economy, although he agreed that there should be a greater degree of concentration and rationalisation of industry. He argued that the basic problem was not one of shortage of manpower, as the OHL insisted, but rather of shortage of jobs available. Compulsory labour for women was quite pointless given the fact that far more women were already looking for jobs than there were jobs available. Higher wages in the armaments industry had already ensured an adequate supply of labour.

Helfferich's thinking was very close to that of Bethmann Hollweg, although the chancellor's objections were more strictly political. He rejected the 'authoritarian measures' suggested by the OHL, and still believed in cooperation rather than coercion. He also argued that the

militarisation of the economy would make peacetime reconstruction all
the more difficult, for the whole complex process would then have to
be reversed.[10]

The war minister was also predictably critical of Hindenburg's
proposals. As early as July 1916 the ministry had come out strongly
against the idea of compulsory labour, on the grounds that it would
appear as an affront to workers who had made such enormous efforts,
and because compulsion would simply result in discontent and in the
reduction of productivity and efficiency. The unions had done much to
maintain 'pleasure in work and discipline', and their work would be
undermined by these measures.[11] Indeed Hindenburg's proposals were
a massive attack on the policies of the war ministry, and an attempt to
bring the ministry under the close control of the OHL. The war
minister was quick to reply to the Hindenburg memorandum, rejecting
the idea of compulsion and stressing how much had been achieved by
voluntary agreements between management and workers.[12] In order to
strengthen his own position Wild created a new procurement agency for
weapons and munitions which was commanded by a very capable
officer, Major General Coupette, thus showing that he was fully aware
of the gravity of the situation.[13]

On 16 September Wild convened a meeting to discuss the economic
situation. It was attended by representatives of the army, navy, the
civilian ministries, and thirty-nine prominent industrialists, among them
Duisberg, Rathenau and Borsig. The ubiquitous Colonel Bauer
represented the OHL.[14] Wild's main speech at the meeting was a failure.
The industrialists who had been pressing for firm control over the
labour force and a reduction of their freedom of movement, were not
pleased with his request that workers should be carefully handled so
that strikes could be avoided. The industrialists welcomed the creation
of a weapons and munitions procurement office (WUMBA), but the
overall impression of Wild's introductory remarks was that little was
promised that might silence the growing criticism of the conduct of the
war ministry by influential sectors of German industry which were
loudly supported by the new OHL.

The captains of industry were outspoken in their attacks on the war
ministry. Duisberg complained about its interminable bureaucracy.
Rathenau claimed that the ministry did not know what it was doing.
Others expressed their indignation at Wild's attempts to interfere with
the smooth running of industry, and with his 'social experiments'. The
war minister's proposals for a real effort to ensure industrial harmony
by giving way to reasonable demands from the workers were severely

criticised by the industrialists. As those present at the meeting were the representatives of the largest companies there was general agreement that the small and inefficient firms should be destroyed in the national interest, and that government contracts should be given to the large and efficient firms.

The conference shows quite clearly how the lines were drawn: on the one hand, the OHL and the industrialists who called for the regimentation of labour, a concentration and monopolisation of industry, and a maximum of interference with the free workings of the economy to ensure the maximum output of war materials. On the other hand, the war ministry and the civilian government who feared that such measures would have a drastic effect on morale, cause labour unrest as well as political dissent, and make economic reconstruction after the war all the more difficult. Economically it was a struggle between monopoly capitalism and economic liberalism, politically a struggle between authoritarian etatism and liberal conservatism, and historically part of a long conflict between the general staff and the war ministry, as well as between the civilians and the military.[15]

Having met with such severe criticism at the conference, the war minister decided not to reply to the OHL's original memorandum, and hoped that a confrontation with Hindenburg and Ludendorff could be avoided. Ludendorff however was not prepared to let the matter rest. He demanded an answer to the memorandum, insisting that freedom of movement for workers in war industries would have to stop and that the war service laws would have to be extended.[16] In spite of the sharp wording of the note to the minister, and of a further note to the chancellor demanding compulsory measures against the workers, Ludendorff did not really know where to turn. He had met with the opposition of the war minister and the chancellor, and as he confessed to Bethmann, he had not yet had time to prepare a detailed reply to criticisms.[17] Thus Wild's policy of waiting on events was not without justification.

The OHL, however, was preparing its second line of attack against the war ministry. The German industrialists had long been pressing for the creation of a new office to control labour questions, an idea that was vigorously supported by Batocki, the head of the war food office (KEA), by General Groener, and by Ludendorff and Bauer. It was agreed that all questions of labour and food should be controlled by a new office to be called the *Kriegsamt* (war office) which would be directly under the OHL, and thus take the critical questions of labour and food away from the control of the war ministry. Groener, with his exceptional organisational talents and his experience at the general staff, was the obvious man to head the new organisation. He was thus promptly sent to Berlin with a memorandum on the creation of the *Kriegsamt* which he was to present to Bethmann Hollweg.[18]

Somewhat to Groener's surprise, Bethmann was enthusiastically in favour of the proposals, and seemed to be unaware of the implications of the memorandum which would lead to a significant increase in the power of the High Command by removing all economic questions from the war ministry. For the chancellor the only problem seemed to be whether Hindenburg's argument that it was a purely military matter that could be settled by a cabinet order from the Kaiser was true, or whether it would have to go through normal legislative channels and thus become a matter for political debate.[19]

While Groener was persuading the chancellor to accept the *Kriegsamt* Wild replied to Hindenburg's memorandum. He rejected the OHL's proposals for compulsory labour, using arguments which are now familiar about the effects of such measures on civilian morale. Insisting that the war ministry had an adequate organisational structure, and that much had already been done to increase the production of war materials, he was only willing to make minor concessions such as raising the military service age to 50 and agreeing to the use of the law on the state of siege only in exceptional circumstances for the restriction of the free movement of labour.[20]

Bethmann's reply to Hindenburg on the proposed *Kriegsamt* slyly pointed out that it could not be a federal authority, as the OHL proposed, without being under the jurisdiction of the chancellor. Thus the only way out of this constitutional dilemma was to place the *Kriegsamt* under the Prussian war minister, and to imply rather than state that it was in practice under the control of the OHL. The chancellor was in a very strong position in arguing this case. However desirable it might have been to centralise control of these pressing economic questions in one really effective central organisation, and however admirable and well qualified General Groener might be, the establishment of an economic quasi-dictatorship under the OHL, based on the powers given to the army by the law on the state of siege, was too radical a break with the established practice of state authority and the parliamentary accountability of the chancellor for economic and social policy.

Ludendorff had to accept the logic of Bethmann's objections, but replied that he was only prepared to accept the counterproposal if Wild were made to resign. If the organisation of the war ministry was to remain more or less intact, then Wild would have to be replaced by a man who was subservient to the wishes of the OHL.

Wild had tried very hard to preserve the authority of his ministry against those who had been determined to undermine its position. He had sensed as early as the end of July that there was a plot to circumvent the war ministry, and he blamed Groener for making endless difficulties and failing to serve the ministry, and through it the commanding generals.[21] He was very bitter that the chief of the military cabinet, General Lyncker, had passed on a memorandum from a group of industrialists which criticised the conduct of the war ministry directly to Ludendorff.[22] He complained that 'interference, criticism, the desire to know better, and what almost amounts to orders from Hindenburg and Ludendorff' meant that one could hardly speak of a 'war ministry of the King of Prussia'.[23] He was well aware that his days as war minister were strictly numbered. Hindenburg, Ludendorff, Bauer and Groener, were determined to see him go. Bethmann would not support him because he had opposed the chancellor's peace moves. He had lost the support of the military cabinet. The Kaiser, faced with such united opposition, was unlikely to save him. On 28 October Wild received a cabinet order which eloquently shows how powerful the OHL had become. It read: 'At the suggestion of General Field Marshal von Hindenburg, His Majesty is obliged to appoint someone else to the position of Prussian war minister.'[24]

Thus the OHL had won the battle over the war minister, and a partial victory over the *Kriegsamt,* but they still could not overcome the objections to a complete regimentation of the labour force. Hindenburg tried to find a way out of the difficulty by demanding that all male Germans between the ages of fifteen and sixty should be enrolled in the army, thus solving all questions of freedom of movement, labour legislation and employment.[25] Hindenburg suggested that all universities in Germany and the occupied countries should be closed, for otherwise they would be filled with women who would take away all the good jobs from the men and forget their natural roles as wives and mothers. He demanded drastic steps against 'female agitation' for equality, and asked that all unemployed or partially employed women should be forced to work in industry and agriculture for the duration of the war.

These ideas were typical of Hindenburg and the OHL. There was no attempt made to gauge the real needs of industry for skilled workers, or to assess how many men would be made available by the means suggested. Instead of a careful analysis of an extremely complex issue, the OHL fell back on demagogic tirades against workers, women, the universities, the parliamentary system and individual freedoms. For the OHL the militarisation of society was almost an end in itself, and no attempt was made to consider the profound consequences of their actions.[26]

Having travelled to Pless to discuss the situation with the OHL, Bethmann returned to Berlin impressed by Groener's arguments that although the situation was very serious, voluntary measures were far more likely to be successful than compulsion. The chancellor put this view to the Prussian ministry of state, adding the argument that placing all males in the army would be seen by the Entente as a definite sign of weakness which would lessen the effect of the peace move which Bethmann was planning as a psychological preparation for a new German offensive and as a boost to German morale.[27]

Meanwhile, with Wild removed, nothing stood in the way of creating the *Kriegsamt*. Wild's successor, General von Stein, was an unimaginative ultra-conservative, with no previous experience of the war ministry, and an attitude typical of an old style Prussian general staff officer towards the politicians and civilians. He promptly countersigned the order creating the new office. The *Kriegsamt*, headed by Groener, was given responsibility for controlling and feeding labour, for the production of raw materials, arms and munitions. Organisations such as the weapons and munitions procurement agency (WUMBA) and the raw materials office (KRA) were placed under the *Kriegsamt*. Stein delegated his authority over the commanding generals in economic matters to the *Kriegsamt*, and Groener was made deputy war minister with a seat in the *Bundesrat*.

The new *Kriegsamt* was in many ways an unsatisfactory compromise. The OHL had not been able to invest Groener with the virtually dictatorial powers they had demanded. A huge bureaucratic apparatus had been reshuffled and placed under an inexperienced new body with ill-defined fields of competence. Groener was a capable, intelligent and experienced man, but without an effective power of command it was doubtful if he could achieve very much. The war ministry was deeply suspicious of the *Kriegsamt*, which it regarded as a dangerous rival. The *Kriegsamt* resented the constant interference in its affairs by the OHL. The industrialists began to feel that the new office was unlikely to be particularly effective, and started to criticise it with increasing frequency.

Having won at least a partial victory over the war ministry with the dismissal of Wild and the creation of the *Kriegsamt*, the OHL could devote all its energies to securing some form of compulsory labour. This

was the origin of the auxiliary labour bill *(Hilfsdienstgesetz)* the basic
notion of which was that every German from the age of sixteen to sixty
was to be obliged to do war service for the fatherland.[28] Bethmann
Hollweg still had serious reservations about such a policy, which
departed so radically from his ideas of the 'politics of the diagonal'; he
found an unexpected ally in General Groener, the OHL's nominee to
the *Kriegsamt.* The OHL countered Bethmann's objections by claiming
that the *Hilfsdienstgesetz* would waken Germans to the harsh reality of
their situation and would thus help the great patriotic effort to win the
war. Far from showing the Entente that Germany's peace moves came
from a position of weakness and even desperation, as the chancellor
argued, it would show her enemies that the Reich was determined to
fight on, sparing no effort to win the final victory. The situation was
confused by the fact that the OHL still hoped that the law would result
in the extension of military service, as they had originally proposed,
rather than a completely new concept of auxiliary service. In any case,
Hindenburg insisted that the law should be passed by the Reichstag so
that the representatives of the people would be made responsible for
the measure, and thus by implication for its failure should it not prove
entirely successful.[29]

Bethmann Hollweg's desire to water down the bill and to reduce the
element of compulsion, met with stiff opposition from some leading
industrialists. Whereas many industrialists welcomed the bill, even in its
amended form as at least a step in the right direction, and were even
prepared to accept a certain amount of union participation in
arbitration committees, the extremists led by Hugo Stinnes attacked
what they considered to be dangerous social experiments fearing that
the bill would greatly enhance the power of the unions to the detriment
of German industry.[30] The rank and file of the union movement were
also deeply suspicious of the law. For the militants on the left it was a
sinister attempt to prolong the imperialist war and to further enslave the
proletariat to German-Prussian militarism. The union leadership,
however, were flattered by the attention shown them by men like
General Groener and by what seemed to be a conciliatory attitude by
some employers, but they were careful to hide the degree of their
commitment to the law from the rank and file who were becoming
increasingly disenchanted with the war.[31] Groener was able to exploit
this situation to the full, and got union agreement to his being made
responsible for binding arbitration. The union leaders, having been
outwitted by Groener, announced that the law was a significant step
towards 'war socialism', and opened the way towards the creation of a

'social peoples' state'.[32]

Groener was thus subtle enough to realise that he could make such concessions to the unions without in any way compromising the position of either the industrialists or the army. But this point was lost on anti-unionists like Helfferich, or the less subtle industrialists like Stinnes, and was unacceptable to the extremists in the OHL. Groener had some difficulty in arguing his case before the Prussian ministry of state, but he eventually managed to convince the ministers that the conciliation boards were essential in order to win union support for the bill, and that they were merely 'safety valves'. The ministers agreed that this was far better than having the right to form coalitions and the right to strike written into the law as the unions had initially demanded.[33] Thus a modified draft was sent, with the Kaiser's approval, to the *Bundesrat* on 14 November 1916.

Hindenburg felt, quite rightly, that Bethmann was deliberately holding up the passage of the bill, and that the longer it was postponed the more modifications would be allowed which would weaken its original intent and purpose. Two days after the bill was sent in draft form to the Bundesrat, Hindenburg sent a blistering telegram to Bethmann saying that unless he was given the necessary support from the home front he would be obliged to 'give up responsibility for the continuation of the war'. The tone of the letter was unforgivable, but to make matters worse, the OHL released the letter to the press so as further to embarrass the chancellor.[34] In spite of Bethmann's insistence that a bill of such complexity could not be rushed through the Reichstag, the Kaiser fully supported Hindenburg, saying that he also refused to accept responsibility for the 'victorious conclusion of the war' unless the bill was passed within the next few days.[35]

Having demanded that the auxiliary labour law should go into effect as soon as possible the OHL then concentrated all its efforts on prodding the *Kriegsamt* into immediate and drastic action. They complained that skilled workers were not being as closely controlled as the seriousness of the situation warranted. They also demanded a more active policy in closing down inessential and inefficient plants, and dismissed out of hand the objections of many of the civilian ministers to such a scheme.[36] Groener, however, took little notice of these diatribes. He continued to strengthen the organisational structure of the *Kriegsamt* and to ensure the close cooperation of the unions. With the consent of the general commission of the trade unions he was able to appoint the president of the metal workers union, Alexander Schlicke, as chairman of a subcommittee on labour relations.[37] The significance of Groener's tactical victory over the union leadership was lost on those who felt that even talking to trade unionists was tantamount to a betrayal of their vital interests.

The bill passed the Bundesrat promptly and with few modifications was sent to the main committee of the Reichstag for discussion on 23 November. These preliminary discussions made it clear that there was likely to be a fairly long and acrimonious debate in the Reichstag over the bill, which was precisely what the government and the OHL wished to avoid. Although there was general agreement in principle that some form of labour law was needed there were severe tactical differences. Mention of controls on profits sent shivers down certain spines, and Helfferich was on the point of resigning when a motion to create workers' councils in the Prussian state railways was narrowly defeated. Although the Reichstag passed the bill, it is hardly surprising that Bethmann was now convinced that there were 'unbridgeable differences' between him and Hindenburg and Ludendorff.[38]

Although some historians have celebrated the auxiliary service law as a 'triumph of labour', it is difficult to see it as anything but a piece of repressive legislation against the working class.[39] The celebration of the bill as a major step towards war socialism by the SPD leadership merely shows how far the party had moved to the right. It was the fourteen votes of the members of the social democratic working group *(Sozialdemokratischen Arbeitsgemeinschaft)* against the bill that represented the authentic voice of German socialism. The law stated that all male Germans between the ages of seventeen and sixty were obliged to perform patriotic duty during the war. The definition of this auxiliary service was so hopelessly vague that it meant in practice that it applied almost exclusively to the working class, for the upper and middle classes could easily describe their activities as essential to the war effort. Under paragraph IX no worker could leave his job without a certificate of release from his employer. However, the worker could appeal against a refusal to grant a certificate if he could show that 'a suitable improvement of working conditions' would result from a change in employment. Section XVIII stipulated that anyone refusing employment assigned to him could be fined up to 10,000 marks or imprisoned for up to one year, or suffer both penalties. Thus the law caused a significant reduction in the workers' freedom of movement and greatly strengthened the relative position of the industrialists. The workers' councils, celebrated as a major triumph by the unions and seen as the first step towards communism by many employers, were in fact without any significant influence. Under section XI workers' councils were to be established in any business which employed more than fifty workers. The duty of the councils, according to paragraph XII was to 'promote a good understanding among the workers and between the workers and their employers'. The councils were also to bring workers' complaints to the attention of the employers.[40]

The auxiliary labour law was designed by the OHL and many industrialists to coerce the labour movement. Bethmann, Groener, the unions and the Reichstag majority hoped that it would smooth over the growing contradictions between capital and labour. To some radical sections of the working class it offered an opportunity for political action. The workers' councils were designed as mere tokenism, but they were determined to use them as platforms for political agitation. Thus in the Leuna works the workers' council became the centre for agitation for the anti-war strike in August 1917.[41]

Such instances of the radicalisation of the workers' councils were infrequent, and it was not for this reason that the OHL and the industrialists turned against the law which they had demanded, devised, and hurried through the Reichstag. The law became a convenient scapegoat for all Germany's economic ills. Inflation, swollen profits, industrial unrest, increasing wages, shortages and shortcomings were all blamed on the law. The contention of the OHL that the law as amended had delivered Germany into the hands of an irresponsible, unpatriotic and selfish working class was ridiculous. The employers had parity on the conciliation committees, and the *Kriegsamt* had the right to make final decisions in cases that could not be resolved by the committees. In some sectors of the economy, particularly in the munitions industry, there were marked increases in wages, and movement of workers towards those branches which offered a 'suitable improvement of working condition'. This, however, was not a direct result of the auxiliary labour law, but rather of a shortage of fully qualified workers in an expanding sector, and partly because of the trend towards further monopolisation as a result of the pressures of wartime and the use of higher wages as part of a deliberate strategy against the smaller and less efficient firms. These wage increases, which in most cases did not keep pace with a dramatic rise in prices, further strengthened the reformist wing of the social democratic party and intensified the divisions within the working class between a 'labour aristocracy' and those who had been unable to profit, even relatively, from the changing situation. Thus these events, which were bemoaned by the OHL and the more outspoken industrialists, in fact served to stabilise the domestic political situation, just as Groener had hoped, but at the same time provided fuel for a small, but increasingly effective revolutionary left. An equally profound efffect of the law was to heighten the contradictions between the traditionally conservative civil administration, which reflected to a marked degree the values and ideology of the Prussian aristocracy, and an industrial bourgeoisie which was frustrated and confined by a superstructure that did not adequately reflect the profound changes in German society since the times of Bismarck.[42]

General Groener was determined to pursue his policy of conciliation towards the unions, and told his subordinates in the *Kriegsamt* that the auxiliary labour law should be seen as a moral imperative rather than simple compulsion.[43] The response from the unions was positive, and union leaders were warm in their praise of Groener's ability to win the confidence of employees.[44] Yet Groener, in spite of his success with the unions, was soon to meet the ferocious opposition of the OHL. Groener was an expert on transport, and he knew that without a marked improvement in transport facilities there could be no question of even approaching the goals of the Hindenburg programme. There was an acute shortage of coal, which further exacerbated the transport problem. But the OHL wanted immediate action. They demanded cuts in wages, a cheapening of raw materials and food, and if possible some sort of control on profits.[45] For the time being Groener decided to ignore these outbursts, and was confident that once the *Kriegsamt* was running smoothly Germany's production problems could be overcome.

By January 1917 such optimism looked somewhat misplaced. Moellendorff, of the weapons and munition procurement agency (WUMBA), estimated that if the auxiliary labour law were used effectively there could be dramatic increase in production by calling on untapped resources. But he made further calculations two weeks later and came to the conclusion that production was bound to decline because of transport shortages, and that it would thus be better to abandon the Hindenburg programme in favour of more realistic goals. Meanwhile Ludendorff complained bitterly to Groener that the targets for January had not been met, and had fallen far short of the OHL's expectations.[46]

The OHL had been prompted into action by the industrialists who complained at the shortages of coal and raw materials, at the transport difficulties and at spiralling wages in some sectors. They demanded action, and Groener was thus expected to act decisively. Groener rejected these demands, insisting that too much compulsion would lead to a drop in productivity, and that war production had to be made attractive to labour in order to reduce to a minimum the amount of compulsion necessary.[47] Ludendorff was obliged to accept the logic of Groener's argument and ordered that there should be a temporary halt to the building of new factories, and an increased effort made to build new locomotives to relieve the chronic deficiencies of the railway system.[48]

This conciliatory attitude by the OHL to Groener and the *Kriegsamt* was short lived. The industrialists continued to bombard the OHL with complaints that the *Kriegsamt* was over-bureaucratised, cumbersome and inefficient.[49] Hugenberg and Stinnes complained that the law had been altered so much by the Reichstag that it created more problems than it solved. They were sharply critical of the arbitration committees which they felt were irresponsible, and blamed the difficulties of the 'turnip winter' of 1916-17 on the shortcomings of the auxiliary labour law.[50] Krupp was soon to join in the chorus claiming that the situation had become so acute that 'only energetic measures by the military and police authorities can save us from the thoroughly dangerous elements'.[51] The association of German employers' organisations asked Groener to support a change in the law which would stop workers from changing jobs at all, and particularly from moving to companies which offered higher wages.[52] Groener would not accept any of these arguments, and continued to try to maintain a compromise between the unions and the industrialists.

For the moment the OHL was unwilling to attack Groener, in spite of mounting pressure from influential industrialists, so they decided to use the obvious shortcomings of the war effort as a stick with which to beat the chancellor. The plan of attack was drawn up by Bauer. He complained that in spite of the demands made by the OHL under the Hindenburg programme, and in spite of the assurances of leading industrialists that the programme could be fulfilled if only certain conditions were met, and in spite of the creation of the *Kriegsamt,* the attempt to increase war production significantly had been a failure. Bauer argued that the appointment of a coal commissar, an idea of Stinnes which had in fact created endless problems because it had been placed under the chancellor rather than under the *Kriegsamt,* had been delayed too long to be effective. Little had been done to overcome the drastic shortages of food. The OHL had asked that military service be extended to cover all ablebodied men and that there should be compulsory work for women, but instead of this they had been given the auxiliary labour law which did more, in Bauer's view, to guarantee rights than to demand duties. The law had caused an upward spiralling of wages and further demands for political rights. A worker in the

munitions industry now earned more than a senior civil servant or a staff
officer in the field, and this was creating serious problems of morale.
The workers were resorting to strikes to press their demands. The
country was going to the dogs, there was an alarming decline of 'German
fidelity, morals and sense of duty', and the accumulation of wealth and
the pursuit of pleasure seemed to be all that mattered. Even more
ominous were the political demands for the extension of parliament's
rights at the expense of the crown. The government had done nothing
to preserve the spirit of 1914, and now Germany was terrorised by the
'Jewish free thinking and international fraternity'. Bethmann Hollweg
was not trusted or respected at home, and the rejection by the Entente
of his peace move showed that he was even less respected by the enemy.
Bauer concluded this diatribe by saying that only a 'real man' could
save the situation.[53]

Bauer's intention was quite clear. Bethmann should go, and a military
dictatorship under Hindenburg and Ludendorff should be created.
Hindenburg was not prepared to go quite so far as Bauer, and preferred
to concentrate his efforts on criticising the government's economic
policies. He demanded that whenever possible the law on the state of
siege was to be used against the 'trouble makers', to silence demands
for higher wages and to end strikes.[54]

Some army commanders were more than willing to use their
authority under the law on the state of siege to intervene in labour
disputes. Thus the commander in the Mark Brandenburg issued an
order forbidding all strikes, or actions which might encourage strikes, in
any enterprises connected with the war effort.[55] The commanding
general of VII army corps issued similar orders and was complimented
by leading industrialists for showing a 'complete understanding for the
misgivings of industry'.[56] The civilian government was horrified at these
actions, and suggested that a 'level headed and experienced officer or
civil servant' should be attached to the staff of the more outspoken
military commanders so as to keep them under control and avoid
actions which would only meet with violent criticisms from the
Reichstag and the entire labour force.[57]

Bethmann replied to Hindenburg saying that the suggestions of
'certain employers in heavy industry' that the law should either be
abrogated or drastically changed would only result in 'well meaning'
labour leaders losing control over workers. If only the employers were
prepared to make certain sacrifices the 'patriotic and sensible elements'
of the labour force would be strengthened. Any coercive measures
would simply cause 'bitterness and excitement'.[58]

April 1917 was a critical month for German labour. The 'turnip winter' was over, but there was little improvement in the food situation. The Russian February revolution gave fresh encouragement to the militant left, and the Russian slogan 'peace, bread and democracy' gained ever more converts. On 7 April the Kaiser issued his Easter message in which he promised to reform suffrage in Prussia, a system which, with its three-class franchise, had long been the object of the particular criticism of democrats. Now the contentious issue of political reform was raised. One week later the flour ration was reduced from two hundred to one hundred and seventy grams per day, and various special allowances of flour were discontinued. As a result of a combination of all these factors the hopes and frustrations of the German working class were expressed in a number of spontaneous strikes that broke out all over the country. These strikes were denounced by the leadership of the unions and by the social democrats. In the course of these strikes there were a number of significant political developments, including the first attempts to establish direct democracy in some factories, events which pointed the way to the development of the notion of industrial democracy in November 1918.[59]

These developments were proof to the OHL that Bethmann and Groener's ideas of conciliation were misguided and dangerous. At headquarters it was widely discussed, even by junior officers when Hindenburg was present, that Bethmann should be removed.[60] Even Groener was beginning to change his tune. He had been convinced that he could solve the labour problem with an ample dose of his Swabian charm, but when this was proved wrong he felt angry and betrayed by the workers and was highly alarmed at the increase in their political demands. He now insisted that in all cases the law on the state of siege took precedence over the auxiliary labour law, and he underlined the fact that the commanding generals had every right to intervene in strikes and to remove agitators. But he still believed that cooperation with the unions and with the social democratic party was possible. The general commission of the unions made a strong statement denouncing the use of unions to secure political aims, and urged a common struggle against the forces of the left. As Friedrich Thimme was to point out at the *Dolchstoss* trial in Munich after the war, the social democrats regarded strikes as treason, and felt it to be their sacred duty to stop strikes of any sort.[61] Groener thus tried to maintain his original policy, but he was becoming increasingly critical of the attitude of a growing section of the working class, and was finding it more difficult to counter the objections of the OHL to his basic attitude towards the labour question.

It was thus something of a sensation when Groener published a declaration on 27 April 1917 which contained the notorious phrase 'anyone who strikes is a scoundrel *(Hundsfott)*', and in which he threatened to use the laws of treason against strikers. The employers were delighted to hear the general speak up against the striking scoundrels, but they did not like his insistence on the rights of labour being respected, nor did they show much enthusiasm for Groener's suggestion that the factories should be organised by the military. Industry wanted to have the full weight of the army behind them to maintain profits and to hold back wage demands, but they did not want to see the army interfering in the day-to-day administration of their companies. The leadership of the workers was still prepared to cooperate with him, and felt that he was a powerful ally against their obstreperous rank and file. They saw to it that there were no political strikes on 1 May, and for Groener that was a major victory. Yet in the long run he could do nothing to counteract the growing disillusionment and radicalisation of the German working class, and few would forgive him for the 'scoundrel decree'.

The OHL left it to Groener to deal with the situation in April, and avoided appearing too openly in the political arena at this time. Their thinking in April is summed up in a political *tour d'horizon* which Bauer wrote at the end of the month.[62] He condemned the government for failing to maintain the *Burgfrieden* and for allowing the 'anti-monarchical and anti-state social democrats' to retain their control over the mass of workers. The socialists and their allies, the 'Jewish liberals', were trying to achieve their goal of a republic by demanding better food, general equality and peace without annexations. The socialists had used the auxiliary labour law to 'terrorise the national-monarchical elements of the people and of the work force'. There was uncertainty in domestic politics, incompetent handling of the food situation and a disastrous foreign policy. Bethmann Hollweg would never again be able to lead the German people. Firm leadership was essential to avoid the desire for peace, to save the monarchy and to preserve Germany from 'internationalist tendencies'. The working class was becoming more radical and was tempted by revolutionary republicanism. This vision of a loyal and staunchly royalist proletariat led astray by a handful of Jewish demagogues shows how little the OHL understood the April strikes. Whereas Groener and Bethmann had been largely successful in coopting the working class, the OHL was now convinced that they had given way to their demands, and that Germany was heading towards a republic, or even towards socialist revolution.

The principal blame for this situation was placed on Bethmann Hollweg, and the OHL was now determined to secure his dismissal.

NOTES

1. Alfred Schröter, *Krieg, Staat, Monopol 1914-1918*, Berlin 1965, p. 96.
2. Helfferich, *Der Weltkrieg* Karlsruhe 1919, p. 279.
3. *Deutschland im Ersten Weltkrieg*, Vol. 2, p. 462; Walter Rathenau, *Politische Briefe*, Dresden 1929, number 40: Erich Ludendorff, *Meine Kriegserinnerungen 1914 bis 1918*, Berlin 1919, p. 216; Bundesarchiv Koblenz, Nachlass Bauer, Band 11.
4. Ludendorff, *Urkunden der OHL*, p. 63. The letter bears all the marks of having been drafted by Bauer. Ludendorff notes that the letter was written for Falkenhayn, but signed by Hindenburg, a fact that seems to have been overlooked by most historians of the period.
5. The draft of the memorandum was by Bauer: Bundesarchiv Koblenz Nachlass Bauer, Band 2. For the final version, with a few minor changes see *Urkunden der OHL*, p. 65.
6. Ludendorff, *Urkunden der OHL*, p. 68. The specific proposals originated from Moellendorff, technical advisor to the WUMBA of the Prussian war ministry, who had made them to Professor Fritz Haber, the organiser of the chemical war industry. The memorandum was then forwarded to the war ministry under Hindenburg's signature. Gerald D. Feldman, *Army, Industry and Labor in Germany 1914-1918*, Princeton 1966. Feldman however exaggerates the importance of Moellendorff's contribution. Such 'corporatist' ideas were prevalent in the OHL and were certainly held by Bauer prior to the memorandum. The notion that Moellendorff's memorandum significantly changed the OHL's thinking from the end of August to the middle of September is not convincing.
7. For the role of the monopolies see particularly Schröter, *Krieg, Staat, Monopol 1914-1918*, and Weber, *Ludendorff und die Monopole*. Dirk Stegmann, *Die Erben Bismarcks*, Cologne 1970, is a very valuable study which is vital to an understanding of the politics of the industrialists.
8. Bundesarchiv Koblenz, Nachlass Bauer, Band 2.
9. Ritter, *Staatskunst und Kriegshandwerk*, Vol. 3, p. 423.
10. Ludendorff, *Urkunden der OHL*, p. 70.
11. Ernst von Wrisberg, *Erinnerungen an die Kriegsjahre im Königlich Preussischen Kriegsdepartments: Band 11 Heer und Heimat 1914-1918*, Leipzig 1921, p. 232. Ritter, *Staatskunst und Kriegshandwerk*, Vol. 3, p. 422. The industrialists were also deeply concerned with the threat posed by the army to the free workings of the economy. On 21 September the *Bund der Industriellen* submitted a memorandum saying that if the war minister and the general commanders were to control industry this would 'kill the ability to work and the joy of work'. The industrialists added: 'the ideas of the highest military authorities about suitable profits for industrial products, the demand for declaration of costs, the request for lists of clients, the legal requirement to show accounts and correspondence even to bodies where the representatives of the interests of rival companies are present, are all measures which are intolerable to business interests.' DZA Potsdam, Reichsamt des Innern, Kriegszustand 12217.
12. *Der Weltkrieg 1914-1918*, Band XI, p. 37.
13. Feldman, *Army, Industry and Labor in Germany*, p. 162 for further details.

14. Excerpts from the protocol in Deist, *Militär und Innenpolitik*, Vol. 1, p. 486.
15. See Kitchen, *The German Officer Corps 1890-1914*, Chapter 1. Feldman, *Army, Industry and Labor*, p. 167 says that the conference showed that the industrialists were 'completely dependent upon the OHL in achieving their aims'. This is only true in a very limited sense, and ignores the degree to which the OHL's thinking was determined by the monopolies.
16. Ludendorff, *Urkunden der OHL*, p. 76.
17. *Ibid.*, p. 77.
18. Wrisberg, *Heer und Heimat*, pp. 124 and 161, and Vol. III, *Wehr und Waffen 1914-1918*, p. 141. Wilhelm Groener, *Lebenserinnerungen. Jugend – Generalstab – Weltkrieg*, Göttingen 1957, p. 553. Summary in Feldman, *Army Industry and Labor*, p. 177.
19. *Ibid.*, diary entry 14-10-16. Groener, *Lebenserinnerungen*, p. 554.
20. This point is made forcefully by Ritter, *Staatskunst und Kriegshandwerk*, Vol. 3, p. 426.
21. Bundesarchiv Militärarchiv Freiburg, Nachlass Wild, N44/2, diary entry 26-7-16.
22. *Ibid.*, diary entry 4-9-16.
23. *Ibid.*, diary entry 29-10-16.
24. *Ibid.*
25. Erich Ludendorff, *Urkunden der OHL*, p. 78.
26. See Groener's notes in Bundesarchiv Militärarchiv Frieburg, Nachlass Groener N46/113.
27. DZA Hist. Abt. Merseburg, Preussische Staatsministerium Rep 90a Abt. B. 111. 2b Nr. 6, Band 165, 27-10-1916.
28. PA Bonn AA Weltkrieg Geheim 34. This is a direct quotation from the Kaiser.
29. Ludendorff, *Urkunden der OHL*, p. 81. Hindenburg to Groener 30-10-16, Hindenburg to Bethmann 1-11-16.
30. Feldman, *Army, Industry and Labor*, p. 204.
31. For examples of protests against the law by the working class see Weber, *Ludendorff und die Monopole*, p. 54. Feldman, *Army, Industry and Labor*, p. 205 finds the attitude of the unions 'paradoxical'. This betrays a certain lack of understanding of the political position of the union leadership.
32. Weber, *Ludendorff und die Monopole*, p. 55.
33. Feldman, *Army, Industry and Labor*, p. 209 gives a detailed account of this meeting.
34. DZA Potsdam, Reichskanzlei Allgemeines 2398/9. For the furious reaction to this move by the General Governor of Belgium, Bissing, and by Lerchenfeld see Ritter, *Staatskunst und Kriegshandwerk*, Vol. 3, p. 258, footnote 10. There is some dispute among historians about the date of the telegram. It was drafted on 15 November by Gauer, and sent to the chancellor on the following day.
35. DZA Potsdam, Reichskanzlei Allgemeines 2398/9.
36. Heeresarchiv Stuttgart, KM Abteilung für allgemeine Armee- und für persönliche Angelegenheiten 1272.
37. *Deutschland im ersten Weltkrieg*, Vol. 2, p. 483.
38. Helfferich, *Der Weltkrieg*, p. 286.
39. 'Triumph of labour' is Feldman's unfortunate expression. Ritter, *Staatskunst und Kriegshandwerk*, Vol. 3, p. 430 also sees the bill as making significant concessions to labour.
40. The text of the law in English in Feldman, *Army, Industry and Labor*, p.535 In German in *Reichsgesetzblatt 1916*, p. 1333.
41. Weber, *Ludendorff und die Monopole*, p. 56.
42. For a theoretical discussion of this point see the brilliant essay by Ernst Bloch, 'Der Faschismus als Erscheinungsform der Ungleichzeitigkeit', in *Erbschaft dieser Zeit*, Frankfurt 1962.

43. Heeresarchiv Stuttgart, KM Abteilung für allgemeine Armee- und für persönliche Angelegenheiten 1272.
44. Paul Umbreit, 'Gemeinsame Arbeit der Behörden und der Gewerkschaften', *Sozialistische Monatshefte*, 26, 1916. Bundesarchiv Militärarchiv Freiburg, Nachlass Groener N46/113.
45. Bundesarchiv Koblenz, Nachlass Bauer le.
46. Groener, *Lebenserinnerungen*, p. 356. Deist, *Militär und Innenpolitik*, Vol. 1, p. 554.
47. Heeresarchiv Stuttgart, KM Abteilung für allgemeine Armee- und für persönliche Angelegenheiten, 1272. Kriegsamt Berlin 29-1-17.
48. Ludendorff, *Urkunden der OHL*, p.160.
49. Bundesarchiv Militärarchiv Freiburg, Nachlass Groener N46/113.
50. Bundesarchiv Koblenz, Nachlass Bauer, Band 14, 'Verein für die bergbaulichen Interessen im Oberbergamtsbezirk Dortmund'.
51. DZA Potsdam, Reichskanzlei, Notständen 2430, Krupp to chancellor 26-2-17.
52. Feldman, *Army, Industry and Labor in Germany 1914-1918*, p. 327.
53. Bundesarchiv Koblenz, Nachlass Bauer, Band 16.
54. Ludendorff, *Urkunden der OHL*, p. 136.
55. DZA Potsdam, Reichskanzlei, Notständen 2431, 19-4-17.
56. The general referred to was General von Gayl. Deist, *Militär und Innenpolitik*, Vol. 1, p. 522, footnote 6, quotes a meeting of the Verein Deutscher Eisen- und Stahl – Industrieller of 16-11-16 where Gayl was characterised as showing 'complete understanding' on the question of arbitration committees.
57. DZA Potsdam, Reichskanzlei, Notständen 2430, Helfferich to chancellor 7-3-17.
58. DZA Potsdam, Reichskanzlei, Allgemeines 2398/10.
59. Erwin Winkler, *Die Bewegung der Berliner revolutionären Obleute im ersten Weltkrieg*, phil. Diss. Berlin 1964; *Archivalische Forschungen zur Geschichte der deutschen Arbeiterbewegung*, Band 4/111: *Der Einfluss der grossen Oktoberrevolution auf Deutschland und die deutsch Arbeiterbewegung*, Berlin 1959; *Dokumente und Materialien zur Geschichte der deutschen Arbeiterbewegung*, Reihe 11, Band 1, Berlin 1958.
60. Bundesarchiv Militärarchiv Freiburg, Nachlass Merz von Quirnheim, Band 23.
61. Hans Herzfeld, *Die Deutsche Sozialdemokratie und die Auflösung der nationalen Einheitsfront im Weltkrieg*, Leipzig 1928, p. 317.
62. Bundesarchiv Koblenz, Nachlass Bauer, Band 2. It is not possible to date the memorandum exactly.

4 FIRST STEPS IN FOREIGN POLICY

The first major question in foreign policy which faced the new OHL, and which led to further differences between the High Command and the chancellor and his civilian advisers, was the issue of Poland. For some time Ludendorff had been thinking in terms of a German satellite state in Poland which could be exploited to provide men and materials for the German war effort. As early as October 1915 he had written to Zimmermann at the foreign office saying that Poland should not fall into the hands of either Russia or Austria, but that it should be a 'more or less independent state under German control *(Oberhoheit)*'.[1] The relative success of the Brusilov offensive, in Ludendorff's parlance 'that *Schweinerei* of the Austrians', brought the Polish question once more into the forefront of his thinking and prompted yet another letter to Zimmermann. He was impressed at the way in which the Poles had fought at Kostiuchnovka and wrote,

> the Pole is a good soldier ... Let us create a Grand Duchy of Poland consisting of Warsaw and Lublin and then a Polish army under German leadership. A Polish army will come sooner or later, and we could use it now. This may be a little difficult politically, but that is a mere nothing considering the importance of the measure for victory.[2]

Meanwhile the politicians had also been active on the Polish question. On 11 and 12 August 1916 Betmann went to Vienna to discuss the issue with the Austrian government, and agreement was reached in principle to a declaration of intent that a Polish state should be formed after the war. Both Austria and Germany were to secure certain frontier rectifications to secure their military security, and the boundaries of Poland were to be pushed as far east as possible. Poland would not be allowed to have an independent foreign policy, and her army would be controlled by the Germans. The question of whether the two powers would have equal economic rights in the new Poland, as Burian hoped, or whether Poland would form part of the German customs area, as Bethmann intended, was to be left to a commission of experts to discuss.[3] On his return to Berlin, Bethmann told the Prussian ministry of state that his intention was to create an 'autonomous' Poland which

would be completely under the control of Germany, but he intended
to pursue a dilatory policy so as to avoid a confrontation at this stage
with Austria over the issue of economic equality in Poland.[4]

Hindenburg had been informed of these negotiations before he was
appointed to the OHL, and was prepared to accept Bethmann's
argument that a declaration of Polish independence should be postponed
because of the possibility of a separate peace with Russia, but at the
same time he insisted that the recruiting of Polish soldiers should begin
immediately.[5] Thus at the outset there were no differences between the
attitudes of Hindenburg and Bethmann over the Polish issue. Both
agreed in principle to the idea of an 'autonomous Poland', that cruel
mockery of genuine independence which would result in Poland
becoming to all intents and purposes a German province. The
differences between them were tactical, but they were of considerable
importance. Firstly the OHL had in mind a far smaller Poland than did
Bethmann, and their notion of 'frontier corrections' was far more
excessive. Secondly there was the question of timing. The OHL, with
its obsession for getting fresh troops from Poland as soon as possible,
was bound to press for a declaration of independence, the *sine qua non*
of obtaining these troops on anything approaching a voluntary basis.
Bethmann was more concerned with the possibility of a separate peace
with Russia and with persuading the Austrians to give in gracefully to
the German demands for economic supremacy in a satellite Poland.

At a meeting in Pless on 2 September 1916, Hindenburg and
Ludendorff were able to win over the German governor of occupied
Poland, Beseler, to their point of view, even though Beseler felt that the
proposal was a 'mixture of undeniable talent with superficiality,
dilettantism and arrogance'.[6] Their next step was to try to undermine
the effects of Bethmann's assurances to the Austrians at the Vienna
meeting at the beginning of August. Thus, without consulting Bethmann,
Hindenburg demanded of the Austrian general staff chief, Conrad,
that the Austrian government at Lublin should be subsumed in the
German general government at Warsaw, thus unifying Poland 'from
above' and from outside and creating the necessary preconditions for
a unified Polish army.[7]

Predictably both Burian and Conrad rejected these proposals out of
hand, so the OHL had now to look for allies at home in order to force
through their Polish policy. They proved to be remarkably successful in
persuading the Prussian conservatives, who had an ingrained horror of
any suggestion of Polish independence, with their spurious 'purely
military' arguments that Polish 'independence' was indeed essential. The

conservatives' principal spokesman in the Prussian ministry of state, Loebell, proved to be a valuable ally to the OHL. Then, somewhat to Hindenburg and Ludendorff's surprise, Bethmann announced that he was a convert to their views on Poland. The foreign office was appalled. The German ambassador in Vienna, Hohenlohe, wrote to Zimmermann complaining about Bethmann, and suggesting that 'they do not seem to be quite right in the head in the Wilhelmstrasse'. Zimmermann replied that Bethmann was a weak character who always hid behind Hindenburg rather than standing up and challenging him.[8]

This united front of the OHL, the conservatives and Bethmann was exceedingly short lived. Almost immediately the conservatives began to have second thoughts, and fears of an independent Poland were widespread. Before long the conservatives were demanding nothing short of outright annexation, and they rejected the OHL's scheme for indirect domination. Bethmann, knowing that the Austrians were most unlikely to agree to the OHL's scheme continued to hope that Russia might begin talks over a separate peace before the winter set in, and a reshuffle of the Russian cabinet gave him further cause for optimism. But the OHL, supported by Beseler, would not listen to these objections, and Beseler wrote to Bethmann saying: 'As the whole question of Poland is concerned not with Poland itself but with the security of Germany and her dominant position in the east, it is primarily a military question and must be dealt with by the OHL, with whom I am in contact.'[9] Bethmann's reply — that the Polish question was not simply a military matter — was pathetic in the extreme.

Beseler travelled to Berlin and arrived on 8 October 1916 to persuade the conservatives that their fears of the OHL's policies were unjustified. He argued that conservative support for Russia was based on the assumption that it was a conservative and autocratic state, but in fact the Stolypin reforms marked the beginning of a democratic wave which could well lead to revolution and the removal of the Tsar. The conservative desire for outright annexation of Poland was also mistaken, for it would bring a lot of undesirable 'catholic Slavs and Jews' into the German Reich. Without a declaration of intent by Germany in favour of Polish independence, there could be no question of recruiting volunteers, and Beseler believed that thirty-six battalions of volunteers could be trained and ready for action within eight months of such a declaration.[10] Beseler's arguments were cleverly presented in terms which were likely to have maximum effect on his audience, and he could assure them that he spoke with the full and unconditional support of the OHL and as a result of his own specialist knowledge of conditions in Poland. Even so the acceptance which he gained for these views was grudging in the extreme.

Bethmann still continued to argue that precipitate action on the Polish question would ruin the chances of a separate peace with Russia, but Hindenburg dismissed these objections out of hand, saying that peace would only come through military victory for which Polish volunteers were needed. The result of this exchange was that Bethmann agreed to a meeting with the Austrians which he felt would have to be followed by a declaration on Polish independence, regardless of the outcome of the talks.[11]

The meeting was held with the minimum of delay at Pless on 18 October 1916. It was attended by Bethmann, Jagow, Hindenburg, Ludendorff and Beseler, and for the Austrians by Burian, Conrad and the ambassador von Merey. On the eve of the conference Bethmann virtually capitulated to the OHL by admitting that he saw no chance of peace with Russia until Rumania was defeated, and by stating that political considerations had to take second place to military imperatives. Little consideration was paid to the question of what policy should be pursued if the Austrians refused to evacuate Lublin. Beseler summed up the army's thinking, and pointed the way to future relations between the allies: 'It is the last phase of the historic struggle between Germany and Austria. Austria must get out of the war.' Thus with no common policy, and with no considered plan of action, the German delegation met with the Austrians.[12]

Burian's reactions to the German proposals were immediate and outspoken. He flatly refused to allow the unification of the two occupied regions of Poland, and he laughed at the suggestion that the Poles would be so stupid as not to be able to see through such a poorly disguised move as combining a declaration of independence with a demand for volunteers. His objections were forcefully seconded by Conrad. These arguments were met with a barrage from the German side, Hindenburg, Ludendorff and Beseler combining to insist that Polish volunteers were needed immediately. Faced with such opposition Burian was forced to give way, and it was agreed that a proclamation should be made as soon as possible, that Polish troops should be recruited in both the German and the Austrian areas of occupation, and that the new Polish army should be controlled by the Germans. It was agreed that the two areas should remain separate, so that Burian was able to win a small and insignificant concession, and the OHL returned from Pless having secured almost all their demands.[13]

The way was now open for the declaration. On 27 October a Polish delegation, representative of no one in particular, duly arrived in Berlin, headed by the rector of Warsaw University, Professor Brudzinski, in order to ask for the proclamation in the name of the Polish people. This pathetic farce was rendered all the more ridiculous by the fact that Brudzinski replied to Bethmann's speech of welcome by saying that his delegation had come to Berlin at the request of the German government, and not on their own initiative.[14] Once these ceremonies were duly completed, and after some final wrangling over the precise wording of the declaration, the proclamation was issued by the governors of Warsaw and Lublin on 5 November 1916.

The declaration began with a pious assurance that the Central Powers would guarantee a happy and prosperous future for Poland by making her an independent state with a hereditary monarch and with constitutional government. It hastily added that the boundaries of the new state were not yet determined, and that only if it were closely connected to Austria and Germany would it have a true guarantee for the full development of its capacity. The organisation, training and leadership of the new Polish army would be decided 'in joint consultation'.[15]

From the very outset there was no hope that the declaration would mark a new and happier era of German-Polish relations. The shortsightedness of German policy in Poland further increased the tension and hatred between the two countries. Those in Poland who hoped that conditions would improve were bitterly disappointed. The deportation of Polish workers continued, and workers who were already in Germany were refused permission to go home. The price paid for an illusory independence seemed to be food shortages, unemployment, sharply rising prices and a black market all of which contributed to an intensification of the class struggle in Poland. Julian Marchlewski summed up the tragic situation in a bitter joke: 'Today's improvisation on the Vistula by Hindenburg and Ludendorff is unique, a joke the like of which the world has neither seen nor dreamed. An "independent" state with unknown frontiers, with unknown government, with an unknown constitution and oh horror, oh shame, a kingdom without a king!'[16]

Hindenburg and Ludendorff brushed aside the objections of the Austrians and of those Poles who were basically sympathetic to the idea of forming a national army, even under such burdensome conditions, and demanded an immediate call for volunteers. Thus, on 9 November, a call for volunteers was published. Austrian fears that the Poles would now realise that the declaration of 5 November was simply a trick designed to get volunteers were soon confirmed. Within hours placards appeared saying 'Without a Polish government, no Polish army!' On 12 November a mass demonstration was held in Warsaw calling for a Polish government, for universal military service and for Pilsudski. A popular slogan was: 'We do not want to be German mercenaries, but Polish soldiers.'[17] The recruiting programme soon proved to be a complete failure. From the beginning a mere trickle of recruits applied to the recruiting offices, most of whom turned out to be unsuitable for use at the front. By the end of April 1917 there had only been 4,700 applications.[18] Thus Beseler's optimistic estimates of Polish recruits proved to be nothing but an illusion.

The declaration of 5 November was the beginning of a period of increasing stress between Germany and Austria, and it immediately became clear that Poland would be a major stumbling block to improved relations between the two allies. Without informing Conrad or the Germans the Austrian government proclaimed the autonomy of Galicia on 5 November in the hope of counteracting Polish irredentist ambitions, and so that Galicia might be the key to eventual Austrian control over Congress Poland. Bethmann was alarmed at this move, but he wanted to avoid placing any undue strain on the alliance and preferred to treat it as an internal matter. Hindenburg was incensed at what he considered the feeble and vacillating policy of the chancellor, and argued that this was a deliberate attempt by Austria to undermine Germany's position in Poland and was thus a threat to Germany's security. For Hindenburg it was not simply a matter of Galicia but of the future relations between the allies. In an angry letter to Bethmann he wrote:

by not interfering in the internal affairs of Austria-Hungary before the war and during the war, our conduct of the war has constantly been made more difficult. If we continue to be afraid of such interference in an area where our interests are directly at stake, we will give up all hope of strengthening Austria-Hungary and the question arises then why we are still fighting for Austria at all.[19]

Bethmann replied angrily to this onslaught by arguing that Hindenburg's policy, if carried to its logical conclusion, could very well lead to Austria seeking some kind of arrangement with England or France.[20] It was left to poor Grünau to placate Hindenburg and Ludendorff, and Hindenburg eventually gave in to Bethmann with singular ill grace.[21]

Hopes that the death of the Emperor Francis Joseph and the

subsequent replacement of Burian by Count Czernin might mark a change in Austrian attitudes towards Poland were soon dashed. Czernin proved to be no more willing to allow Germany to unite the two occupation areas under her leadership than had been Burian, and for all his suave aristocratic charm he was every bit as stubborn as his predecessor. On 6 January 1917 it was agreed that a conference should be held to end what Bethmann called the *Tohuwabohu* between the two allies over Poland. The OHL blundered into the meeting demanding that the new Polish army should take an oath of allegiance to the German Kaiser, thus confirming all the worst suspicions of the Austrian delegates. It was thus hardly surprising that Czernin categorically refused to accept the idea of joining Lublin and Warsaw, for he was suspicious of German motives, fearful that the loss of Lublin might well be followed by the loss of Galicia, and lastly he was determined to use the Austrian position in Lublin as a bargaining counter for Eastern Galicia and the Bukovina. Thus the conference achieved nothing but an agreement to disagree, and a pious expression of hope that serious differences could be avoided.[22]

The Germans had thus achieved little but the formation of a small, demoralised, poorly disciplined and militarily dubious Polish legion and the mounting suspicions of the Austrians when the situation was further complicated by the effects of the Russian February revolution on Poland. On 27 March the Petrograd Workers' and Soldiers' Council published a declaration calling for the full independence of Poland, a move which eventually forced the bourgeois provisional government to make a similar declaration some two days later.[23] There followed a wave of strikes throughout Poland, protests not only against intolerable economic conditions but also against the occupation forces whose policies had done so much to cause this increasing hardship. This powerful wave of anti-German feeling was so strong that the Polish auxiliary force became increasingly demoralised until it had virtually no military value. By the end of August 1917 the Germans managed to fob the auxiliary force off on to the Austrians, and the OHL's Polish policy was in ruins.

Whereas the prime reason for the OHL's intervention in Poland had been to secure additional troops, in Germany's other main area of occupation, Belgium, a systematic exploitation of the economic resources of the country had been instigated by the civilian and military authorities. By the summer of 1915 the deportation of Belgian workers to the armaments factories in Germany had begun. A state controlled organisation was created under the aegis of the German Industry Bureau, established in Brussels at the beginning of the war by the *Verein deutscher Eisen- und Stahlindustrieller,* and fully supported by the general governor of Belgium, Bissing. With full cooperation between the German military and civilian organisations in Belgium about five hundred workers were deported per week from June 1915 to October 1916.[24]

With the appointment of Hindenburg and Ludendorff to the OHL there was a marked intensification of the exploitation of the occupied territories. The industrialists renewed their efforts to secure Belgian labour and the OHL warmly supported their demands. The heavy industrialists were convinced that the Belgians were enjoying such a high standard of living as a result of Herbert Hoover's relief commission's efforts that they were reluctant to 'volunteer' for work in Germany, and they therefore demanded that their rations should be reduced.[25] Ludendorff agreed with this argument and promptly wrote to the administrations of occupied Poland and Belgium that 'social and legal considerations should be regarded as secondary', as Germany needed more workers for the Hindenburg programme.

General Bissing was determined to preserve his prestige and authority as general governor of Belgium, and was reluctant to become a mere mouthpiece to the OHL. Thus he replied that such a policy would cause a violent reaction in the neutral countries and from Hoover's commission, and therefore he could not accept responsibility for it.[26]

Bissing's high minded objections are in marked contrast to the more sordid reality. He decided to treat all workers who were 'unwilling to work', in other words the unemployed, as criminals because they failed to obey an order by the general governor. Since they were regarded as provocateurs who endangered law and order in Belgium they clearly had to be deported. That Bissing could claim that this was in any way substantially different from the demands of the OHL, or that the reaction in Belgium and abroad would be significantly different, is indeed extraordinary. Bissing was seventy-three years old and had a critical heart condition – he died in April 1917 – and it might possibly be argued that he was no longer able to deal with a situation that he felt was unfortunate, but for which he could find no viable alternative. Ludendorff refused to accept any of Bissing's objections, and the general governor offered his resignation to the Kaiser, but this was refused.[26] Bethmann also chose to ignore Bissing's warnings of the likely results of deportations and preferred to listen to the mounting chorus of industrialists, men like Duisberg, Kirdorff, Krupp, Vögler, Beukenberg and Rathenau, all of whom were demanding workers from Belgium.[27]

After a number of exchanges of memoranda and rancorous meetings Bissing agreed to the OHL's request for 200,000 workers to be sent directly to Germany. His only stipulation was that they should be sent as prisoners, for he still held the extraordinary belief that if the workers were treated as criminals the objections to the deportations by the neutral states would not be so severe. He also suggested that the chancellor should be asked to make a final decision on the issue of deportations from Belgium.[28]

Bethmann, true to the politics of the diagonal, was attempting to reconcile his Flemish policy, designed to bring the Flemings into close association with Germany by political means, with the forcible deportation of workers. How the Flemings were supposed to become increasingly pro-German whilst they were being forcibly deported was a problem that not even Bethmann's political geometry could solve. The chancellor accepted the need for deportations, but hoped that they could be done carefully so as to cause the minimum of reaction abroad. In a similar spirit it was agreed that the camps where the Belgian workers were housed were not to be called 'concentration camps', but 'accommodation for industrial workers'. The reality of the situation was thus to be concealed by legalistic dialectics and etymological ingenuity.[29]

The deportations were carried out with considerable brutality and with frequent disregard for basic human dignity. 'Volunteers' were recruited by using all kinds of chicanery and by wearing down the resistance of the Belgians. Massive unemployment and poor working conditions were deliberately created in order that it might seem that conditions would probably be better in Germany. Families were rent asunder. The workers were transported in cattle trucks to the camps in Germany, camps which the war ministry had to admit were unsuitable for human habitation and which were breeding grounds for bronchial ailments and tuberculosis. It seemed as if Belgium was rapidly becoming a vast slave market for German industry.

With the intensification of the deportations the OHL had won a significant victory over those like Bissing and Bethmann who had some reservations about the possible political effects of the policy, and they had given sterling support to their friends among the heavy industrialists. Hindenburg and Ludendorff were now determined to drive home their advantage and end the semi-autonomy of the general governor, placing Belgium under the control of the OHL.[30] After an initial round, in which Bethmann supported Bissing against the attacks of the OHL, Hindenburg proposed that the general governors of Belgium and Poland should take their orders directly from the chief of the general staff as far as the economic exploitation of the occupied areas was concerned. Hindenburg wrote: 'In my opinion all political considerations have to be ignored in the light of our own desperate situation.'[31] When Bethmann rejected this suggestion, as was to be anticipated, it was suggested that representatives of the *Kriegsamt* should be attached to the general governments and act as intermediaries between the general governors, the OHL and the war ministry.

It soon became apparent that the deportations were creating more problems than they solved. The number of deported Belgians soon was greater than could be absorbed by German industry. Not only were there insufficient work places available at short notice, but employers were often reluctant to employ men who were in poor physical condition and who were bitterly resentful and reluctant to work. As a result, according to one report, only one fifth of the deported workers were in fact employed.[32] The neutral countries protested strongly against the deportations. The violent reaction in Belgium made it unlikely that Bethmann's Belgian policy would have any chance of success. The chancellor thus called for moderation in the deportations, but little was changed. In the next few months a further 120,000 workers were deported.[33]

With the failure of the deportation policy, due to the inability of German industry to absorb the workers, increasing emphasis was placed on the deportation of machinery rather than men.[34] But Hindenburg was still not satisfied. In a note to Bethmann he stressed that there was a considerable contrast between the exploitation of those areas which were directly controlled by the OHL, and Poland and Belgium. He pointed out that 'everything possible has been taken from the occupied territories which are under the command of the OHL', and suggested that the gravity of the situation made it imperative that the same should happen in the general governments.[35] Hindenburg was unable to increase his authority in Belgium, and Bissing put up a strong resistance to any attempt to encroach upon his prerogatives. Hindenburg continued with his straightforward argument.

The greater the shortage of men in Germany who are able to work and of raw materials as a result of the length of the war, the greater become the demands of the military in the face of the constantly improving methods of attack of our enemies, and thus it is even more important that the still rich economic resources of Belgium should be used for the good of our war effort.

This could only be achieved, Hindenburg argued, if the OHL could extend its power over Belgium.

> If the OHL is not given the necessary influence in the economic exploitation of the general government immediately the only alternative would be to extend the area behind the lines *(Ettapengebiet)* so far that it is large enough to provide for the needs of the army and then place it *in every respect* under the army alone. It is surely of far less import for the chancellor's policy that there should be a complete exclusion of the general governor from large areas of what was the kingdom of Belgium, than that the OHL should have what I consider to be the necessary influence over the economic exploitation of the country.[36]

Such measures, even if they had been carried out to the degree that Hindenburg insisted was necessary, would not have been enough to solve the contradictions of the German position in Belgium. The immediate and drastic exploitation of Belgian resources, which in any case could not be absorbed by German industry, the Flemish policy of Bethmann Hollweg, and the annexation or association of the country after the war were three policies that were mutually irreconcilable. German policy pulled in three directions, and this ensured the failure of all three and the implacable hatred of the people of Belgium.

Differences between the OHL and the chancellor over Poland and Belgium made it seem desirable to Hindenburg for Bethmann to produce a list of minimum war aims, for this would force the chancellor to make a stand and there could then be a debate between the civilians and the military over concrete proposals. Hindenburg gained the support not only of the war minister, von Stein, but also from the Kaiser, and on 5 April 1917 he asked Bethmann to discuss the question of minimum war aims.[37] Bethmann wanted at all costs to avoid being tied down to any definite proposals, and at first did not even wish to reply to Hindenburg's request. Eventually, prompted by Grünau, who warned that his enemies would make considerable political capital out of the fact that he did not reply, he answered that he did not want to be tied down to a definite war aims programme as he was still trying to achieve a separate peace with one of Germany's enemies and thus split the Entente.[38]

Bethmann's procrastination was not merely due to his policy of attempting to split the Entente, and the resulting refusal to be tied to fixed and immutable war aims, but also because of the increasingly

tricky relations with Austria-Hungary. The steady worsening of the
position of Austria-Hungary had led to a fruitless attempt to negotiate
a separate peace in the first weeks of 1917. Kaiser Karl and his
brother-in-law Prince Sixtus of Bourbon-Parma had tried to negotiate
with the French behind Germany's back. Poincaré and Briand named
four preconditions for serious talks — Alsace-Lorraine was to be restored
to France, Belgium was to be given full sovereignty and lose no territory,
Austria was to make no demands on the Straits of Constantinople, and
Serbia would also be given full sovereignty and integrity. Czernin
promptly tried to prevail upon the Germans to agree to give up Alsace
and Lorraine in the interests of general peace. Bethmann replied that
Alsace and Lorraine would never be abandoned by Germany, and that
he intended to hold on to Belgium and occupied France as bargaining
counters for eventual peace negotiations.[39] A few days later Bethmann
made it clear that as far as Belgium was concerned the *status quo ante
bellum* was unacceptable to Germany, and that Germany 'needed Briey
because of its ore', insisting that this would not matter to France as she
had considerable quantities of ore in Normandy, and in any case much
of the Briey holdings had been in the hands of German interests before
the war.[40]

Thus when the OHL began to press its demands for fixed war aims
there is clear evidence that Bethmann had no intention of abandoning
imperialist aims. Unlike the OHL, however, he realised that certain
concessions had to be made, and that effective control over other
countries need not be in the form of outright annexation. Indeed it was
often preferable to disguise domination in the form of economic treaties
and trade agreements. This was particularly true when it seemed that
Austria might possibly be tempted away from the alliance and would
not support excessive German demands.

In order that there should be a better understanding between
Germany and Austria over the issue of war aims, Bethmann and Czernin
agreed to a maximum and minimum programme which was embodied in
the so-called 'Vienna document' which they jointly signed on the
conclusion of their meetings.[41] The minimum programme stated that
neither power would withdraw their forces from occupied territories
until there was a guarantee of the territorial *status quo ante bellum*.
The maximum programme was deliberately vague. Austria was to get
Rumania, and Germany would make annexations mainly (though not
exclusively) in the east. Bethmann had thus ensured that the Austrians
would not accept the French terms for a separate peace, and as the
maximum programme was geared to the comparative contributions to

the war effort it was certain that Germany would get the lion's share of
the spoils in the event of victory.

Meanwhile Bethmann still hoped for a separate peace with Russia.
Kolyshko, who had been under state secretary in the finance ministry
under Witte before the war, who was married to a German lady, and
who had been offered a post in the provisional government in Russia,
asked another amateur diplomatist and arch busybody, the catholic
politician Erzberger, to travel to Stockholm to discuss the possibility of
a negotiated peace between Russia and Germany.[42] Bethmann's
optimism and the OHL's anger at this move was soon dispelled when,
on 29 March, the provisional government announced its determination
to continue the war until Germany was defeated. But the provisional
government, although supported by a chauvinist and ambitious
bourgeoisie, was faced with the mounting opposition of the Petrograd
Soviet, the mouthpiece of the workers and peasants who opposed the
war. Thus the provisional government was forced to make some
concessions to the soviet's demands, and the Germans, mistaking
appearance for reality, were again encouraged by what seemed to be a
significant change in attitude.[43]

Erzberger, eager to play the role of international statesman and
architect of a separate peace with Russia, began another period of
frantic activity which, even without the determined opposition of the
OHL, would almost certainly have led nowhere. The OHL, disgusted
with what they considered to be Bethmann's weak-kneed domestic
policy and his vacillating foreign policy, was determined to frustrate his
efforts to secure a compromise peace with Russia, and was thus
determined to tie him down to a shopping list of minimum war aims.
This determination was further strengthened as the demand for a peace
without annexations or compensations was increasingly heard,
particularly in social democratic circles.

For the chancellor, the talks with Kolyshko were an excellent
excuse for avoiding Hindenburg's request. He argued that if the war
aims were too excessive it would make Russia all the more determined
to fight on, and if they were too modest they would appear to the
Entente to be a confession of weakness. He pointed out to the Kaiser
that Germany was simply not in a position to dictate peace terms, and
that therefore the position of the OHL and its Pan German supporters
was utterly unrealistic. Furthermore Germany was likely to have to
negotiate peace terms before America began to make an effective
contribution to the war. Excessive and direct demands would make a
negotiated peace impossible, would have a disastrous effect on the

alliance with Austria and would further strengthen the growing opposition to the war at home. It was only in these terms that Bethmann was prepared to discuss the war aims issue with Hindenburg.[44]

Hindenburg replied that a peace with Russia on the basis of the territorial *status quo* was a military impossibility. The annexation of Courland and Lithuania he deemed 'indispensable'. He complained bitterly that he had not been properly informed of the peace feelers, and had therefore been unable to give the proper military support to these diplomatic initiatives. He begged Bethmann to discuss the whole range of problems as soon as possible.[45] The Kaiser promptly ordered Bethmann to come to headquarters at Kreuznach on 23 April 1917 to discuss the question of war aims with the OHL.[46]

The situation on the eve of the Kreuznach meeting was particularly critical. On 19 April the executive committee of the social democratic party published a declaration that warmly supported the Russian February revolution, and which called for peace on the basis of the Petrograd formula against the 'dreams of power of ambitious chauvinists'. At the same time there was a strike of Berlin munitions workers. Hindenburg visited the Kaiser on 21 April when he was lying in bed with heart trouble. He bluntly demanded that Bethmann should be dismissed on the grounds that he could no longer control the social democrats. It would seem that in the first moment of shock the Kaiser agreed, but he was then persuaded by Valentini, the chief of the civil cabinet, to reject the idea. Once he had changed his mind the Kaiser was furious that Hindenburg was meddling so actively in politics, and acting as the spokesman for 'other powerful forces'. But the army did not give up so easily. On the following day the war minister, von Stein, ended his audience with the Kaiser with a long diatribe against the chancellor who, he insisted, was leading Germany headlong down the path to revolution. He was supported in this attack by Lyncker. Once again Valentini had to step in and made an impassioned defence of Bethmann; even Stein had to admit that a change of chancellor at that particular moment was somewhat risky.[47]

The meeting was duly held on 23 April. The OHL came well prepared with detailed maps and lists of demands, all couched in terms of military imperatives. Bethmann gave way to these demands, merely adding the rather obvious rider that they could only be attained if Germany were in a position to dictate peace terms.[48] These aims included the annexation of Courland and Lithuania and other parts of the Baltic provinces including the islands of Dagö, Moon and Ösel; the military, political and economic domination of Poland, the annexation of a frontier strip to the Narev and along a line from Ostroleka to Mlawa and around Thorn and Kalisch to secure the Silesian industrial area. This frontier area was to be fully Germanised. The Polish frontier in the east would be pushed back into Russia, and Russia compensated in East Galicia and Moldavia. Austria would in turn be compensated in Rumania and Serbia, although Germany would have substantial rights in the Rumanian oilfields. Serbia could be joined with Montenegro and Albania to form a South Slav state, and then joined to Austria-Hungary. Bulgaria would regain the Dobrudja as in the frontiers of 1913, but the railway from Cernavoda to Constanta would remain Rumanian, in other words would be controlled by German interests. In the west, Belgium would remain under military control until effective treaties were signed. Germany would take Liège and the Flanders coast including Bruges. The Belgian railways would be under German control. The area round Arlon in the south was to be annexed as there was ore in the region. Luxemburg would become incorporated into the German Reich. Longwy-Briey would be annexed, and there would be further frontier rectifications along the French border. Questions of the Balkans, Asia Minor, naval bases and the colonies would be discussed at a later date.

In a note to the chancellery after the meeting Bethmann wrote that he believed that the OHL had deliberately brought up the issue of war aims in order to overthrow him, but he said that he had no intention whatever of resigning over a question of 'fantasies'.[49] Although it is quite true that Bethmann had capitulated to the OHL without attempting to assert the political rights of the chancellor against the generals, it would be a mistake to imagine that such subsequent reservations about the Kreuznach agreement amounted to a rejection of it in principle.[50] The fact that these conditions could only apply in the event of a German victory was a glimpse of the obvious that not even Ludendorff was prepared to deny. Bethmann's insistence that he would ignore the stipulations of the Kreuznach protocol if peace negotiations would be in any way prejudiced by them, must also be seen in the light of the fact that he did not see any immediate chance of such negotiations, even with Russia. He also had no reason to doubt the OHL's repeated insistence that the war would be won in the near future, an opinion that seemed all the more plausible as the U-boat campaign seemed to be even more successful than had been hoped. Lastly, the Kreuznach protocol cannot be seen as an isolated document, but has to be situated in the course of the development of Germany's war aims since September 1914. Seen in these terms there is no great difference between the aims of the OHL and of the chancellor.[51] Nevertheless it is clear that Kreuznach was a further victory of the OHL over the chancellor, which restricted his freedom of action and which marked a further step towards his dismissal. It would not be too fanciful to suggest that Bethmann's insistence that he would not be bound by the Kreuznach decisions was prompted by his frustration and his realisation that he had been outwitted.

Immediately before the Kreuznach meeting, Erzberger and Kolyshko, somewhat carried away by an inflated sense of their own importance, worked out the details for a draft armistice between Germany and Russia.[52] The document was sent to Admiral Müller who did not take it seriously as a step towards peace, and thought that it might well be part of some sinister political intrigue. He thus handed it to Grünau to discuss with Ludendorff.[53] Hindenburg and Ludendorff were furious that a meddlesome amateur like Erzberger should attempt to undermine their authority. They pointed out that an armistice was a military matter, and further that the terms suggested by Erzberger were far too lenient.[54] The foreign office replied to these charges by saying that Erzberger had been instructed not to make any proposals and had therefore exceeded his instructions.[55]

Ludendorff was being exceedingly disingenuous over the Erzberger affair. He knew all about the negotiations in Stockholm through his spies, and at once sent his friend Stinnes to Stockholm in order to bribe Kolyshko not to negotiate further with Erzberger and to become a German agent on his return to Russia. This proposal was angrily rejected, but Kolyshko was unable to decide quite what was going on at the top levels of government in Germany, or to know with whom he was really negotiating.[56] His refusal to accept Stinnes' bribe did not help him very much. Shortly after his return to Russia he was arrested as a German agent.

One of the reasons why the OHL was so angry about the Erzberger mission was that it was busy with its own efforts to achieve a peace settlement in the east by means of propaganda sent to the Russian troops at the front. Immediately after the February revolution the OHL, with the active and enthusiastic support of the foreign office, bombarded the Russian lines with propaganda material which argued that the war had been caused by the warlike and dishonest policies of the Tsarist regime. Germany was willing to support the Russians' desire to be free, and they were ready to give Russia economic support. Germany wanted nothing more than an 'honourable peace' which would enable the two countries to live side by side in peace and friendship. As the Russian provisional government was the puppet of the Entente it was hoped that the Russian troops at the front would begin direct negotiations with the German troops for an armistice. It was to be expected that if this came about there would be total confusion in Russia resulting from disagreements between the army and the provisional government.[57]

This trench propaganda turned out to be something of a mixed blessing to the Germans. There were frequent instances of Russians and Germans crossing no-man's-land and creating a kind of *de facto* armistice in many parts of the front. Although this was encouraged at first by the Germans it soon turned out that the Russians were at least as successful in revolutionising the German troops as the Germans were in demoralising the Russians. Senior officers became worried that their men were increasingly attracted by social revolutionary, menshevik and even bolshevik ideas, and they therefore began to press for an end to all contacts between the two sides. This tendency for pacifist and socialist sentiments to increase among the German troops was also encouraged by the growth of radical socialism at home, the growing disillusionment with the war and the increasingly frequent strikes. The army now began to fear that what had happened in Russia might also occur in Germany.[58]

Although the propaganda offensive seemed to be a failure, encouraging news came that Stecklow of the Petrograd Soviet was prepared to discuss peace terms with an SPD party comrade from Germany. The right wing social democrat, David, was suggested as a suitable ambassador. In the course of discussions between the OHL and the chancellor on armistice terms Bethmann and Zimmermann suggested that in order to make the idea of annexations more palatable for the Russians they could be disguised by demanding that Courland and Lithuania should become independent states, but that they should in fact be bound politically, economically and militarily to Germany. The OHL wanted direct annexations in the form of 'frontier rectifications'. This is an example of the 'fundamental difference of principle' between the OHL and the chancellor that some historians have tried to divine.[59] Less than three weeks later there was full agreement between the two parties, but nothing came of the negotiations. Stecklow did not appear for the meeting.

The OHL was determined that the chancellor should stick to the terms of the Kreuznach agreement of 23 April 1917, and as the position of Austria seemed increasingly uncertain, Ludendorff suggested that there should be a meeting beeting between the German and the Austrian chiefs of staff to discuss the question of war aims in the east in terms of the agreement.[60] The foreign office tried to stop this proposal, feeling that it would only serve to exacerbate further the already strained relations between the two countries, but the OHL was able to overrule these objections, and a conference was set for 17 and 18 May, to be held in Kreuznach.

On the eve of the conference Hindenburg outlined his ideas on future German policy in a letter to Bethmann.[61] He was convinced that whatever the outcome of the war England would try, as soon as possible after the war, to attack Germany before she was fully prepared. Therefore Germany had to achieve an economic and military position at the peace that would enable her to withstand any such attack, and the peace settlement would further have to make it impossible for the Entente to launch such an attack. The answer was 'fortress Germany', supplied by a vast merchant fleet made up of captured enemy vessels. 'New German land' would have to be provided with adequate supplies of phosphates, animals and machinery. Germany would have to have enough food to withstand a further three years of war, even if the harvest were bad. Germany would also have to control such a large share of the world's shipping that the Entente countries would only be able to ensure an adequate flow of imports by using German ships.

Such then was the overbearing atmosphere in the OHL on the eve of the Kreuznach meeting with the Austrians. The conference was a triumph for the OHL. Czernin agreed that the Germans should annex Courland and Lithuania and control Poland. In return Austria was to have Rumania, apart from the Bulgarian Dobrudja, but Germany was to have a majority share of all sources of oil production, control of shipping and of the railways. Austria would establish a small 'new Serbia' without access to the sea and in close association to the monarchy. Valona which was to be vacated by the Italians, was to become a German naval base. Salonica would be controlled by German interests in Macedonia and by control of the railway. Constanta would be the German base for the economic exploitation of Rumania and act as a springboard to the Orient.[62]

The OHL was understandably pleased with the results of the Kreuznach meeting. Even Hindenburg had to admit, however grudgingly, that Bethmann had done well, for he had gained Czernin's consent to the OHL's war aims.[63] In fact it was not until 18 June that Czernin was able to write to Zimmermann informing him that the government of Austria and Hungary agreed to the Kreuznach proposals. Czernin asked that the fact that Austria was no longer interested in the 'condominium' in Poland should be kept secret. This information enabled the Kaiser to reject out of hand Kaiser Karl's proposals of 7 June for negotiations for peace on the basis of the *status quo* for he now knew that the Kreuznach proposals were acceptable to the governments of Austria and Hungary.[64]

Thus the OHL's first excursions into the field of foreign policy resulted in a number of significant victories over the more cautious chancellor. Hindenburg and Ludendorff had imposed their Polish policy on the civilians. They had succeeded in intensifying the exploitation of Belgium, even though they had not been able to secure all their aims. They had managed to get a list of war aims from the chancellor, in spite of his protests that this would be most undesirable, and they were able to gain the support of the Austrians for these demands. Most important of all they had managed to make it seem as if these major policy decisions were the work of the civilians, so that if they failed they could be blamed for formulation of unworkable policies. Thus the failures of German policy in Poland and Belgium, the worsening of relations with Austria-Hungary, and problems caused by demanding unrealistic war aims could all be used by the OHL, who were the original force behind the policies, as ammunition to use against Bethmann Hollweg as they began to work for his removal from office. Thus in many ways Bethmann Hollweg was sacrificed to absolve the OHL from the blame for policies which had failed, and Hindenburg and Ludendorff could turn even their failures into victories.

NOTES

1. Werner Basler, *Deutschlands Annexionspolitik in Polen und in Baltikum 1914-1918,* Berlin 1962, p. 132.
2. *Untersuchungsausschuss IV Reihe,* Band 7:1, p. 364.
3. Scherer Grunewald, *L'Allemagne et les problemes de la paix,* Vol. 1, p. 427.
4. *Ibid.,* p. 447.
5. Werner Conze, *Polnische Nation und deutsche Politik im ersten Weltkrieg,* Cologne 1958, p. 195.
6. *Ibid.,* p. 196. These remarks are contained in a letter to his wife 3-9-16.
7. Ritter, *Staatskunst und Kriegshandwerk,* Band 3, p. 268.
8. *Ibid.,* p. 269.
9. Conze, *Polnische Nation und deutsche Politik,* p. 203.
10. Scherer Grunewald, *L'Allemagne et les problemes de la paix,* Vol. 1, p. 492.
11. *Ibid.,* p. 515. Ritter makes Ludendorff the author of the telegram, *Staatskunst und Kriegshandwerk,* Vol. 3, p. 273.
12. Conze, *Polnische Nation und deutsche Politik,* p. 213.
13. *Ibid.,* p. 214 based on the notes of von Hevnitz and of Burian in H.H. und Staatsarchiv, Vienna, Geh. XLVII/3-12. Jagow's memorandum on the results of the meeting in Scherer Grunewald, *L'Allemagne et les problemes de la*

paix, Vol. 1, p. 520. Ritter, *Staatskunst und Kriegshandwerk,* tries to excuse Bethmann's feeble attitude towards the OHL by suggesting that he might have wanted them to go ahead with their Polish plans, fail, and thus make fools of themselves. If this were so – and Ritter produces no evidence to suggest that it was – it would be proof of outstanding irresponsibility on the part of Bethmann. It is more likely that Ritter's hero had feet of clay.

14. Basler, *Deutschlands Annexionspolitik,* p. 153. Hutten-Czapski, *60 Jahre Politik und Gesellschaft,* Band 2, p. 301.
15. Paul Roth, *Die Entstehung des polnischen Staates,* Berlin 1926, p. 129.
16. *Spartakusbriefe,* p. 273.
17. Conze, *Polnische Nation und deutsche Politik,* p. 233.
18. DZA Reichsamt des Innern: Das polnische Heer, 19831. Ludendorff wrote 16-9-17 that the Polish army should be as small as possible as the soldiers were 'unreliable' and there was a danger of there not being enough security in the rear of the eastern army. The Polish army was 'politically tainted' and 'militarily useless', and therefore the army should not be larger than one or two infantry battalions to act as training battalions, this would also make sense for reasons of economy.
19. PA Bonn AA Oesterreich Nr. 95, Band 4: PA Bonn AA Weltkrieg Geheim, Band 34, 7-11-16.
20. PA Bonn AA Oesterreich Nr. 95, Band 4, Bethmann to Hindenburg 10-11-16.
21. PA Bonn AA Weltkrieg Geheim, Band 35, Grünau to Bethmann 13-11-16. (handwritten letter).
22. Scherer Grunewald, *L'Allemagne et les problemes de la paix,* Vol. 1, p. 663.
23. Basler, *Deutschlands Annexionspolitik,* p. 179.
24. Willibald Gutsche, 'Zu einige Fragen der staatsmonopolistischen Verflechtung in den ersten Kriegsjahren am Beispiel der Ausplunderung der belgischen Industrie und der Zwangsdeportation von Belgiern', in *Politik im Krieg 1914-1918;* Fernand Passelecq, *Déportations et travail forcé des ouvriers et de la population civile de la Belgique occupée,* Paris/New Haven 1928: Ritter, *Staatskunst und Kriegshandwerk,* Vol. 3, p. 433 is far too apologetic about Bissing on the grounds that he said a 'squeezed lemon has no value, a dead cow gives no milk' – hardly an attitude designed to win friends in Belgium for Germany's annexationist plans. Ritter was unable to use the files of DZA Potsdam Reichsamt des Innern which has valuable material on this topic. For Bissing's prewar activities see Kitchen, *The German Officer Corps 1890-1914,* pp. 139, 164 and 165.
25. Ritter, *Staatskunst und Kriegshandwerk,* Vol. 3, p. 438.
26. Lancken, *Meine 30 Dienstjahre,* p. 234; Groener, *Lebenserinnerungen,* p. 553; *Untersuchungsausschuss IV Reihe,* Band III.I pp. 345-8; Ritter, *Staatskunst und Kriegshandwerk,* Vol. 3, p. 440.
27. *Untersuchungsausschuss IV Reihe,* Band III.I p. 382.
28. *Ibid.,* p. 368.
29. Ludendorff, *Urkunden der OHL,* p. 127. Bundesarchiv Koblenz, Nachlass Bauer Nr. 14.
30. DZA Potsdam Reichsamt des Innern: Einrichtung einer Zivilverwaltung in Belgien 19352.
31. DZA Potsdam Reichskanzlei Notständen 2427/1.
32. Ritter, *Staatskunst und Kriegshandwerk,* Vol. 3, p. 447.
33. *Deutschland im ersten Weltkrieg,* Vol. 2, p. 496: Gutsche, 'Staatsmonopolistische Verflechtung', p. 88.
34. H. Pirenne, *La Belgique et la guerre mondiale,* Paris 1928.
35. DZA Potsdam Reichskanzlei, Notständen 2429. Hindenburg to Bethmann 27-2-17.

36. DZA Potsdam Reichsamt des Innern, Deutsch-Polnisch Militärkonvention, 19683.
37. Scherer Grunewald, *L'Allemagne et les problemes de la paix,* Vol. 2, p. 80.
38. *Ibid.,* p. 114.
39. *Ibid.,* p. 32.
40. German holdings in Briey before the war were indeed considerable. Bethmann's remarks about Normandy should be seen in the light of the fact that there were no German troops in Normandy, and in any case about three quarters of the ore holdings in Normandy were in German hands before the war. For details see Hans W. Gatzke, *Germany's Drive to the West,* Baltimore 1950, p. 32; Fritz Fischer, *Krieg der Illusionen,* Dusseldorf 1969, p. 462. Fischer's book contains some useful charts and maps to illustrate this point.
41. Ludendorff, *Urkunden der OHL,* p. 373.
42. Epstein, *Erzberger,* p. 165.
43. Fischer, *Griff nach der Weltmacht,* p. 488; Scherer Grunewald, *L'Allemagne et les problemes de la paix,* Vol. 2, p. 59.
44. *Ibid.,* p. 126.
45. *Ibid.,* p. 132.
46. *Ibid.,* p. 134.
47. *Ibid.,* p. 135. Valentini, *Kaiser und Kabinettschef,* p. 151; Müller diary 21-4-17.
48. Scherer Grunewald, *L'Allemagne et les problemes de la paix,* Vol. 2, p. 149.
49. Graf Westarp, *Konservative Politik im letzten Jahrzehnt des Kaiserreiches,* Band 2, Berlin 1936, p. 85.
50. This is argued by Ritter in *Staatskunst und Kriegshandwerk,* Vol. 3, p. 507. A similar, but rather more differentiated view in Epstein, 'The development of German-Austrian War Aims in the Spring of 1917', *Journal of Central European Affairs,* Vol. XVII, April 1957.
51. This latter point is made forcefully by Fischer in *Griff nach der Weltmacht,* p. 459.
52. Scherer Grunewald, *L'Allemagne et les problemes de la paix,* Vol. 2, p. 136. Text also in Epstein, *Erzberger,* p. 170. Erzberger's extraordinary overestimation of his own importance seems to escape his biographer's attention.
53. Müller diary 24-4-17.
54. *Ibid.,* 25-4-17. Scherer Grunewald, *L'Allemagne et les problemes de la paix,* Vol. 2, p. 152, draft version on p. 156.
55. *Ibid.,* p. 153.
56. Epstein, *Erzberger,* p. 174.
57. Scherer Grunewald, *L'Allemagne et les problemes de la paix,* Vol. 2, p. 88.
58. Erich Otto Volkmann, *Der Marxismus und das deutsche Heer im Weltkriege,* Berlin 1925, p. 286.
59. Scherer Grunewald, *L'Allemagne et les problemes de la paix,* Vol. 2, p. 179; Ritter, *Staatskunst und Kriegshandwerk,* Vol. 3, p. 511 tries to excuse Bethmann by saying that he was 'forced into making this dubious compromise', but as he offers no evidence to support this theory it does not convince.
60. Scherer Grunewald, Vol. 2, p. 152.
61. *Ibid.,* p. 189.
62. *Ibid.,* p. 205.
63. Müller diary 19-5-17.
64. Ritter, *Staatskunst und Kriegshandwerk,* Vol. 3, p. 532, attributes the slowness of Czernin's reply to the crisis in the Hungarian government. It would seem far more probable that the Austrians were trying to find some way out of committing themselves to fighting for Germany's fantastic war aims. Hence

Kaiser Karl's peace appeal of 7 June. Czernin was also well aware that Germany wanted to 'take the core in Rumania and leave Austria the skin'. Scherer Grunewald, *L'Allemagne et les problemes de la paix,* Vol. 2, p. 212.

5 UNRESTRICTED SUBMARINE WARFARE

By the late summer of 1916, and particularly after the failure of the
Verdun offensive, the question of the use of unrestricted submarine
warfare became central in the discussions between the government and
the military. The question was whether the submarines would be able to
inflict such damage on allied shipping that the worsening of relations
with the neutral countries and the risk of war with the United States
could be regarded with equanimity. As might be expected, the political
right had long been pressing for unrestricted submarine warfare as the
only possible way of winning the decisive victory which alone would
enable them to realise their territorial and economic ambitions. The
conservative party, acting as the mouthpiece of the Prussian Junkers;
the right wing of the national liberals, on behalf of the Rhenish-
Westphalian heavy industry; chauvinist elements within the centre
party; the Pan German league, and the majority of the influential
military and naval personalities, all pressed for the use of the weapon,
and blinded by often highly dubious calculations and statistics they
ignored the grave political consequences of such action. On the other
hand, many representatives of industry, banking and ship building had
serious reservations about the use of unrestricted submarine warfare.
Men like Walter Rathenau and Albert Ballin, supported by such liberal
writers as Hans Delbrück and Friedrich Naumann, and by many liberal
politicians and civil servants, formed an influential and powerful group
that was able for a considerable time to stand up against the
arguments of the pro-submarine faction. This group was supported by
Bethmann Hollweg, who also felt that unrestricted submarine warfare
was at the very most an extremely risky gamble, and at worst would
have such dire consequences that it might lead to the eventual defeat of
Germany.[1]

The military crisis which led to the appointment of Hindenburg and
Ludendorff was so severe that it became increasingly difficult for the
moderates to counter the argument that Germany would have to use
every means at her disposal to win the war, and that in this desperate
situation the land forces could only be relieved by the full use of
submarines. So grave was Germany's predicament that any political
objections would have to be overruled, and an all-out effort would have to
be made to inflict really appreciable damage on allied shipping.

111

Immediately after their appointment to the OHL Hindenburg and Ludendorff met Holtzendorff, the chief of the admiralty staff, and Capelle, the state secretary of the navy, Bethmann, Jagow and Helfferich at a conference in Pless, where among other issues the question of unrestricted submarine warfare was discussed at some length. Somewhat unexpectedly Hindenburg and Ludendorff argued that the situation on land, particularly in the south-east, should be stabilised, before running the risk of bringing the United States, and possibly some of the neutral states into the war. They agreed, in principle, that unrestricted submarine warfare was desirable, but felt that it should be postponed until the military situation was more stable. Only when Rumania was defeated could troops be withdrawn from that front to be ready in reserve to meet the eventuality of Denmark and Holland declaring war, a possibility that Bethmann stressed was very real. Both Holtzendorff and Capelle tried to defeat this argument by insisting that unrestricted submarine warfare should begin at once, and they attempted to show, on the basis of some highly dubious statistics that England could be brought to her knees by the end of the year if only the submarines were given the chance to strike now when the British economy was already in a precarious state. But the admirals were almost alone with such arguments. Jagow and Helfferich forcefully supported the view that Germany could not afford to risk the intervention of the United States and the neutrals, and Helfferich further suggested that the navy's statistics were highly suspect.[2]

At first sight it might seem that Bethmann and the moderates had secured a major victory at Pless over the submarine enthusiasts. In fact Hindenburg had clearly favoured unrestricted submarine warfare. He had assured the conference that the situation on land was not so critical as some timid souls had suggested, and thus unrestricted submarine warfare was simply to be postponed. The most serious implication of the conference was that Bethmann was clearly thinking of submarine warfare in military rather than political terms, and was content to follow the lead of the OHL in this sensitive matter. Hindenburg was so confident about the overall military situation that he demanded that the submarine issue be discussed again in two weeks time, thus trapping the chancellor into what seemed likely to be a very limited time schedule if he were to pursue his peace initiative.[3]

The comparative reticence on the part of Hindenburg and Ludendorff at Pless can easily be explained. They wanted a quick and spectacular victory in Rumania, and did not want unrestricted submarine warfare to distract from this aim. Newly appointed to the

OHL they did not yet have a clear picture of the overall military situation, nor had they yet found their true place within the political structure of the country. Lastly there was some rivalry between the new OHL and the admiralty. How impressive were the victors of Tannenberg by contrast to the modest achievements of the navy! In a most illuminating letter to his wife, written in April 1916, Colonel Bauer wrote: 'Our navy!!! In peacetime it took money and men away from the army, in war it has achieved nothing – for basically the successes of the submarine are just pinpricks for England. And for that to make an enemy of the whole world!. . .Naturally I am pretty much alone with these views, and it would be funny, were it not so sad.'[4] As the OHL came to echo the policies of the extremist groupings in Germany they were encouraged to demand unrestricted submarine warfare, and Bauer was to forget all his well founded arguments against it, arguments that were almost identical with those used against the OHL in the ensuing weeks.

While Bethmann was using the possibility of unrestricted submarine warfare as a threat to force President Wilson to act as a peace intermediary in the course of a heavy-handed peace initiative, the navy began to work on Hindenburg and Ludendorff, whom they knew held the key to the situation. Ludendorff's initial reaction to the navy's arguments were unexpectedly sudden and severe. He continued to insist that the military situation was still too uncertain, rejected the navy's argument that Bethmann's appraisal of the situation was too pessimistic, and even went so far as to say that such a decision at that moment would be irresponsible. The blame for this situation he placed on the Austrians, whom he described as a military sieve – the more that was poured in, the more it flowed out of the bottom. Ludendorff reiterated the position of the OHL at Pless. He was in favour of unrestricted submarine warfare, but he could not support it until the military situation on land was more satisfactory.[5]

The navy continued its offensive. Trotha, the chief of staff of the high sea fleet, seems to have won over Hindenburg to the idea of unrestricted submarine warfare to start as soon as possible in the course of a conversation on 12 September.[6] Holtzendorff got Ludendorff to agree to earmark divisions for the Dutch and Danish borders by the middle of October, by which time unrestricted submarine warfare could begin.[7] Bethmann was highly alarmed at these developments, for he feared that the 'submarine fanatics' might gain the upper hand and thus jeopardise his diplomatic initiative in Washington. He promptly sent Kühlmann, the German envoy to the Hague, to headquarters with the news that the Dutch would be able to put 500,000 men into the field. This news seems to have made some impression on Ludendorff and Holtzendorff.[8] For the next few days the OHL was particularly conciliatory towards Bethmann, making profuse confessions of loyalty and frequent denials of any political ambition.

As time passed Hindenburg became increasingly concerned that Bethmann might use his diplomatic initiative towards Washington to postpone almost indefinitely the decision to begin unrestricted submarine warfare. He was also worried that the submarine lobby might blame the OHL for postponing a decision which they felt was in the vital interests of Germany. Bethmann had cunningly told members of the Reichstag that the decision to postpone the submarine war was the responsibility of the OHL, so that a highly controversial decision would now have to be made openly by the OHL and Hindenburg and Ludendorff were unable to shift all the blame for whatever decision was taken on to the chancellor. Bethmann knew that Hindenburg wanted to make the final decision on submarine warfare, but at the same time he wished to cover himself against his critics who might begin to think that he was prevaricating.

The OHL's position thus seemed to become all the more uncomfortable as the pro-submarine groups became louder and cruder in their criticism of the government's policies. The heavyweights of the movement, Tirpitz, General Keim, the master propagandist of the extremist and chauvinist groups, and the historian Dietrich Schäfer, demanded that the government and the OHL abandon their reservations about unrestricted submarine warfare. On 10 September the six economic lobbies *(Wirtschaftsverbände)* demanded that all possible measures should be taken to knock Britain out of the war. This was followed by a similar memorandum from the Hamburg *Kaufmannschaft*. The criticisms of such influential groups were a matter of some concern to the OHL, for it was precisely from these sectors that they would normally expect their strongest support. They therefore called upon Carl Duisberg of the Bayer chemical firm, and a frequent visitor to supreme headquarters, to urge these leading industrialists and ultra politicians to moderate their criticisms. On 15 September Duisberg told a meeting of Schäfer's 'Independent Committee for a German Peace', an organisation of professional men and academics who supported the annexationists, that Hindenburg did not want any further open discussion of the submarine question, as the real reason why unrestricted submarine warfare had to be postponed could not be discussed in public for reasons of military security. The result of

Duisberg's action was that pro-submarine propaganda became somewhat muted in the following weeks, though there were some furious protests from the more extreme members of the group.[9]

Yet for all these differences and misunderstandings there was a certain degree of agreement between the OHL and Bethmann in September and October 1916 on the issue of unrestricted submarine warfare. The OHL had little sympathy for the diplomatic subtleties of Bethmann's attempt to find a third way, to allow unrestricted submarine warfare without provoking the Americans and the neutral states to enter the war, but for the time being at least they felt that the military situation was not stable enough to enable them to run the risk of further engagements on the Dutch and Danish borders.[10] Similarly, Bethmann was grateful for the OHL's comparative moderation, the more so as he was under heavy pressure from the politicians to begin unrestricted submarine warfare as soon as possible. Within the Reichstag he had virtually no support and the pro-submarine faction comprised almost all parties except the social democrats and the progressives. Indeed it seemed as if Bethmann's political future rested on the outcome of the submarine question. The crown prince wrote to his father saying that as only the Jews and the social democrats supported him on this issue he should 'throw him out'.[11]

For the time being the OHL was still prepared to support Bethmann. They were convinced that the peace initiative was bound to be a failure, and could thus give it lukewarm support in order to take the ground from under the feet of the pacifists, anti-annexationists and socialists, thus strengthening the home front, and appeasing the neutrals whose relations with Germany were becoming increasingly strained. Hindenburg and Ludendorff still wanted to defeat Rumania before unleashing the submarine warfare, and had no fears that the diplomatic initiative would lead to a 'feeble peace'. The OHL was able to tie the hands of the chancellor still further by insisting that the peace move be preceded by the declaration on Polish independence and by the auxiliary labour law. Although the ostensible reason for this demand was that Germany should only embark on a peace initiative from a position of strength, it is clear that an ulterior motive was that these moves would make it all the more unlikely that the allies would begin serious negotiations.

The peace initiative was further delayed owing to differences with the Austrians, and further discussions with the OHL on war aims. Rumania's resistance finally collapsed and on 6 December 1916 the troops of the Central Powers entered Bucharest. Now the military objection to unrestricted submarine warfare which the OHL had raised in August no longer held good. The navy increased its efforts to persuade the OHL to agree to the beginning of unrestricted submarine warfare, for they were afraid that the British would put off discussions of the peace proposals as long as possible and thus be able to import the new harvest with the minimum of interference, so that Germany would lose the opportunity to deal Britain a real economic blow. The submariners were also straining at the leash, for nearly all British merchant vessels were now armed so that the *Prisenordnung,* which required submarine commanders to give due warning to merchant shipping, was becoming increasingly hazardous. With the help of Admiral Müller, Bethmann was able to restrain the navy for the time being, but Bethmann was 'tortured with doubts as to whether he should insist upon even stronger restrictions on underwater torpedoing in order to avoid the possibility of a clash with America'. On the other hand Müller had to admit that if Holtzendorff ordered any further restrictions it would virtually amount to an end of submarine warfare.[12]

Such was the situation when on 8 December Hindenburg launched another attack on the chancellor's policies. He argued that the military situation had changed so significantly that the war should be pursued without any restrictions, not only on land but also with submarines. The government must be convinced that Germany could negotiate a peace as she needed, and to secure this end submarine warfare should no longer be restricted as of the end of January.[13]

The Kaiser forwarded these views to Bethmann who replied that the phrase 'the peace that Germany needs' was so vague that it was almost meaningless. He refused to be tied to any timetable on the submarine question, and tried to answer Hindenburg with the somewhat delphic statement that 'should our peace offer be rejected our position on the question of armed merchant vessels must be made perfectly clear to America'. He thus hoped to postpone still further any decision on unrestricted submarine warfare, and as a compromise supported Holtzendorff's demands for the treatment of armed merchantmen as warships, and to use this as a real alternative to unrestricted submarine warfare.[14]

Bethmann returned to Berlin from this visit to Pless convinced that he had scored s significant victory over the OHL. He was more confident than ever that he could extend the submarine war without bringing America into the conflict, in other words that his 'third way' could work.[15] But as soon as he was back in Berlin he had to face the mounting criticisms of the right wing politicians who were convinced

that Germany was heading for a 'feeble peace'. His critics feared that
their ambitious war aims designed to establish Germany as an
undisputed world power could not be achieved if a peace were to be
negotiated at that moment.[16] The army's propaganda machine was used
to considerable effect sytematically to undermine the peace effort,
such as it was. Bethmann was too weak and full of doubts to stand up
to this attack, and his concept of the 'third way' was seriously flawed.
In his Reichstag speech on 12 December he made bombastic references
to Germany's invincible strength and the desperate position of the
Entente; hardly a fortunate tone of voice to choose for the opening of
peace negotiations.

As they waited for the reply to the peace move both Bethmann and
the OHL became increasingly nervous. Bethmann began to fear that the
Entente might in fact begin serious negotiations, so that he would not
be able to provide the diplomatic cover for stepping up the submarine
war. The OHL feared that negotiations might begin before they had
been able to convince the chancellor of the need for their minimum war
aim plan. Thus Hindenburg used Lloyd George's remark that he did not
want to 'buy a pig in a poke' as a pretext for demanding increased
submarine warfare, adding that the situation on the western front was
such that submarines would have to be used to the utmost. Zimmermann
tried to restrain the OHL, but Ludendorff's reply exploded like a
bombshell. He announced that he and Hindenburg would resign if the
politicians did not agree to the opening of unrestricted submarine
warfare by the end of January, adding that unless it was begun as soon
as possible Germany would be defeated.[17]

Hindenburg supported Ludendorff's move with two further
telegrams to the chancellor sent on 23 December. He demanded a rigid
timetable for submarine warfare, that all armed merchantmen should be
torpedoed on sight, and drew up a list of annexationist demands which
would make sure that Bethmann's peace move could not possibly
succeed.[18] In a further note to the chancellor, Hindenburg insisted that
if there were an armistice it could not be made to include the navy, for
this would give Britain an unacceptable advantage.[19] Hindenburg and
Ludendorff were acting in the interests of the Reichstag majority and
of most industrialists, so that Bethmann was left to rely on the uneasy
and unwilling support of the left.

Bethmann's reply to this threat was an almost pathetic appeal for
restraint, and a request that the OHL should await the Entente's reply
before demanding unrestricted submarine warfare.[20] Holtzendorff, who
had been prepared to moderate his views on unrestricted submarine

warfare, now gave the full weight of the admiralty's support to the OHL. Armed with a document known as the Kalkmann memorandum, which was designed to show that Helfferich's statistics in August 1916 were hopelessly pessimistic, the navy now tried to argue that within five months of the beginning of unrestricted submarine warfare some 39 per cent of shipping going to Britain would be rendered unoperational, 600,000 registered tons of shipping would be sunk each month, and two fifths of the neutral ships which normally went to Britain would no longer risk the voyage. The resulting devastation of Britain's economic and military position would lead Britain to beg for peace.[21]

On 24 December Holtzendorff met Hindenburg at Pless and they both agreed that the military situation was such that Germany could afford to risk America's entry into the war. Admiral Müller had a hard time convincing Holtzendorff that if America were to enter the war the war might be somewhat prolonged.[22] For the time being Holtzendorff preferred to hide behind Hindenburg and wait for the outcome of the clash between the OHL and the chancellor on unrestricted submarine warfare before showing the Kalkmann memorandum to the chancellor.

On 29 December Bethmann, accompanied by Helfferich and Zimmermann, arrived in Pless to confront the OHL.[23] Lersner met the party at the station and informed them that Hindenburg refused to invite the chancellor to luncheon, and that the OHL did not wish Helfferich to attend the discussions. Bethmann replied that it was his perfect right to bring whomsoever he wished to conferences, and Hindenburg reluctantly had to give way. Before the talks began the OHL accused the chancellor of trying to drag the OHL into politics by publishing statements to the effect that there was complete unanimity between the chancellor and the OHL over the question of unrestricted submarine warfare, and they accused 'people in Berlin' of trying to oust Ludendorff. They also demanded that Helfferich should be removed.

Bethmann was understandably enraged by this disgraceful behaviour, and he demanded to know the names of the 'people in Berlin', for if they were indeed plotting against Ludendorff their actions would be treasonous. Hindenburg, who was never able to stand up to determined criticism, collapsed and either agreed with Bethmann, or denied any knowledge of the accusations which had been made.

After such a dramatic beginning the conference which ensued was uneventful. No decision was reached. Bethmann returned to Berlin complaining of the OHL's 'dictatorial desire to dominate and their aim, which they followed deliberately, to militarise the entire life of the state'. Müller was convinced that Hindenburg was now determined to overthrow the chancellor.[24] Helfferich felt that the conference had been a waste of time, for the OHL was not interested in unrestricted submarine warfare against armed merchant vessels, the subject of the conference, but wanted nothing short of unrestricted submarine warfare. As Hindenburg and Ludendorff were not seriously interested in the problem, agreement with Bethmann was of little consequence.[25]

Immediately after the conference the representative of the naval staff at headquarters, von Bülow, asked Ludendorff to make yet another attempt to convince the chancellor of the need to begin unrestricted submarine warfare.[26] Ludendorff replied somewhat testily that he was tired of always having to fight the chancellor on behalf of the admiralty, and added that he 'must preserve [his] energies for a more important matter'. Bülow took the hint and suggested that Hindenburg should face the Kaiser with the choice — 'Bethmann or Hindenburg'. Ludendorff muttered that he would do whatever he thought was right, and he did not need the advice of the naval staff. Thus the question of unrestricted submarine warfare had also become a question of Bethmann's political future. Bethmann knew that with their wide popular support and their important circle of contacts the demigods of the OHL were in a far stronger position than the chancellor. If it came to a choice between Hindenburg or Bethmann there was no doubt who would win. Yet rather than fight against the dictatorial ambitions of the OHL, about which he was fully aware, he prefered to take the line of least resistance, and rationalised his own weakness as a selfless attempt to preserve the political unity of the Reich.

On 31 December the Entente's reply to the German peace initiative arrived in Berlin.[27] The note rejected Germany's account of the outbreak of the war, accused the German government of trying to use a peace move to attain war aims they would never be able to gain by military means, and added that it was a propaganda attempt to undermine public opinion in the Entente countries. The move was designed to improve morale in Germany, pull the wool over the eyes of the neutral countries, and further cover up German crimes: submarine warfare, deportation of workers, enslavement of nationals and their conscription to fight against their own countries, and further violations of neutrality. The Kaiser was furious at the note. Czernin deplored its 'impertinent' tone, but still hoped that there was a faint possibility that a dialogue might be established.[28] Bethmann realised that the note skilfully outwitted his attempt to find the 'third way'. He still hoped to further involve the neutral states so that the effect of the peace move would not be entirely lost.[29]

The OHL had no such scruples. It demanded that a total rejection of the Entente's note should take the form of an army order. The order made the OHL's attitude quite clear: 'In justified revulsion at the insolent malice of the enemy, and in the will to defend our most sacred possessions and to secure a happy future for the Fatherland, you must become as hard as steel.'[30] Yet it was the navy which brought matters to a head. Admiral Scheer, the chief of the high sea fleet, was fed up with what he considered to be the equivocal attitude of the naval staff. He therefore sent Captain von Levetzow to Holtzendorff in order to tell him that he no longer enjoyed the confidence of the navy, and that he had left the navy virtually without leadership owing to his dilatory handling of the submarine question.[31] Holtzendorff, Ludendorff's refusal to do his dirty work fresh in his memory, was thus forced into action. First he sent the Kalkmann memorandum to Bethmann, and then travelled to Pless to gain the Kaiser's consent to unrestricted submarine warfare.

Much to Holtzendorff's surprise and delight he found that Admiral Müller had come to the conclusion that unrestricted submarine warfare was the 'last shot in the locker' which should be used since the peace offer had been so roundly rejected.[32] Hindenburg and Ludendorff agreed with Holtzendorff that if the chancellor did not agree to unrestricted submarine warfare he should be forced to resign. Hindenburg promptly forwarded a request to the chancellor that unrestricted submarine warfare should begin on 1 February.[33] Bethmann spoke to Holtzendorff on the telephone the following day and asked that the decision might be postponed until he had completed his 'diplomatic preparations', and he still suggested that unrestricted submarine warfare would not necessarily lead to America entering the war if only the proper diplomatic preparations were made. This extraordinary view was shared by Zimmermann.[34] Bethmann thus wanted to postpone the decision and hoped for the best.

The news that Bethmann intended to visit headquarters the following day prompted Hindenburg, Ludendorff and Holtzendorff into further action. At 7 o'clock that evening they had an audience with the Kaiser. They demanded either unrestricted submarine warfare or the dismissal of Bethmann. Faced with such united and determined opposition the Kaiser gave way, quickly insisting that it was obviously a purely military matter, and therefore no concern whatever of the chancellor. He announced that he had no intention of even discussing the question with Bethmann in the morning. Müller and Holtzendorff urged the

Kaiser not to dismiss Bethmann for fear that the decision might seem a desperate *coup* and not the result of carefully considered policy.[35]

Bethmann duly arrived at Pless on 9 January, suffering from a severe cold, the decision virtually made against him. There was no fight left in him. At 11:15 a.m. he met Hindenburg and Ludendorff, and it seemed as if he was trying to convince himself that unrestricted submarine warfare was justified. He had a curious obsession that Switzerland might enter the war, but Hindenburg promptly dismissed this fear. After a few comments about the possibility of America entering the war he concluded that 'when, however, the military authorities consider submarine warfare to be necessary, I am not in the position to contradict', and when Hindenburg assured him that the opportunity for success was particularly good he added, 'Yes, when success is on the horizon we must act.' The chancellor was further reassured by the OHL's insistence that the threat from America was nothing compared to the damage that unrestricted submarine warfare would do to the Entente's war effort. Thus the chancellor capitulated to the generals, and the remaining discussions were almost formalities.[36]

Hindenburg and Ludendorff had argued that the allies were planning a second offensive on the Somme, and that everything possible had to be done to stop the enemy building up reserves of arms, men and supplies. The troops at the front demanded unrestricted submarine warfare, and it was essential for their morale that it should begin as soon as possible before the spring offensive could be mounted. The admiralty was convinced that they could bring Britain to her knees within a few months. Against these military arguments, backed by impressive statistics and presented with over-brimming confidence, the chancellor had nothing tangible to offer. His peace move had failed, and he could hardly threaten to resign for it would merely be seen as a confession of failure. He realised that if unrestricted submarine warfare were to start it would have to be with the full support of the chancellor, for otherwise the political effects on Germany's allies, and on the neutral states, would be utterly disastrous.[37]

The crown council met at 6 o'clock that evening.[38] By this time Bethmann had given up the struggle. He did not even make use of a carefully argued telegram which Helfferich had sent to him from Berlin, which tried to refute the navy's statistical arguments, and which reached the chancellor after his initial meeting with Hindenburg and Ludendorff.[39] All he could do was mumble about the danger from Switzerland, reservations which were drowned in a torrent of outspoken bravado from Hindenburg, Ludendorff and Holtzendorff. The Kaiser closed the discussion by quoting a few highly optimistic figures taken from a newspaper article and announced his determination that unrestricted submarine warfare should start as soon as possible. He told the chancellor that it was his business to try to keep the United States and the neutral powers out of the war, but that if the United States did declare war 'so much the better'.

Bethmann was understandably depressed by such irresponsible talk. Valentini agreed, and wrote in his notebook 'finis Germaniae!'.[40] Bethmann pointed out to Müller that the Kaiser had done irreparable harm to the Hohenzollern dynasty by alienating his sovereign power to the 'demigods' at the OHL.[41] In a most significant comment to Müller that evening as he gloomily sipped his champagne, Bethmann pointed out that unrestricted submarine warfare would prolong the war and eventually force Germany to sign a 'modest peace'. Here was the crux of the matter. Bethmann believed that the decision would make it more difficult for Germany to achieve her ambitious annexationist aims for which he had been working since September 1914; whereas the OHL felt that it was the only way to achieve their even more exotic demands. Thus fundamentally the argument was over means rather than ends, a fact that is so often obscured by the ramifications of the issues and the slightly more subtle approach of the chancellor which was incomprehensible to the narrow-minded militarists of the OHL and their ultra supporters.

The OHL was now determined to press home its victory on the submarine question and to demand the removal of the chancellor. On 10 January Hindenburg told the Kaiser that Bethmann was weak and indecisive and that the OHL could no longer work with him. The Kaiser left it to Valentini to placate Hindenburg, and Valentini was easily able to point out that a change of chancellor at that particular juncture would be political folly. In the course of their conversation it became clear that it was Ludendorff who was behind the move to get rid of Bethmann, and Hindenburg rather pathetically asked Valentini to convince him that it would be unwise to do so.[42] Valentini met both Hindenburg and Ludendorff on the following day and made a convincing and eloquent appeal to Ludendorff not to press for Bethmann's dismissal. Ludendorff reluctantly agreed, but let it be known that it would not be long before the OHL demanded the heads of Bethmann, Helfferich and Zimmermann all of whom were men whom the OHL regarded as dishonest and with whom it was impossible to work.[43] Thus the OHL placed itself at the head of a powerful anti-Bethmann faction and was more deeply involved than ever in politics.

Unable to keep the United States out of the war by diplomatic means, the chancellor now hoped that the threat of unrestricted submarine warfare would act as such a deterrent that war could be avoided. What had been something near to a policy had now become little more than wishful thinking. The United States, faced with unrestricted submarine warfare, with a threat to her considerable war profits, with the possibility that Germany might win the war and that the Entente would not be able to repay its debts, and anxious about the possibility of revolution in Europe, declared war on 6 April. America was no longer able to conceal her bid for world power behind the mystifying rhetoric of international law and neutrality; she was pushed out into the open by force of circumstance.[44] That the United States entered the war was not surprising, indeed it was an inevitable result of her attitude to the war, but what was truly extraordinary was the ignorance of America's policies and intentions, to say nothing of her immense economic and military power, shown by the military and political elites in Germany. Only men like Warburg, Ballin and Dernburg, who had important business interests in America, warned against the danger from that quarter. At the OHL Major Wetzell was almost alone with his deep concern for the tremendous military potential of the United States.[45]

The confidence of the Kaiser, the OHL and the submarine lobby was overwhelming, and the exceptionally high risk involved seemed to make them even more confident, as if they wished to push from their minds the desperate situation in which they were placed. This was the third great *va-banque* play in the war. The Schlieffen plan, the Verdun offensive, and now unrestricted submarine warfare were all desperate attempts to achieve that breakthrough which alone would enable Germany to achieve her far-reaching imperialist ambitions. As frustrations grew more intense, and as the contradictions between Germany's schemes and her means of attaining them became increasingly severe her determination to make a last desperate effort became all the stronger. Armed with highly dubious calculations of how many ships could be sunk, and refusing to even consider the military potential of the United States — the Germans regarded the American navy as worthless, the army as useless — and since the war would be over before it arrived in Europe, it could be completely discounted. On 31 January 1917 Admiral Capelle told the budgetary committee of the Reichstag that 'they will not even come, because our submarines will sink them. Thus America from a military point of view means nothing, and again nothing, and for a third time nothing.'[46] This

euphoric mood seemed also to affect the normally cautious Admiral
Müller. On 6 February he argued that the war would be over before
August. He was warned not to be over-optimistic by none other than
General Ludendorff.[47] The absurdity of such optimism can be clearly
seen in the actual effectiveness of the submarines. Two million
Americans were to arrive safely in Europe, and not one single troopship
was sunk. But for the moment the OHL was in a mood of confident
optimism, having triumphed yet again over the chancellor and having
further enhanced their already excessive power.

NOTES

1. Andreas Michelson, *Der U-Bootkrieg 1914-1918*, Leipzig 1925; Der Krieg zur
See 1914-1918, Band 3, Berlin 1934; Hans-Jürgen Schwepke, *U-Bootkrieg und
Friedenspolitik*, phil. Diss. Heidelberg 1952; K.E. Birnbaum, *Peace Moves and
U-Boat Warfare. A Study of Imperial Germany's Policy Towards the United
States April 18, 1916 – January 9, 1917*, Stockholm 1958; Arno Spindler,
*Wie es zu dem Entschluss zum uneingeschränkten U-Bootkrieg 1917
gekommen ist*, Göttingen, Historisch-politische Hefte der Ranke Gesellschaft,
Heft 2; Baldur Kaulisch, 'Die Auseinandersetzungen über den
uneingeschränkten U-Boot-Krieg innerhalb der herrschenden Klassen im
zweiten Halbjahr 1916 und seine Eröffnung in Februar 1917,' in *Politik im
Krieg 1914-1918*, Berlin 1964.
2. *Untersuchungsausschuss IV Reihe*, Band 2, p. 170. PA Bonn AA Gr. HQ
42 U-Bootkrieg, Band 3 for the report by Hindenburg to Prince Max 16-10-18
on the Pless meeting. Weizsäcker noted in his diary that the appointment of
Hindenburg and Ludendorff to the OHL was a victory for the U-boat
enthusiasts, but he tended to overemphasise the purely military aspects of the
change in the OHL in these early days. Weizsäcker diary 30-8-16.
3. Birnbaum, *Peace Moves and U-Boat Warfare*, p. 136.
4. Bundesarchiv Koblenz, Nachlass Bauer, Band 34.
5. Ludendorff, *Urkunden der OHL*, p. 302. Ritter, *Staatskunst und
Kriegshandwerk*, Band 3, p. 325 exaggerates Ludendorff's 'loyalty' towards
Bethmann in these discussions with the navy. His arguments were 'purely
military' in Ludendorff's sense that the division between politics and military
affairs was scarcely defined and he insisted on the OHL having the right to
decide when unrestricted submarine warfare should be begun as the question
was 'purely military' and he did not care about the 'political questions'.
6. Müller diary 12-9-16.
7. *Ibid.*, 20-9-16.
8. Ritter, *Staatskunst und Kriegshandwerk*, Vol. 3, p. 326. Kühlmann talked to
Müller of 700,000 men: Müller diary 1-10-16. Ritter is therefore wrong in
accusing Bethmann of exaggeration when he also spoke of 700,000 men.
Clearly Kühlmann scaled it down for the OHL's benefit.
9. *Deutschland im ersten Weltkrieg* Band 2, p. 559. For the *Unabhängige
Ausschuss für ein Deutschen Frieden* see Karl-Heinz Schädlich's well researched
article in *Politik im Krieg*, p. 50.
10. Birnbaum, *Peace Moves and U-Boat Warfare*, pp. 125, 149, 169 and 299
argues that Bethmann thought that there was a remote possibility of finding

his 'third way'. Fischer, *Griff nach der Weltmacht,* p. 368 supports Birnbaum, as does *Deutschland im ersten Weltkrieg,* Band 2, p. 561. Ritter, *Staatskunst und Kriegshandwerk,* Band 3, p. 647, footnote 7 feels that this is neither proven nor probable. The argument is over the interpretation of Bethmann's remarks: 'The probable rejection of our appeal by England and her allies, while we accept that it will form the basis for us being able to withdraw our guarantee to America, and we will then be able to justify this morally to the world, particularly to the European neutrals, and therefore we will be able to influence their probable future attitude.' Bethmann to Grünau 1-10-16, *Untersuchungsausschuss IV Reihe,* Band 2, number 162, p. 191. Ritter argues that this was a tactical move to appease Ludendorff. Other historians have preferred to take it, to my mind correctly, at its face value.

11. Müller diary 14-10-16.
12. *Ibid.,* 3-12-16.
13. Scherer Grunewald, *L'Allemagne et les problemes de la paix,* Vol. 1, p. 609.
14. Birnbaum, *Peace Moves and U-Boat Warfare,* p. 240.
15. Even Ritter has to admit that this is true, even though it contradicts the views he expresses earlier in the book. *Staatskunst und Kriegshandwerk,* Band 3, p. 350.
16. Westarp, *Konservative Politik,* Band 2, p. 74.
17. Ludendorff, *Urkunden der OHL,* p. 312; *Untersuchungsausschuss IV Reihe,* Band 2, *Beilagen,* p. 221; Birnbaum, *Peace Moves and U-Boat Warfare,* p. 277.
18. Ludendorff, *Urkunden der OHL,* p. 315; Scherer Grunewald, *L'Allemagne et les problemes de la paix,* Vol. 1, p. 630.
19. *Ibid.,* p. 640.
20. Ludendorff, *Urkunden der OHL,* p. 316.
21. Ritter, *Staatskunst und Kriegshandwerk,* Band 3, p. 370; Birnbaum, *Peace Moves and U-Boat Warfare,* p. 279.
22. Müller diary 24-12-16.
23. Bethmann Hollweg to Valentini 31-12-16, Valentini, *Kaiser und Kabinettschef,* p. 241.
24. Müller diary 30-12-16.
25. Helfferich, *Der Weltkrieg,* p. 361.
26. Bülow's memorandum is printed in full in Birnbaum, *Peace Moves and U-Boat Warfare,* p. 370.
27. Scherer Grunewald, *L'Allemagne et les problemes de la paix,* Vol. 1, p. 651.
28. *Ibid.,* p. 654, Wedel to foreign office 1-1-17.
29. *Ibid.,* p. 654, Bethmann to Kaiser 2-1-17.
30. *Ibid.,* p. 661. Grünau to foreign office 4-1-17.
31. Birnbaum, *Peace Moves and U-Boat Warfare,* p. 305.
32. Müller diary, 8-1-17.
33. *Untersuchungsausschuss IV Reihe,* Band 2, p. 334.
34. See Zimmermann's instructions to Bernstorff 7-1-17 with the rather pathetic appeal for suggestions on how submarines could be used without America breaking off relations with Germany. Scherer Grunewald, *L'Allemagne et les problemes de la paix,* Vol. 1, p. 668.
35. Müller diary 8-1-17.
36. Ludendorff, *Urkunden der OHL,* p. 322; Valentini, *Kaiser und Kabinettschef,* p. 144 says that Holtzendorff and Müller were present but Bethmann Hollweg, *Betrachtungen zum Weltkriege,* Band 2, Berlin 1922, p. 137 specifically states that he was alone with Hindenburg and Ludendorff. There is no mention of this meeting in Müller's diary. Holtzendorff and Müller are not mentioned in the protocol of the meeting drawn up by Bartenwerffer in Ludendorff, *Urkunden der OHL,* p. 322.

37. Helfferich, *Der Weltkrieg*, p. 368.
38. No protocol could be found of this meeting. The most detailed accounts are Valentini, *Kaiser und Kabinettschef*, p. 145, and Müller's diary, 9-1-17. There are minor discrepancies between the two accounts.
39. Helfferich, *Der Weltkrieg*, p. 364. *Untersuchungsausschuss IV Reihe*, Band 2, p. 226.
40. Valentini, *Kaiser und Kabinettschef*, p. 146.
41. Müller diary 9-1-17.
42. *Ibid.*, 10-1-17, Valentini, *Kaiser und Kabinettschef*, p. 146.
43. *Ibid.*, p. 148.
44. Botho Leberke, *Die wirtschaftlichen Ursachen des amerikanischen Kriegseintritts* 1917, Berlin 1940; Jürgen Möckelmann, *Das Deutschlandbild in den USA 1914 bis 1918 und die Kriegszielpolitik Wilsons*. phil. Diss. Hamburg 1964.
45. PA Bonn AA Weltkrieg 28 Geheim, Band II: PA Bonn AA Weltkrieg 23 Geheim, Band 28, Bethmann to Prince Max 23-10-18 in which Bethmann said that he was helpless against Hindenburg on the U-boat question as he was opposed by the army and navy, the political parties and 'basically all those who, as a result of the unfortunate development of our political life, were fond of considering themselves to be the sole possessors of national feeling'.
46. Fischer, *Griff nach der Weltmacht*, p. 400.
47. Müller diary 6-2-17.

6 THE JULY CRISIS 1917 AND ITS CONSEQUENCES

The quarrels between the OHL and the chancellor over war aims, over Poland and Belgium and on the question of unrestricted submarine warfare were all symptoms of the profound tensions and conflicts which were beginning to threaten the very foundations of the social order. As the demands of the right became increasingly strident and out of all proportion to the relative strength of the Central Powers, the political demands of the left for reform at home and peace without annexations appeared increasingly attractive. As the war dragged on into its third year, and the hardships of the winter of 1916-17 revealed the deep-rooted contradictions within German society, many politicians felt that some political concessions would have to be made if the total collapse of the truce of 1914, the *Burgfrieden,* were to be avoided. There were those who felt that even the magic names of Hindenburg and Ludendorff, and the peculiar form of bonapartist rule by the OHL, was not enough to overcome the mounting disgust with the senseless slaughter in the trenches and the pangs of empty stomachs at home. It was hoped that political reform could be used to take some wind out of the sails of the radical socialists, counteract the considerable effect of the Russian revolution in Germany, and neutralise the idealistic rhetoric of President Wilson on the subject of democracy and autocracy.

One of the aspects of the Bismarckian constitution that was most obviously in need of reform was the Prussian franchise with its three class system which guaranteed a conservative hold on the *Landtag.* Yet such a change would fundamentally alter the structure of the imperial constitution which had been so ingeniously designed to reconcile liberal nationalism and Junker domination. Electoral reform in Prussia would seriously threaten the position of the conservatives in Prussia and of Prussia within the Reich, and was thus a matter of far greater importance than a mere correction of the franchise. It would be an important step towards the development of parliamentary government in Germany, and therefore a significant strengthening of the power of the Reichstag majority. As such it would to a certain extent counterbalance the excessive power of the OHL.

Such reform had been discussed by the Prussian government as early as December 1914, but the conservatives resisted the proposals so vehemently that little progress was made. In the spring of 1915 a liberalisation of German politics after the war was announced in the Reichstag, and in the speech from the throne in January 1916 electoral reform was promised. Such was the violent reaction of the conservatives that the promise had to be watered down to become a vague and unsatisfactory assurance. Bethmann's belief in the need for a degree of reform, and his apparently more moderate views on war aims resulted in the growing opposition of the conservatives, and the determination in some extremist circles that Bethmann should go. In order to placate his critics on the right the chancellor allowed the Prussian *Landtag* to discuss a bill on changes in the laws of entailment of Junker estates (*Fidei Commiss* bill) in January 1917, but this was such a flagrant attempt to strengthen the economic position of the Junkers that the debate had to be tabled out of consideration for the *Burgfrieden*.

The *Fidei Commiss* bill led to an intensification of the political debate and the beginnings of a new political alignment in favour of moderate reforms which might strengthen the home front thus giving Germany a better chance to win the war and achieve her war aims. Thus the national liberals, the centre and the independents joined with the social democrats to demand domestic reform as the *quid pro quo* for the *Fidei Commiss* law.[1] Bethmann was prepared to accept the idea of reform after the war, but his assurances satisfied neither side. The left was not content with vague promises, the right felt that the chancellor now believed in parliamentary democracy and the end of conservative privilege.

Hindenburg and Ludendorff, who were determined after the squabbles over unrestricted submarine warfare that Bethmann should go, were more than willing to use the political crisis in Prussia over electoral reform for their own ends. Carl Duisberg visited Pless on 24 January 1917 and shortly afterwards gave a widely reported speech in Munich in which he called for a strong man to save the country from otherwise certain defeat. Duisberg was also busy organising the 'Adlon Action', which brought together leading figures of heavy industry and the political right who were determined to remove Bethmann and secure the appointment of Hindenburg as chancellor and head of the OHL. The group met at the Hotel Adlon in Berlin, and its activities were reported and supported by the army's propaganda machine.[2]

At first the OHL was tempted by Duisberg's plan for an outright military dictatorship, but they soon began to have serious reservations. Although they were anxious that Bethmann should be removed, they were increasingly reluctant to take over direct political responsibility, preferring to hide behind a new chancellor who they hoped would be subservient to their wishes. Hindenburg and Ludendorff were particularly anxious to retain their popularity, for they were keenly aware that much of their power rested on this pseudo-democratic popular support. They were thus disturbed by the fact that Duisberg and the Adlon group were unable to gain much support, for there was a growing awareness that not even right wing political goals could be achieved without some political concessions, and that a military dictatorship as the Adlon group proposed would lead inevitably to a worsening of the domestic political situation and provide useful ammunition to the left. Thus the 'Adlon Action' misfired, due in part to skilful leaking of information to hostile newspapers which was used to discredit the movement.[3] But even though the 'Adlon Action' had failed, the OHL made yet another attempt to get rid of Bethmann Hollweg. On 14 March Hindenburg asked the Kaiser to dismiss Bethmann, but the request was refused. Indeed the Kaiser seems to have become most upset at the intrigues of the radical right.[4]

By the end of March there was an overwhelming majority in the Reichstag in favour of suffrage reform, and Bethmann was determined to use this movement to combat his critics and enemies on the right. He cunningly revived William II's dreams of becoming a 'people's Kaiser' which had been so appealing to him at the beginning of his reign in 1888, so that he was willing to overlook the hostility of the OHL and agreed to make a statement on suffrage reform in Prussia in his Easter message scheduled for 7 April.[5]

Bethmann had considerable difficulty in convincing the Prussian ministry of state that reform was indeed essential. Finding himself with a majority of only one, and well aware that he was heading for yet another serious confrontation with the OHL, Bethmann agreed that the reform should be postponed until after the war and should be indicated in the negative sense of an end to the three class system rather than the positive form of equal suffrage. These modifications were incorporated into the Kaiser's speech on Easter Sunday in which he announced that the Prussian *Landtag* would be reformed after the war and added that 'after the tremendous efforts of the entire people in this war there can be no place, in my opinion, for a class suffrage'.

The OHL bitterly complained that it had been kept in the dark about the preparations for the Easter message, and indeed Bethmann, knowing full well the attitude of the OHL to any such proposals had preferred to wait and ride the storm after the Kaiser had made his speech, rather than run the risk that the OHL might make the Kaiser change his mind for some spurious 'military' reason.[6] For Ludendorff the Easter message was a 'kowtow to the Russian revolution' and a direct cause of the April strikes, which in turn were the 'insolent answer of the proletariat to a policy dictated by fear'.[7] But the OHL found itself in a very delicate situation. On the one hand they wished it to be assumed that the OHL regarded the proposed reforms as the thin end of the republican wedge and a craven concession to illusory fears of revolution, but at the same time they were anxious that Hindenburg's implacable opposition to suffrage reform should not be too widely known, for it would be correctly interpreted as meddling in politics.[7] Thus for the time being the OHL was content to use the Easter message as a weapon to attack the chancellor, and their main concern was to ensure that all such reforms were postponed until after the war.[8]

There were some officers at the OHL who felt that the army would gain tremendous popularity and boost morale if it came out in favour of suffrage reform.[9] When Merz von Quirnheim, a prominent proponent of this idea, asked Bauer how universal suffrage could be avoided after the war, Bauer replied 'with a devilish sarcastic grin: "we still have the machine guns"'. But not even Bauer could have dreamed that the machine guns were later to be used at the request of the SPD against German socialists. The OHL was successful in postponing discussion of the suffrage question, and it was not until 5 December 1917 that the first reading of the bill took place in the house of representatives.[9]

By the middle of June 1917 it was clear that a major political crisis was on the horizon. It was not simply a matter of the mounting hostility between the OHL and the chancellor which had been further intensified by the question of reform of the Prussian franchise – it was also the result of growing disappointment with the course of the war. Submarine warfare, on which so many exaggerated hopes had been pinned, failed in its primary objective of bringing England to her knees, in spite of some initial successes. Hopes for a separate peace with Russia were dashed. Sharply rising prices and excessive profits in some sectors caused widespread discontent and an appreciable radicalisation of the labour movement. The enormous increase in the cost of warfare put an intolerable strain on the already grossly overextended financial resources of the Reich. Towards the end of June the secretary of the treasury, Graf Roedern, announced that the war credits would be exhausted by the middle of July, and that the Reichstag would have to be recalled to vote for new credits. The session was likely to be stormy, for the *Burgfrieden* was strained to breaking point by the end of the previous session.[10] Bethmann hoped to placate the SPD with promises of future reform, the OHL intended to use the inevitable crisis to remove the chancellor.

In order to keep up the pressure on the Kaiser to dismiss Bethmann, Hindenburg invited the Kaiser's old friend, the president of East Prussia, to headquarters. Von Berg turned out to be an admirable choice for the OHL. He agreed fully with Hindenburg and Ludendorff's views, and promptly went to the Kaiser and told him that Bethmann's dismissal was demanded by 'all patriots'.[11] Berg also complained about Valentini, and it was clear that he hoped to succeed him as chief of the civil cabinet. Masterminding this whole plot was the Kaiser's adjutant, von Plessen, who had first suggested to Hindenburg that Berg should be invited to Kreuznach, and who urged Berg to speak up against Bethmann and Valentini during his conversations with the Kaiser. It was noted that Plessen treated Valentini with 'special, almost obsequious politeness'.[12]

When Bethmann arrived in Kreuznach to argue the case for moderate reforms in order to win the support of the Reichstag majority in the forthcoming debates, he found that Berg had effectively undermined his position.[13] The Kaiser, although he was not yet prepared to join Hindenburg and Ludendorff in their attack on Bethmann, was not prepared to support the chancellor against the encroachments of the OHL into the political field. He relapsed into nervous inactivity, a mood which grew even worse when in the course of the day Hindenburg and Ludendorff threatened to resign.[14] Bethmann was without friends at headquarters, for even Valentini as a staunch conservative was opposed to any further parliamentarisation. Without something approaching a political revolution he could not maintain his position against the will of the conservative forces in Germany, the army, the bureaucracy and the leaders of industry and finance. The constitutional position of the Reichstag was such that it had virtually no influence on the decision making process, and was almost powerless against the overwhelming strength of Prussian conservatism. In the last resort the chancellor was dependent on the goodwill of the Kaiser, not on any possible coalitions in the Reichstag, and he had good reason to doubt that he had William's support.[15]

In fact the chancellor was steadily losing support in the Reichstag: each day criticism of government policy mounted, reaching a climax on 6 July when Erzberger made a sensational speech which stressed the gravity of the military situation, the failure of the submarine campaign, and the collapse of Germany's allies. Erzberger suggested that Germany should disavow any territorial expansion, and since there was no likelihood of obtaining extensive war aims, negotiations for a peace should begin immediately.[16] The speech caused a sensation because Erzberger was known to have close contacts with the military and political leadership. Indeed Erzberger's gloomy assessment of the military situation and the superiority of the Entente in men and materials was in part due to a conversation he had with Bauer on 10 June, and Czernin had told him how grave was the situation in Austria-Hungary. Many politicians were convinced that Erzberger was speaking in a semi-official capacity, though this was an unfounded belief. Another reason for the impact of the speech was that he had managed to articulate the feelings that many on the main committee of the Reichstag shared but dared not voice. But the speech was exceptionally ambiguous, and almost any peace settlement would have been consistent with the principles he enunciated, short of an outright annexationist peace. If Scheidemann could speak of the 'conversion of Matthew', no one could be quite certain what new faith he had espoused.

The war minister, von Stein, hearing of Erzberger's speech and alarmed at the possible consequences, immediately telephoned the OHL asking Hindenburg and Ludendorff to come to Berlin at once to discuss the military implications of the speech with the Kaiser. The generals arrived the next day in Berlin, hoping to be able to give Bethmann the *coup de grace,* but they were disappointed. The Kaiser first discussed the affair with Bethmann before meeting Hindenburg, and the chancellor was able to convince him that as negotiations with the main committee were still in progress the whole affair might blow over, or the final result might well be acceptable. When Hindenburg and Ludendorff arrived for their audience they were given a long lecture by the supreme warlord not to meddle in matters which were of no concern to them, and they were ordered to return to headquarters immediately.[17]

While Hindenburg and Ludendorff were engaged with the Kaiser, Colonel Bauer dined with Erzberger and Stresemann and stirred up their anger against Bethmann by saying that the chancellor had denied them the right to discuss the military situation with Hindenburg and Ludendorff.[18] The following day Ludendorff let the party leaders know that he was in favour of bringing politicians into the government, but that the chancellor had made open discussions between the Reichstag members and the OHL impossible. That Ludendorff had the nerve to pose as the champion of parliamentary democracy against a reactionary chancellor is grotesque enough, but that an experienced politician like Erzberger should have believed such nonsense is truly remarkable. But if a man could believe that the most suitable successor to Bethmann, and the man most likely to bring about a negotiated peace, was that suave windbag Bülow, then he could believe almost anything.[19]

The OHL was thus playing a double game. To the politicians in the Reichstag they were suggesting that they supported greater political power for the Reichstag, but at the same time they bombarded the government with protests against their weakness towards the demands of the Reichstag. As soon as they arrived back at headquarters the OHL telegraphed both the chancellor and the state secretary that a resolution by the Reichstag which called for a peace without territorial gains, and which insisted that Germany was fighting a purely defensive war, would be highly undesirable and would undermine the efforts of the army.[20] The object of both these approaches was to secure the dismissal of Bethmann by convincing both the government and the Reichstag that he was deliberately frustrating their policies. Both arguments were backed by the almost magical figure of Hindenburg who by some fascinating quirk of mass psychology seemed to become more invincible and infallible the more it was realised that Germany had little hope of ever winning the war. Thus it was possible for one and the same man to continue to have absolute faith in Hindenburg and at the same time vote for the peace resolution, in spite of the fact that only the shrewdest politicians realised that there was not so much difference between a 'Hindenburg peace' and certain annexationist interpretations of the Reichstag resolution.

On 8 July Bethmann found himself deadlocked with the Prussian ministry of state over the issue of franchise reform. Loebell threatened that the entire ministry would resign if equal suffrage were declared; Bethmann countered by threatening his own resignation. That evening the Kaiser discussed with Valentini the possible candidates for Bethmann's position, for he was convinced that he would have to resign.[21] Two days later Bethmann again offered to resign, telling the Kaiser that some sort of reform was inevitable and spoke so passionately that even Valentini, staunch conservative though he was, was convinced by his arguments. After the interview the Kaiser sadly remarked to Valentini: 'I am supposed to dismiss that man who stands head and shoulders above all the others.'[22]

The next day, 11 July, the crown prince also arrived in Berlin, well primed by the OHL with arguments against Bethmann, in order to persuade his father to dismiss the chancellor. But the Kaiser and Valentini were able to persuade him that a change of chancellor at that particular moment would be most unwise, and the crown prince remarked that only an idiot could fail to see the logic of this argument.[23] But Colonel Bauer was waiting for the crown prince after the audience, and he found it easy to persuade him to join the movement against Bethmann and to forget the unassailable logic of the Kaiser's defence of the chancellor. Bauer suggested that the crown prince should meet leading members of the Reichstag in the morning, while Bauer hid in the anteroom taking notes. Westarp, Erzberger, Stresemann, Mertin, Payer and David were invited, a list that made it certain that Bethmann would appear in the worst possible light.

This extraordinary meeting took place on the morning of 12 July.[24] It was certainly a constitutional novelty. It was the first time in the history of the German empire that representatives of the Reichstag were asked about their attitudes towards the dismissal of a chancellor, and asked not by the Kaiser, who alone could appoint and dismiss the chancellor, but by the crown prince acting as the messenger boy of the OHL. Only Payer seems to have thought the whole affair ridiculous and undignified, for it reminded him of the mustering of recruits. If he had known that Bauer was hiding behind a curtain taking extensive notes of the proceedings he would have been even more outraged. For Bauer the meeting was a tremendous success. All the politicians, except Payer, spoke out against the chancellor, so that the crown prince was given the totally false impression that the Reichstag was solidly in favour of getting rid of the chancellor.

In order further to heighten the crisis, Bauer announced that Hindenburg and Ludendorff would resign if Bethmann did not go. The faithful Payer promptly reported this to the chancellor, who immediately sent a telegram to Kreuznach demanding to know if it was true. Ludendorff's reply was artfully cryptic: 'I have not ordered any officer to tell any member of the Reichstag that I can no longer work with the chancellor von Bethman Hollweg.'[25] Bauer stayed in Berlin, and was busy lobbying the political parties to stop supporting the chancellor. To the right wing parties he argued that Bethmann was too conciliatory and was heading Germany towards a revolution, to the left he insisted that he was a hindrance to peace and a major obstacle to a good understanding between the OHL and the politicians. Bauer did his work well. Both the national liberals and the centre party announced that they could no longer support the chancellor.[26]

The war minister, von Stein, had also been active. In the course of the afternoon of 12 July he telegraphed the OHL saying that the Reichstag majority was still uncertain about the wording of what he incorrectly called a 'peace offer'. He asked the OHL to tell the Kaiser that if the chancellor agreed to a document which could be construed as a 'peace of renunciation' it would have a disastrous effect on the army. Without even seeing the resolution, and even though Stein's telegram was singularly poorly expressed, Hindenburg immediately telegraphed the Kaiser, saying that the resolution was an obvious sign of weakness that would diminish Germany's fighting ability and strengthen the determination of the Entente. He concluded by asking the Kaiser to part with Bethmann.[27]

It was thus hardly surprising that Bethmann received a frosty welcome on his arrival at Schloss Bellevue that evening. Even though he had discussed the Reichstag peace resolution with Bethmann two days ago, the Kaiser claimed never to have seen the document. He then ordered that the document should be read to Hindenburg over the telephone so that he could have a chance to comment. Hindenburg's reply arrived within half an hour. He insisted that a sentence which read 'Forcible seizure of territory and political, economic, or financial acts of force are not commensurate with such a peace' should be removed. He knew that this was the key phrase in the resolution, and he was not going to have his imperialist dreams shattered by a handful of politicians and a weak-kneed chancellor. The Kaiser fully supported his chief of general staff.[28]

Shortly after Hindenburg's reply was known, General Lyncker informed the Kaiser that the resignations of Hindenburg and Ludendorff were on the way, for they felt that they could no longer work with the chancellor.[29] The Kaiser was furious at the OHL for blackmailing him in this shameless fashion, but Lyncker persuaded him to order Hindenburg and Ludendorff to come to Berlin, rather than refuse their resignations by post.[30] Bethmann then asked the Kaiser to be relieved of his position, for although he was confident that he could control the Reichstag, and was even prepared to accept Hindenburg's amendment to the peace resolution, he knew that it would be impossible to continue working with the OHL. The Kaiser was now placed in an intolerable position. He had to agree with Bethmann that it would hardly be possible for the chancellor and the OHL to work together, but if he accepted the chancellor's logic then he would be giving way to pressure from the OHL, a thought that was abhorrent to a man so concerned with his prerogative. On the other hand the dismissal of Hindenburg and Ludendorff would cause such an uproar that Bethmann's position would become untenable. Unable to resolve this dilemma the Kaiser ended the meeting with some angry remarks about Hindenburg and Ludendorff's insolence. After the meeting Bethmann told Payer to amend the resolution to meet Hindenburg's objections, but to defer any further discussions until Hindenburg and Ludendorff arrived in Berlin. In other words he had relinquished control over foreign policy and given it to the OHL.[31]

The following morning, before the generals arrived in Berlin, the Kaiser accepted Bethmann's letter of resignation, and approved his suggestion that Hertling should be his successor. However, Hertling told Valentini that he was too old and too tired to think of becoming chancellor, and that he had serious differences of opinion with the OHL on the question of war aims. In the course of further discussions the Kaiser agreed to appoint Bernstorff, provided that Hindenburg found him acceptable. It was agreed that Lyncker would pass this message on to Hindenburg, but Lyncker flatly refused, saying that Bernstorff was quite unsuitable. There then occured one of the most extraordinary episodes in the constitutional history of the Reich. Plessen arrived on the scene quite by chance, and began to discuss with Lyncker the question of a successor to Bethmann Hollweg. Plessen suggested Michaelis, a worthy figure of no great prominence. Valentini felt that under the circumstances Michaelis, who was felt to be an honourable and firm personality, would be suitable, even though he had no experience of foreign affairs.

They all then piled into a car, which Plessen had waiting outside, and drove to see Hindenburg in order to propose not the man whom the Kaiser had agreed to accept, but another who had never even been mentioned to him, and to ask the approval of Hindenburg who had not the slightest constitutional right to be in any way concerned with the appointment of a chancellor. Bernstorff's name was mentioned to Hindenburg, but not as a serious candidate, and as was to be expected the suggestion was gruffly repulsed. Michaelis was then suggested and was warmly approved by Hindenburg and Ludendorff. Valentini then reported back to the Kaiser who was understandably amazed at these antics, the more so as he had never even heard of Michaelis. Under the icy gaze of Ludendorff the Kaiser gave in, and ordered Valentini to visit Michaelis and ask him to accept. Michaelis was astounded, but pressed by Valentini he agreed, muttering 'with God's help I will give it a try!'. When Michaelis arrived at the palace the Kaiser had gone to dress for dinner, so that the unfortunate man was kept waiting. When the Kaiser eventually arrived he spoke throughout the interview so that Michaelis was unable to get a word in edgeways. He was then taken by Valentini to meet Bethmann.

The senior civil servants who supported Bethmann were naturally hostile towards Michaelis, and Bethmann was also prepared to give him a cool reception. But they soon warmed to the new chancellor and realised that he was in no way responsible for the circumstances of his appointment. Indeed it is impossible not to feel sorry for him. He had suddenly been appointed chancellor in a crisis and without any prior knowledge. He had not wished to become chancellor, and his appointment was due to the plotting of the generals rather than to due constitutional process. He seemed to face the implacable opposition of many senior officials who felt that his appointment was a deliberate insult – Michaelis had been a civil servant – and who were rightly appalled at the circumstances of his appointment.[32]

News that Bethmann had resigned was greeted with wild enthusiasm by the army. Equal suffrage in Prussia and the possibility of parliamentary reform threatened the unique position of the army within German society, and these reforms were closely associated with Bethmann Hollweg. When the chancellor fell, the Bavarian military plenipotentiary reported that this 'success' was celebrated with numerous parties, and all the worries about the peace resolution and the failures of the Austrians on the Dniester were forgotten.[33] Hindenburg and Ludendorff were immensely relieved that Hertling had not been appointed, and were so full of their triumph over Bethmann that they granted a series of interviews with leading members of the Reichstag.[34] They painted an optimistic picture of the situation. The western front was safe, the Russian army was demoralised, the submarines had been successful, for although America had entered the war the material position of the Entente had worsened and the Americans would pose no threat to the Central Powers until the summer of 1918. Victory was certain if the people would give their full support to the army. When pressed, Ludendorff had to admit that offensives which would end the war were no longer possible, and he suggested that the demoralisation of the Entente was the only possible way of achieving victory, insisting that the peace resolution would make this all the more unlikely.

The politicians would not give up the idea of a peace resolution, and so the OHL decided that it would have a hand in the drafting of the proposal. This led to another ludicrous scene. Ludendorff was to be seen jovially joking with the social democrat Scheidemann, whom until that moment he had regarded as the next best thing to a traitor, and they worked together on a resolution which Ludendorff had insisted would undermine the fighting power of the army. But Scheidemann had already told the OHL that the resolution was so worded that 'necessary territorial gains and compensations are not precluded'.[35] Hindenburg summed up the OHL's thinking by saying that he wanted a 'little more pepper' in the resolution. Michaelis defeated the original intention of the resolution by accepting it in the Reichstag on 19 July 1917 with the proviso 'as I interpret it'. Writing a few days later to the crown prince, Michaelis explained that with the resolution as it stood he could make any peace he wanted.[36]

When the generals returned to headquarters they had good reason to be pleased with their work. They had removed a chancellor whom they loathed and had replaced him with a man they felt to be of their own heart. They had ensured that the peace resolution of the Reichstag was a meaningless and empty formula. Above all they had established the precedent that the OHL could make or break a chancellor, and that it could even have a final say in the drafting of resolutions in the Reichstag. The triumph of the OHL seemed complete.

The appointment of Michaelis was obviously something of a compromise and there was an unspoken understanding that he was unlikely to remain chancellor for very long. The Adlon group who had hoped to replace Bethmann with a military dictatorship were disappointed. The OHL supported Michaelis, but would probably have preferred either Bülow or Tirpitz. The Kaiser could not forgive Bülow for his conduct during the 'Daily Telegraph' affair, and Tirpitz was too closely associated with the Pan Germans and his appointment would be bound to cause endless rancour.[37] Michaelis was thus in many ways the ideal choice for an interim chancellor. He appealed to the OHL because of his conservatism and his memorandum of April 1916 in which he had called for an extensive militarisation of the economy along the lines that were later to be suggested by Colonel Bauer. Perhaps his greatest asset was that he was virtually unknown. As a senior Prussian civil servant responsible for food policy he had hardly appeared in public, and he had no political experience. The OHL therefore hoped that he would be subservient to their wishes, and on the whole they were not disappointed.

In order to make his position quite clear Hindenburg drew up a list of reasons why the OHL had opposed Bethmann, and the list was intended as a clear warning to Michaelis. Bethmann's foreign policy had been feeble, and he had refused to consult closely with the OHL. He had dithered too long on the submarine issue. He was entirely to blame for the Polish fiasco, the OHL being completely innocent, and also for the failure of the policy towards the Belgian workers. He had not been sufficiently energetic in his economic policy, particularly with regard to food, war production, transport and coal. He had not fully mobilised the power of the people *(Volkskraft)*. He had failed to mount an adequate propaganda effort, and as a result there was a general and widespread demoralisation, pessimism, and worst of all, strikes. He had no proper control over the press. He had gravely damaged the prestige of the monarchy. Hindenburg assured Michaelis of his support, but this support was conditional on his correcting these grave errors of his predecessor.[38]

Michaelis was quite unable to escape the consequences of Bethmann's policies. He was certainly more cooperative than Bethmann in his relations with the OHL, but he could not overcome the serious divisions within German society that had grown worse under the pressure of three years of war. Bethmann Hollweg's removal did not end the problems which he had tried in his own way to solve. Michaelis, for all his qualities, was rapidly to find himself stuck between the antagonistic factions which Bethmann had tried to assuage, between capital and labour, between reaction and reform, between the OHL and their supporters and the Reichstag majority, and was to be left without any support. He lacked any political understanding and cunning, and was faced with problems that would have floored even a politician of real stature. From the first few weeks of his chancellorship it was apparent that he would not remain in office for long.

The first major political event in his chancellorship was the peace resolution of the Reichstag of 19 July 1917. At first it seemed that he would be successful with his policy. The social democrats voted for the war credits. The OHL indicated that any objections that might have been voiced by them were not ones of principle, but simply about means of bringing a peace which everyone desired so profoundly.[39] But it was not long before a massive attack began from the right, starting with a blistering protest from the Army League *(Wehrverein)*. The iron and steel interests soon followed suit. Right wing opposition to the peace resolution was organised in a new party, the *Vaterlandspartei,* which was founded by Admiral Tirpitz and Wolfgang Kapp, who was later to lead the putsch against the Weimar republic. The *Vaterlandspartei* was to win the sympathetic support of the army which used its propaganda apparatus to further the aims of the party, and it soon became a vast organisation. Within a short time there were one and a quarter million paying members.[40] The *Vaterlandspartei* became the organised mass political support for the policies of the OHL, thus formalising the pseudo-democratic dimension of the bonapartism of the OHL. Thus within a few days Michaelis no longer had the unqualified support of the political and economic leadership, and the tensions which marked the chancellorship of Bethmann Hollweg were far from being overcome.

One of the main complaints made by the OHL against Bethmann was his mismanagement of the Polish question. The German ambassador in Vienna, Wedel, had come to the conclusion that the only way out of the muddle caused by the Kreuznach agreement which seemed to satisfy neither Germany nor Austria, would be to revive the Austro-Polish solution.[41] These ideas were suggested to Hindenburg by the Austrian representative at headquarters, General von Cramon, in an informal manner. Hindenburg objected strongly to the suggestion, and on 28 July he instructed Ludendorff to write to Michaelis pointing out that the Austro-Polish solution would encourage Polish irredentism which would spread to the Polish parts of Prussia and to Lithuania. Hindenburg even went so far as to suggest that it would be better to give Poland to Russia than to Austria. He ended by calling for the speedy unification of the two occupation governments and the appointment of Albrecht of Württemberg as Regent of Poland.

Further discussions were held between the OHL and Michaelis on the question of Poland at a meeting in Kreuznach 9 August. It was agreed that an Austrian Poland was 'impossible' and that Hindenburg's suggestions on 28 July should form the basis of German policy towards Poland. If this scheme failed the only possible solution would be the 'fourth partition of Poland', which would involve an even more drastic frontier change with Germany.[42]

Czernin arrived in Berlin on 14 August, hoping to renegotiate the Kreuznach agreement. Ludendorff made it quite plain on the eve of Czernin's meeting with Michaelis that the OHL would not tolerate any changes, and even talked of an *Anschluss* of Poland to Germany.[43] Poor Czernin was submitted to such an onslaught from Ludendorff the following day that he broke out in tears of frustration and humiliation.[44]

Ludendorff had by now lost all patience with Austria. On the day after the meeting with Czernin in Berlin he suggested to Michaelis that Germany should simply annex parts of Poland, and he told the chancellor that the chief of the civil government in Poland, von Kries, had told the OHL that the Poles would not object to this provided that they were promised compensation in the east.[45] A further memorandum was sent to the chancellor, drafted by Colonel Bauer, saying that Germany might have to tolerate an independent Poland, but she would have to ensure that this new Poland was a failure so as not to give 'our Poles' irredentist ideas. This could best be achieved by leaving Poland to its own devices, for it would soon collapse owing to 'Jewish-Polish incompetence'.[46]

With the failure of the OHL's Polish policy, a failure which was blamed on Bethmann Hollweg, came a renewed interest in Rumania. German demands for the future domination of Rumania were formalised in 1916. On 7 December the 'Association for the Protection of German Interests in Rumania' was formed; it acted as a powerful lobby for the interests of German industrial and financial interests in Rumania, and did all that was possible to use the German occupation of parts of Rumania to strengthen Germany's economic stranglehold.[47] The work of the Association was supported by the OHL which was increasingly dissatisfied with the economic benefits likely to come to Germany if the Kreuznach agreement on Rumania were ever put into effect. On 4 September 1917 Ludendorff wrote to the military governor of Rumania that by far the best solution as far as Germany was concerned would be if Rumania were bound as closely as possible to Germany. The implication of this letter was that the Kreuznach proposal should be stood on its head. The OHL would be prepared to accept the Austro-Polish solution, but with many unspecified reservations, and in return Rumania would be annexed by Germany.[48] Later in September the Kaiser visited Rumania. The intoxicating sight of the mountains and the petroleum fields of Campina convinced him that Germany must annex the country.[49] As his imagination carried him away he had visions of the wealth of Rumania pouring into Germany, of Germany with access to the Black Sea, and of Rumania as a pistol pointed at Austria should there ever be any serious differences between the two allies.

Even the most enthusiastic advocate of the annexation of Rumania realised that nothing could be done without the support of Hindenburg and Ludendorff. The Kaiser therefore tried to persuade the OHL to accept the Austro-Polish solution. The supreme warlord went down on his knees before the generals and begged them to accept his suggestions. At first he thought he had been successful, but it soon became apparent that he was once again indulging in wishful thinking. Michaelis agreed with the Kaiser's proposals. He saw the obvious economic advantages of a German-dominated Rumania, and felt that by giving Poland to Austria the Austro-German alliance would be strengthened, for the Austrians seemed to be particularly anxious to secure the domination of Poland. The chancellor insisted that Germany would have to establish military and economic footholds in an Austrian Poland, and suggested that these questions should be discussed with the OHL before sending a proposal to the Austrian government.[50]

Michaelis was being hopelessly optimistic. The Kreuznach agreement could not be so easily reversed. While the OHL agreed that Germany should have economic, political and military control over Rumania, it was opposed to the Austro-Polish solution on the grounds that it would lead to a strengthening of the anti-German elements in the Austrian empire, and would also mean the encirclement of Germany. If there was indeed no alternative to the Austro-Polish solution, then Germany should be given wide-ranging guarantees which would in effect make Poland a German rather than an Austrian dependency.[51]

The proposed conference took place at Kreuznach on 7 October 1917.[52] Ludendorff opened the case for the OHL and listed the military objections to the Austro-Polish solution and the danger of Polish irredentism. Hindenburg supported Ludendorff's arguments, but got even more carried away. In the blackest of terms he spoke of a vast increase in Austrian power that would make the Hohenzollern the vassals of the Hapsburgs, and would lead to another war between Austria and Germany for the hegemony of Central Europe. Austria had done nothing but intrigue against Germany, and now the time had come to strike back. In his summing up he said: 'We must have a deployment area in the east, and if there is no other way then an agreement must be made with Austria with every precaution taken for the security of our interests.' At the end of the conference a list of demands were drawn up as compensation for the Austro-Polish solution. They included a German-controlled railway system for Poland, control over the export of ore, the right for German citizens to own land and mining rights in Poland, guarantees for the rights of the German potash monopoly, and the denial of the right to immigrate into Prussia of Poles and Jews – although workers could be brought in for the harvest. The OHL's demands were thus quite clear. The Austro-Polish solution was only acceptable if it contained guarantees for German economic and military supremacy.

Hindenburg backed up his objections to the Austro-Polish solution in a lengthy memorandum to the chancellor and the state secretary, Kühlmann, written shortly after the Kreuznach meeting.[53] His twenty-four point programme included new demands for the expulsion of the Jews from the new German-Polish territories, the so-called Polish frontier strip, and Jews were to be forbidden from serving in the Polish army. Here one is tempted to see the influence of the most virulent anti-semite in the general staff, Colonel Bauer. Further points were designed to secure an even greater degree of economic penetration of Poland, and the cession of Austrian Silesia to Germany so that Germany would control a direct railway link to Hungary and Rumania.

Hindenburg also insisted on full Austrian support in the Dobrudscha question, so that the Germans could establish their position in Constanta, and the acceptance of all German demands concerning the shipping on the Danube and the transit through Hungary and Rumania. He also demanded a German base on the Adriatic at either Valona or Cattaro, and what amounted to unconditional support by the Austrians for all Germany's war aims. In yet another note Hindenburg said that 'German blood was lost that Austria might defeat Poland and Serbia and that Galicia, the Bukovina and Transylvania might be won back'. He suggested that Austrian Silesia (Teschen) would be the minimum compensation required to appease German public opinion for this sacrifice.[54]

The OHL's thinking on Poland thus combined the traditional anti-Polish and anti-semitic prejudices of the Prussian conservatives with the crude annexationist ideas of a significant sector of heavy industry, and was made all the more extreme by their conviction that a war with Austria was inevitable. It seems that Michaelis agreed with this analysis, so that Kühlmann had little support for his idea of using Austria as the main unit in a German-dominated *Mitteleuropa* designed to extend German power and influence over so large an area at so low a cost militarily, economically and politically.[55]

It was left to Kühlmann to negotiate with the Austrians, the OHL glowering in the background. On 22 October he met Czernin.[56] Kühlmann's handling of Czernin was masterly, the concessions he obtained from the Austrians extraordinary. The Austro-Polish solution was accepted, the Kreuznach agreement reversed, but the Austrians were left with an empty shell. Under Article III of the 'suggested guidelines' it was agreed that the 'Kingdom of Poland and Austria-Hungary are to be joined militarily and financially to the German Empire'. Austria was also obliged to sign a twenty year defensive pact *(Schutz- und Trutzbündnis)* a military convention and an economic agreement designed to remove tariff barriers between the two countries. The only concession Czernin managed to get in return was an exceedingly vague assurance that German policy in Belgium should not form a 'hindrance to peace' and that Austrian interests in Rumania would be respected.

The reversal of the Kreuznach agreements was not the only major question to plague the chancellor in his short term of office. The problem of the war economy still remained to be solved. A major new debate was opened when Captain Merton, Groener's adjutant in the *Kriegsamt,* presented him with a memorandum on profits on 12 July

1916. Merton's argument was that although German industry made much of its sacrifices, heroic efforts and patriotic sense of duty, its main concern, just as in peacetime, was to make the largest possible profits. Industry was able to blame higher prices on higher wages, and use spiralling wages as an excuse for ever higher profits. Merton suggested that it was the steadily rising prices of coal, iron and steel that was the main cause of the sharply rising prices, and argued that the producers of these raw materials should either be obliged to enter into longer term contracts for prices, or that there should be a price stop, profits being high enough to absorb any further increases in wages. Merton made three basic proposals: contracts should be based on fixed prices, so that there could be no increase in prices before, still less after, delivery; there should be a steep profits tax so that war profits could in fact be eliminated; the government should be empowered to take over any firms which refused to accept the prices demanded by the *Kriegsamt,* or which were involved in industrial disputes that the two sides could not resolve.[57]

Richard Merton, general director of the *Metallbank* and of the *Metallurgische Gesellschaft,* Frankfurt, was a representative of light industry, as were many of the advisors to General Groener. As a businessman he had every reason to distrust heavy industry, and as an expert at the *Kriegsamt* he was fully aware that the massive profits of heavy industry would have to be cut back if the *Kriegsamt's* efforts to control the economy were to be at all effective.[58] The struggle which was to begin over the Merton memorandum was part of a more fundamental economic struggle between the coal, iron and steel group which was particularly associated with the OHL after the appointment of Hindenburg and Ludendorff, and the electro-chemical group which tended to be more closely associated with the war ministry, the KRA, the *Kriegsamt* and the consolidation committee (SAZ).[59]

Groener entirely agreed with Merton's proposals, and forwarded the memorandum to Michaelis to gain the chancellor's approval. Michaelis in turn gave it to Helfferich for his comments. Helfferich, as a typical economic liberal, resented any interference with the freedom of the market place and thus opposed the suggestion that profits should be controlled. Helfferich had become extremely critical of Groener, accusing him of empire building and saying that his military approach to economic problems posed a threat to free enterprise. Michaelis also had little faith in Groener. As a traditional conservative he had little sympathy for Groener's approach, and he could easily be persuaded that the *Kriegsamt* was being too favourable to labour. The Merton memorandum was therefore filed away unanswered.

The OHL, and even the war minister, was becoming increasingly critical of Groener. In spite of the *Hundsfott* declaration it was felt that Groener was too conciliatory in his attitude towards labour, so much so that he was given the name of 'red geneial'. His attitude during the strikes in Silesia which broke out in May, when he had attempted to restrain the rather ferocious commanding general of the VIth army corps, von Heinemann, convinced the OHL that a firmer hand was needed against labour and against the attempts of the *Kriegsamt* to act as an intermediary between capital and labour. At the beginning of July the OHL and the war minister agreed on a set of proposals to put before the chancellor.[60] Workers should be bound to the factory where they worked, individual productivity would have to be increased, industry should only produce goods essential to the war effort, there should be total control over employment, and more efforts made to employ women. Pressed by the OHL, von Stein told the commanding general in Silesia to ignore the *Kriegsamt's* efforts to conciliate and to put down the strikes by military force. Ludendorff then issued a general appeal to the commanding generals to render all agitators harmless.[61]

The industrialists were quick to use the wave of strikes in the summer of 1917 as further argument against the auxiliary labour law which they were now determined either to abolish or drastically to modify. In August the Association of German Iron and Steel Industrialists launched a massive attack on the policies of the *Kriegsamt* and on General Groener who seemed to them to be the evil genius behind the policy of conciliation.[62] Groener agreed that the auxiliary labour law should be redrafted in order to meet the objections of the OHL and the industrialists, and his attitude towards labour became noticeably tougher. But this was too late to save his position. The OHL, prompted by Duisberg, began their campaign to remove Groener at the end of July. At first Michaelis was somewhat reluctant to support this move as Groener still had considerable support in the Reichstag and among the labour leaders. On 14 August he gave in and signed a cabinet order which placed the *Kriegsamt* firmly under the control of the war ministry. This move was taken without Groener's knowledge, and had he known he would most likely have resigned. As it happened he was dismissed before the Kaiser countersigned the order.

Groener had travelled to headquarters on 15 August, but Ludendorff was careful to avoid any contentious issues and was exceedingly polite to Groener. That evening Schleicher, who was enjoying one of his first tastes of political intrigue, telephoned Merton to say that Groener was about to be dismissed.[63] On the following day Groener was officially informed that he had been appointed to command the 33rd division. On 19 August Ludendorff sent him a telegram thanking him for his efforts in the *Kriegsamt,* and wishing him every possible success. Groener was stunned and angry at this unexpected turn of events and the extraordinary conduct of Ludendorff.

The dismissal of Groener was the result of disagreement over means, rather than fundamental differences as to ends. Groener had tried to carry out the task imposed by the Hindenburg programme, to increase war production and the productivity of individual workers, but he attempted to do this with a degree of consent rather than help create a military dictatorship in economic affairs. The heavy industrialists, led by Duisberg and Stinnes, were angry with Groener for attempting to hold back the commanding generals, and accused him of being too conciliatory towards labour. The OHL fully agreed with these views, but the issue of the control of profits was probably of far less concern to them. Hindenburg, Ludendorff and Bauer all continually paid lip service to the idea that profits in industry were excessive, and that they should be controlled in some way. The soldiers' notion of an authoritarian corporate state had little place for excessive profits and the amassing of vast wealth. It also seems that the Merton memorandum was withheld from Ludendorff, although Bauer and Duisberg obviously knew of its contents.[64] Ties between heavy industry and the OHL were so close, and the OHL's understanding of economics so crude, that there was full agreement between them that Groener should be removed, and that for the time being the issue of profits should be ignored. Groener, however, was convinced that it was the threat to profits which caused his downfall, and this view was shared by many newspapers and liberal politicians.[65] Duisberg was quick to tell Groener that the widely held view that he had been dismissed because of pressure from heavy industry was a perfidious lie, and that he himself was entirely innocent of any such action.[66] Groener knew full well that this was quite untrue, but he still could not see that factors other than the threat to profits had been critical in bringing about his downfall.[67]

Duisberg had convened a meeting of the Dusseldorf Industry Club to meet on 19 August in order to discuss the question of the freedom of workers and the 'attack on the employers' posed by proposed profit controls. In other words Groener, the *Kriegsamt* and the Merton memorandum were to come under attack. Colonel Bauer was invited to attend. In spite of the unexpected dismissal of Groener the meeting took place as arranged.[68] Duisberg opened the proceedings by blaming a drop of 20 per cent to 40 per cent of productivity per worker on the auxiliary labour law, because workers knew that they would not be sent to the front. He felt that the workers' councils were extremely dangerous institutions and should be stopped. The unions were far too powerful, created industrial unrest and undermined productivity. He countered the attacks on high profits with the extraordinary argument that firms which declared high dividends were contributing directly to the war effort since more taxes could be collected from those incomes which were increased by the payment of larger dividends. Duisberg insisted that the auxiliary labour law should be modified so that the employers could become 'masters in their own house', an echo of the 'Stumm era' before the war. Overall control of the economy could then be vested in the OHL. In other words Duisberg was arguing for a kind of economic *Führerprinzip,* seeking the support of the army against the working class, while at the same time trying to ensure the minimum of army interference with the actual running of industry. Bauer gave Duisberg his full support; he agreed that the influence of the workers would have to be curtailed, that the abuses of the auxiliary labour law needed rectification, and that further steps should be taken to close down small and inefficient firms. The civilian Lewinski from the war ministry was one of the few to dampen the general feeling of enthusiasm by pointing out that the Bundesrat could not simply remove paragraphs IX and XII from the law; they would have to abrogate the entire law. This the industrialists knew was most unlikely.

On 10 September Hindenburg suggested to Michaelis that the Auxiliary Labour Law should be removed and that full use should be made of the law on the state of siege. Hindenburg also repeated Duisberg's charge that workers were deliberately producing as little as possible in order to avoid being sent to the front. The successor to Groener as head of the *Kriegsamt,* Scheüch, who had worked his way up through the war ministry, was not the kind of man to support such radical suggestions, and preferred instead to reform the implementation of the law, rather than to press for major changes. He thus continued with Groener's policy and cooperated with Legien and Gustav Bauer to get the unions to support measures to stop workers from changing their jobs too often.[69]

Michaelis realised that it was a political impossibility to tear up the auxiliary labour law, and hoped that the OHL would eventually realise this truth. The OHL continued to press the chancellor for changes in the law, repeating all the familiar accusations, but paradoxically the more frustrated they became the more they came round to a position very similar to that of Groener. Michaelis' representative at headquarters thus reported that Bauer was now calling for a

> united and voluntary effort of all concerned people in order to achieve an increase of the productivity of labour on a nationwide scale during the winter. Certain political concessions can be considered — for example, the creation of labour committees in cooperation with the unions on the basis of the existing workers' councils for the duration of the war.[70]

On 12 October Legien and Gustav Bauer and other prominent labour leaders were invited to headquarters, and the OHL was delighted to receive their assurances that they would be able and willing to prevent any serious strikes or disturbances.[71]

In a remarkable memorandum to the *Kriegsamt* Ludendorff summed up his impressions of this meeting.[72] He was impressed by the 'good intentions' of the labour leaders, but felt that they had little concern or understanding for those who were less well off than the workers. He accepted the complaint that workers' councils had often not even been formed, and that employers showed an unreasonable reluctance to discuss wages and profits. He also suggested that workers often had a justified fear that the provisions of the law were being used by the employers to control labour to an unnecessary degree, and that the army was seen to be too much on the side of the employers. His conclusion could almost have been written by Groener. There should be discussions between employers and labour under the aegis of the commanding generals, but at the same time it should be made perfectly clear that strikes were tantamount to treason.

The negotiations over Pope Bendict XV's rather pathetic peace appeal of mid-August 1917 to the belligerent governments brought the question of German aims in Belgium once more into the centre of the political arena.[73] On 30 August the Papal Nuncio for Bavaria Pacelli wrote to Michaelis calling for a firm declaration of German intentions to respect the full independence of Belgium, for reparations for war damage, and further to specify German guarantees for the political, economic and military independence of Belgium.[74] Michaelis tried to persuade the OHL that if there were close economic links between Belgium and Germany there would be no need to annex Liège. Germany would then have secure access to the raw materials of western Europe, special tariffs on the railways and canals, privileges in the port of Antwerp, influence over the pro-German Flemish movement in Belgium, expulsion of British interests from the Flanders coast and Northern France, and the return of Germany's colonies as compensation for not annexing the Flanders coast. In the east, Germany would still control Poland, Lithuania, Courland, the Ukraine, Finland and Rumania. Michaelis then appealed for the support of the OHL against the extremist annexationists like Westarp.[75]

Michaelis' hopes were soon dashed. Hindenburg replied that the navy and 'patriotic circles' would be so upset by the loss of the Flanders coast that massive compensations would be needed probably in the form of naval bases throughout the world. Belgium would have to be under military occupation 'for many years' if the economic links with Germany were to be effective. Hindenburg thus had no sympathy whatever for Michaelis' view that the economic dependence of Belgium on Germany would make military occupation unnecessary, and argued that without military occupation there could be no economic exploitation.[76]

Included with Hindenburg's reply was a memorandum from Ludendorff.[77] He argued that the military and domestic position of the Central Powers was stronger than that of the Entente, but he was prepared to accept the idea of a peace before the end of the year provided that it gave Germany the essentials for her domestic development and the military and economic position from which she could successfully fight a defensive war. Such 'minimum demands' included extensive frontier rectifications in Poland; Courland and Lithuania to be under German control; economic control of Rumania, and in the west frontier rectifications in France, annexation of the Maas line and Liège, the military occupation of Belgium and control of Holland. The Russian market would have to be under German control as would South America. Germany would have to have an extensive empire in Africa and naval bases throughout the world. Last but not least Denmark would have to be under the economic control of Germany.

The OHL remained completely intransigent over Belgium and thus Michaelis had to reply to the papal note by refusing to give any 'definite declaration of the intentions of the imperial government with regard to Belgium and on the guarantees that we wish'.[78] The Vatican took this letter to mean a rejection of their peace move, even though Michaelis tried to argue that this was not the case.

Michaelis' position was now becoming increasingly precarious. His foreign policy had pleased no one as he had tried ineffectively to steer a middle course between those who would have nothing to do with the peace feelers, and those who wished to use them to improve Germany's diplomatic position. On the auxiliary labour law he had also seemed to be lacking in a sense of direction. His attitude towards the peace resolution and franchise reform in Prussia had satisfied none of the political parties. The chancellor seemed to be without any effective support at a time when the problems facing the government were becoming increasingly difficult with a steady growth of anti-war sentiment, of strikes and unrest in the navy. On 22 October the majority parties of the Reichstag, the SPD, the progressives, the centre party and the national liberals demanded tha Michaelis be replaced by a chancellor who would agree to a five point programme of political principles which included making the German reply to the papal note of 20 September the basis for future policy, prompt reform of the franchise and the relaxation of censorship. The chancellor's extraordinarily inept handling of the naval mutiny convinced many, including Kühlmann who had agreed with the outline of his foreign policy, that he would have to be replaced. But there were two major obstacles to be overcome. A successor would have to be found who would be generally acceptable, and there was a general agreement among the Kaiser's advisers that if Michaelis were in fact replaced at that time it would appear as if the crown had given way to the social democrats, and this would create a precedent that would seriously undermine its power.

The immediate initiative for the dismissal of Michaelis thus came from the Reichstag majority, but others were soon to join the fight. On 25 October the Kaiser received a letter from the crown prince asking that Michaelis be replaced by the candidate of the OHL and the heavy industrialists, Bülow, who also had a talkative supporter in Erzberger. Predictably the Kaiser promptly rejected this suggestion. Helffferich then advised the Kaiser to persuade Hertling to accept. In spite of many misgivings, the Bavarian minister president decided to accept the post. On 1 November 1917 he was appointed chancellor.[79]

The OHL played little part in the overthrow of Michaelis. They had been delighted with his reaction to the peace resolution of the Reichstag, and Bauer announced that he was the chancellor of the OHL, and that there was only one mistake he could make, and that would be to try to act independently of the army.[80] Yet the situation was not quite as clearcut as Bauer imagined. The OHL had mobilised the Reichstag majority against Bethmann Hollweg, and by doing so had strengthened the authority of parliament. Michaelis could not afford to risk the opposition of the Reichstag majority, as Bauer felt he could, and he was far more dependent on the Reichstag than Bethmann had been. The politicians' initiative against Michaelis was thus the price the OHL had to pay for using the majority parties against Bethmann. The OHL was reasonably satisfied with Michaelis, he was a weak politician who was usually prepared to give way to the OHL's demands, and his conservative position was acceptable to the generals. When Michaelis' position became increasingly precarious the OHL was at a loss to know what to do, for there was still no obvious alternative candidate, and they still did not want to establish the direct dictatorship of the army. On the other hand the Kaiser's advisers were anxious that the chancellor crisis should be settled as soon as possible, before the OHL came to Berlin at the beginning of November. The atmosphere at headquarters was depressed. The OHL did not like Hertling, and had made this plain in July when he had been suggested as a possible successor to Bethmann. Hindenburg had a long-standing quarrel with him: not only was he a catholic, even worse he was a Bavarian. Hindenburg and Ludendorff were also deeply conscious of the fact that he had been appointed without them being consulted, a bitter pill to swallow after their triumph over Bethmann Hollweg.[81] But they decided to cooperate and agreed to accept Hertling. Hindenburg even went as far as to apologise for the differences between the OHL and Hertling in the spring of 1917 over the Polish question, and Ludendorff agreed with unaccustomed humility to Hertling's request to try to keep Colonel Bauer from meddling in politics.[82] Hertling for his part proved to be substantially in agreement with the broad aims of the OHL, who hoped that he would at last succeed where Michaelis had failed and would be able to combine subservience to the wishes of the OHL with enough political acumen to preserve the *Burgfrieden* and restore some degree of harmony to a seriously divided country.

NOTES

1. L. Bergstrasser, *Die preussische Wahlrechtsfrage und die Entstehung der Osterbotschaft 1917*, Tübingen 1929; Reinhard Patemann, *Der Kampf um die preussische Wahlreform im Ersten Weltkrieg*, Düsseldorf 1964.
2. DZA Potsdam Reichsamt des Innern, Deutsch-Polnisch Militärkonvention 19683.
3. For the leaks to the press see Conrad Haussmann, *Schlaglichter. Reichstagsbriefe und Aufzeichnungen*, Frankfurt 1924, p. 103. Haussmann played an important role in discrediting the conference by leaking information to the press.
4. PA Bonn AA Gr.HQ 29, Band 1, Grünau to Bethmann 14-3-17. William II wrote

to the chief of the military cabinet on 27-12-17: 'The representatives of heavy industry. . .are engaged in activities that can only be described by the word "treason", particularly in time of war.' He suggested that they should all be sent to Spandau jail. 'For me the most serious aspect of this affair is the carefully prepared impression that the hounding of the chancellor has been set in motion with at least the silent approval of the high command, certainly with their cognizance. Before I take steps against this revolutionary attack on the power of the crown and of the supreme warlord, which is a slap in the face of all the traditions of Prussia I should like to hear your opinion and also that of Valentini.' Bundesarchiv Koblenz, Nachlass Schwertfeger, Band 212.

5. PA Bonn AA Gr. HQ 247.

6. PA Bonn AA Polit. Abt. Preussen Nr 3 Nr 2, Band 5.

7. Bundesarchiv Koblenz, Nachlass Bauer, Band 17. Bauer's very contrived answer to Roedern 20-6-17.

8. *Ibid.,* Band 11, Besprechung mit Unterstaatsserkretär Drews, 29-4-17.

9. Patemann, *Der Kampf um die Preussische Wahlreform,* p. 123.

10. Helfferich, *Der Weltkrieg,* p. 437.

11. Valentini, *Kaiser und Kabinettschef,* p. 154.

12. Bundesarchiv Koblenz, Nachlass Schwertfeger, Nr. 212. Berg had been educated with the Kaiser and was friendly with him.

13. Bethmann Hollweg, *Betrachtungen zum Weltkriege,* Band 2, p. 218.

14. Valentini, *Kaiser und Kabinettschef,* p. 156.

15. Ritter, *Staatskunst und Kriegshandwerk,* Band 3, p. 558. Ritters says that Bethmann was now dependent on the support of the Reichstag if he were to realise his plans against the powers of political reaction and militarism. This implies that Germany was already a parliamentary democracy, when in fact the Reichstag was still to a large extent the 'fig leaf of absolutism'.

16. *Untersuchungsausschuss IV Reihe,* Band 8, p. 108 for an extract from Erzberger's speech. The reference in Epstein, *Erzberger,* p. 190 is incorrect.

17. The origins and the effects of Erzberger's speech are discussed in Epstein, *Erzberger,* p. 182.

18. *Deutschland im ersten Weltkrieg,* Band 2, p. 753 states incorrectly that Ludendorff met Erzberger and Stresemann. Ritter, *Staatskunst und Kriegshandwerk,* Band 3, p. 567 says that their belief that Ludendorff was unable to attend the dinner because of Bethmann's activities was unfounded. This objection is true only in the most literal sense. Bethmann's objections to Hindenburg and Ludendorff's visit to Berlin influenced the Kaiser to order them to return to HQ and it was for this reason that they were invited to the palace. It should also be noted that Erzberger was not a *persona non grata* to the OHL after his speech and he remained in close contact with Bauer.

19. PA Bonn Weltkrieg AA Gr. HQ 29, Band 1. Wahnschaffe to Ludendorff 8-7-17.

20. PA Bonn AA Weltkrieg 15 Geheim, Band 4. Ludendorff to Bethmann and to Zimmermann 8-7-17.

21. Valentini, *Kaiser und Kabinettschef,* p. 159. No decision was reached as the Kaiser refused to consider Bülow, Hatzfeldt or Roedern.

22. Valentini, *Kaiser und Kabinettschef,* p. 162.

23. Valentini, *Kaiser und Kabinettschef,* p. 162.

24. *Ibid.,* p. 164. Valentini writes that the Kaiser as far as he knew was not asked to give his permission for this meeting. Ritter, *Staatskunst und Kriegshandwerk,* Band 3, p. 577 says that he was, but he stresses that the move was 'incredible' (*unerhört*). For details of the meeting see Bauer's protocol in Ludendorff, *Urkunden der OHL,* p. 408; F. von Payer, *Von Bethmann Hollweg bis Ebert. Erinnerungen und Bilder,* Frankfurt 1923; Erzberger, *Erlebnisse im Weltkrieg,* Stuttgart 1920, p. 262; Bauer, *Grosse Krieg,* p. 141; Valentini, *Kaiser und*

Kabinettschef, p. 164; Helfferich, *Der Weltkrieg,* p. 450; Westarp, *Konservative Politik,* Band 1, p. 357; Bethmann Hollweg, *Betrachtungen zum Weltkriege,* p. 234; *Untersuchungsausschuss IV Reihe,* Band 2, p. 153; Band 7.1, p. 16, 104, 359, Band 7.2, p. 398, Band 8, pp. 79, 167; Epstein, *Erzberger,* p. 198.
25. Helfferich, *Der Weltkrieg,* p. 450. Marvin L. Edwards, *Stresemann and the Greater Germany,* New York, 1963, p. 146 gives a rather garbled version of Stresemann's activities during the July crisis, and is blissfully unaware of most of the significant literature on the subject. See also PA Bonn AA Gr. Hauptquartier 247, Reichskanzler Nr. 29, Band 1, Wahnschaffe to Lersner 12-7-17 saying that Ludendorff had threatened to resign if Bethmann was not removed. Wahnschaffe thought this 'incredible', and could hardly believe it.
26. Helfferich, *Der Weltkrieg,* p. 451.
27. Ludendorff, *Urkunden der OHL,* p. 405.
28. For texts of the peace resolution see Matthias, Morsey, *Der Interfraktionelle Ausschuss,* Teil 1, p. 110. Also Bethmann's account of the interview in *Untersuchungsausschuss IV Reihe,* Band 2, p. 154. This is a perfect transcription of DZA Potsdam Reichskanzlei und Gr. HQ 2403/5.
29. According to Ludendorff, *Urkunden der OHL,* p. 406, Lyncker received the news of Hindenburg and Ludendorff's impending resignations at 2.50 p.m. Quite why there was such a delay in informing the Kaiser is unclear. Certainly the news was broken at the best possible moment for the OHL's purposes, but the archives provide no evidence as to whether this was accident or design.
30. Ludendorff, *Urkunden der OHL,* pp. 406, 408.
31. Helfferich, *Der Weltkrieg,* p. 452.
32. Valentini, *Kaiser und Kabinettschef,* p. 167 gives an excellent account. Helfferich, *Der Weltkrieg,* p. 453 adds further details. Also *Untersuchungsausschuss IV Reihe,* Band 2, p. 155.
33. Bayerisches Hauptstaatsarchiv Abteilung IV Kriegsarchiv, M.Kr. 1831, Bevollmächt. in Gr. HQ 1917.
34. Ludendorff, *Urkunden der OHL,* p. 412 for the protocol of these meetings. The protocol was made up by Harbou, who in Scheidemann's often inaccurate account in *Zusammenbruch,* p. 92 appears as 'Hauptmann von Haarbaum'.
35. Ludendorff, *Urkunden der OHL,* p. 416.
36. *Untersuchungsausschuss IV Reihe,* Band 7.2, p. 390.
37. Weber, *Ludendorff und die Monopole,* p. 106. In fact Bülow was rather more moderate than many of his supporters imagined. Writing to the Kaiser in the autumn of 1917 he said that all wars necessitated a degree of democratisation, and concessions would have to be made if the monarchy were to survive. Bülow also suggested that the army should be placed under political control, and insisted that war aims should not be too excessive. Bundesarchiv Koblenz, Nachlass Bauer, Band 2.
38. Fischer, *Griff nach der Weltmacht,* p. 525. *Untersuchungsausschuss IV Reihe,* Band 7.2, p. 390; Erzberger, *Erlebnisse im Weltkrieg,* p. 265.
39. Bauer to Erzberger 9-9-17, Bundesarchiv Koblenz Nachlass Bauer, Band 19.
40. *Untersuchungsausschuss IV Reihe,* Band 12.1, p. 147; Stegmann, *Bismarcks Erben,* p. 497.
41. Scherer Grunewald, *L'Allemagne et les problemes de la paix,* Vol. 2, p. 376; Z.A. Zeman, *The Break-up of the Habsburg Empire. A Study in National and Social Revolution,* London 1961, p. 150.
42. Scherer Grunewald, *L'Allemagne et les problemes de la paix,* Vol. 2, p. 207.
43. PA Bonn AA Weltkrieg 15 Geheim, Band 4.
44. Ritter, *Staatskunst und Kriegshandwerk,* Band 4, p. 48.
45. PA Bonn AA Weltkrieg 15 Geheim, Band 4. Ludendorff to chancellor 15-8-17.

46. Scherer Grunewald, *L'Allemagne et les problemes de la paix*, Vol. 2, p. 413.
47. *Deutschland im ersten Weltkrieg*, Band 3, p. 204.
48. Carl Mühlmann, *Oberste Heeresleitung und Balkan im Weltkrieg 1914-1918*, Berlin 1941, p. 202.
49. DZA Potsdam ReichskanzleiAllgemeines 2398/11.
50. Scherer Grunewald, *L'Allemagne et les problemes de la paix*, Vol. 2, p. 458.
51. PA Bonn Oesterreich 95, Band 4.
52. Scherer Grunewald, *L'Allemagne et les problemes de la paix*, Vol. 2, p. 487; Fischer, *Griff nach der Weltmacht*, p. 569.
53. Scherer Grunewald, *L'Allemagne et les problemes de la paix*, Vol. 2, p. 495.
54. *Ibid.*, p. 500.
55. Fischer, *Griff nach der Weltmacht*, p. 573 for further discussion of this point. Ritter, *Staatskunst und Kriegshandwerk*, Band 4, p. 509 for his criticisms of Fischer's analysis.
56. Scherer Grunewald, *L'Allemagne et les problemes de la paix*, Vol. 2, p. 521.
57. Groener, *Lebenserinnerungen*, p. 520; Merton, *Erinnernswertes aus meinem Leben*, p. 367.
58. The question of how far Merton's memorandum was 'honest' is irrelevant for there was no conflict of interests involved. Merton's position as a businessman was particularly threatened because part of his company's interests was in aluminium which, being so dependent on large supplies of power, was particularly vulnerable to takeovers from heavy industry. See Schröter, *Krieg, Staat Monopol 1914-1918*, p. 150.
59. Kuczynski, 'Die Barbarei', *Zeitschrift für Geschichtswissenschaft*, Heft 7, 1961. Typical for the latter group was Rathenau, representative of the AEG and the *Metallurgische Gesellschaft* and the architect of the KRA.
60. DZA Potsdam Stellvertreter des Reichskanzlers 53. 'Notizen für die Besprechungen mit dem Herrn Reichskanzler 1-7-18.'
61. Ludendorff, *Urkunden der OHL*, p. 186.
62. Feldman, *Army, Industry and Labor in Germany*, p. 379.
63. Schleicher had served under Groener in the general staff before the war, and they had been close associates. Schleicher managed to get quite a good job for Merton. Thilo Vogelsang, *Kurt von Schleicher*, Göttingen 1965.
64. Feldman, *Army, Industry and Labor*, p. 400 gives a lengthy and convincing account of the reasoning for this point. Groener did not send the memorandum to the OHL. See Bundesarchiv Militärarchiv Freiburg, Nachlass Groener N46/117.
65. Bundesarchiv Militärarchiv Freiburg, Nachlass Groener, N46/113 and N46/117.
66. *Ibid.*, N46/112.
67. *Ibid.*, N46/117.
68. *Ibid.*, N46/113. DZA Potsdam, Reichsamt des Innern. Die Stimmung im Lande 12476.
69. Bundesarchiv Militärarchiv Freiburg, Nachlass Haeften N35/7. After the war Waldersee accused Scheüch of being a revolutionary freemason (!), of undermining the power of the crown and the morale of the army, of failing to support the army against the Reichstag and allowing the civilians to get the upper hand over the army, etc. The court of honour acquitted Scheüch of all Waldersee's charges.
70. DZA Potsdam Vertreter des Reichskanzlers bei der OHL, Band 7, report dated 14-9-17.
71. *Deutschland im ersten Weltkrieg*, Vol. 2, p. 779.
72. Ludendorff, *Urkunden der OHL*, p. 94. DZA Potsdam, Reichsamt des Innern, die Stimmung im Lande, 12476.

73. Pacelli handed the document to Treutler 13-8-17. For the full text see Scherer Grunewald, *L'Allemagne et les problemes de la paix,* Vol. 2, p. 307.
74. *Ibid.,* p. 376.
75. *Ibid.,* p. 421.
76. *Ibid.,* p. 429.
77. Ludendorff, *Urkunden der OHL,* p. 428. The memorandum is a repetition of the speech he made to the crown council.
78. Scherer Grunewald, *L'Allemagne et les problemes de la paix,* Vol. 2, pp. 441. 443, and 445 for some of the correspondence.
79. Hertling wrote to the Abbess of St Walburg in Eichstätt that 'the acceptance of the post of chancellor is the greatest sacrifice I have ever made in my life'. Bundesarchiv Koblenz, Nachlass Hertling, Band 40.
80. Bundesarchiv Militärarchiv Freiburg, Nachlass Merz, Band 25. Merz felt that Michaelis had made a serious error by letting everyone 'see the cards in his hand'. Bauer was well aware that by using parliament against Bethmann he would have a tougher struggle with the Reichstag in future.
81. Bayerisches Hauptstaatsarchiv Abteilung IV Kriegsarchiv, M.Kr. 1831, Bevollmächt. in Gr. HQ 1917. The military plenipotentiary reported on 30-10-17 that the OHL was depressed at the prospect of Hertling's candidature for the position of chancellor because of differences in the past, because the whole affair had been managed without the OHL being consulted and because now 'the two most important positions in the Reich' were held by Bavarians.
82. *Ibid.,* 8-1-17. Hertling complained to Merz about Bauer. Merz defended him but passed on Hertling's remarks to Ludendorff. Bauer was then given a rather meaningless reprimand to make Hertling happy and the military plenipotentiary reported that Bauer was from then on extremely pleasant to him.

7 BREST LITOVSK

From the very early months of the war, the German government had been in touch with Russian revolutionaries in exile, hoping that the revolutionary movement could be used to undermine the Russian war effort. Parvus Helphand was the rather dubious intermediary between the German government and the exile groups which were determined to overthrow the Tsarist regime, and considerable sums of money were paid to these revolutionaries.[1] This policy was extremely risky to the ruling class in Germany, for in the short term interests of keeping Russia out of the war, they were running the far greater risk of helping to establish some form of socialist regime in Russia, which was bound to have a tremendous effect on the German proletariat – already becoming dangerously disenchanted with the course of government policy. But so great were the contradictions between Germany's ambitions and her means of carrying them out that such considerations seem to have been forced to the back of political consciousness. General Hoffmann wrote: 'Just as I fire grenades at the enemy trenches, and attack him with poison gas, as an enemy I have the right to make use of propaganda against his men.'[2]

The February revolution, which was in no sense the result of the efforts made by the Germans to assist the exiled revolutionaries, seemed to be the signal that Russia was on the point of imminent collapse and would shortly withdraw from the war. Ludendorff was convinced that Russia would no longer be able to mount an offensive, and therefore troops could be withdrawn at once from the eastern front, a movement which could be increased as Russia continued to collapse. Germany would thus gain a preponderance on the western front, leading to an overall improvement of the military situation in spite of the likely declaration of war by the United States.[3]

Men like Lvov, Miliukov and Kerensky seemed to be the heralds of a new era to the German social democrats, and they were hardly alarming to the German government. It seemed that the February revolution was the ideal solution to Germany's problems, but this feeling of euphoria did not last for long. The Lvov-Miliukov government declared its determination to continue the war and the new government was promptly recognised by the Entente: President Wilson gave another starry-eyed performance in praise of the new democratic regime. But the new Russian government had come to power largely because the Russian people were war weary, and yet it promised to continue the war. Thus it earned the implacable hatred of the workers and peasants organised in the soviets. On 27 March 1917 the Petrograd Soviet denounced the militaristic and imperialist foreign policy of Miliukov and proclaimed its demand for a peace without compensations and annexations – a document of such forcefulness that the government had to make a pious, if somewhat empty gesture of accepting it in principle on 4 April.[4] Just as there was a marked contrast between the airy idealistic notions of Wilson in the senate speech of 22 January and the concrete declaration of the Petrograd Soviet on 27 March, so there was an irreconcilable gap between the demands of the proletarian socialist soviets and the bourgeois liberals of the government. The German government, realising that the establishment of bourgeois liberalism in Russia might mean the strengthening of Russia's war ability, decided to support the socialists in their bid for power.

Germany might possibly have been able to come to terms with the provisional government in Russia, but that would mean that Germany would have to abandon most of her imperialist ambitions in the east. Socialist revolution in Russia was thus seen as the most effective way of achieving Germany's war aims.

Graf von Brockdorff Rantzau, the leading figure in Germany's revolutionising policy in Russia, and the foreign office agreed that Lenin admirably fitted the bill. Parvus had little enthusiasm for Lenin. As he was a right wing social democrat and had a curious vision of a 'dual alliance of Prussian bayonets and Russian proletarian fists' that was hardly likely to appeal to the bolsheviks. But on the other hand he wanted to see an end to Russian autocracy and the defeat of the imperialism of the Entente. Thus there was general agreement that Lenin should be sent back to Russia to destroy the provisional government.

On 23 March 1917 Zimmermann asked the OHL for permission to send Lenin and his fellow exiles back to Russia. The OHL had no objections to the scheme, and suggested that the revolutionaries should sent through Germany in an escorted train, the details to be worked out by Department 111b of the general staff in Berlin.[5]

Although the OHL had promptly agreed with the suggestion that the revolutionaries should return to Russia the subsequent actions of the army High Command threatened to undermine the scheme. Prince Leopold of Bavaria, with General Hoffmann as his chief of staff, launched a new offensive against the bridgehead across the Stochod at

Toboly, hoping to exploit the political weakness of Russia to gain a major military victory. The offensive, mounted on 3 April was a complete success, but it convinced many Russians that it would be foolish to accept German assurances that they wanted peace in the east, and it threatened to unite the Russians in a patriotic struggle against the Germans in which political differences would be forgotten. For this reason the OHL ordered the cessation of any further offensives in the east, a decision which was affected by the realisation that the situation on the western front was such that the army could not fight a full-scale war in the east. The result of this order was that something very closely resembling a ceasefire existed on the eastern front.[6]

On the night of 10 to 11 April the train passed through Germany with thirty-two emigrés, of whom nineteen were bolsheviks. It was the result of the most curious temporary alliance in Germany. The OHL, the chancellor, the foreign office, the Kaiser, the SPD and the unions all worked together. None of these groups really understood the motives of the others, and none understood Lenin. Ludendorff tried to conceal his real motives for agreeing to the foreign office's suggestion. In 1922 he wrote that he did not really know very much about Lenin, and that he had agreed to the chancellor's request to halt operations on the Stochod in accordance with Clausewitz's formula that military considerations were secondary to political matters. The OHL supported the policy in the hope that it would lead to peace in the east.[7] These arguments are not convincing. Ludendorff knew full well that Lenin was a revolutionary socialist, and it was precisely for this reason that he had agreed to send him back to Russia. A negotiated peace might well have been possible with the provisional government on the basis of the Petrograd formula, but Ludendorff had supported the return of the revolutionaries in order to gain extensive annexations. On 5 April Hindenburg told the chancellor that the war was nearing its end and that a maximum and minimum war aims programme should therefore be worked out. It was in pursuit of these maximum aims that the OHL agreed to allow Lenin to return to Russia. Within a few months it seemed that Germany's policy towards Russia was about to be crowned with spectacular success.

The Soviet peace proposals of 8 November, the appeal for a general armistice on 28 November, the negotiation of a four week armistice which was finally agreed upon 15 December, and the opening of the Brest Litovsk conference on 22 December 1917 presented particularly thorny problems to both the Russian and the German governments. The Soviet government had to fulfil its promise to bring peace or its position at home would become untenable but at the same time it would have to combat the annexationist intentions of the Germans. The Germans for their part had to find some artful way of securing their annexations without seeming flagrantly to violate the principle of self-determination, the powerful slogan of 8 November. The situation was further complicated by the determination of the government to resist the OHL's intentions of having a decisive say on the question of the future political relations between Germany and Russia.[8]

In the course of preliminary discussions between the government and the OHL, held in Berlin on 6 and 7 December, it became clear that there was little hope of the OHL submitting to the wishes of the civilians.[9] They insisted that military control over the occupied territories in the east would have to continue for years to come. The OHL said that an autonomous Lithuania and Courland was unacceptable from a military point of view. Hoffmann, who was to represent the OHL at the negotiations at Brest Litovsk, insisted that the Russians should remove all their troops from Finland, Livonia and Estonia as they were running amok, and law and order could not be restored until they went. Thus from the very beginning the OHL made certain that military questions would not be separated from political ones, and that they would have a decisive influence on the negotiations for a peace with Russia.

On 16 December Ludendorff instructed Hoffmann on how he was to approach the negotiations at Brest Litovsk.[10] He was to demand that Lithuania and Courland, as well as Riga and the offshore islands should be annexed by Germany 'so that we can feed our people'. Poland was to be closely associated with the Central Powers. The Russians were to evacuate Finland, Estonia, Livonia, Bessarabia, East Galicia and Armenia. Germany should gain a decisive influence on the Russian economy and help to reorganise the transport system. Grain, oil and other raw materials were to be delivered by the Russians to the Germans at favourable prices. Russia was to pay compensation for the prisoners of war held in Germany. These instructions went far beyond the decisions made at the Berlin conference on 6 and 7 December, and their openly annexationist character made it quite impossible to disguise them in accordance with the principle of the self-determination of peoples which had been accepted, largely for propagandistic reasons, by the German government as the basis for peace negotiations.

The demands of the OHL, although more extreme than those of the more cautious diplomatists and politicians in Berlin, were in full accord with the annexationist ambitions of wide sections of the German ruling class. The government was flooded at this time with requests from various sectors of industry, from commercial interest groups and chambers of commerce, asking that their particular interests should be taken into account in the forthcoming negotiations at Brest Litovsk.[11] The discussions and debates that were to ensue were essentially about the way in which these aims were to be achieved, the OHL believing in outright annexation, the civilians in the creation of a chain of dependent but 'autonomous' states.

On 18 December further discussions were held in Kreuznach between the government and the OHL, with the Kaiser presiding, about policy to be adopted at the peace talks.[12] After an initial disagreement between the OHL and Kühlmann on policy towards the Baltic, it was agreed that the Baltic states should remain under military administration for some considerable time after the war, and that the inhabitants of Livonia and Estonia should be allowed to make use of their right of self-determination; in other words they should be convinced of the advantages of seeking German protection.

Negotiations began at Brest Litovsk on 22 December. The OHL was furious that the negotiations were to be made public. Czernin, although he detested the bolsheviks, resented the Germans' annexationist ambitions for he wanted peace as soon as possible at almost any price. The Turkish and Bulgarian delegations were as determined as the Germans to get their pound of flesh, and it took all of Kühlmann's considerable diplomatic skill to persuade them to conceal their intentions and not to be so crudely, openly and undiplomatically greedy.[13]

The proceedings opened with a six point peace proposal made by Joffe which was substantially similar to the declaration of 8 November, which called for the evacuation of all occupied territories, the full independence of all peoples who had lost their independence during the war – no compensations or contributions were to be paid.[14]

Joffe's proposals were certainly an embarrassment to the Central Powers. The Turks wanted guarantees that Russian troops would be removed from the Caucasus; the unfortunate Bulgarian, Popoff, spoke no French or German and thus had difficulty in articulating his objections to a peace which would not include annexations of parts of Serbia and Rumania. Kühlmann and Czernin managed to assuage the anxieties of most of the delegates and to render Joffe's points innocuous. Then at the very last moment the German military threatened to sabotage the reply to the Soviet note by expressing the fear that the Entente might indeed accept the invitation to general peace talks before the Central Powers had won their victory in the west. Czernin could hardly contain his rage, and he now began to fear a German victory in the west as this would almost certainly lead to German demands becoming so excessive that peace negotiations could well become impossible.[15]

The reply was presented to the Soviet delegation at the plenary session on Christmas Day.[16] While seeming to go most of the way towards meeting the conditions laid down in Joffe's note, and thus apparently opening the way for a general peace, in fact it made subtle changes in each of the six points so that Germany's expansionist aims in the east could be achieved. The agreement in principle to most of Joffe's proposals was made conditional upon the acceptance of those principles by the Entente, which Czernin and Kühlmann knew would almost certainly not be forthcoming. Thus the Central Powers could demonstrate their genuine desire for peace without running the risk of being taken seriously.

In one important matter the diplomatists at Brest Litovsk made a serious miscalculation. The reply was seen by most people in Germany as frivolously throwing away the opportunity of making those territorial gains that the defeat of Russia had made possible. At the head of this movement stood the OHL, but it included almost all the political parties apart from the independent socialists.[17] Hindenburg promptly telegraphed to both Kühlmann and Hertling with a bitter attack on the course of the peace negotiations.[18] For him the reply to the Soviet note was an outright renunciation of annexations and compensations, and he was seriously worried that the Entente might accept the invitation to begin peace negotiations on the basis of the reply. He had the impression that the diplomatists simply refused to realise that Russia was militarily defeated, and that therefore Germany was in a position to dictate peace terms. The narrow and unimaginative minds of the OHL failed to see through the deceptions of the reply, but then so too did the Soviets who indulged in a little wishful thinking that they had won a significant diplomatic victory over the Central Powers.[19]

It was general Hoffmann who pointed out to the Soviet delegation that their optimism was misplaced. Acting with the full consent of Kühlmann he unofficially informed the Soviet delegation that Poland, Lithuania and Courland would be separated from Russia and associated with the Central Powers, and further, that German occupation troops would not be withdrawn from the area. Hoffmann claimed that this was in full accordance with his reading of the principle of the self-determination of peoples, and cited the appeals which the German government had so carefully engineered as free expressions of the will of the people. The Soviet delegation was shattered by this news. Prokrovsky crying that there could be no talk of a peace of understanding *(Verständigungsfrieden)* when eighteen government districts were to be torn away from Russia.[20]

Hoffmann's informal remarks made across the luncheon table were formalised the following day at a meeting of the political commission.[21] Kühlmann insisted that the Baltic provinces and Poland had freely asked for independence from Russia in accordance with the Soviet peace proposal. The Soviet delegation asked that these areas should first be evacuated and then referenda should be held to determine the real wishes of the peoples; in the meantime elected representatives of the people should take on all administrative functions.

Thus by 27 December the lines were clearly drawn. Kühlmann insisted that the declarations of self-determination had already been made, and that German annexationist ambitions could therefore be commensurate with the Soviet peace proposals. The Soviets for their part realised that their optimism of 25 December had been cruelly misplaced, and were now faced with annexations so great that even a regime as weak as their own had to threaten to break off negotiations, and had to face the ghastly prospect of continuing a war in which, but for some miracle, they were bound to be defeated.

Joffe threatened to break off negotiations, which filled the Austrians with alarm. Czernin promptly threatened to sign a separate peace with Russia, but this was an empty gesture. Neither Kühlmann hoped to use this Austrian threat in order to strengthen his own position against the mounting criticism of the OHL. Hoffmann, in characteristic fashion told Czernin that it was a splendid idea, for Germany could then withdraw twenty-five divisions from the Austrian front, and use them to put pressure on Russia.[22]

The Soviet threat did not have to be put to the test immediately, for it had already been agreed that the conference should adjourn for ten days, ostensibly so that the Entente could be given sufficient time to decide whether they wished to join in negotiations for a general peace. This break came at a time that was particularly welcome for all the main protagonists. Joffe was now, as Helfferich remarked, a 'political corpse'. Czernin was anxious to consult his government to decide how best to restrain the Germans. Kühlmann hoped to return to Berlin to overcome the resistance of the OHL which he expected, even though he had gone far to meet their objections on 27 December. The onslaught that awaited him was to exceed his worst fears.

The OHL, and their Pan German supporters, could never forgive Kühlmann for the 'treachery of 25 December'. The left could not forgive him for dashing their hopes for a real peace of understanding with his annexationist declaration of 27 December. The OHL continued to regard Kühlmann as the man of 25 December, and refused to believe that he had undergone a change of heart. Thus Hindenburg and Ludendorff hurried to Berlin spoiling for a fight; within the OHL, Colonel Bauer and Major Bockelberg were particularly active in the campaign against Kühlmann. He was accused of indolence and complaisance in his capacity as a negotiator, even though many in Berlin, and even within the OHL, knew that this was not the case, and that the argument was essentially one over means rather than ends.[23]

On 29 December Hindenburg's letter of protest against Kühlmann and the course of the negotiations at Brest Litovsk arrived at the chancellery.[24] He was particularly angered by the idea that the separation of the Baltic states and Poland would have to be ratified, according to Kühlmann's and Czernin's joint declaration of 28 December, by a vote of the people concerned, and he refused to see this concession to the Soviet peace principles as a sham. He would not accept any kind of plebiscite, however fraudulent, to settle the question of the Polish frontier, for this was to him a purely military question.

As soon as Ludendorff arrived in Berlin he demanded of Hoffmann why he had allowed the declaration of 25 December to happen. Hoffmann replied haughtily that since the OHL had discussed the tactics to be used at the peace conference at the Kreuznach meeting he had assumed that there was general agreement about the course to be pursued.[25] He could have added that he was merely an observer at the peace conference, but that argument would hardly have cut much ice with Ludendorff. Hoffmann now seemed to be stuck between the OHL and Kühlmann. He had little sympathy for Kühlmann, and he had the traditional mistrust of a Prussian officer for 'ink-pot men'. His approach was always bluff and direct, and Kühlmann's sly and smooth strategems were not at all to his taste. On the other hand he was too much of a realist to be entirely taken in by the fantasies and excesses of the OHL, and they in turn tended to blame him for Kühlmann's policies.

Hindenburg's preliminary attacks were followed by a lengthy memorandum to the chancellor on 31 December 1917.[26] He expressed his disgust with the course of the negotiations, and insisted that the OHL would have to have more influence on them, for matters of vital military importance were involved.

For the future course of the proceedings I must therefore have a greater influence and the definite right to approve all suggestions and decisions. In order to judge in each particular case all the consequences of any suggestion and decisions I will ask General Hoffmann to send me the wording by telegram, and not just by telephone, so that I can make my position known.

Conveniently forgetting that Hoffmann was nothing but an observer at the negotiations, Hindenburg threatened that he would not allow his representative to sign a 'weak peace' which was not in accordance with the 'honour and dignity of the Throne and the Fatherland'. He then outlined his demands, which included the annexation of Lithuania, Courland, Riga and the islands of Dagö and Moon, to which Russia was to agree. There was to be no self-determination of peoples in the occupied areas. Finland would have to become independent from Russia. Poland would have to pay for the German fortifications on the frontier, and undertake not to build forts or airfields on their side of the border. The frontier with Poland was to be drawn in accordance with the needs of the military.

Both Kühlmann and the OHL looked around in Berlin for support. Kühlmann concentrated on the Reichstag. He met the party leaders on 1 January and tried to steer his usual elegant course between the left and the right. To the right he pointed out that it was an unfortunate fact that the vast majority of the peoples in the east did not care for the Germans, and certainly did not want any sort of *Anschluss*. At the same time he outlined his policy of concluding separate peace treaties with states such as the Ukraine which had been parts of Russia, in order to force the Soviets to make concessions. But Kühlmann's presentation was full of obvious contradictions. The most glaring of these was that he claimed that the declarations from the Baltic states and Poland were true expressions of the will of the people, but when pressed by Scheidemann he admitted that this was not strictly true. Most of the leaders of the majority parties could at least agree that he was preferable to the OHL, but men like Stresemann complained that he took no interest in German economic ambitions in the east, and the left found little comfort in his assurances, leaving the meeting convinced that he was different from the OHL only in degree.[27]

Ludendorff concentrated his energies on the *Bundesrat* committee for foreign affairs which he addressed shortly before attending a meeting of the crown council on 2 January.[28] He insisted that the Russian army would hardly be able to continue to fight, and thus

Germany could renounce the armistice at any time. The situation on the western front was steadily improving because troops could now be moved from the east, even though there were problems with the treachery and unreliability of the troops from Alsace-Lorraine. Ludendorff stated that the overall military situation was so good, that there was a distinct possibility that the war could be won in the west. Germany was so strong that she no longer needed the military support of Austria-Hungary. Turkey was now more of a hindrance than a help. Bulgaria was equally useless. The neutral states were no longer needed as sources of supplies. The Reich stood alone, and this was a great advantage. Germany could now pursue her annexationist aims unhampered by considerations for her allies, or the likely reactions in the neutral countries. Ludendorff then outlined once again the demands of the OHL: annexations to protect the natural wealth of upper Silesia, Lorraine and the lower Rhine; the division of Belgium under a customs union with Germany; a military regime in Alsace-Lorraine and the rejection of the idea that it should become a state within the Reich; rejection of the Austro-Polish solution which would render Silesia indefensible in the event of war between Germany and Austria, and the occupation of the Baltic provinces which were needed as a deployment area for a future war against Russia. Just as the officer corps after 1871 felt that the final decision had not yet been made in the historic struggle for supremacy in Europe, so a growing and influential number of officers, with Ludendorff as their spokesman, began to feel that whatever the outcome of the World War it would not be decisive. Therefore Germany was fighting for a strong economic and strategic position from which to fight this final battle. The annexationist demands of the imperialist forces could thus be rationalised as 'purely military considerations', and the economic domination of foreign states could be seen as military self-protection.

Kühlmann could find little support in the *Bundesrat* committee against the OHL, for the committee's reservations about the OHL's policies were almost exclusively due to concern about state rights and fear that the policy would lead to an excessive increase in the power of Prussia. It was hardly possible for Kühlmann to use anti-Prussianism as a weapon against the OHL, for this would make it impossible for him to gain the support of the Kaiser which he now so badly needed.[29]

In spite of his failure to win the support of the *Bundesrat* committee he was greatly encouraged by the fact that the Kaiser assured him of his full support in the course of a private audience held immediately before the meeting of the crown council. Knowing that he could count

on the support of Hertling, he thus went to the crown council in a
confident mood.[30] Kühlmann opened the meeting with an outline of
his policy at Brest Litovsk which was supported by the Kaiser. Rapidly
the meeting seemed to degenerate into an exchange of bland generalities.
The Kaiser introduced the topic of Poland into the discussion, which he
hoped would not be particularly controversial as general agreement had
already been reached at Kreuznach on policy towards Poland. Poland
was a topic uppermost in the Kaiser's mind, as he had discussed the
Polish question with General Hoffmann over breakfast that morning.
Hoffmann had argued that it was undesirable to increase the number of
Poles living in Prussia, as it was hard enough to cope with those who
were already in the country. For this reason he rejected the 'Germano-
Polish solution', and also the frontier rectifications demanded by the
OHL which would mean that two million Poles would be included in
the Reich. Hoffmann had argued that a few minor frontier changes
would be sufficient to secure the safety of the coal fields of upper
Silesia, Soldau and the bridgehead at Osowiec. The Kaiser, who had lost
much of his enthusiasm for large-scale annexations in Poland ever since
Rumania had become his main concern, eagerly supported Hoffmann's
suggestions.

Hoffmann had hoped to explain his position to Ludendorff before
the crown council met, but he had been unable to do so. It was
therefore much to his embarrassment that the Kaiser suddenly produced
a map with a modified and extended version of Hoffmann's frontier
outlined on it, and announced that these were to be the official frontier
demands from Poland.[31] He then announced that his new plan for the
Polish frontier was the result of discussions with Hoffmann, whom he
particularly valued as an expert on eastern affairs. Hindenburg and
Ludendorff were livid with rage, convinced that a subordinate officer
had been plotting behind their backs, and that their man at Brest
Litovsk was in fact one of Kühlmann's agents. Hindenburg and
Ludendorff began to talk so loudly with one another, that all present
could hear their biting criticisms of the Kaiser. The scene was extremely
unpleasant for all concerned, for their behaviour was felt to show an
unprecedented lack of respect for the supreme warlord, to say nothing
of a breach of ordinary good manners. The Kaiser, realising that the
discussions had reached an *impasse,* broke off the session with the
remark that he awaited further comments from the OHL. Ludendorff
stormed out of the room slamming the door behind him.

Ludendorff, who had rejected the Kaiser's proposals for a new
frontier with Poland with the arrogant remark that 'the OHL is opposed

to the suggestion', decided to go over at once to the attack.[32] On 4
January 1918 he offered his resignation to the chief of the military
cabinet, and at the same time mounted a press campaign in which
rumours were circulated that Ludendorff was being forced to resign,
and the dire consequences of such a fateful step were emphasised.[33]
The OHL also began a vicious press attack on Hoffmann. Dark hints
were made that his wife came from 'semitic circles', and that she
organised 'parliamentary tea parties' to which members of alarmingly
liberal persuasion were invited. From this it was concluded that
Hoffmann had high political ambitions.[34]

   The campaign seemed at first to be highly successful. The Kaiser was
swamped with telegrams from outraged patriots who feared that
Ludendorff was in danger of being forced to resign. The army issued a
pointed order forbidding any officer to attend 'political tea parties'.[35]
Colonel Bauer won over the crown prince to the OHL's side in the
struggle against his father with a lengthy memorandum on the situation.[36]
He argued that Germany was faced with two possible choices: either
that offered by the army — a 'strong' peace that alone would make the
sacrifices of war worthwhile, and which would leave Germany militarily
powerful, with the prospect of economic development and peace; or
Germany would cease to be a great nation both militarily and politically,
collapse economically, and run the risk of being overrun by bolshevism.
Bauer insisted that Germany was militarily victorious and that the
politicians and diplomatists simply refused to see this fact. The only
people who profited from this appalling situation were the 'Red and
Golden Internationals'. The Kaiser therefore faced a simple choice.
Either he supported the OHL, and accepted every demand they made,
or he sided with his political advisers, Kühlmann, Valentini, Hoffmann
and Müller, in which case he chose chaos, defeat and communism.

   Although the Bauer memorandum was widely circulated, and even
reached the hands of Crown Prince Rupprecht of Bavaria who was
enraged at such shameless political meddling by the OHL, it was
Hindenburg's memorandum of 7 January, addressed directly to the
Kaiser, which had a far greater impact.[37] Hindenburg complained that
the government had not finally given up the idea of autonomous state
rights for Alsace Lorraine, and that military considerations were being
ignored in the Belgian question. The Kaiser's proposals for frontier
rectifications with Poland would make the Austro-Polish solution
unacceptable to the OHL. The declaration of 25 December at Brest
Litovsk had created a dangerous sense of uncertainty in the east.
Hindenburg placed the blame for what he considered to be the totally

unsatisfactory outcome of the negotiations at Brest Litovsk on inadequate preparation by the foreign office, and by their compliant attitude towards the demands made not only by Germany's enemies, but also her allies. The fact that the Kaiser had listened to Hoffmann was 'a sign that Your Majesty disregards our judgement on a question which affects the life of the German Fatherland'. He added that since the negotiations at Brest Litovsk were being carried out in a 'diplomatic' rather than a 'strong' fashion, the impression was being created that Germany needed peace just as badly as Russia. This was having a disastrous effect on the morale of the army. Should the offensive in the west bring victory, and should this victory not achieve the peace that was needed to make Germany a world power politically, economically and militarily as a result of the shortcomings and failures of the diplomatists, there would be severe disappointment among the soldiers as they returned home, for they would feel that their sacrifices had been in vain. This in turn would have 'unforeseeable consequences', a phrase which the Kaiser carefully underlined. Hindenburg concluded by insisting that the Kaiser had to choose between the OHL and Kühlmann, between strengthening the position of the monarchy and of Germany, and a downhill path from the heights to which 'Your Majesty and Your Majesty's esteemed ancestors have guided Prussia and Germany'. Given this choice Hindenburg and Ludendorff threatened to resign if they did not get their way: 'Your Majesty would not order honest men who have loyally served Your Majesty and the Fatherland to have their authority and their name involved in actions that they realise with their profoundest feelings to be harmful to crown and Reich.'

This belligerent letter to the Kaiser crossed with a conciliatory letter to Hindenburg from Hertling.[38] The chancellor assured Hindenburg that the question of the Polish frontier was still open, and that as the OHL had not been presented with a *fait accompli* there was no need for Ludendorff to think of resigning. Hertling appealed to Hindenburg to preserve unity and to present a united front as the negotiations were about to resume. He pointed out that Kühlmann's policy had been successful, for the Entente had not accepted the invitation to join in the peace talks on the basis of the Russian proposals, and that therefore Germany was free to pursue her war aims.

Hindenburg replied to this letter on 9 January.[39] He pointed out that both he and Ludendorff agreed that the Kaiser had made up his mind on the Polish question, and that unless the chancellor was able to obtain a definite statement from the Kaiser to the contrary, he too would hand in his resignation. On the other hand he expressed his delight that the German delegation to Brest Litovsk had now decided to adopt the 'language of the victor' and would henceforth take a much tougher attitude against the Soviets. But he complained bitterly about the course of the economic negotiations, and called for the dismissal of Johannes, the director of the economic and commercial section of the foreign office, and the appointment of men with 'practical experience'. Finally he expressed his delight that the Western allies had not taken up the peace offer, but he hastily added that this had been a *va-banque* play that should not be allowed to happen again.

Hertling met Hindenburg and Ludendorff in Berlin on 12 January in a further attempt to restore some semblance of unity between the government and the OHL.[40] The OHL used its usual tactics; Ludendorff said he would resign if Kühlmann was not dismissed, and a further attack was launched on Valentini, who was soon to be sacrificed to the OHL in place of Kühlmann.[41] In spite of this virulent and ill-mannered attack, Hertling stood his ground. He argued that the OHL was trying to usurp the power that was constitutionally vested in the government, and he was determined to settle the question of the delineation of authority between the imperial government and the OHL.

A draft of a letter by Hertling to Hindenburg on this question is still in the files, and although it was never sent it offers an interesting summary of the chancellor's thoughts on the question which he decided to bring up during his meeting with the OHL.[42] He pointed out that he alone bore the constitutional responsibility for the political leadership of the Reich, and this responsibility could not be shared. In a curious slip of the pen, Hertling even wrote that he was 'responsible to parliament alone', but realising the mistake he crossed out the phrase and substituted 'constitutionally responsible' *(staatsrechtlich verantwortlich).* Thus the OHL could advise the government, but could not bear any political responsibility. Contrary to the arguments of the OHL, Hertling insisted that the question of Germany's frontiers and the problem of the future of Alsace and Lorraine could not be seen as purely military affairs. Frontiers which contained the seeds of fresh wars must be rejected on political grounds. For political reasons it was desirable that Lithuania and Courland should be joined as closely as possible to Germany, but this could not be achieved by means of annexations. Self-determination plus 'persuasion' could be used to work to Germany's advantage. Returning to the question of the stand taken at Brest Litovsk on 25 December, he argued that Kühlmann had acted with the full support of the representative of the OHL, and that there could thus be no question of the civilians working behind the backs of the military. Lastly he rejected Hindenburg's criticisms of the *va-banque* play by saying that the Entente would not accept the invitation, and thus there was no risk involved.

This document is the furthest Hertling ever went in his attack on the excessive powers of the OHL, and it is significant that it was never despatched. In the version which he finally sent to Hindenburg after the meeting he significantly modified his position.[43] Hertling admitted that the OHL should advise the chancellor not only on military matters, but also on questions of industry, transport and labour in as much as these were directly concerned with the conduct of the war or the morale of the troops. If there were any conflicts between the OHL and the chancellor then the Kaiser would have to decide, and if the decision went against the chancellor then he would feel obliged to resign.

Such a letter was hardly likely to alarm Hindenburg, who expressed his agreement with Hertling's interpretation of the constitution, except that he felt that such was the position of the OHL in the eyes of the German people that they would have to share responsibility for shaping the peace settlement. Hindenburg also stretched the already elastic definition of military matters in Hertling's letter to include the future frontiers of the Reich and relations with foreign countries.[44]

Ignoring the subtle changes which Hindenburg had made to his original letter, Hertling was pleased with the reply and felt that there was now a general understanding between them.[45] The OHL was also delighted that they had outwitted the chancellor. The Bavarian military plenipotentiary reported back to Munich that although the OHL could not forgive Kühlmann, and were now determined to secure the dismissal of Valentini, they still regarded Hertling very highly. 'As before, the OHL has a very good relationship with Hertling. They appreciate very much the distinction and the parliamentary skill of the chancellor.'[46]

This exchange between Hindenburg and Hertling provides an excellent summary of the OHL's thinking about its position within the Reich, and about the nature of the war. They continued to insist on their right and duty to influence and even decide vital political decisions, all the while insisting that they were offering merely military advice. This encroachment of the military into the political sphere could be justified by bonapartist appeals to their popular support, which was such a new departure for the traditionally aloof officer corps. Behind all their demands at Brest Litovsk was the insistence that the war had to be fought until victory was won, because without a victory Germany would be faced with a revolution; the longer the war lasted the more likely this revolution would be. A 'strong' peace, with massive annexations was thus designed to place the political and social order in quarantine and prop up the antiquated structure of the Reich which was threatened by the forces of a new and hostile age. The OHL was always determined that the chancellor should have the appearance of political power, while they controlled the substance. Thus the OHL could decide policy, and the chancellor bear the responsibility for any failures.

The OHL now concentrated its efforts on securing the dismissal of Valentini, who now found himself in an extremely awkward position. He was perspicacious enough to realise that some concessions to the Reichstag were necessary, even though he was a staunch conservative and felt that Hertling had gone too far in that direction by appointing Payer as vice-chancellor and Friedberg as vice-president of the ministry of state. In November 1917 he told the Empress that parliament should be given greater power in such troubled times, but she was highly alarmed and exclaimed: 'I would rather place my neck on the executioner's block than allow any rights of the crown to be diminished.'[47] Such remarks convinced the Empress and the crown prince that Valentini was the sinister man behind the creeping parliamentarianism which threatened to undermine the power of the crown.

The OHL enthusiastically joined in the attacks on Valentini. Hindenburg asked the Kaiser to replace him with his old school friend, the arch-reactionary Berg.[48] Valentini offered his resignation, but the Kaiser refused to accept it. The crown prince saw Valentini as the 'evil spirit of the monarchy', and demanded his dismissal, adding that Hertling should be replaced by Bülow.[49] Again the Kaiser refused, whereupon the OHL mounted another scurrilous attack on Valentini in the *Deutsche Zeitung* and the *Alldeutsche Blätter,* calling him a traitor because of some remark he had reputedly made that the battle of the Skagerrak had ruined any chances of peace with England.

On 12 January 1918 Hindenburg and Ludendorff arrived in Berlin to demand the dismissal of both Kühlmann and Valentini. Again the Kaiser refused. This served to increase the anger and frustration of the OHL who were determined if they could not get rid of Kühlmann, with whom they had long been engaged in battle, then at least to secure the dismissal of Valentini. They had no concrete criticisms of Valentini, their aim to get their own man, Berg, appointed to the important position of chief of the civil cabinet, and thus undermine the position of Kühlmann. Valentini was thus to be the whipping boy of the OHL.

The following day the crown prince spoke to Valentini. He was in a state of great agitation, chain smoking his habitual Turkish cigarettes. He told Valentini that unless he resigned, Hindenburg and Ludendorff would resign. Valentini replied that he had the full confidence of the Kaiser. He accused Hindenburg and Ludendorff of being puppets in the hands of the Pan Germans and extremists, and asked the crown prince what they had against him. The crown prince was unable to answer this question, muttered quite untruthfully that he personally had every confidence in him, and shamefacedly took his leave.[50]

On the morning of 14 January Hindenburg went to the Kaiser and bluntly informed him that unless Valentini was replaced by Berg both he and Ludendorff would resign. When pressed for a reason Hindenburg came up with the preposterous argument that Valentini was entirely to blame for the leftward swing in the government, and suggested the fate of the offensive on the western front depended in some mysterious way on whether Valentini was dismissed. The Kaiser was disgusted at such shameless attempts at blackmail and stormed out of the room in a towering rage, slamming the door and yelling that he had no need for Hindenburg's paternal advice.[51]

That evening the Kaiser poured out his heart to Colonel von Winterfeldt, who acted as the liaison officer between the OHL and the chancellor. He bitterly complained that he was being forced to make a choice between Valentini and Hindenburg and Ludendorff, and that although the generals had been unable to make any case against Valentini, he was convinced that this time they were serious about their intention to resign. Winterfeldt, whose sympathies lay with the OHL, replied that in that case the resignation of the chief of the civil cabinet was the only way out.

Winterfeldt spoke to Valentini the following day, told him all that had passed, and, insisting that he was speaking purely as a private individual, asked Valentini to resign to release the Kaiser from the intolerable situation in which he was placed. Valentini then consulted Lyncker, who confirmed most of what Winterfeldt had said. He then went to Bellevue and offered the Kaiser his resignation. The Kaiser accepted it graciously, and later in the day told Berg bitterly: 'I have been asked to make you chief of the civil cabinet.'[52]

These words spoke a bitter truth. William II knew that his imposing title of supreme warlord was merely an empty phrase, and that he had lost his authority over the army. It is true that Hindenburg and Ludendorff had failed in their primary objective, to secure the dismissal of Kühlmann and a tougher policy at Brest Litovsk, and had been given Valentini's head as a compensation. The crown prince, however, seemed to understand the implications of an action in which he had played a vital role. To Hindenburg and Ludendorff he said: 'You cannot demand of my father that he dismiss a statesman every five minutes just because you don't like him.' It seems almost as if he had woken up to the idea that he was, by his willing complicity with the OHL, undermining the authority of the crown which he one day hoped to wear.

Valentini was succeeded by Berg, a man described by Kühlmann as a 'protestant jesuit in German national colours' and the 'grave-digger of the monarchy'.[53] He was an avid admirer of Ludendorff and Tirpitz, was convinced that Bethmann and Valentini were disasters, and he firmly believed in victory. He was a close associate of the OHL, well known in Pan German circles, and an old friend of the Kaiser. He was a second rate man of extremist views, perfectly willing to follow the lead of the OHL.[54] As Admiral Müller wrote to Valentini, Berg was an 'effective representative of the H-L company'.[55]

Meanwhile Graf Roedern from the treasury and von Radowitz from the chancellery had been working on the final draft of a memorandum which was based on a paper of Kühlmann's and was to serve as a detailed justification of Hertling's constitutional position and an attack on the encroachments of the OHL.[56] The memorandum repeated many familiar arguments, but it went much further than any previous attempts to delineate fields of competence between the chancellor and the OHL. It argued that although Hindenburg and Ludendorff, owing to their unique position and the confidence which the German people had in them, had won an unusually powerful position, but this did not mean that the government would have to give way to their demands in the political sphere. Indeed it was highly improper that the OHL should use the threat of resignation in order to attempt to force through their political demands. If the political and military executive power were to be united in the hands of the OHL, this would amount to overthrowing the fundamental principles of the constitution, to say nothing of a serious curtailment of the authority and dignity of the crown. Questions of the future frontiers of the Reich could not be regarded as purely military, for true defence rested on the future political situation, in that security was not a question of establishing frontiers so powerfully defended that no enemy could cross them — no such frontiers could ever be found — but rather the establishment of friendly relations with neighbouring states. 'Purely military' frontiers would merely be an invitation to further wars. Thus questions of the future of Poland, Belgium, Alsace-Lorraine, and particularly relations with Austria-Hungary were first and foremost matters of grave political importance and could not be considered as military questions. He supported Kühlmann's policy at Brest Litovsk, but condemned the Reichstag peace resolution as a 'momentary opinion'.

Hertling now seemed to be falling between two stools, that of the OHL and their annexationist plans and the Reichstag resolution. It seemed unlikely that he would be able to defend this position against a man as determined as Ludendorff. The OHL was prepared to agree to the memorandum, for it was so full of loopholes that it could settle nothing. They were also in a sufficiently conciliatory mood to accept a compromise solution to the question of the Polish frontier strip. But at the same time they urged that there should be a speedy conclusion to the peace talks so that more troops could be withdrawn for use on the western front. Failing this a separate peace should be signed with the Ukraine.[57]

Meanwhile the negotiations at Brest Litovsk had recommenced on 9 January. Kühlmann and Czernin both announced that they no longer felt themselves bound by the declaration of 25 December, as the Entente had refused the peace offer; therefore it was now a question of negotiating a separate peace, and thus the underlying assumptions would be quite different. Faced with such intransigence, Trotsky, who now headed the Soviet delegation, could only hope that the Soviet peace offer would stimulate the proletariat of German and Austria-Hungary to political action that would undermine the efforts of the diplomatists at Brest Litovsk. This calculation was shrewd, for political strikes were soon to break out in Germany, Vienna and Budapest; but Trotsky's own position had been weakened by the serious tactical blunder of allowing the Ukrainian Rada the right to appear at the peace conference as an equal partner, and thus allowing Kühlmann to outmanoeuvre the Soviet delegation on the Ukrainian issue by insisting that the Rada was the legitimate government of the Ukraine even though its authority rested on the power of the German army of occupation.

Trotsky's position rested on hopes that must have seemed faint, and was weakened by serious tactical errors. But the Central Powers also faced severe problems. Austria-Hungary was desperate that peace should be concluded as soon as possible. The principle of self-determination threatened the very foundations of the dual monarchy, there was a severe shortage of food, the German government supported the Ukrainian claim to the Cholm, and the question of Poland was still undecided between the allies. Kühlmann's position was also uncertain. There was growing unrest at home over the prolongation of the war, unrest which was to become manifest in the great January strikes, and yet he was being pushed by General Hoffmann to ignore all principles of abstract justice and to negotiate as a victor over the Soviet government. He also knew that he lacked support in the government, and was under attack from the OHL. Hoffmann in turn was becoming increasingly alienated from the OHL who uncritically voiced the extreme annexationist demands of the heavy industrialists and the Pan Germans, and who had no sympathy for Hoffmann's somewhat more realistic appraisal of the limits of German power and of Germany's ability to absorb hostile nations. Lastly the OHL itself was beginning to realise the contradiction within its own thinking, between the desire for far-reaching annexations and prolonged military occupation and administration of the eastern area, and the need to bring back troops from the east for the final decisive battle on the western front. With these growing tensions and with little hope for an immediate solution, the position of those who demanded that the war should be continued in the east until the Soviets were forced to their knees was greatly strengthened.[58] No one understood the situation clearer than Lenin who, in the seventh of the twenty-one January theses pointed out that the Soviet government was now faced with the clear alternative of continuing the war, or of being forced to accept an annexationist peace.[59]

Discussions were held in Berlin between the Austrians and the Germans on 5 February 1918 in the hope of resolving some of these problems. Czernin talked of restoring the *status quo ante bellum,* and Kühlmann muttered something about it being a defensive war. Hertling tried to avoid making any stand. It was Ludendorff who characteristically let the cat out of the bag. Impatient with the duplicity of the civilians he told Czernin: 'A peace that simply guaranteed the territorial *status quo* would mean that we have lost the war. Such a peace was never discussed as far as the east is concerned. In the west there is still a lack of clarity. If we keep our old frontiers there we will be in a less advantageous military position after the war than we were before.' Ludendorff's argument that annexations were a military necessity was supported by Payer, a man of dangerously liberal ideas in the eyes of the OHL.[60]

The meeting was adjourned until 4.30 that afternoon in the hope that some of these differences could be settled in the meantime. Ludendorff began by speaking in favour of breaking the armistice with Russia not only to secure German war aims in the east but also to topple Trotsky and the bolsheviks. To Czernin's objections that peace should be made as soon as possible he replied that if nothing were done the bolsheviks would over-run the Ukraine. It was then agreed that if the Russians did not agree to the peace terms the war should be continued. Ludendorff had in fact already given orders to prepare an operational plan for an attack on Soviet Russia.[61] Thus the Germans had no intention of continuing the negotiations, and the foreign office and OHL began a massive anti-communist campaign which was designed in part to counteract the effects of the January strikes. Thus Rosenberg telegraphed from Brest Litovsk asking the German delegation in Petrograd to send 'daily reports of atrocities, murders, suspensions of political rights etc., so that we have material to supply our press with frightening pictures of Russia'.[62]

Whereas Kühlmann still hoped to negotiate with the Soviet delegation, Hindenburg was determined that the war should be fought to the finish. He told Hoffmann to issue an ultimatum that either Russian troops were withdrawn from Livonia and Estonia or the armistice would be broken. Kühlmann managed to head off this move by saying that he must first receive his instructions from the chancellor, as this went beyond the Kreuznach agreement of 18 December 1917.[63]

Prompted by a further message from Hindenburg that the Soviets were encouraging the German soldier to disobey orders, the Kaiser sent two telegrams. The first, to Hoffmann, said that 'Neither I nor His Excellency Fieldmarshal von Hindenburg can tolerate or allow such a state of affairs! It must be brought to an end at once.' In a second telegram to Kühlmann he added: 'Trotsky is *immediately* to be given the ultimatum − a peace according to *my* conditions with the evacuation of Livonia and Estonia, or an immediate cessation of discussions and an end to the armistice.'[64] Kühlmann, who had already protested to the chancellor about Hindenburg's first attempt to sabotage the negotiations at Brest, replied to the Kaiser that the course of action which he proposed would not be accepted by the Austrians, who would then be obliged to seek a separate peace with Soviet Russia. He asked the Kaiser to reconsider his order by 5.30 that afternoon when negotiations were due to recommence, adding that otherwise he would have to offer his resignation.[65] Hertling supported Kühlmann's stand and also offered to resign.[66] Faced with this opposition the Kaiser agreed to wait one more day.

When negotiations resumed the initial wrangles over General Hoffmann's frontier proposals and the presence of Russian troops in Finland were almost ignored, for all the delegates were waiting for the Soviet reply to the German peace proposals. Suddenly Trotsky announced that he would not accept the German terms, which he denounced as imperialist and annexationist, and yet at the same time he told the astonished assembly that the Russian army was to be demobilised. So great was the amazement that only Hoffmann's cry of 'disgraceful' *(unehört)* broke the silence.[67] Trotsky refused to discuss the matter any further, and announced that the Soviet delegation would return to Petrograd immediately.

Trotsky's surprising moves were carried out against the express wish of Lenin, who had urged that the German demands be accepted. Furthermore Trotsky issued an order to begin the demobilisation of the army, an order for which he had no authority, and which was countermanded the following day by Lenin in the name of the Council of Peoples' Commissars.[68] Although Lenin voted for the Sverdlov motion presented to the central executive committee which approved the actions of the delegation at Brest Litovsk, it was with a heavy heart and with serious misgivings. He could not share Trotsky's unbounded optimism that the Germans would be restrained from continuing the war.[69]

General Hoffmann's first reaction to Trotsky's strategy was to demand that the armistice be renounced at once and that the war be resumed. Kühlmann argued against this policy in a lengthy telegram to the chancellor.[70] He pointed out that a military solution was hardly possible owing to the vast size of Russia, the enormous numbers of troops needed to occupy the country and the need for troops from the eastern front for the spring offensive in the west. A continuation of the war in the east would be enormously unpopular in Germany, and would strengthen the position of the left wing socialists. Kühlmann suggested that the Germans should simply wait until troops could be spared from the west for further operations in the east, for the Soviets were in no position to do the Germans any damage.

Hindenburg would not listen to these arguments. He insisted that the situation in the east would have to be cleared up before an offensive could be mounted in the west. The longer Germany waited, the greater would be the danger of bolshevism spreading to the Baltic provinces and Poland. He said that if the chancellor refused to agree to a resumption of hostilities in the east then the whole matter should be brought before the Kaiser for his decision.[71] Hertling again resolutely refused to take sides, saying that as Trotsky had in effect renounced the armistice there was no point in the German government making a formal declaration on this point.[72] Once again the matter was postponed for a major meeting to be held in Homburg.

The crown council duly met. Among those present were Hertling, Kühlmann, Hindenburg, Ludendorff, vice-chancellor Payer and Admiral Holtzendorff.[73] Kühlmann agreed that the 'centre of revolutionary pestilence' should be destroyed, but he warned that a continuation of the war into Russia would enable the bolsheviks to appeal to national sentiments, and a united Russia would be almost impossible to defeat, quite apart from the risk of guerilla warfare in the Baltic which would lead to a 'massacre of the Baltic barons by the bolsheviks'. The only possibility of an effective intervention in Russia would be if there was a genuine support by the Russians themselves against the bolsheviks, but Kühlmann doubted that this existed. Hindenburg dismissed these arguments out of hand by simply saying that the war was still on, and therefore it was not a question of starting a new one. Without a decision in the east the Ukraine would be over-run by the bolsheviks, the English would establish a bridgehead in Estonia, and it would not be possible to withdraw troops for use on the western front where the war would be decided. The ensuing debate consisted of variations on these two basic positions. When Payer talked of possible political repercussions at home over continuation of the war in the east the Kaiser replied that he could not tolerate such 'republican conditions' where the Reichstag could interfere with military operations. The Kaiser fully sided with the OHL. He argued that Totsky had gone to Brest Litovsk to make revolution not peace, adding that 'Bolsheviks want revolution, they want to make mince-meat'. They supported the Entente, and also the strike movement in Germany, therefore they had to be removed as soon as possible. 'Bolsheviks are tigers, round them up, and shoot them.' Summing up he argued that the Russians had now become prey to the Jews, and that the bolsheviks formed part of a world-wide Jewish conspiracy, aided by that other sinister international, the freemasons. The future policy should therefore be out of carefully orchestrated 'cries for help' from the Baltic followed by police actions against the bolsheviks. After this confused and confusing speech the Kaiser left the meeting.

It was thus agreed that the armistice should run out by 17 February, and then 'police actions' should be carried out to restore 'law and order'. Particular emphasis was placed on the need to secure grain from the Ukraine. This compromise did little to clear the air between the OHL and the civilians. Most people realised that little more than a breathing space had been achieved. For Admiral Müller the only compensation was that Hertling's compromise was better than the open military dictatorship at which the OHL seemed to him to be aiming.[74] Ludendorff was triumphant, and was bitterly scornful that Kühlmann, had not done the honourable thing and resigned.[75] Kühlmann. however, convinced himself that the difference between his position and Hertling's compromise was simply a matter of political expediency, and was not one of principle. Few confessions are so frank as to the fundamental agreement between the objective aims of men like Kühlmann and the OHL and the social forces which they represented, however bitter the quarrels over 'expediency'.[76]

The compromise scarcely restricted Hindenburg and Ludendorff's course of action. They could now send troops to Finland and the Ukraine at will, provided that cries for help were forthcoming − and this presented no problem to such masters of the theatrical. They were confined to Dünaburg and Walk for their operations, but military necessity could be claimed for more extensive operations. Similarly the distinction between police operations and annexations was hardly likely to trouble the OHL when it came to operations in Livonia and Estonia.

The Soviet government was informed on the evening of 16 February that hostilities would begin on 18 February. A German force of fifty-two divisions met with little resistance from a demoralised Russian army, and the campaign rapidly became much like a summer manoeuvre, as in most cases the Russians did not even destroy the railway lines. Dünaburg was reached on the first day, and five days later the area around Pskov was occupied. By 1 March Kiev was reached, and the position of Petrograd was becoming increasingly perilous.[77]

With no signs of revolutionary activity in either Germany or Austria it became clear that the Soviet government would have to accept Lenin's arguments in favour of accepting the peace terms of the

Central Powers. The central committee met on 18 February and
agreed by the narrowest of margins to accept the German
conditions. This decision was forwarded to the Germans on the
following day, but Hoffmann's initial reaction was to ignore it, and
to wait for official confirmation with proper signatures.[78]

The speed with which the military operations were carried out,
the lack of any powerful reaction at home against the
continuation of the war, and the submission of the Soviet
government further strengthened the position of the OHL, and
seemed to be a triumphant vindication of their policies. Kühlmann, who
had tried so hard to frustrate the OHL's plans at the crown council
now completely reversed his position. In a lengthy and carefully
considered speech to the main committee of the Reichstag on
19 February he showed that he was now in almost full agreement with
the policy of the OHL.[79] He spoke with heavy pathos of the
'terrible oppression, plunder and murderous acts' in Estonia and
Livonia, of the 'profoundly moving cries for help', and contrasted
the Germany policy of bringing law and order to the Baltic
provinces and to Finland and the Ukraine with the 'rape' of these
areas by the bolsheviks. He now knew that the Soviets would sign
a peace which would be satisfactory to Germany. This was of course
the exact opposite of the arguments he had used at the crown council.
Clearly 'political expediency' which had weighed so heavily with
Kühlmann at Bad Homburg now dictated full support for the
'compromise' solution over which only a few days before he had
thought of resigning.

The German demands reached Petrograd on 23 February.[80] They
included the drawing of a new frontier from Dünaburg to the
eastern frontier of Courland; German control of the Baltic provinces;
Russia was to sign a peace with the Ukraine, and both the Ukraine
and Finland were to be evacuated by Russian troops and Red Guards;
the army, navy and the Red Guards were to be demobilised immediately;
a trade agreement based on the Russo-German trade agreements of
1904 was to be signed which would greatly favour German interests;
compensation was to be paid by the Soviet government for losses
incurred by German citizens, and for the cost of prisoners of war;
the Soviet government was to desist from sending any propaganda
material to Germany or to the German troops; and lastly the Soviet
government was given forty-eight hours to accept these conditions.

The central committee met immediately to discuss the German
ultimatum. It was agreed by seven votes in favour, four against and

four abstentions that the conditions would have to be accepted.
Lenin had won another significant victory over the left wing led by
Bukharin, whose revolutionary adventurism would almost
certainly have resulted in the total destruction of the fragile power
of the Soviets. But it was a bitter victory, and Trotsky, accusing
Lenin of subjectivism, resigned as foreign minister. Bukharin also
resigned from the central committee. There was, however, full
agreement that preparations should begin at once for a
revolutionary war against Germany.[81] The following day the
central executive committee agreed to accept the ultimatum by a
vote of 116 to 84 with 26 abstentions.

Hertling announced the news of the Soviet acceptance of the
ultimatum in the Reichstag on 25 February, stating categorically
that Germany had only acted on the initiative of the peoples of
the Ukraine and the Baltic who had asked for help against
bolshevik terror, and added that Germany had no territorial
ambitions whatever with regard to these states.[82] Hindenburg was
highly alarmed by such statements, by similar comments from
Kühlmann, and by the suggestion that the OHL favoured a peace
without annexations, and the principle of self-determination. To
Kühlmann he wrote that he 'rejected such an insinuation with
indignation'.[83] So bad were the relations between Kühlmann and
the OHL, and so poor the communications between them, that
Hindenburg was clearly unaware of the significant change in the
state secretary's attitude towards the operations in the east.

The negotiations reopened at Brest Litovsk on 1 March, but they
were hardly worthy of the name. Kühlmann had already left for
Bucharest to negotiate the peace with Rumania, and his deputy,
Rosenberg, made it quite clear that the Soviet delegation had
a simple choice, either to accept the German terms or continue
the war. Sokolnikov, the leader of the Russian delegation, stated that
he had come to sign the treaty and not to negotiate, and by
underlining this fact as heavily as possible he hoped that the Soviets
would appear to the world as the innocent victims of German
militarism and imperialism. Thus on 3 March 1918, at five o'clock
in the afternoon, Sokolnikov signed the instruments of the treaty
of Brest Litovsk, and as a final gesture gnashed his teeth whilst
signing his name.[84]

The treaty was a triumph for the policy of the OHL, since the
indirect imperialism of the foreign office was now no longer evident.
Lithuania, Courland, part of White Russia and Poland were to be taken

away from the Russian sphere of influence and further: 'Germany and Austria-Hungary intend to determine the future destiny of these areas in consultation with the inhabitants.' The East Anatolian provinces, and the districts of Erdehan, Kars and Batum were to fall into the Turkish sphere of influence. Estonia and Livonia, Finland and the Aaland Islands were to be evacuated by the Russians. The Ukrainian government was to be recognised by the Russian government. Germany's 'police role' in Estonia and Livonia was to be accepted by the Soviets. The Russian army was to be demobilised, and the navy to return to port immediately.[85]

It is hardly surprising that the treaty of Brest Litovsk was regarded by world public opinion with horror. Although accurate figures are not available, about one million square kilometres of territory with fifty million inhabitants were taken away from Russia. About 90 per cent of Russia's coal mines, 54 per cent of Russian industry, 33 per cent of the Russian railway systems, 32 per cent of Russia's agricultural land, 34 per cent of the population, 85 per cent of the sugar beet production and virtually the entire oil and cotton production was taken.[86] With such rich prizes it is hardly surprising that the OHL was able to stomach the opposition of the foreign office to a direct assault on Petrograd, at least for a while. Yet the treaty of Brest Litovsk did not mark the end of fighting between German and Russian troops. The Germans were to continue their advance in the hope of realising the increasingly fantastic dreams of the OHL; and Lenin and the bolsheviks had no intention of accepting this 'scrap of paper' which Lenin boasted he would neither read nor execute.

If the treaty itself was bad enough, the attitude of the political parties, and particularly the social democrats, was even more disgraceful. It needed the most extraordinary intellectual acrobatics to surpass the contradictions between the declaration of 4 August and the Reichstag resolution and the treaty of Brest Litovsk. For the social democrats not to disclaim a treaty which stood in flagrant opposition to their avowed aims and policies a singular lack of principle was needed. Westarp for the conservatives complained that the peace was too weak, but Scheidemann for the social democrats announced that his party would abstain from voting on the grounds that the treaty had brought peace in the east, even though there were some points in the treaty with which he could not agree. Only the USPD spoke out strongly against the treaty, and voted against ratification. Hugo Haase warned the Reichstag that the treaty created a dangerous precedent: 'He who sows the wind, reaps the whirlwind.' He also pointed out that the government claimed to be marching into the Baltic provinces to restore law and order and save the area from red terror and bolshevik barbarism, but on the other hand part of the treaty called for the immediate opening of diplomatic relations between Berlin and the terrorist barbarians in Petrograd.[87]

If the treaty of Brest Litovsk marks the highest point of German power, and another victory of the OHL over the civilian government, it also showed to the world the true nature of this imperialist war. No longer could the pious assurances of the government and the Reichstag be taken seriously, and the majority of Germans gave their full support to the annexationist ambitions and the power political illusions of the government and the OHL.

NOTES

1. Z.A.B. Zeman, *Germany and the Revolution in Russia,* London 1958; Z.A.B. Zeman, W. B. Scharlau, *Parvus Helphand. Freibeuter der Revolution,* Cologne 1965; W. Hahlweg, *Der Diktatfrieden von Brest Litovsk 1918 und die bolshevistische Weltrevolution,* Münster 1960.
2. Max Hoffmann, *Die Aufzeichnungen des Gen. -Maj. M. Hoffmann,* ed. K.F. Novak, 2 Vols., Berlin 1929, Vol. 2, p. 174.
3. Hahlweg, *Der Diktatfrieden,* p. 11.
4. Fischer, *Griff nach der Weltmacht,* p. 478.
5. Zeman, *Germany and the Revolution in Russia,* p. 25. IIIb was not merely responsible for military passports as Zeman seems to suggest. See Chapter 2 of this book.
6. Ritter, *Staatskunst und Kriegshandwerk,* Vol. 3, p. 486.
7. Ludendorff, *Kriegsführung und Politik,* p. 270, with a very dubious reading of Clausewitz.
8. *Deutsch-Sowjetische Beziehungen von den Verhandlungen in Brest Litovsk bis zum Abschluss des Rapallovertrages,* Hrsg. von Ministerium für Auswärtige Angelegenheiten der DDR und von Ministerium für Auswärtige Angelegenheiten der UdSSR, Dokumentensammlung I, 1917-1918, Berlin 1967, p. 44.
9. *Ibid.,* p. 62.
10. *Ibid.,* p. 118.
11. *Deutschland im ersten Weltkrieg,* Vol. 3, p. 104 for details.
12. PA Bonn AA Weltkrieg 15 Geheim, Band 5.
13. Ottokar Czernin, *Im Weltkrieg,* Berlin 1919, p. 299; Kühlmann, *Erinnerungen,* p. 523.
14. *Deutsch-Sowjetische Beziehungen,* p. 167.
15. Czernin, *Im Weltkriege,* p. 307.
16. *Deutsch-Sowjetische Beziehungen,* p. 194.
17. Fischer, *Griff nach der Weltmacht,* p.647; Ritter, *Staatskunst und Kriegshandwerk,* Vol. 4, p. 114. Ritter tends to emphasise the desire for peace in Germany, without stating on what terms. *Deutschland im ersten Weltkrieg,* Band 3, stresses that the war aims were the work of the ruling class, not the German people, but tends to minimise the extent of

public support for these aims. Ritter thus exaggerates the moderation of German policy, while the authors of *Deutschland im ersten Weltkrieg* tend to exaggerate potential class consciousness.

18. *Deutsch-Sowjetische Beziehungen*, p. 203.
19. Ritter, *Staatskunst und Kriegshandwerk*, Vol. 4, p. 493, quoting from Kennan, *Russia Leaves the War.*
20. Hoffmann, *Aufzeichnungen*, Vol. 2, p. 197.
21. *Deutsch-Sowjetische Beziehungen*, p. 206.
22. Hoffmann, *Aufzeichnungen*, Vol. 2, p. 202.
23. Bayerisches Hauptstaatsarchiv Abteilung IV Kriegsarchiv, M. Kr. 1831 Bevollmäch. in Gr. HQ 1917.
24. Ritter, *Staatskunst und Kriegshandwerk*, Vol. 4, p. 117.
25. Hoffmann, *Aufzeichnungen*, Vol. 2, p. 203.
26. PA Bonn AA Gr. HQ 232 Kriegsziele 16a, Band 1.
27. Matthias, Morsey, *Der Interfraktionelle Ausschuss*, Vol. 2, p. 3.
28. *Archivalische Forschungen* 4/11, p. 879; *Untersuchungsausschuss IV Reihe*, Band 2, p. 130; *Deutsch-Sowjetische Beziehungen*, p. 232; W. Baumgart, K. Repgen, *Brest Litovsk*, Göttingen 1969, p. 50.
29. Ritter, *Staatskunst und Kriegshandwerk*, Band 4, p. 122 sees the meeting as an 'approval of his policy' by the *Bundesrat* committee, but even his own account of the meeting suggests the opposite. Kühlmann, *Erinnerungen*, p. 525, writes: 'The *Bundesrat* committee for foreign affairs was a cover-up invented by Bismarck in his wisdom to make it as easy as possible for Bavaria to give up having her own independent foreign policy.' Kühlmann was also unable to give a lengthy account of his policy as he was called to the Kaiser in the middle of his exposé
30. Hoffmann, *Aufzeichnungen*, Vol. 2, p. 203; Ludendorff, *Kriegserinnerungen*, p. 438; Czernin, *Im Weltkriege*, p. 314; Hertling, *Ein Jahr in der Reichskanzlei*, p. 52; Kühlmann, *Erinnerungen*, p. 527; Payer, *Bethmann Hollweg bis Ebert*, p. 174; Müller diary 15-1-18. There is no protocol of the meeting in the archives.
31. For a useful map see Geiss, *Grenzstreifen*, p. 131.
32. *Untersuchungsausschuss IV Reihe*, Band 2, p. 4. It should be stressed that the Kaiser was part of the OHL, and therefore the remark was particularly wounding.
33. Valentini, *Kaiser und Kabinettschef*, p. 190; Ludendorff, *Kriegserinnerungen*, p. 439.
34. Bayerisches Hauptstaatsarchiv Abteilung IV Kriegsarchiv, M. Kr. 1832 Bevollmäch. in Gr. HQ 1918, 6-1-18.
35. *Ibid.*, 7-1-18.
36. Bundesarchiv Koblenz, Nachlass Bauer, Band 2.
37. DZA Potsdam Verkehr des Reichskanzlers mit den Gr. HQ 2403/6.
38. *Deutsch-Sowjetische Beziehungen*, p. 258.
39. *Ibid.*, p. 269.
40. Kühlmann, *Erinnerungen*, p. 537; Hertling, *Ein Jahr in der Reichskanzlei*, p. 55.
41. On 14 January Ludendorff stormed around headquarters announcing that he would resign if Kühlmann was not dismissed. To Haeften he said that 'the German people are more important to me than the Kaiser'. Bundesarchiv Militärarchiv Freiburg, Nachlass Haeften N35/3.
42. DZA Potsdam Verkehr des Reichskanzlers mit den Gr. HQ 2403/6.
43. Ludendorff, *Urkunden der OHL*, p. 455.
44. *Ibid.*, p. 456.
45. Hertling, *Ein Jahr in der Reichskanzlei*, p. 59.

186   *The Silent Dictatorship*

46. Bayerisches Hauptstaatsarchiv Abteilung IV Kriegsarchiv M. Kr. 1832 Bevollmäch. in Gr. HQ 1918, 15-1-18.
47. Bundesarchiv Koblenz, Nachlass Schwertfeger, Band 206. The notes on the conversation 9-11-17 written 10-10-1918.
48. Valentini, *Kaiser und Kabinettschef,* p. 186. Kaiser's interview with Hindenburg on 17-11-1917.
49. Bundesarchiv Koblenz, Nachlass Bauer, Band 16. The Kaiser wrote that Bülow was 'certainly not the man' to secure international peace and win the war.
50. Valentini, *Kaiser und Kabinettschef,* p. 191.
51. DZA Potsdam Hist. Abt. Merseburg Preussisches Staatsministerium Rep 90a Abteilung B, III, 2b, Nr. 6, Band 167.
52. Bundesarchiv Koblenz, Nachlass Berg, Band 1.
53. Kühlmann, *Errinerungen,* p. 548.
54. Bundesarchiv Koblenz, Nachlass Berg, Band 1 which gives a very good picture of the man.
55. DZA Hist. Abt. Merseburg Rep 92 Nachlass Valentini Nr. 15, Briefwechsel mit Müller, 30-3-1918.
56. Bundesarchiv Koblenz, Nachlass Bauer, Band 18; Nachlass Schwertfeger Band 206. It was very typical that Ludendorff was given full blame for a letter signed by Hindenburg.
57. *Deutsch-Sowjetische Beziehungen,* p. 314.
58. *Schulthess' Europäischer Geschichtskalender 1918,* Teil 2, p. 660.
59. Lenin, *Selected Works,* Vol. 2, Moscow 1970, p. 533.
60. *Deutsch-Sowjetische Beziehungen,* p. 353.
61. *Der Weltkrieg 1914-1918,* Band 13, p. 363.
62. *Deutsch-Sowjetische Beziehungen,* p. 345.
63. *Ibid.,* p. 389. The treaty was actually signed 9 February.
64. *Ibid.,* p. 390.
65. *Ibid.,* p. 391.
66. *Ibid.,* p. 393.
67. Wheeler-Bennett, *Brest-Litovsk,* p. 228.
68. *Deutschland in ersten Weltkrieg,* Band 3, p. 190.
69. J. Bunyan, H.H. Fisher, *The Bolshevik Revolution 1917-1918,* New York 1961, p. 511.
70. Hahlweg, *Diktatfrieden,* p. 65.
71. *Deutsch-Sowjetische Beziehungen,* p. 398.
72. *Ibid.,* p. 397.
73. Bundesarchiv Koblenz, Nachlass Schwertfeger, Band 119; *Deutsch-Sowjetische Beziehungen,* p. 403; Baumgart, Repgen, *Brest-Litovsk,* p. 57.
74. Müller diary 13-2-1918.
75. Ludendorff, *Kriegserinnerungen,* p. 446.
76. Kühlmann, *Erinnerungen,* p. 549. Ritter, *Staatskunst und Kriegshandwerk,* Vol. 4, p. 140 attributes Kühlmann's reasoning to 'opportunism', but this is situating Kühlmann's policy regardless of its determining factors.
77. For an account of these operations see *Der Weltkrieg 1914-1918,* Band 13, p. 365.
78. *Deutsch-Sowjetische Beziehungen,* p. 417.
79. Baumgart, Repgen, *Brest Litovsk,* p. 82.
80. *Deutsch-Sowjetische Beziehungen,* p. 425.
81. Baumgart, Repgen, *Brest Litovsk,* p. 123.
82. *Stenographische Berichte,* 25-2-1918.
83. *Deutsch-Sowjetische Beziehungen,* p. 437.
84. Ritter, *Staatskunst und Kriegshandwerk,* Vol. 4, p. 144. For the negotiations

see *Schulthess' 1918,* Teil 2, p. 680.

85. *Deutsch-Sowjetische Beziehungen,* p. 455; and Wheeler-Bennett, *Brest-Litovsk,* for the text of the treaty in German and English.
86. *Deutschland im ersten Weltkrieg,* Vol. 3, p. 197; Bunyan, Fisher, *Bolshevik Revolution,* p. 523; *Foreign Relations 1918,* for the report of Summers; Ritter, *Staatskunst und Kriegshandwerk,* Vol. 4, p. 145. Ritter's argument that the treaty was a war measure brought about by the precarious economic position of the Central Powers as a result of the allied blockade, that most of the territorial settlement was arranged before Brest, that the Polish question was solved according to 'historical necessities', his insistence that the economic clauses rested on principles of reciprocity, that the treaty was provisional and in no sense a peace of annexation is a further example of his conservative prejudice and nationalist feelings standing in marked contradiction to the evidence which, as a painstaking and conscientious historian, he presents beforehand. Ritter's work, based on the meticulous, detailed and wrong-headed research of his pupil Steglich, does not convince.
87. *Stenographische Berichte,* Band 311, 19-3-1918.

8 THE TREATY OF BUCHAREST

One of the main reasons for the increasingly strained relations between Germany and Austria during the negotiations at Brest Litovsk was the still unsettled question of the future of Poland and Rumania, a question which now had to be settled as Kühlmann and Czernin had left for Bucharest to negotiate a peace with Rumania even before the final details of the Brest Litovsk peace had been settled.

At a crown council held on 5 November 1917 the Germans had agreed to Kühlmann's proposals for the Austro-Polish solution. The Kaiser had argued that Poland was hardly worth bothering about, saying that 'for hundreds of kilometres it looks like the Jüterbog artillery ground' and vividly contrasting this valuable country to the potential riches of Rumania. Countering the murmurs of dissatisfaction from the OHL he added that 'the Austrians must be hit with conditions that will really make their eyes roll'.[1]

Thus the Austro-Polish solution was accepted, but under terms that were likely to make such a solution unworkable. Germany was determined that the frontier with Poland should be pushed east, for the OHL and the annexationists were adamant, although even Hindenburg seems to have rejected at least for the time being the favourite idea of the *Ostmarkenverein* and the Pan Germans, that the inhabitants of the frontier strip should be removed forcibly from the area. There was also deadlock over the question of the military convention with Austria, the OHL continuing to insist that they had no intention of strengthening Austria, and Kühlmann clinging to his *Mitteleuropa* concept.

On the following day the Germans met the Austrians again in Berlin to discuss the revision of the Kreuznach agreements.[2] Ludendorff at once launched into an attack on the Austro-Polish solution saying that it would result in the defence of the eastern borders of Prussia and Germany being in the hands of Austria, adding with a certain irony 'it is always better to have the defence of one's frontiers in one's own hands, rather than in those of one's best friend'. He then produced a map with a new frontier with Poland marked on it which would give Germany still further gains in the east. Czernin pointed out that this new frontier would amount to a new partition of Poland, and was clearly incompatible with the declaration on Polish independence. Kühlmann tried, with a very little success, to calm down the ensuing argument between Ludendorff and Czernin. Ludendorff's argument was that the Austro-Polish solution gave Austria enormous advantages which would not be adequately compensated by German control of Rumania. It is difficult to find the reasoning behind such arguments. Perhaps Ludendorff was thinking in purely military terms, for once, and saw the great strategic importance of Poland to Germany. On the other hand he was fully aware of the enormous economic potential of Rumania, and may simply have been bluffing the Austrians in the hope of getting the highest possible price for the Austro-Polish solution. The confusion was not simply a matter of pure greed, that in the last resort Ludendorff wanted both Rumania and Poland; it was also a reflection of deep divisions within the officer corps and German society. Recruited traditionally from the ranks of the aristocracy, the officer corps had been forced to make concessions to a rising bourgeoisie. Its aristocratic ideology was becoming rapidly infused with an aggressive capitalist imperialism of middle-class provenance. The aristocrats could not tolerate an independent Poland, or a Poland dominated by Austria. The middle class was far more inclined to accept the annexation of Rumania, and make do with indirect control of Poland along the lines of Kühlmann's *Mitteleuropa* scheme. Objectively, as Kühlmann rightly argued, there was little to choose between the two positions, but subjectively there was a great deal, and this subjective moment was crucial. Seen in this light the clash over Poland and Rumania was much more than a debate over war aims, it was a conflict of class consciousness.

At the afternoon session of the meeting, Hindenburg and Ludendorff were not present, but this afforded little comfort to Czernin. Kühlmann argued on the basis of the OHL's brief, but did not mention the critical question of Belgium, or the fact that Austria would be required to continue fighting until Germany had achieved all her war aims. Even so it was clear that Kühlmann's interpretation of the Austro-Polish solution amounted to little more than an Austro-German condominium over Poland, which was hardly what Czernin wanted. No final agreement could therefore be reached, and the issue of a military convention was not even raised. It was agreed that a draft treaty between Austria and Germany should be discussed at some later date.

It was at this moment, when the whole question of the future of the Austro-German alliance was so much in question that the October revolution heralded the beginning of a new era in world politics. The impact of the bolshevik revolution on Poland was considerable. The desire for full Polish independence was strengthened, but at the same time conservative circles in Poland were alarmed at the possibility of the revolution spreading to Poland.[3] Through leaks to the press, probably the work of Bülow, the Poles learned of the Austro-Polish solution, and they were predictably angry at such a flagrant violation of the declaration of 5 November, but again there were those who favoured a conservative union with Germany, rather than Austria, as the best guarantee that bolshevism would not spread to Poland. Whatever the final outcome of this new and dynamic situation there was nothing to encourage Czernin, who saw his hopes for the Austro-Polish solution, the cornerstone of his policy, further diminished.

Safely back in Vienna, Czernin decided to go over to the offensive. He was convinced that the OHL was the principal hindrance to the realisation of his plans, for he had received sympathetic and rather pathetic assurances from Kühlmann that he would try to moderate German demands on Poland, but there was little indication that he could succeed. In his desperation Czernin even considered mounting a propaganda campaign against the OHL, but this was quite ludicrous. For such a campaign to succeed the support of the anti-war efforts of the extreme left in Germany and of the anti-Austrian Polish patriots would have been necessary, and this the Austrians could not even consider.[4]

In the course of further meetings in December the Germans were unable to agree on a policy towards Poland.[5] Meanwhile on 6 December 1917 General Stcherbatschev, the commander of the Ukrainian army, and the Rumanian General Lupescu were received by the Germans at Focsani. The Ukrainians and the Rumanians were unable to continue fighting without Russian support, and both countries were becoming increasingly concerned with fighting bolshevism rather than the Central Powers. Three days later an armistice was signed, enabling the Germans to withdraw some troops to the western front, and the Ukrainians and Rumanians to prepare for their crusade against bolshevism.

The armistice was simple to achieve, but the negotiations for the peace were liable to be extremely difficult. The problems of the revision of the Kreuznach agreement, of the Austro-Polish solution, and future relations with Austria-Hungary had yet to be settled in Berlin. The Germans were encouraged by the fact that the Rumanian negotiators, Carp and Marghiloman, favoured close cooperation with Germany as the best way of ensuring the territorial integrity of their country, and wished to replace King Ferdinand by a German prince. On the other hand the Hungarians wanted to annex vast tracts of the Carpathians, and the Austrians, frustrated by the Germans over Poland were thinking in terms of reviving the Austro-Rumanian solution. Thus at a crown council in Vienna on 22 January 1918 Kaiser Karl summed up the results of the debate as follows: 'For the time being, however unfortunate it might be, the Austro-Polish solution must be put in the background, and we must concentrate on the *Anschluss* of a debt free Rumania to the monarchy.'[6] To complicate matters still further the Kaiser had promised the Bulgarian minister president, Radoslavov, the entire Dobrudja in the course of an audience in December 1916.[7] The German foreign office was loath to renege on a solemn promise made by the Kaiser to an ally, but German financial interests had their eyes on the railway from Constanta to Cernavoda and on the port of Constanta, and the Turks demanded compensation which included the area around Adrianople, the Maritsa and all Turkish territory lost during the Balkan wars in return for Bulgarian control of the Dobrudja. The Bulgarians would not hear of these claims, and even threatened to leave the alliance if they were pressed.[8]

The German military on the spot, Field Marshal von Mackensen, Colonel Hentsch and the head of his political department, Horstmann, agreed that Carp would not be able to overthrow the Rumanian monarchy unless he was given a guarantee of the territorial integrity of Rumania, and particularly an assurance that the northern Dobrudja would not go to Bulgaria. Their motive was to ensure that Germany would control all of Rumania, but there were fears in Berlin that this would place too great a strain on the Bulgarian alliance, and fail to satisfy those powerful interests in Germany which wanted to control Constanta and the railway.

Mackensen believed that the price for German domination of Rumania would have to be the Austro-Polish solution, but the OHL still would not accept this argument. The fact that the Polish question seemed unlikely to be solved in the immediate future did not seem to the OHL to be any hindrance to Germany acting in what they called, with a familiar euphemism, 'military interests' in Rumania.[9] Ludendorff's thinking was at least straightforward. Rumania should be a 'viable' state, but all excess production beyond that which was needed to satisfy the immediate

needs of the people, should simply be shipped off to Germany.[10]
The OHL, which was now convinced of the inevitability of war with
Austria, wanted to strengthen Bulgaria as an ally against Austria,
and thus wished to give the Dobrudja to Bulgaria, provided that
Germany controlled Constanta and the railway. The Kaiser was most
upset at these suggestions, for he feared that the intransigence of the
OHL over the Austro-Polish solution would make it impossible for
Germany to achieve her aims in Rumania.

Owing to the negotiations at Brest Litovsk the Germans waited
until 28 January before they issued an ultimatum to Rumania to
begin the peace talks. On 4 and 5 February a Rumanian delegation
headed by General Lupescu began preliminary negotiations with
Mackensen's chief of general staff, Generalmajor Hell, and with
delegates from Austria-Hungary, Bulgaria and Turkey at
Focsani.[11] At the same time Kaiser Karl, with Czernin's approval,
sent Colonel Randa on a secret mission to Jassy. Randa's mission
was to assure the King of Rumania that the Central Powers would
sign an 'honourable peace', and to assure the Rumanians of help
against bolshevism. The Rumanian minister president, Bratianu,
was uncertain whether to accept this rather dubious offer of
help, the main object of which was to frustrate German designs
on Rumania, and on 8 February he resigned. His place was taken
by General Averescu, an arch-conservative who feared bolshevism
more than the Central Powers, and who was a close friend of
Mackensen. Negotiations soon began, but the Austrians stayed in
Jassy, the Germans in Focsani.[12]

On 4 February Ludendorff was invited to address the council
of state in Berlin on the Polish question, for discussions were due
to begin the following day with Czernin to establish guidelines
for the peace talks with Rumania.[13] The arguments he used were
familiar but they were presented with new emphasis. He argued
that the Austro-Polish solution would almost certainly lead to
war between Germany and Austria, for the irredentist Poles would
look to Vienna for support. A militarily defensible frontier with
Poland was therefore essential, even though the OHL was
prepared to make a few minor concessions to the diplomatists. For
Ludendorff the main problem with the proposed frontier
rectifications was that the number of Poles living in Germany would
be increased, and this was highly undesirable. The OHL suggested
that one sixth of the frontier strip should be used as a military
exercise area, and all the Poles there would therefore have to be

removed. In the remainder of the frontier strip, all the Jews, who were mostly of Russian origin, were either to be removed *(verpflanzt)*, or forced to emigrate to America. Poles who owned land in the area would be forced to exchange it for land held by Germans in Poland. Polish state lands would be confiscated. Some landless labourers would be allowed to remain to work for the Germans – dangerous, but necessary elements. Put in plain terms the OHL was proposing the forced removal of something like two million people and the confiscation of their property. This was the beginning of a new and barbarous era in the history of imperialism when millions of people would be displaced, uprooted and massacred in the name of national interest and security. The enormity of the OHL's proposal did not seem immediately apparent to the ministers, and only the minister of the interior timidly suggested that it might cause an unfavourable reaction in Poland! Once again the OHL had triumphed. Not a voice had been raised against the basic conception of the OHL that parts of the richest industrial and agricultural areas of Poland should be annexed in the name of military necessity. The only discussion had been about the extent to which this should be carried out. The suggestion that the Poles and the Jews should be removed was hardly even discussed. 'Military necessity' had triumphed not only over political wisdom, but also over common humanity.[14]

On the morning of the following day further discussions were held with Czernin at the chancellery in Berlin.[15] After the preliminary discussion of Brest Litovsk, where there was general agreement, Czernin introduced the Polish question by bluntly stating that if the OHL insisted on their demands in the east the Austro-Polish solution would be impossible. As Gratz pointed out, if the Germans controlled the Polish railways, seized the Dombrowa and the crown lands, and had considerable control over the Polish economy, all Austria would get out of Poland would be the doubtful privilege of paying for the deficit in the budget. The Germans were not prepared to back down, and Czernin said that there was little point in further discussion. Since the Austro-Polish solution was unacceptable to the Austrians without far-reaching changes in the German plan, and since, in Czernin's words, Germany wanted to leave Rumania like a 'squeezed lemon', there was little point in thinking of *Mitteleuropa*. Kühlmann could do little to salvage his *Mitteleuropa* scheme, and was further harassed by Ludendorff who was convinced that he had agreed to the Randa mission, and was trying to frustrate the OHL's plans to remove the king of Rumania.[16]

There was thus no agreement between Germany and Austria on the future of either Poland or Rumania when, on 17 February, the carefully orchestrated cry for help against the bolsheviks came from the Ukranian puppet government. In a brief moment of panic the OHL thought of using Rumanian troops in the Ukraine, and suggested that the Rumanians should be given Bessarabia as compensation for this effort. General Mackensen met his old friend Averescu for the first time on 18 February, and acting on orders from the OHL, made this suggestion to him, adding that Rumania could rely on German support against the Austrians and their designs on the Rumanian-Hungarian frontier.[17] Averescu was most suspicious of these proposals, and wanted confirmation from the Austrian and German foreign offices. This understandable caution turned out to be most convenient to the OHL. The thrust of German troops into the Ukraine had been remarkably swift. Kiev was held, and thus there was no immediate danger from the bolsheviks to the Rada government. No longer in need of Rumanian help in the Ukraine against the bolsheviks, and now in a position to attack Rumania from the rear with the troops in the Ukraine, the OHL could demand the immediate commencement of the peace negotiations. On 24 February Averescu met Kühlmann and Czernin in Buftea, but he refused to even consider the cession of the Dobrudja to Bulgaria. Czernin then met the King of Bulgaria at Racaciuni in occupied Moldavia on 27 February in the hope of continuing negotiations. The discussion lasted a mere twenty minutes. The King insisted that Rumania could not continue to exist without the Dobrudja, and that Bessarabia was 'poisoned with bolshevism'. The meeting ended with Czernin painting an impressive picture of the military superiority of the Central Powers, and issuing a forty-eight hour ultimatum.

The situation was now critical. Kaiser Karl refused to allow Austrian troops to fight in Rumania if the ultimatum were not accepted. The Bulgarians would not fight unless they were given guarantees for further expansion at the expense of Rumania. Turkish support for a further campaign in Rumania was uncertain. German troops were already badly over-extended in the east after the campaign in the Ukraine. Kühlmann understood the situation clearly, but could see no acceptable solution. To Hertling he wrote:

> They [the Austrians] are afraid of falling between two stools:
> economically to get a really bad deal in Rumania and getting
> very little, or nothing, in Poland. The influence of an
> irresponsible policy has already had a disastrous effect on our
> relations with Austria. As this policy is irresponsible it has
> no need to worry about positive solutions, but is content to
> reject individual solutions which are needed for an overall
> policy.[18]

On 1 March a Rumanian note agreed in general terms to the
conditions of the Central Powers, but it was couched in such vague
terms that Czernin did not find it acceptable. The Rumanians
were given a further twenty-four hours to reconsider the note.
Ludendorff managed to obtain a promise from Kaiser Karl that the
Austrian army would fight if the Rumanians did not accept the
preliminary conditions. Averescu was then told that military
operations would resume on 5 March if the reply was not
satisfactory.[19] On the same afternoon Averescu accepted the
preliminary conditions, of which the principal was the loss of
the Dobrudja to Bulgaria, and agreed to begin negotiations for a
peace settlement. The Germans and Austrians, however, used the
dubious excuse that the Rumanian reply had come a few hours late
to increase their demands. The Rumanians were now told that
unless they accepted the loss of the entire Dobrudja as far as the
Danube and Hungarian demands for frontier rectifications in the
Carpathians, agreed to 'appropriate economic measures', moved
their forces to the east against the Soviets in Bessarabia, and
allowed troops from the Central Powers to march through
Rumania to attack the Ukraine and the Crimea, fighting would be
resumed on 5 March. Averescu argued that these terms had to be
accepted if Rumania was to retain Bessarabia, and on 5 March the
Rumanians signed the preliminaries for the peace treaty.[20]

Three days later Averescu resigned, and his place was taken by
the pro-German Marghiloman, the arch-conservative opponent of
Bratianu and friend of Czernin. The change resulted in the
formation of the most curious alliances in the struggles over
Rumania. Kühlmann was to support Marghiloman and his new
government against the onslaughts of the OHL. The OHL, and their
amenuensis in Rumania, General Hell, wanted the German military
government to remain in Rumania for a considerable time after the
peace was finally signed. Kühlmann agreed with Marghiloman that his

government could only combat liberalism and democracy at home if it was given a free hand.[21] The OHL also wanted massive compensation from Bulgaria in return for German support for their claim to the Dobrudja. This included the port of Constanta and the railway, a military convention which would give the Germans effective control over the Bulgarian army, the payment of the Bulgarian war debt by German loans that would mean German control of the Bulgarian capital market, and far-reaching economic control of the entire Dobrudja 'for the time being'.[22]

Kühlmann's main problem as a negotiator was not the intransigence of the Rumanians, but rather the attacks from the OHL and differences with Germany's allies. Whereas Hindenburg and Ludendorff were eager to resume fighting in Rumania in order to get the whole affair settled as quickly as possible to their satisfaction, Kühlmann, who claimed to be supported by Mackensen and Hell, felt that this would result in the overthrow of the Marghiloman government which was proving most cooperative.[23]

For the OHL this was merely an excuse for inaction. Ludendorff complained that the negotiations were being allowed to drag on far too long, and far too much consideration was being shown to Austria-Hungary and Bulgaria. To the foreign office he complained: 'Above all, the economic advantages which we have gained in Rumania as compensation for the great sacrifices we have given and which take the place of annexations and indemnities have been much reduced and shared by our allies, to such an extent that, compared to Austria-Hungary and Bulgaria, Germany has certainly not got her due.' These general criticisms were followed by a flood of specific complaints often about the minutist details of the negotiations, all at a time when the OHL was supposed to be fully engaged in the offensive on the western front.[24]

During the negotiations a chorus of complaint came from the OHL and the industrialists who had investments in Rumania. As one report said: 'The Deutsche Bank roars, Stinnes fumes, Ballin yelps, and they are all men whose voices are heard.'[25] These complaints make extraordinary reading when they are compared to the articles of the treaty of Bucharest, which reduced Rumania to the position of a vassal state of Germany, with its sovereignty a mere shadow. Of the fifteen Rumanian divisions five were to be demobilised and the remaining ten to be sent to Moldavia and Bessarabia to fight against the Soviets. The question of the Dobrudja remained unsolved. Bulgaria regained that part of the Dobrudja which she had lost in 1913, but the Northern Dobrudja was placed under a condominium of the four powers, and administered by the high commands. Field Marshal Mackensen was given final power of decision should any differences arise between the four powers. The solution was disappointing to the Bulgarians who had hoped to get all of the Dobrudja, and also to Ludendorff, who wanted the Northern Dobrudja under exclusive German control.[26] The OHL was also unable to secure Constanta as a German port. Under the terms of the treaty it was to become a free port, but with the degree of German economic domination in Rumania the distinction was largely academic. Rumania was at least guaranteed free passage to the Black Sea.

The financial obligations of Rumania towards Germany were exceptionally onerous. Rumania had to pay the full cost of the occupation forces, and compensation for the cost of maintaining Rumanian prisoners of war. Rumania was also obliged to cover the value of the money which had been issued by the Banca Generala Romina during the occupation either in lei or in any legal tender. This operation would then release over one million marks worth of kronen and marks which had been deposited in Berlin to provide the initial cover for the 'new' or 'German' lei in the occupied parts of Rumania. Kühlmann reckoned that the profit to Germany from this dubious operation would be between 2.5 and 2.75 billion marks.[27]

In spite of the objections of Czernin and Kühlmann, the OHL was able to ensure the continued occupation of Rumania until 'a date to be determined later'. A German civil servant was appointed to supervise each Rumanian ministry and was given absolute right of veto and the right to dismiss any Rumanian civil servant he wished. The telegraph, railways and posts were controlled by the occupation forces. The Central Powers also had the right to requisition agricultural products, wood and oil.

Under the petroleum agreement all the oilfields that were under state control were placed under the 'oil-field lease company' *(Oelländereien Pachtgesellschaft)* for thirty years. This company had been formed in 1916 by the Deutsche Bank, the Discontogesellschaft, the Darmstädter Bank and the Dresdner Bank. It proved to be a most effective lobby, and enjoyed the full support of the OHL. Not only did Germany thus control all the state owned oilfields, and all oilfields owned by enemy interests such as Standard Oil, but the entire oil industry in Rumania was to come under an Austro-German monopoly which fixed prices, decided the amount of oil to be used for domestic purposes in Rumania, and controlled all sales and purchases of crude oil. With the dominant position of the big German banks, the four 'D's', German finance capital effectively controlled Rumanian oil.

The trade agreement specified that all 'surplus' agricultural production should be delivered to the Central Powers. This was to remain an optional right until 1926, but was to be enforced until 1918 whatever happened. 'Surplus' was determined by the relationship between domestic consumption and export from 1908 to 1913. A commission was to be established to determine prices, and the Central Powers could ban the export of any commodity they wished to specify.

Yet even these terms were not harsh enough for the OHL. Ludendorff had tried to torpedo the negotiations by ordering Hell not to sign the treaty unless Germany was given full control over the shipyards at Giurgiu. Kühlmann managed to persuade Hell that as all the delegates were assembled in full ceremonial uniform for the official signing of the treaty it was hardly the time to quarrel about what he described as an insignificant workshop.[28] Ludendorff then announced that he would only agree to the petroleum clauses of the treaty if the Austro-Polish solution were abandoned.[29] At the Spa conference on 11 May he announced that as Germany had not been given the position in Rumania which she had been promised in October he could no longer support the Austro-Polish solution.[30] That Austria-Hungary should get one quarter of Rumanian oil exports was too much for the OHL, even though the remainder went to Germany.

The treaty of Bucharest was ratified by the Reichstag in June 1918. Some dissatisfaction with the treaty was voiced by the right, particularly by the conservative leader Westarp. From the left, silence, but for Ledebour speaking for the independent socialists who condemned the treaty as undemocratic, expansionist and reactionary. The SPD voted for the ratification, thus taking yet another step away from their socialist principles.[31]

There were two men who really understood the treaty of Bucharest. Field Marshal Mackensen expressed his satisfaction in typical terms for a Prussian officer: 'This time the pen has secured what the sword has won.' Kühlmann confided in a Saxon diplomat that he 'would rather be attacked for apparently granting too favourable conditions for peace, than let the public know the real nature of the agreements'.[32] Such cunning was not enough either to placate the OHL, or to save Kühlmann.

The attacks which the OHL had launched against the secretary of state during the negotiations at Brest Litovsk were further intensified during the discussions at Bucharest. Hindenburg and Ludendorff were now prepared to go to any lengths to discredit their rival. Major von Kessler, Ludendorff's personal representative at Bucharest, was instructed to collect as much material as possible which could be used against Kühlmann, and he eagerly sent reports back to the OHL. Kessler had a network of officers acting as his agents, men whose imaginations were as vivid as their dislike of Kühlmann was intense.[33] On the basis of such reports Hindenburg reported to the Kaiser, in tones of the deepest distaste and approbation that Kühlmann spent his time at Brest Litovsk playing 'an American game of chance by the name of poker'. Kühlmann was obliged to explain patiently that as Germany's 'eastern allies' spoke little German and liked to play cards after dinner, he sometimes joined them in a hand of poker. Kühlmann told the Kaiser that he personally hated card games, was a poor player, and had thus lost considerable sums of money, but he had sacrificed himself in the interests of the Reich.[34] Further shocked reports came from Bucharest that Kühlmann was spending all his time shooting duck with Czernin and deliberately prolonging the negotiations because he did not believe that the Rumanians would fight.[35] A photograph was circulated among German officers at Bucharest purporting to show Kühlmann gaily waving a champagne glass and in the company of a notorious Bucharest whore. Investigations later showed that the man in the photograph was a young secretary from the German delegation.[36]

Kühlmann certainly enjoyed the good things of life. He was a man of considerable culture who spent most of his leisure time at Bucharest not at brothels and shooting lodges, as the OHL insisted, but examining the art collections in the museums and palaces of the city. His only major vice was to consume inordinate quantities of caviar which had to be confiscated by the German army on the Black Sea coast.[37] He took little notice of the constant attacks from the informants until the *Deutsche Zeitung* published an article based on information given by the OHL accusing the state secretary of taking part in bacchanalian orgies. Kühlmann sued for libel, and although the case was adjourned and later fell under a general amnesty, he had the satisfaction of finding out that the source

of these particular rumours had been his driver at Bucharest who had
been placed at his disposal by the OHL.[38] Hertling was disgusted with
these attacks, but with his distinguished aristocratic manners and the
political naievety of an old style professor of philosophy, he was
unable to imagine that Hindenburg and Ludendorff were the men
behind these attacks.[39]

Kühlmann's position after Bucharest was perilous indeed. His
Mitteleuropa policy was in ruins as the alliance with Austria became
increasingly strained, and as the Austro-Polish solution clearly had
little chance of success. He also knew that even a modest success
on the western front would trigger off a new set of annexationist
demands, for now more than ever the cry was 'world power or
collapse' *(Weltmacht oder Untergang)* and the ultras abandoned all
restraint.

At the beginning of May 1918, Colonel Haeften, the
representative of the OHL at the foreign office suddenly suggested
to Kühlmann that he should meet Ludendorff and discuss the
possibility of ending the war. Kühlmann replied that as long as the
OHL refused to change its policy towards Belgium there could be
no fruitful discussions between them, and rather testily added that
if Ludendorff had any political demands to make he should
address them to the foreign office. A few days later Haeften
discussed the overall situation with Ludendorff who insisted that if
he could not get an additional 200,000 men there was no
possibility of winning the war militarily. Ludendorff added that the
chancellor and the war minister had both made it plain that the
reserves could not be found. Haeften therefore returned to Berlin
convinced that diplomatic and political action was needed
immediately to relieve the desperate military situation. He therefore
began work on his 'peace offensive'.[40] His memorandum was
finished on 3 June.[41]

Haeften's document is further evidence of the astonishing lack
of political realism among the German ruling class in the summer
of 1918. He believed that a peace move could be used as a weapon
of psychological warfare to undermine the fighting ability of the
Entente, and make up for the 200,000 missing men on the western
front. Peace rallies were to be held throughout Germany which would
inspire pacifists in the enemy countries to do likewise. Germany
would be shown as the guarantor of 'basic human rights' and of
'moral and economic values' against the menacing threat of
bolshevism. According to Haeften 'order and freedom' were guaranteed

by the treaty of Brest Litovsk, and it would be a simple matter to
counter the Entente's claims that it was an annexationist peace.
Another weapon in Haeften's arsenal was Bismarck's social
legislation and insurance schemes which should now become a
German war aim that would win Germany the 'sympathy of the
working classes of the entire world' and could well lead to strikes
and revolutionary outbreaks, particularly in England. Haeften
hoped that his campaign would be unleashed during a pause in the
German offensive, and if the timing was right the Entente would
be forced to see the futility of continuing the war. The basic
argument was that military successes, such as Chemin des Dames,
were alone not enough, but if they were coupled with a 'political
victory behind the enemy lines' they could well result in a
'statesmanlike peace'.

Haeften showed his paper to Ludendorff with considerable
trepidation, for the OHL was in a mood of ecstasy after the
successful attack on Chemin des Dames. Much to his surprise and
delight Ludendorff agreed with the argument and ordered the
memorandum to be sent immediately to the chancellor. In his
covering letter Ludendorff said that as the Compiègne offensive
had yet to be launched the time was suitable for the type of political
offensive which Haeften suggested.[42]

Back in Berlin Haeften discussed his scheme with Hertling,
Kühlmann, Payer and Radowitz. In order to give a sense of urgency
to his plan, he stressed the critical military situation which made it
imperative to take immediate steps to end the war. For Hertling
and Kühlmann the main problem was the OHL's attitude to
Belgium, but Haeften replied that he was convinced that Ludendorff
would be conciliatory on the Belgian issue if the government were
vigorous with the peace offensive. There was then general agreement
that the Haeften plan should go ahead, and Kühlmann suggested that
Haeften himself, assisted by an experienced diplomat, should
organise the peace offensive. Haeften agreed to accept, provided that
the OHL granted him permission to take on this duty.[43]

Such unanimous approval of Haeften's ill-conceived and unrealistic
proposal is extraordinary, and there were few criticisms. The
chancellor's press chief, Deutelmoser, was almost alone in writing a
detailed and perceptive criticism. Deutelmoser pointed out that
the OHL could well have come to the same conclusion a year ago
and 'they might have presented the power idea a little less crudely
on some other occasions in matters of foreign policy'. For

Deutelmoser political unity at home was the essential precondition for any such peace initiative, and this would not be achieved unless the OHL gave its full support to the programme of electoral reform in Prussia, and become fully involved with the peace initiative.[44]

The OHL also believed in political unity, but to them this meant the removal of Kühlmann, and also Hertling whom they felt to be too old, tired and sick to be effective.[45] The politicians imagined that the cry for help from the military promised the restoration of the authority of the civilian government in matters of foreign policy and the beginning of more harmonious relations with the OHL. This was a misunderstanding which was to have fatal consequences, and could possibly have been avoided had there been adequate consultation between the OHL and the civilians over the peace initiative instead of leaving everything to Haeften.

Meanwhile on 1 June Hertling received a letter from Crown Prince Rupprecht of Bavaria in which he argued that Germany could not defeat the Entente. At best there could be a few limited successes, so the unpleasant consequences would have to be accepted and peace negotiations begun at once. Once the new offensive had been launched there would be nothing with which to threaten the Entente. According to Rupprecht, even Ludendorff no longer believed in military victory, and was hoping for some *deus ex machina* in the form of the internal collapse of the western powers. Rupprecht believed that this was mere wishful thinking, for the Entente was not as rotten *(morsch)* as Russia. A peace on the basis of the *status quo* in the west could still be a victorious peace if the gains in the east were secured. Hertling, however, did not share this pessimistic but realistic appraisal, and refused to grant Rupprecht an interview.[46]

Hertling was due to speak in the Reichstag on 24 June on foreign policy, but two days beforehand he asked Kühlmann to take his place, claiming that he was too exhausted to make the speech himself. Kühlmann's speech was hardly remarkable. He insisted on Germany's right to hegemony in the east, and carefully concealed her aims in the west. It seemed to be firm enough to satisfy the right, but if offered the possibility that the negotiations with the British government on the exchange of prisoners currently taking place in The Hague could lead to peace talks between the two countries. But Kühlmann made a serious miscalculation. His speech contained a phrase, clearly based on his interpretation of the Haeften memorandum, which was to prove his downfall.

> As long as every attempt to open discussions is immediately
> and roundly condemned by the opponents of any discussion in
> the various countries, it is impossible to see how any exchange
> of ideas can begin that might lead to peace. With the incredible
> magnitude of this coalition war and the number of powers,
> including overseas powers, that are engaged in it, without such
> exchanges a purely military decision without diplomatic
> negotiations can hardly be expected to bring about an absolute
> end.

The cries of approval from the left to this remark marked the end
of Kühlmann's political career.

Horrified at this remark Graf Westarp promptly telephoned the
OHL from the Reichstag building.[47] He then returned to the
chamber to deliver a blistering attack on the state secretary for failing
to see that the war was a question of 'to be or not to be' between
two fundamentally different ideologies. Here Westarp was echoing
the Kaiser's words in his thirtieth jubilee speech when he said:
'Either the Prussian-German Germanic *Weltanschauung* – Justice,
Freedom, Honour, and Morals be respected, or the Anglo-Saxon
Weltanschauung will triumph, and that means sinking into the
worship of Mammon. In this struggle one *Weltanschauung* is bound
to be destroyed.'[48] Westarp insisted that the Flanders coast and
Belgium would have to remain in the German sphere of
influence. Accusing Kühlmann of defeatism he argued that
negotiations could only be brought about by military victory,
and without such a victory there could be no peace.[49] This
speech was greeted with the rapturous applause of the right wing
parties. Stresemann said that there had never been less reason to
doubt a German victory, and added that Kühlmann's speech was
'shattering', a phrase which was eagerly pounced upon by the
OHL.[50]

Hindenburg promptly sent two telegrams to Hertling in which he
demanded to know whether the idea that the war could not be
won by military means alone was merely Kühlmann's personal
view, or whether it was shared by the chancellor. He also spoke
of the 'shattering effect' of the speech on the troops, and
demanded that Haeften's peace offensive be dropped as it had been
ruined by Kühlmann's blundering.[51] Hertling replied by loyally

supporting Kühlmann and denying Hindenburg's charges.[52]

At a press conference on the morning of 25 June Major Würz, speaking for the OHL, said that Kühlmann's view that a military victory was not possible in no way corresponded with the view of Hindenburg and Ludendorff. That day's edition of *Vorwärts* was banned in the army because of the headline: 'No End to the War by a Military Decision.'[53] That the OHL had the right to censor the speeches of the state secretary was an alarming innovation, but that the government did so little to protest was even more remarkable.

With this massive onslaught on Kühlmann, Hertling gradually began to disassociate himself from the state secretary. Kühlmann's second speech to the Reichstag was a feeble effort. He almost apologised to Westarp rather than going over to the attack, so that it seemed to Scheidemann that he had given way to pressure from the 'gentlemen at supreme headquarters'. As Helfferich remarked, after these two speeches Kühlmann was finished, and what followed was 'a struggle over his political corpse'.[54]

On 1 July Hertling arrived at headquarters in Spa, and he discussed the Kühlmann affair the same day with Hindenburg and Ludendorff. Hindenburg suggested that Kühlmann was involved in a sinister liberal plot which involved the *Frankfurter Zeitung*, the *Berliner Tageblatt* and the Reichstag majority. Hertling excused Kühlmann's performance in the Reichstag by saying that he had not had time to eat a proper breakfast. His attempts to criticise the OHL for the press conference on 25 June were countered by Hindenburg's categorical statement that he could no longer work with the state secretary.[55]

The conference on war aims, which began the following day, and which lasted for two days, was a clear indication that Kühlmann's dismissal was now only a matter of time. He was not even invited to attend the conference at which a large number of civilian and military leaders were present. The consensus of the meeting, particularly with regard to the Flanders coast and Belgium, was annexationist, and there was general agreement that military victory was within their grasp. The protocol of the Spa conference makes astonishing reading with the vivid contrast between the extent of German demands and the actual military situation. All the warnings that the chancellor had received from the more far-sighted army leaders were forgotten, the Haeften memorandum thrown aside, and Kühlmann's attempt to combine

expansionist ambitions with some sense of political realism was
scorned. Yet these sentiments were not confined to the extremists
in the OHL. They were shared by the Kaiser, the majority of the
civilian leaders, many politicians, and probably the majority of the
German people. It was as if the nation was trying to repress the
growing realisation that the war could not be won in one final
burst of imperialist fantasy. Yet within a few weeks even
Ludendorff was to realise in a moment of panic that the war was
lost.[56]

After the conference Hindenburg and Ludendorff left for their
operational headquarters at Avesnes. Kühlmann arrived in Spa on
6 July. Hertling was old, weary and in poor health, and was not
prepared to fight any longer. On 8 July the Kaiser met Kühlmann in
the park, and bluntly told him that their ways would have to part.
Kühlmann, unable to persuade the Kaiser to let him stay in office
a little longer so as to see the outcome of the meeting in The
Hague, parted from his sovereign with the archaic and somewhat
flamboyant gesture of kissing his hand. So ended the career of this
sauve aristocrat whose very real abilities as a diplomatist were so
greatly underestimated by his peers. Unable to share the more
wild fantasies of the OHL and the Pan Germans he earned their
implacable and unwaranted hatred.[57]

Kühlmann was succeeded by Admiral von Hintze, a particular
favourite of the Kaiser. He accepted the job with some reluctance
largely because as a naval officer he felt that he would be regarded
as an outsider by the foreign office, but in the end he gave way
to Berg's cajoling and the accusation that it would be
unpatriotic if he did not accept.[57] The OHL had long thought of
Hintze as a suitable state secretary. In May 1917 the anti-semitic
extremist, Dr Fleischer, a confidant of Bauer's, suggested that
Hintze would 'realise in a determined fashion the political ambitions
of the OHL'.[58] On 30 June 1918 Ludendorff told Haeften that he
was determined that Hintze should be Kühlmann's successor.
Haeften at once objected, saying that Hintze was unreliable and 'an
extremely dangerous and ambitious opportunist who always
puts his personal interests above those of the fatherland'.
Ludendorff ignored these objections and argued that he was a
'national man' and was suitably close to the Pan Germans.[59]
Heye, the head of the operations division at the OHL also relates
how Ludendorff and the other officers had full confidence in
Hintze as 'a fine German, a good diplomat and soldier'.[60]

Hintze was smooth and blasé, highly ambitious and something of a trimmer. In many ways he resembled Kühlmann, but he lacked his predecessor's experience and cunning. But his deviousness was, in one important way, an asset. He was able to continue Kühlmann's policies and still remain on good terms with the OHL. He was appointed to be the political architect of the 'victory peace' which would realise the expansionist dreams of the Spa conference at the beginning of July. The mood on the eve of the German offensive at Rheims was optimistic, so much so that on 14 July William turned down Wilson's request for German conditions for peace. On the following day the offensive began. Admiral Müller noted in his diary that the Kaiser was 'slightly less ebullient than usual. I have the impression that the day's objectives have not been reached.'[61] From then on the military position of the Central Powers was to get steadily worse, and Hintze far from presiding over the victory of German arms, was to witness total defeat.

NOTES

1. Conze, *Polnische Nation und deutsche Politik,* p. 326.
2. Scherer Grunewald, *L'Allemagne et les problemes de la paix,* Vol. 2, p. 533.
3. Hutten-Czapski, *60 Jahre Politik und Gesellschaft,* Band 2, p. 434.
4. Ritter, *Staatskunst und Kriegshandwerk,* p. 199.
5. PA Bonn AA Weltkrieg 15 Geheim, Band 5.
6. *Deutschland im ersten Weltkrieg,* Vol. 3, p. 205.
7. *Ibid.,* p. 206. Kühlmann reports that the Kaiser had said to Radoslavov in December 1916: 'The Dobrudja is guaranteed to you by treaty. You have everything that you want.' This assurance by the Kaiser was to prove most embarrassing to the foreign office, the more so as it was constantly pressed by German finance capital for the railway from Constanta to Cernavoda. Kühlmann, *Erinnerungen,* p. 552.
8. *Deutschland im ersten Weltkrieg,* Vol. 3, p. 206.
9. PA Bonn AA Weltkrieg 2 Geheim, Band 55.
10. PA Bonn AA Weltkrieg 23 Geheim, Band 14.
11. Margot Hegemann, 'Der deutsch-rumänische Friedensvertrag in Mai 1918 – ein Vorstoss der imperialistischen Reaktion gegen die junge Sowjetmacht', *Zeitschrift für Geschichtswissenschaft,* Heft 5, 1957, p. 990.
12. Czernin, *Im Weltkriege,* p. 356. *Deutschland im ersten Weltkrieg,* Band 3, p. 207. The Randa mission was no secret to the Germans, see *Deutsch-Sowjetische Beziehungen,* p. 357.
13. PA Bonn AA Weltkrieg 20c Geheim, Band 22; Bundesarchiv Koblenz, Nachlass Heinrichs, Band 24; DZA Hist. Abt. Merseburg, Preussisches Staatsministerium Rep 90a Abt. B III 2b Nr 6, Band 167 with the OHL's suggestions of making the frontier with Poland into a gigantic military exercise area.
14. For further details on the frontier strip see Imanuel Geiss, *Der polnische Grenzstreifen 1914 bis 1918. Ein Beitrag zur deutschen Kriegszielpolitik*

im Ersten Weltkrieg, Lübeck-Hamburg, 1960, p. 128. Ritter, *Staatskunst und Kriegshandwerk*, Vol. 4, p. 206 says that the suggestions of the OHL for the removal of the Poles and Jews from the frontier strip were strongly opposed by the civilians and the foreign office in particular; but on p. 207 he writes that 'the settlement plans of the OHL . . . were hardly discussed'.

15. PA Bonn AA Kriegsziele Nr. 16a, Band 1.
16. Ludendorff, *Kriegserinnerungen*, p. 456.
17. Czernin, *Im Weltkriege*, p. 357.
18. DZA Potsdam Reichskanzlei Rumänien 2458/3.
19. Ritter, *Staatskunst und Kriegshandwerk*, Band IV, p. 225.
20. *Deutschland im ersten Weltkrieg*, Vol. 3, p. 210. Hegemann, 'Der deutsch-rumanische Friedensvertrag', *ZfG* Heft 5, 1957, p. 995 for details of the Buftea agreement of 5 March.
21. DZA Potsdam Reichskanzlei Rumänien 2458/3.
22. Fischer, *Griff nach der Weltmacht*, p. 694.
23. DZA Potsdam Reichskanzlei Rumanien 2458/3.
24. *Ibid.*
25. *Deutschland im ersten Weltkrieg*, Band 3, p. 210; Fischer, *Griff nach der Weltmacht*, p. 696.
26. DZA Potsdam Reichskanzlei Rumänien 2458/3. According to Hauptstaatsarchiv Stuttgart E 74 (1) Berliner Gesandschaft, Krieg 1914-18, Politische Berichte 168, Ludendorff told the chancellor 6-4-18 that Rumania should give up the Dobrudja to the Central Powers, and that it should go to Bulgaria only when German demands on Bulgaria had been fully met. The chancellor made a rather feeble protest against this drastic view.
27. *Deutschland im ersten Weltkrieg*, Band 3, p. 212.
28. Kühlmann, *Erinnerungen.*, p. 561.
29. PA Bond AA Rumänien Politisches Nr. 1, Band 9.
30. Fischer, *Griff nach der Weltmacht*, p. 698.
31. *Stenographische Berichte*, Band 313, p. 5542 and 5748.
32. *Deutschland im ersten Weltkrieg*, Band 3, p. 214.
33. Bayerisches Hauptstaatsarchiv Abteilung IV Kriegsarchiv M. Kr. 1832.
34. Kühlmann, *Erinnerungen*, p. 563.
35. DZA Potsdam Reichskanzlei Beschwerden über die Führung der Friedensverhandlungen in Bucharest 2458/4. According to Kühlmann *Erinnerungen*, p. 560 the Austrians had a luxury yacht ready to sail down the Danube to the delta for a day of duck shooting to celebrate the signing of the treaty.
36. Kühlmann, *Erinnerungen*, p. 564.
37. *Ibid.*, p. 560.
38. *Ibid.*, p. 564; *Deutsche Zeitung* 23-4-18.
39. DZA Hist Abt. Merseburg Preussisches Staatsministerium Rep 90a Abteilung B, III, 2b, Nr. 6, Band 167.
40. *Untersuchungsausschuss IV Reihe*, Band 2, p. 188.
41. Ludendorff, *Urkunden der OHL*, p. 478. DZA Potsdam Stellvertreter des Reichskanzlers, Presse, Band III.
42. *Untersuchungsausschuss IV Reihe*, Band 2, p. 196. Ludendorff to chancellor 8-6-18.
43. Payer, *Bethmann Hollweg bis Ebert*, p. 257.
44. *Untersuchungsausschuss IV Reihe*, Band 2, p. 199.
45. Helfferich, *Der Weltkrieg*, p. 626.
46. Hertling, *Ein Jahr in der Reichskanzlei*, p. 139; *Untersuchungsausschuss IV Reihe*, Band 2, p. 191.

47. Kühlmann, *Erinnerungen*, p. 575.
48. Fischer, *Griff nach der Weltmacht*, p. 838.
49. *Stenographische Berichte*, Band 313, p. 5635. Westarp, *Konservative Politik*, Band II, p. 608.
50. Marvin L. Edwards, *Stresemann and the Greater Germany*, p. 155 places little emphasis on this speech and manages to get the date wrong in the text.
51. DZA Potsdam Reichskanzlei Allgemeines 2398/11; DZA Hist. Abt. Merseburg Rep 89 H XXXVI Militaria II; Bundesarchiv Koblenz, Nachlass Hertling, Band 41.
52. DZA Potsdam Reichskanzlei Allgemeines 2398/11.
53. Matthias, Morsey, *Der Interfraktionelle Ausschuss*, p. 415, footnote 8.
54. *Stenographische Berichte,* Band 313, p. 5640; Matthias, Morsey, *Der Interfraktionelle Ausschuss*, p. 419, footnote 3; Helfferich, *Der Weltkrieg*, p. 631.
55. Ludendorff, *Urkunden der OHL*, p. 491; Bundesarchiv Koblenz, Nachlass Hertling, Band 41; *Untersuchungsausschuss IV Reihe*, Band 2, p. 203. The version in *Urkunden der OHL* is incomplete, and does not mention Hindenburg's remark that the the the OHL could not work with Kühlmann.
56. PA Bonn AA Gr. HQ Kriegsziele 16a, Band 1, Fischer, *Griff nach der Weltmacht*, p. 842 gives a characteristically trenchant analysis of the Spa conference.
57. Bundesarchiv Koblenz, Nachlass Berg. Aufzeichnungen. Baumgart, *Deutsche Ostpolitik* p. 89, footnote 91, has transcribed Berg's ghastly handwriting.
58. Bundesarchiv Koblenz, Nachlass Bauer, Band 13.
59. Bundesarchiv Militärarchiv Freiburg, Nachlass Haeften N35/4.
60. *Ibid.,* Nachlass Heye N18/5. Lebenserinnerungen.
61. Müller diary 15-7-18.

9 THE BALTIC AND FINLAND

The Baltic states and their future played an important part in the negotiations at Brest Litovsk and Bucharest and in discussions with the Austrians on the question of war aims. Lithuania and Courland, unlike Poland and Belgium, were directly under the command of the *Oberkommando Ost* and did not have civilian governors. Hindenburg and Ludendorff had tried to get Poland placed under military government, but Falkenhayn had refused. Ludendorff vented his anger at this decision in a letter to Zimmermann: 'Since they have taken Poland from me, I must find another kingdom for myself in Lithuania and Courland.'[1]   From the very outset of the war Hindenburg and Ludendorff, supported by a wide cross-section of German opinion and inspired by romantic visions of regaining the lands of the Teutonic knights, combined with a more prosaic land hunger, regarded Lithuania and Courland as being already annexed to Germany, and began to work out the details of colonisation plans, regardless of the effect that this policy might have on the chances of a separate peace with Russia.[2]

Thus Hindenburg and Ludendorff's close associate at *Oberost*, Freiherr von Gayl, suggested that all the Russians, Latvians and Jews who had been driven out of the area should not be allowed to return, and that 50,000 new farms should be settled with immigrants from the Reich.[3] When Hindenburg and Ludendorff were appointed to the OHL these ideas became the basis of their policy and grandiose schemes which contained a sinister racialist component were developed to move whole populations so that the Western Slavs could be separated from the Eastern Slavs, and Poland surrounded by German colonies. The Baltic states were thus to form part of a new German frontier from the Baltic to the Ukraine which would place Poland in a German stranglehold.[4]

At the war aims conference in Kreuznach on 23 April 1917 the OHL was enabled to continue its military operations in the Baltic so that by September Riga was captured, by the middle of October the islands of Oesel, Dagö and Moon were in German hands, and in February 1918 Livonia and Estonia were also occupied. The Baltic states were to be given 'autonomy' but, in accordance with Bethmann Hollweg's 'window dressing instructions' *(Frisieranweisungen)* of 7 May 1917 they would be under the economic, military and political control of Germany.[5] This policy could then be presented to the Austrians as the renunciation of any annexationist claims to the Baltic so that they could be convinced to make a similar sacrifice of parts of Galicia in the interests of a separate peace with Russia. Ludendorff made this quite clear in a note to the foreign office in which he stated that the OHL had renounced annexations in Lithuania and Courland, but would never renounce Lithuania and Courland 'as such'.[6]

On 31 July 1917 a conference was held at Bingen to discuss the future of the Baltic states. On the eve of the conference Ludendorff suggested that Germany should declare her intention of striving for the personal union of Prussia and the Baltic states, and further that there should be a call for the help and protection of the Reich.[7] At the conference the representative of the foreign office expressed his full approval of the scheme. As he so delightfully put it, 'It is not a question of annexing countries, but of satisfying the wishes of the population of Courland and Lithuania which aims at *Anschluss* with Germany.' In order to make certain that the true wishes were in fact expressed it was agreed to set up a council *(Vertrauensrat)* in the province of Courland, making certain that it had a German majority. The council would then send a message to the Kaiser placing their destiny in the hands of His Majesty. It was somewhat more tricky to establish a council in Lithuania which would be submissive, but Fürst zu Isenburg, the administrative head of Lithuania, felt that it could be done by September and sovereignty *(Staatshoheit)* over Lithuania could then be vested in the King of Prussia.

The new chancellor, Michaelis, approved of the OHL's plans for the Baltic. The Bingen proposals could now be implemented. In Courland everything went according to plan. In Lithuania there were considerable difficulties from the very outset. It was difficult to find anyone who was prepared to cooperate with the army of occupation which was so heartily disliked by all patriotic Lithuanians. Only the threat of outright annexation forced them into a grudging cooperation. Persuasion and blackmail could not disguise the fact that in both Courland and Lithuania the Germans were hated, and democratic elections would have resulted in a crushing defeat for German policies. The army was blatantly using its power to maintain the dominant economic position of the Baltic Germans, who were now in ever increasing danger of being caught in a crossfire between the hatred of the indigenous population, and the threat to their economic domination posed by the bolsheviks. Ludendorff boasted of the efforts to build up the communications system and the economy in his 'kingdom', but to most Lithuanians and Courlanders it seemed as if he was merely creating the conditions for the more effective exploitation of the area.

With the complete failure of the OHL's Polish policy it was inevitable that Poland and Germany would be enemies. The OHL's policy towards Lithuania was therefore to extend her frontiers to the south so as to include parts of Poland. With Wilna as capital with its large Polish population Lithuania and Poland were likely to be in an almost permanent state of conflict, regardless of whether the Austro-Polish solution were adopted or not, and Lithuania could become an ally in a common struggle against the Poles. Hindenburg summed up this policy: 'With these dubious elements the principle of *"divide et impera"* is correct.'[8] In order to maintain the fiction of the self-determination of peoples, the two states were to be joined in personal union with Prussia, but the pretence of autonomy maintained by their treatment from the point of view of international law as foreign countries.

Conditions in the Baltic states were terrible. Starvation was rife. Workers and peasants were forced to work in conditions which amounted in everything but name to slave labour. Banditry was rife.[9] These conditions were used by the OHL as further evidence that the Baltic states were unable to stand on their own feet and would therefore have to be bound closer to Germany, and the local population forced into the Prussian army to give Germany sufficient military protection against Russia. There should thus be less emphasis on 'autonomy'; Hindenburg insisted that the Kaiser should become Duke of Lithuania.[10]

The extension of the bolshevik regime to Livonia and Estonia, the abolition of the large estates, the expropriation of the aristocracy, and the establishment of Soviets had resulted in the ruling class of the provinces seeking the protection of Germany against the threat posed to their position by the bolsheviks. Thus on 4 December 1917 the Knights' Council *(Ritterschaft)* of Livonia appealed to the OHL for armed intervention.[11] Hertling and Kühlmann were opposed to this idea largely because it would make future relations with Russia extremely delicate. Hindenburg argued that the provinces were essential for the defence of the Reich, and that Germany needed Riga. The Kaiser supported the OHL, saying that Russia did not need a port in the Baltic, and could equally well have a port in the Persian Gulf. The OHL were further convinced that the panic striken cries of the Baltic barons was adequate evidence of the will of the people.[12]

At a further conference at Bad Homburg on 13 February 1918 it was decided that formal 'cries for help' should be ordered from Estonia and Livonia. Kühlmann was somewhat dubious about the OHL's policy. He remarked: 'When the bolsheviks see that the barons have called the Germans there will be a great revenge on the barons.' But everyone knew that the barons were doomed in any case, unless they could get military support from the Reich.[13] The Bavarian military plenipotentiary reported to his government: 'The agreement on our policy in the east consists of getting the Estonians and Latvians (he should of course have said the Livonians) to ask for protection against the bolsheviks, and then going into these provinces and occupying them, which should not present any difficulties.'[14] This is an admirably terse summary of the OHL's policy. The army acted rapidly, and the provinces were occupied by 23 February.

It was far more difficult to control the situation in Lithuania. The intransigence of the Lithuanians and the difficulties over the negotiations at Brest Litovsk, however, merely encouraged the OHL and their crude approach. When the council of state met in Berlin on 4 February Ludendorff had demanded that Courland and Lithuania should be made fully dependent on Germany, and that the Baltic states should be seen as a deployment area for the 'punic war' which would finally settle the destiny of Germany.[15] On 16 February the Lithuanian *Taryba* (parliament) announced the repudiation of article 2 of their declaration of 11 December which called for binding treaties with Germany. The situation was particularly difficult because the negotiations at Brest Litovsk had just reached an *impasse,* and the OHL had begun military operations and had taken Dünaburg by the time news of the *Taryba's* defiance had reached them.

Once the treaty of Brest Litovsk was signed the foreign office wanted formal recognition of the independence of Lithuania, but the OHL wanted to put this off until there was a Lithuanian bishop of Wilna, until the debentures *(Pfandbriefe)* of the *Wilna Agrarbank* were bought up, and until the questions of the bank itself and of Polish landholdings in Lithuania had been settled.[16] By this time the OHL was determined to keep the Baltic states under the control of the army and to ward off attempts by the civilians, led by Keyserlingk, to establish a civilian administration that would be directly responsible to the Kaiser. Ludendorff objected vigorously to this scheme.[17] Keyserlingk only lasted for six weeks in the Baltic. His place was taken by the civilian Falkenhausen from *Oberost* who was more than willing to cooperate with the OHL.

The Lithuanians could now do nothing but accept the inevitable. The *Taryba* requested independence, and on 23 March 1918 Lithuania was recognised by the German government as an independent state. Lithuania remained under military control, and neither the government nor the military were willing to allow the Lithuanians any say in the government of their country. The words 'free and independent' in the declaration of independence were thus a bitter mockery.

On 25 March the Kaiser made a formal declaration of recognition of the independence of Courland which, with its powerful German element in the *Landesrat* could easily be controlled by the Germans. On 9 April Estonia's *Landesversammlung* declared its independence from Russia, and Livonia followed suit on the following day. On 12 April the 'United *Landesrat* of Livonia, Estonia, Riga and Oesel' met in Riga. This body had a large majority of Baltic Germans, and it was hardly surprising that on the first day of its deliberations it requested the German Emperor to place Livonia and Estonia under permanent military protection, and further asked that the Baltic provinces should be united by personal union with the Kingdom of Prussia.[18] Hertling was deeply moved by this touching display of the self-determination of peoples, but he was unable to go ahead with his schemes for personal union with some new thrones for Princes from Saxony, Württemberg, Bavaria and Baden to keep the federal states happy, because of likely hostile reaction from the Reichstag.[19] The future of Germany policy in Livonia and Estonia was further jeopardised by the running battle between the OHL and the government, or more precisely between Lundendorff and Keyserlingk. Keyerserlingk argued that the almost criminal lack of concern for the peoples of the Baltic shown by the army of occupation, and the inefficiency of its administration would make the government's policy of indirect annexation impossible. It is hardly surprising that Keyserlingk did not survive for long as the OHL maintained furious attacks on what they considered the unwarranted interference in purely military affairs by an ignorant and troublesome civilian.

At the big conference at Spa on 2 July the OHL insisted that Germany needed Reval as a naval base, that one third of the land of Livonia and Estonia should be seized for German settlements, that the frontier should be extended to the east of Lake Peipus and that Germany should control the railway from Riga to Dünaburg.

The civilians tried to frustrate these schemes, and Erzberger made a picturesque effort to break the deadlock by getting the *Taryba* to appoint the Duke of Urach, a relative of the King of Württemberg, as king of Lithuania, with the delightful name of Mindaugas II. This affair was typical of Erzberger's self-important meddling, and was carried out without any consultation with the German government who therefore promptly denounced the scheme.

As the battle between the civilians and the OHL over the Baltic states continued there was a growing realisation that all these plans for the future of the area had little chance of ever being realised. Prince Max of Baden tried to win over the Lithuanians to accept German designs by making some minor concessions along the lines of his flexible liberal imperialism, but by now it was too late. Even the German troops in the Baltic were becoming demoralised, the position of the bolsheviks stronger and the *Taryba's* position consequently more precarious. On 3 November the Kaiser formally ended the military administration of the Baltic, and five days later Prince Max terminated the *Reichskommissariat,* the office held by Keyserlingk and later Falkenhausen. On the following day revolution broke out in Berlin, but the dream of a German colony in the Baltic lived on.[20]

The cornerstone of German policy in the Baltic was Finland. The Germans had a favourable situation to exploit, for with the outbreak of the war in 1914 there was a growing desire among Finns for national independence. The problem was to find support for this movement abroad. The Swedes had no great love for the Finns, and were certainly not willing to sacrifice their neutrality from which they were making such considerable economic and political profits. Russian democrats showed little sympathy, and in any case had more pressing problems. Approaches were made to the Entente powers, but they were naturally unwilling to betray the interests of their Russian ally. It was therefore to Germany that the nationalists turned, ignoring the warnings of the Finnish democrats who feared that Finland might well become the victim of German imperialism.[21]

In the early stages of the war the Germans were anxious not to become too involved in Finland. A Finnish regiment was formed of some 2,000 volunteers in the *Königlich Preussische Jäger Bataillon 27* which was used on the Düna front. The Finnish nationalist, Wetterhoff,

formed the'Bureau Wetterhoff' in Berlin which acted as the political
centre of the movement for Finnish independence in these early years of
the war. It was not until the Russian February revolution-that the
situation began to change rapidly. Kerensky tried to appease the Finnish
activists by restoring Finland's autonomous rights, and by pardoning some
political prisoners, but the attempt was a failure. The Finnish nationalists
would be content with nothing but complete independence. The
Finnish *Landtag,* which had a moderate and badly divided socialist
majority, proclaimed that henceforth sovereignty was vested in the
Landtag. The right had serious misgivings about this step, for they
feared that an independent Finland might well be a socialist
Finland. The left were also under constant pressure from an increasingly
radical and bolshevik proletariat, and a wave of strikes showed that
the Finnish workers were not satisfied with the compromise of the
left in the *Landtag.* The situation became even more tense when
Kerensky refused to accept the *Landtag's* demands for complete
independence. In October 1917 elections were held which returned
a small bourgeois majority, a vote against the left as much as for any
positive alternative. Finland was now on the brink of civil war.
The right organised white guards; the left, inspired by the example
of the bolsheviks, formed red guards to protect themselves from the
whites and to back up their demands for far-reaching social reform.
The reformist social democrats in the *Landtag* and the union leaders
tried to find a middle path between the reds and the whites, but merely
earned the hatred of both sides. By January full-scale civil war had
broken out, the whites controlling the north and the reds Helsinki.[22]

In August 1917 the foreign office approached the OHL asking
for support for their scheme of using the Finnish desire for
independence to further German ambitions in the Baltic. Ludendorff
promptly replied that he was in favour of training the Finns in the
techniques of guerilla warfare.[23] Discussions also took place in
August between the representative of the political section of the
general staff and a leading nationalist figure, Edward Hjelt, the vice-
chancellor of the university, and it was agreed that the Germans
would send arms to the nationalists.[24] It was not until November,
after the bolshevik revolution, that the OHL developed its plans
for the future of Finland. Ludendorff told Kühlmann: 'I do not
ask for an open declaration from Finland right now. But we must
do everything to prepare the ground so that the desire for an
Anschluss with Germany will really be expressed when the time
comes.'[25] Hjelt met Ludendorff in Kreuznach on 26 November, and

said that he hoped that Finland would be closely associated with Germany and form 'the northern part of a chain of states which will build a European wall against the east'.[26] Ludendorff, however, hoped to achieve these ends by means of the peace treaty with Russia, and wanted to avoid costly and massive intervention. Thus he would not allow grain to be sent to Finland as Germany was short of it in any case, and it would probably fall into the hands of the Russian *Soldateska*. These Russian troops would have to be removed before any aid was sent to Finland.[27]

By 4 January 1918 the Finnish government had good reason to be grateful to Germany. Germany had formally recognised Finnish independence, had forced the Soviet government to do the same, and had delivered arms to the nationalists via the S.S. *Equity* and the U.C. 57. As yet Germany had asked for nothing in return. It was the sharpening of the conflict in Finland, and the breaking off of the negotiations at Brest that was to mark the beginning of a new phase in German-Finnish relations.

In the initial stages of the Finnish civil war the situation of the whites seemed to deteriorate. Hjelt, who had been given plenipotentiary powers by the nationalists, therefore requested that the *Jäger* battalion should be sent to Finland. This was supported by the OHL, but the foreign office were reluctant to enter on a course of action which seemed likely to make the peace negotiations with Russia all the more difficult.[28] The OHL therefore conjured up the nightmare vision of a socialist Finland, and told the government that unless something were done quickly the nationalists would fall.[29] Ludendorff was also very concerned that there was a move afoot in the foreign office to secure the neutralisation of Finland. He wrote to the foreign office: 'Germany has no military interest in the declaration of independence. Before the declaration of independence we must secure the greatest advantages that we need in the future of Finland and in the Baltic, by means of a military and economic agreement with Finland, which would be very difficult for us to achieve after a declaration of neutrality.'[30] By the end of January Kühlmann and the foreign office gave way, and agreed that the *Jäger* should be sent to Finland, but asked that no weapons should be sent so as not to get into a 'tricky situation' with the Russians. The *Jäger* were also to be sent as civilians, and not as a military unit.[31] The *Norddeutsche Allgemeine Zeitung* published an article to prepare the way for this move. 'Latest reports from Finland give us a vivid picture of what the self-determination of peoples and their freedom are worth if the Bolshevik rulers implement these beautiful theories.' It was a question of 'ethical obligation' and 'normal responsibility' to save these western areas of the old Russian empire from the curse of bolshevism. The OHL simply ignored the foreign office's request that no arms should be sent to Finland. Twelve Russian guns with 12,000 rounds of ammunition, 70,000 Russian rifles, and 150 Russian machine guns along with other weapons and ammunition were promptly despatched.[32]

Just as German military involvement was stepped up, even before negotiations were broken off at Brest Litovsk, so economic demands on Finland were beginning to emerge more clearly. Ludendorff had always insisted on the necessity of using the Finnish crisis to strengthen Germany's economic position, and in doing so he was once again closely associated with the leaders of German capitalism. As Germany became increasingly involved in Finland the demands of the leaders of German industry and finance became more far-reaching. The *Reichsbank* also refused to repay 50 million marks of Finnish assets on the grounds that Germany was still formally at war with Finland, preferring to keep the money as a bargaining counter for later negotiations.[33]

By early February the foreign office seemed to be caught in an uncomfortable cross-fire. The Finnish government was demanding more help against the reds, but the foreign office was loath to compromise the peace negotiations with Russia and was also concerned not to alienate neutral Sweden. On 1 February, Hjelt pressed Kühlmann either to send troops, or to bring more pressure to bear on the Russians to withdraw all their troops.[34] Meanwhile the Swedish press carried stories of arms shipments to Finland, carried on Swedish vessels, and the foreign office denied the story by lamely saying that the shipment was only salt from Hamburg.[35]

By breaking off the Brest negotiations and proclaiming the formula of 'neither peace nor war', Trotsky precipitated a series of events that was to lead to German intervention in Finland, the indirect approach having failed. Future policy was discussed at the meeting of the crown council in Homburg on 13 February.[36] Kühlmann telegraphed his instructions to the foreign office: 'In order to carry out the decisions of the chancellor made today it is necessary to get declarations from the Estonians, Livonians, Finns, and if possible the Ukrainians which mention the existing anarchy and continual danger of life and property and appeal to us to intervene to establish order.'[37]

Hjelt drew up a memorandum requesting German intervention to restore order in Finland without even consulting his government. On 18 February Ludendorff told the foreign office that he was ready to send the troops to Finland, and that he had discussed the operation with the Admiralty 'some days ago'. He suggested the Aaland islands as a base.[38]

The suggestion that the Aaland islands should be used gave the foreign office further cause for concern, for the islands were claimed by Sweden. The Queen of Sweden protested to the Kaiser when she heard of the German plans, but the Kaiser replied that he had no territorial ambitions on the islands and warned 'Delay impossible without the ruin of Finland and the grave danger of the bolshevik floods pouring into the rest of Europe and particularly Sweden.'[39] The Swedish government accepted this assurances with serious misgivings, and published the German note in the hopes that this would deter them from making any moves to annexe the islands.

Relations between Germany and Finland were formalised by the treaties signed on 7 March and ratified on 3 June. The intention behind the treaties was to tie Finland closely to Germany, economically, militarily and politically, and to make Finland as much of a client state of Germany as the Ukraine or Rumania.[40] Politically, Finland was severely restricted in her freedom of action by the stipulation that she could not ally with a foreign power without the prior permission of the German government. Militarily, the Finnish army was to accept a number of German 'advisers', German military and naval bases on Finnish soil, and close military cooperation. The Finnish army was to be closely linked to the Prussian army by interchange of personnel and the adoption of Prussian training methods, so that Germany would have a decisive voice in Finland's military planning. Most onerous of all was the economic treaty. German goods were to enter Finland free from duty, but Finnish goods sent to Germany would be subject to tariffs. This was to retard the development of Finnish industry, and make Finland into a dumping ground for German industrial goods, and a source of cheap raw materials for German industry.[41]

With the signing of the treaty of Brest Litovsk there was a strong feeling among the civilians that the expedition to Finland should at least be postponed. Hindenburg reacted violently to these suggestions. He refused to accept Hertling's argument that the expedition was undesirable because it would mean an extension of the war which the Reich, with its already over-extended financial resources, could not afford, and that the expedition would endanger the chances of peace with Russia. He believed that Hertling wanted to put off the expedition altogether, and was not just thinking of postponement. He therefore outlined his reasons for thinking that the expedition was essential for German interests. Russia would only respect the treaty of Brest Litovsk if she saw that any attempt to win back the border states was doomed to failure. With a strong position in Finland and Estonia, Germany would be able to apply a 'healthy pressure' on Petersburg. The operation in Finland would secure Germany's rear against the western powers both during the present war and afterwards. He also stressed the economic importance of Finland, and the importance of Finnish raw materials for the war effort.[42]

At the crown council meeting at Schloss Bellevue the final decision was made on 12 March. The OHL, supported by the navy and the Kaiser won a decision that the expedition should be mounted, against the serious misgivings of Hertling and the civilians. Weather conditions, however, came to the help of those who were arguing for postponement. The ice was so thick that the expedition could not be launched until the end of March or the beginning of April.[43]

Mannerheim, who commanded the white army, had at first objected to the idea of German intervention, but he began to feel that the would be unable to defeat the reds unless he had German support. Thus Mannerheim was prepared to accept the Germans once they gave a meaningless guarantee not to interfere with the internal affairs of Finland.[44] The German force under von der Goltz met with little opposition in southern Finland, as the reds were unwilling to risk a fight with the Germans.[45] On 13 April Goltz reached Helsinki. The Brandenstein section sent by *Oberost* landed on the south coast of Finland on 10 April and took part in a joint operation supported by Goltz's Baltic division to the west, and Mannerheim's whites to the north. This successful operation brought military operations in Finland to an end.[46] Mannerheim, however, was soon to resign. His demand for a large Finnish army was rejected by the government who wished to save money. He felt that Finland was becoming dangerously dependent on Germany, in spite of the guarantee that had been given, and he had ambitions to overthrow the bolsheviks by marching on Petersburg.[47] Furthermore Mannerheim by this time did not think that the Germans had any chance of winning the war, and therefore he felt that Finland was backing the wrong horse.[48]

With the departure of Mannerheim and with the Finnish president, Svinhufvud, so blatantly pro-German, nothing stood in the way of strengthening the ties between Finland and Germany to the distinct advantage of Germany. Men like Thyssen, Stinnes and Ballin began to press for further advantages, and for the annexation of the Aaland islands so as to secure the port of Lulea from which ore would have to be shipped if the British controlled Narvik.[49] For the politicians these excessive, and often ludicrous, demands of industry and the OHL threatened the carefully drafted economic treaty which gave Germany such enormous advantages. As Bussche pointed out to Hindenburg: 'On the basis of existing agreements German industry will be in the position to secure its interests to an extent that is agreeable to us.'[50] Hintze used similar arguments in a letter to Hindenburg written in characteristically serpentine prose: 'With regard to the economic demands which Your Excellency has deemed desirable, I would like to suggest that we do not disregard the point of view that we must avoid everything that might create the impression of the economic exploitation and subjection of Finland by us.'[51] Clearly there would have been further conflict between the industrialists and the OHL with their blatant approach, and the civil government with their more sophisticated and disguised form of economic exploitation had not the end of the war brought an end also to Germany's ambitions in Finland.

Once the fighting in the Finnish civil war was over, demands for eastward expansion at the expense of the Soviets became louder. A regime which had been fighting for its life only a few weeks before was now openly expansionist, and was encouraged in its ambitions by the OHL. Thus the OHL prompted the Finns to demand the fort of Ino from the Russians, as the fort had considerable strategic importance for the defence of Petrograd.[52] The German navy was, however, extremely reluctant to undertake the bombardment of the fort, as the Finns requested, for it was well fortified and equipped with powerful modern guns. Hertling felt than an attack on Ino would be a senseless provocation of the Russians, and that as Ino was essential for the defence of Petrograd and the vital interests of Finland were hardly at stake, therefore the German government should use its influence to persuade the Finns to accept the Russian presence in Ino.

Meanwhile Ludendorff was beginning to have second thoughts. He was now concerned to have Finnish support against the allied landing in Murmansk, and suggested that the Finns should be given a stretch of the Murman coast in return for leaving Ino alone. But the Russians had already acted. Fearing the loss of Ino they destroyed all the installations on 14 and 15 May, and the Finns took possession of piles of rubble.[53] Although the Russians were willing to negotiate, the Finns refused to abandon their position at Ino.

In spite of the powerful German position in Finland, the OHL seems to have been unaware of the activities of the allies in Murmansk until a remarkably late date. It was not until 21 April, and then only on the basis of an inaccurate newspaper report, that the German government protested to the Soviet government about the presence of enemy troops in northern Russia. Chicherin flatly denied these reports, and continued to do so until the end of May, but he promised to send an observer to the region.[54] This was an extraordinary piece of bluffing, for the British had landed in Murmansk with the express permission of the Soviet authorities given on 2 March in a moment of extreme crisis when Trotsky feared that the negotiations at Brest were about to be broken off.[55] Ludendorff did not want to send German troops to the Murman coast, as Hertling feared, but hoped that the Finns could be used to drive the British from their positions.[56] This scheme suited Kühlmann who feared that the Finns might be tempted to march on Petrograd. Both Kühlman and Hintze after him wanted to preserve the bolshevik regime at least for the time being, fearing that a government to the right of the bolsheviks might well continue the war on the side of the Entente. Chicherin found himself in a most uncomfortable dilemma. He wanted to avoid the Finns and the Germans intervening in Murmansk, but he also feared a strong Entente bridgehead in the north of Russia. It was therefore with a heavy heart that he asked Trotsky on 24 June to send troops to Murmansk.

The Murmansk question was rapidly becoming another cause for disagreement between the foreign office and the OHL. The foreign office, and even the Kaiser in his curious way, hoped that the Finns and the Russians would cooperate to throw out the British. Hindenburg and Ludendorff wanted the exact opposite. For them the greater the differences between the two countries the better. Germany was fighting both the Entente and bolshevism, and for this purpose the Finns were essential. Ludendorff summed up the OHL's thinking thus: 'The basis of the quarrel is this: the foreign office thinks that the Russians are honest, the OHL thinks they are dishonest.'[57] In point of fact it was more a matter of timing. Kühlmann and the foreign office were just as strongly opposed to the bolsheviks as the OHL, but they felt that for the time being the bolshevik regime had an important role to play in keeping Russia in a state of chaos and anarchy and thus of no use to the Entente.

The Russians were extremely reluctant to cooperate against the British on the Murman coast, but Ludendorff was still unwilling to send German troops to the area, for this would be a flagrant violation of the treaty of Brest Litovsk. He tried to get round this problem by arranging an exchange of territory between Russia and Finland, so that the English would suddenly find themselves on Finnish, not Russian soil. Talks were indeed begun, but the Finns' demands were so extreme that they had to be broken off.

The Murman question was soon to become involved in a problem of far greater moment – the very survival of the Soviet regime. On 29 July Lenin reported to the central executive committee on the situation in Russia. The picture he painted was indeed black. Allied strength on the Murman coast was growing, and now American troops were reported there. In the east the Czechs were approaching the Red army headquarters in Kazan. In the south – east Alekseev's army was making considerable advances. In Baku the local Soviet had appealed to the British for support via Persia. Lenin saw the socialist revolution encircled by British and French imperialists, and the future of the revolution now seemed to depend on the military situation. In this desperate situation Lenin took the only step left to him. He appealed to Germany for help.[58] On 2 August Helfferich, who had received the request directly from Chicherin, forwarded the message to Berlin. The Russians requested a joint German and Finnish intervention against the Entente on the Murman coast, but owing to the pressure of public opinion, an open alliance between the three countries was not desirable. Petrograd would be avoided by the German troops, and the political status of Karelia and the Murman should not be prejudiced by the intervention. Chicherin also asked that the Germans should no longer support Krasnov's army in the Don and should actively cooperate against Alekseev in the Kuban.

In a covering letter Helfferich suggested that Germany should exploit the fact that the bolsheviks were in such a desperate position and should ally with the cossacks to overthrow the Soviet regime. Hintze, who wished to preserve the bolsheviks in power for the time being, and who also knew that the cossacks were pro-Entente, rejected this proposal, and suggested that the Soviet request be met, provided that troops were available for the operation on the Murman coast. Ludendorff agreed to send troops, provided that they did not have to fight alongside bolshevik troops, and added that a German operation against the English would only be possible if they could use Petrograd as a base, and have access to the Murman railway. It was a foregone conclusion that the Soviet government would not accept the OHL's demand to occupy Petrograd, for this would leave the regime at the mercy of the German army. Indeed Ludendorff told Hintze that he intended to overthrow the bolsheviks with the help of Krasnov. Hintze argued that it was in Germany's interest to keep a political stalemate in Russia, rather than help to establish a new government firmly in power. Ludendorff reluctantly agreed with Hintze, but he was still prepared to send troops. Thus on 10 August Ludendorff told the foreign office that he was ready to move against the Entente on the Murman coast if only the Soviets would allow the German army to use Petrograd and the railway.[59] This last note is a clear indication that the reason for Germany not marching into the Murman was not because of the failure on the western front on 8 August, as some historians have suggested, but because of the refusal of the Soviets to allow German troops to enter Petrograd.[60] This was an insoluble problem. Even if the OHL had no ulterior motives it is difficult to see how the Germans could have mounted a successful operation against the Murman coast without entering Petrograd and using the Murman railway. On the other hand it would have been suicidal for the Soviet government to permit this move.

On 9 August Lenin, clearly suspicious that the German fleet intended to sail on Petrograd and Kronstadt, probably under the guise of taking part in operations in the Murman, ordered mines to be laid in the bay of Kronstadt. The move was in direct violation of the treaty of Brest Litovsk. The German foreign office protested vigorously, but both Chicherin in Moscow and Joffe in Berlin denied the reports. Lenin's fears were indeed fully justified, for as early as the beginning of July Ludendorff and the naval staff had discussed the possibility of a Finnish attack on Petrograd supported by the Germans, a plan which was given the code name *'Schlussteinoperation'* (operation coping stone). Holtzendorff had agreed that the navy could be used to secure the gulf of Kronstadt. On 11 and 12 August *Schlusstein* was discussed further by Hoffmann and representatives of the navy. It was decided that the attack on Petrograd should be supported by two infantry divisions from Narva, two divisions from Pskov, and Goltz's Baltic division from Finland. Thus while Ludendorff was negotiating with the Russians over intervention against the Entente, and hoping that the Soviet government would give him the keys to Petrograd, he was also instructing *Oberost* to plan a direct attack on Petrograd. The result of either policy, had it been successful, would have been the overthrow of the bolshevik regime, a policy which was in direct contradiction to that of the foreign office, who felt that for the time being at least a weak bolshevik government, fighting for its life against enemies both at home and abroad best suited German interests.

On 27 August the supplementary treaty to Brest Litovsk was signed, and under paragraph 5 Russia agreed to use all possible means to expel the Entente troops from northern Russia. Germany guaranteed that the Finns would not attack Russian territory during these operations, and specifically not Petrograd. However the Russians were warned that if they did not begin immediately the Germans and the Finns would be obliged to intervene, in which case the Germans would have to use Petrograd and the Murmansk railway. So the situation remained until 27 September when *Oberost* received the order from the OHL that the operation *Schlusstein* was cancelled, and that preparations should be discontinued. The collapse of the Balkan front had saved Petrograd.[61]

From the very early days of the war the Finnish nationalists had thought in terms of a close political association with Germany, and men like Mannerheim who resisted this policy were very much in a minority. Finland was to be part of a chain of states from the White Sea to the Black Sea in close association with Germany, forming a barrier against bolshevism. Part of this scheme was a proposal that a German prince should become king of Finland.[62] Svinhufvud was a staunch proponent of this scheme. His own government was extremely weak, a minority government which could only survive because most of his opponents were in jail, including the right wing social democrats. He also had had territorial ambitions in Karelia for which he needed German support.

A major problem was to select a suitable German prince. The Kaiser wanted his son, Prince Oscar, to have the throne. The Bureau Wetterhoff in Berlin wanted the Duke of Mecklenburg-Schwerin. The OHL wanted a Württemberg or Saxon prince.[63] Gradually the OHL came round to the view that a Prussian prince would be the most suitable, as they supported Svinhufvud's designs on Karelia and felt that a Prussian prince would be the best guarantee of German support for this policy.[64] Meanwhile the Kaiser was less enthusiastic. The monarchy was to be elective, an idea that was abhorrent to William II with his exalted ideas of a monarchy by the grace of God, and there was also the sneaking suspicion that the Finnish parliament would not vote for the prince which would be a disastrous setback for the house of Hohenzollern, and also that the monarchy was unlikely to last very long in a country which had a republican majority. Hindenburg and Ludendorff continued to support Svinhufvud's proposals, and even agreed to Prince Oscar, against the objections of the Kaiser and the foreign office.[65] Faced with the refusal of the Kaiser to allow his son to be considered for the Finnish throne, Ludendorff and Svinhufvud had to accept his compromise proposal that Prince Friedrich Karl of Hessen, a brother-in-law of the Kaiser, should be candidate.[66] On 8 October the prince was elected king.[67] As Prince Max of Baden pointed out, the parliament was a rump, the agrarians had abstained, and there was little enthusiasm for the monarchy among the Finnish people. He urged the prince to ask for time to think things over.[68] But the prince's problems were shortly to be solved for him. The military defeat of Germany meant that the prince lost his appeal even to the strongest pro-German factions in Finland. With the abdication of the Kaiser and of the German princes his position was further weakened. Finally, on 14 December 1918 he announced his resolve not to accept the invitation of the Finnish parliament.

NOTES

1. Conze, *Polnische Nation*, p. 87; Egmont Zechlin, *Die deutsche Politik und die Juden im ersten Weltkrieg*, Göttingen 1968, p. 230; *Der Weltkrieg 1914-1918*, Band 13.
2. Fischer, *Griff nach der Weltmacht*, p. 355, quoting Robert Stupperich, 'Siedlungspläne im Gebiet des Oberbefehlshabers Ost (Militärverwaltung Litauen und Kurland) während des Weltkriegs', *Jomsburg*, 5, 1941. Stupperich's article is otherwise of little value, being little more than an apology for Ludendorff. Groener felt that the attack on Courland was the first 'political raid' of Ludendorff. He also thought that the move was a deliberate attack on Falkenhayn. The occupation of Courland certainly seemed to Ludendorff as a 'means to immortality'. Bundesarchiv Militärarchiv Freiburg, Nachlass Groener, N46/63.
3. Fischer, *Griff nach der Weltmacht*, p. 356; Zechlin, *Die deutsche Politik und die Juden*, p. 231. This would have involved about 82 per cent of the Lithuanian Jews.
4. PA Bonn AA Weltkrieg, Band 15.
5. PA Bonn AA Weltkrieg 15 Geheim, Band 3. Scherer Grunewald, *L'Allemagne et les problemes de la paix*, Vol. 2, p. 149; Ritter, *Staatskunst und Kriegshandwerk*, Vol. 4, p. 98; Fischer, *Griff nach der Weltmacht*, p. 456. On p. 493 Fischer argues that Ludendorff did not agree to Bethmann's autonomy policy until after Bethmann had fallen from power, at the Bingen conference on 31 July. This is true in the strict sense, although the above letter suggests that Ludendorff had no serious objections to the autonomy proposal as early as May.
6. PA Bonn AA Weltkrieg Geheim, Band 38, Lersner to foreign office 25-6-17.
7. PA Bonn AA Gr. HQ 147 Russland 31a, Band 2.
8. DZA Potsdam Reichskanzlei 2, 11, Kr. 4(2), Band 1, Fischer, *Griff nach der Weltmacht*, p. 605; Ritter, *Staatskunst und Kriegshandwerk*, Vol. 4, p. 101.
9. DZA Potsdam Reichskanzlei, Kurland, 2404.
10. PA Bonn AA Gr. HQ Russland 31a, Band 1.
11. Fischer, *Griff nach der Weltmacht*, p. 611.
12. PA Bonn AA Weltkrieg 15 Geheim, Band 5.
13. DZA Potsdam: Reichskanzlei: Verkehr des Reichskanzlers mit den Gr. HQ 2403/6.

14. Bayerisches Hauptstaatsarchiv Abteilung IV Kriegsarchiv M.Kr. 1832. Report 14-2-18 on the Homburg discussions.
15. Bundesarchiv Koblenz, Nachlass Heinrichs, Band 34.
16. PA Bonn AA Gr. HQ Kriegsziele 16a, Band 1. Lersner to Kühlmann who was then in Bucharest, 7-3-18.
17. DZA Potsdam; Reichskanzlei, Kurland und Litauen, 2406. Lersner to foreign office 19-3-18.
18. Fischer, *Griff nach der Weltmacht*, p. 811. Fischer describes events as following the directions of Ludendorff, but unfortunately does not present any evidence. On the other hand this was exactly what Ludendorff wanted to happen, and follows the general pattern of events in the Ukraine and Finland.
19. Janssen, *Macht und Verblendung. Kriegszielpolitik der deutschen Bundesstaaten 1914-1918*, Göttingen 1963, p. 204.
20. J.W. Hiden, 'The Baltic Germans and German Policy towards Latvia after 1918', *Historical Journal*, Vol. XIII, No. 1, for a recent account which argues that German policy was of 'self-interest but responsible' after 1919 until the Nazis came to power.
21. General Graf Rüdiger von der Goltz, *Meine Sendung in Finnland und im Baltikum*, Leipzig 1920, p. 37; J.O. Hannula, *Finland's War of Independence*, London 1939; Eino Jutikkala, *Geschichte Finnlands*, Stuttgart 1964; G. Mannerheim, *Erinnerungen*, Zurich 1952; Erkki Räikkönen, *Svinhufvud baut Finnland*, Munich 1936; M.G. Schybergson, *Politische Geschichte Finnlands 1809-1919*, Gotha and Stuttgart 1925; C. Jay Smith Jr., *Finland and the Russian Revolution 1917-1922*, Athens, Georgia 1958; W. Hubatsch, 'Finnland in der deutschen Ostseepolitik 1917/18', *Ostdeutsche Wissenschaft*, Band 11, 1955.
22. Jutikkala, *Geschichte Finnlands*, pp. 344-9.
23. PA Bonn AA Gr. HQ 36 Finnland A-Z 10, Band 1 (allgemeine Lage Juni 1915-Feb. 1918) Zimmermann to GHQ 4-8-17, Lersner to foreign office 7-8-17.
24. Fischer, *Griff nach der Weltmacht*, p. 677.
25. PA Bonn AA Gr. HQ 36 Finnland A-Z 10, Band 1. Ludendorff to Kühlmann 13-11-1917.
26. Fischer, *Griff nach der Weltmacht*, p. 677, quoting Schybergson.
27. PA Bonn AA Gr. HQ 36 Finnland A-Z 10, Band 1. The Bussche referred to is of course Hilmar Frhr. von dem Bussche-Haddenhausen who should not be confused with Erich Frhr. von Bussche-Ippenburg, major in the operational division of the general staff. See also the correspondence in PA Bonn AA Russland 63, Band 18.
28. Hubatsch, 'Finnland in der deutsche Ostseepolitik', p. 53; PA Bonn AA Russland 63, Band 18. Lersner to foreign office 12-1-18.
29. PA Bonn AA Russland 63, Band 18.
30. *Ibid.*, and PA Bonn AA Gr. HQ Finnland A-Z 10, Band 1.
31. PA Bonn AA Russland 63, Band 18.
32. PA Bonn AA Gr. HQ Finnland A-Z 10, Band 1, Bussche to Grünau 5-2-18.
33. PA Bonn AA Russland 63, Band 18, Reichsbank to foreign office 22-1-18.
34. *Ibid.*, Band 20.
35. PA Bonn AA Russland 63, Band 20. Stellv. St. Sec. AA to Gesandter Stockholm 9-2-1918.
36. *Deutsch-Sowjetische Beziehungen*, p. 403. Baumgart's account in: *Deutsche Ostpolitik*, Chapter III tends to exaggerate the degree of Kühlmann's opposition to the OHL's plans in Finland.
37. PA Bonn AA Russland 63, Band 20.
38. *Ibid.*, Band 21; Gr. HQ 36 Finnland A-Z 10, Band 1.

39. PA Bonn AA Russland 63, Band 7.
40. Fritz Fischer, *Griff nach der Weltmacht*, p. 678. Baumgart's account is a little confused owing to his errors in dating, so that in his version replies are sometimes sent before the original documents are received. *Deutsche Ostpolitik*, p. 94, especially footnote 9. The text of the treaties in PA Bonn AA Gr. HQ Finnland A-Z, 10 Allgemeine Lage, Band 1.
41. Bundesarchiv Militärarchiv Freiburg, Marine Akten 75600 Ostsee Finnland, Band 1. Hindenburg sent a considerable staff with Goltz to Finland which included sections for propaganda, press, film propaganda, counterespionage and a group responsible for watching all telegrams sent to and from Finland. A communications system was set up using German equipment and engineers. Bussche reported to Lersner 30 August 1918 that the treaty was ruinous to Finland and that Finland was looking for support against Germany from Petrograd. He also reported that German troops were behaving incredibly badly in Finland. PA Bonn AA Gr. HQ 39 Finnland A-Z 10, Band 3, Teil 2. Further material in DZA Potsdam Reichskanzlei Finnland 2406/4.
42. PA Bonn AA Gr. HQ 37 Finnland A-Z; 10, Band 2.
43. Fritz Fischer, *Griff nach der Weltmacht*, p. 682.
44. Jutikkala, *Geschichte Finnlands*, p. 356; Räikkönen, *Svinhufvud baut Finland*, p. 2. PA Bonn AA Gr. HQ Finnland 10, Band 2.
45. C. Jay Smith, *Finland and the Russian Revolution 1917-1922*, p. 75.
46. Ludendorff, *Meine Kriegserinnerungen*, p. 505. Fischer, *Griff nach der Weltmacht*, p. 682, gives the wrong date, and so does Jutikkala, *Geschichte Finnlands*, p. 356.
47. Goltz, *Meine Sendung in Finnland und im Baltikum*, p. 82.
48. Jutikkala, *Geschichte Finnlands*, p. 360.
49. PA Bonn AA Russland 63 Nr I Die Aalandinseln, Band 9. The letter was on behalf of Gewerkschaft Deutscher Kaiser, Gelsenkirchner Bergwerks Aktiengesellschaft, Eisen und Stahl Werk Hoesch, Phoenix, Deutsch-Luxemburgische Bergwerks und Hütten — Aktiengesellschaft, Gutehoffnungshütte, Fried, Krupp, and Rheinische Stahlwerke.
50. Bussche to Admiralstab 21-9-18. Bundesarchiv Militärarchiv Freiburg, Marineakten 75660 Ostsee — Finnland, Band 1.
51. *Ibid.*, Hintze to Hindenburg 30-8-18.
52. Baumgart, *Deutsche Ostpolitik*, p. 99; Wheeler Bennett, *Brest Litovsk*, p. 332.
53. Wheeler Bennett, *Brest Litovsk*, p. 334.
54. PA Bonn AA Gr. HQ 41 Finnland A-Z 10a, Band 1.
55. Wheeler Bennett, *Brest Litovsk*, p. 332.
56. PA Bonn AA Gr. HQ 232 Kriegsziele Nr 16a, Band 1. On 29 May Ludendorff suggested to the foreign office that the Finns should move into Karelia and Murman 'without the Russians knowing anything about this step of ours'.
57. Bundesarchiv Militärarchiv Freiburg, Marine Akten 75660, Ostsee-Finnland, Band 1. Report by the Vertreter ASd.M at Gr. HQ 12-6-18 on a conversation between Ludendorff and Kriege.
58. Baumgart, *Deutsche Ostpolitik*, pp. 106, 237; Helfferich, *Der Weltkrieg*, p. 652; E.H. Carr, *The Bolshevik Revolution*, Vol. 3, p. 92; Gunter Rosenfeld, *Sowjetrussland und Deutschland 1917-1922*, Berlin 1960, p. 119.
59. PA Bonn AA Weltkrieg 23 Geheim, Band 14.
60. Carr, *The Bolshevik Revolution*, Vol. 3, p. 93; Rosenfeld, *Sowjetrussland und Deutschland*, p. 121; Baumgart, *Deutsche Ostpolitik*, p. 108.
61. Baumgart, *Deutsche Ostpolitik*, pp. 113-17 gives a good account. See also *Der Weltkrieg 1914-1918*, Band XIII and *Der Krieg zur See 1914-1918. Der Krieg in der Ostsee*, Band 3, for details of the military operations. Goltz, *Meine Sendung*, pp. 90-2. PA Bonn AA Gr. HQ 40 Finnland A-Z 10, Band 4.

62. C. Jay Smith Jr., *Finland and the Russian Revolution,* p. 10.
63. PA Bonn AA Gr. HQ 37 Finnland A-Z 10, Band 2. Lersner to Hertling 12-3-18. DZA Potsdam Reichskanzlei, Finnland 2406/4.
64. PA Bonn AA Gr. HQ 39 Finnland A-Z 10, Band 3 (Teil 2). Berckheim to foreign office 6-7-18. Jutikkala, *Geschichte Finnlands,* p. 360.
65. PA Bonn AA Gr. HQ 39 Finnland A-Z 10, Band 3, Teil 2. Bussche to Lersner 16-7-18, Hertling to Grünau 15-7-18, Lersner to foreign office 18-7-18; DZA Potsdam Reichskanzlei, Finnland 2406/4, Lersner to chancellor 18-7-18, Hintze to chancellor 26-7-18, Hindenburg to chancellor 16-7-18; PA Bonn AA Gr. HQ 38 Finnland A-Z 10 Allgemeine Lage, Band 3, Ludendorff to foreign office 24-8-18.
66. PA Bonn AA Gr. HQ 38 Finnland A-Z 10 Allgemeine Lage, Band 3.
67. PA Bonn AA Gr. HQ 40 Finnland A-Z 10 Allgemeine Lage, Band 4.
68. *Ibid.,* Prince Max to Grünau 10-10-18.

10 EASTERN POLICY 1918

The treaty of Brest Litovsk did not mark the end of German eastward expansion, but rather the beginning of a new phase. Two factors decided the course of this policy: the determination of the Germans to exploit the resources of the Russian empire, and the course of the civil war in Russia. Thus at Brest Litovsk they had managed to secure the grain and the raw materials of the Ukraine, but the Rada government, with whom the treaty had been signed, represented nobody. The government had fled from Kiev on 7 February, two days before the treaty was signed, and even before that date had lost contact with the delegation at Brest Litovsk.[1] By the time the treaty was signed the Rada government was in full flight, Kiev was in the hands of the bolsheviks whose appeal was so great that the last act of the Rada had been to abolish private property in land, establish the eight hour day and state control over the means of production and exchange. A richly comic end to its pathetic career.

The Central Powers had managed to reduce the Ukraine to a satellite state by the treaty of Brest Litovsk, but the instrument of their control, the Ukrainian Rada, had no authority over the country. A solution to this problem was found at the crown council at Bad Homburg when it was decided that the Ukrainians, along with Finland and the Baltic states, should appeal to Germany for help. At first the OHL hoped that the Ukrainians would be able to drive out the bolsheviks of their own accord, for they were planning an attack on Petrograd, and did not want to get involved in a sideshow. The delegates of the Rada at Brest Litovsk managed to convince the Germans that they had no chance of returning to power in the Ukraine without German help. On 12 February they appealed to the German people for help against the 'enemies of our liberty who have invaded our native land in order to subjugate the Ukrainian people with fire and the sword'.[2] The OHL promptly decided on intervention on the basis of the Homburg decision.

Military and political operations in the Ukraine were in the hands of General Groener, who was now chief of staff to Field Marshal Eichhorn. Groener made brilliant use of the railways, as might be expected from the general staff's foremost expert on the military use of railways, and the country was rapidly over-run.[3] He was given virtually a free hand, the OHL having given him no detailed order. On 1 March Kiev was in German hands, the bolshevik troops were driven back to Russia, much of their supplies and equipment falling in to the hands of the Germans. The advance developed such momentum that Groener asked permission of the OHL to continue. By the end of April the Crimea was in German hands, Rostov was captured at the beginning of the following month, and the Donets basin was occupied. Within a few weeks the German generals had carved out an enormous empire in the east, and their boundless ambition and fanatical anti-communism was to give rise to further struggles with the foreign office. They announced that they had come to restore law and order, remove the bolsheviks, reinstate the Rada and open what was euphemistically called trade relations. At first the Rada tried to convince itself that the Germans meant what they said, that they genuinely wished to help establish a peoples' republic on social reformist lines, and that they had no intention of interfering with the internal affairs of the state. They were soon disillusioned.

At first Ludendorff hoped that Groener could be given plenipotentiary powers, but Kühlmann managed to avoid this by securing the appointment of Mumm von Schwarzenstein as diplomatic representative to the Rada. Mumm's task, in the typically blunt words of General Hoffmann, was to 'provide the necessary legal basis for the force that the military will have to use in order to get the grain'. It is hardly surprising that Mumm, surrounded by hostile army officers, felt himself to be like Robinson Crusoe.[4] The main problem facing both Groener and Mumm was that the Rada government was useless for any purpose whatever, and could not even be used as a fig leaf to disguise German ambitions in the Ukraine. They knew that the Rada could not last, but as yet they were unwilling to overthrow it, hoping to maintain the fiction that Germany had come as a friend of the Ukranian government.

This fiction was becoming increasingly hard to uphold. In some areas the peasants were effectively protecting their grain from being requisitioned, often by resorting to the use of rifles and shotguns.[4] On April 6 Eichhorn, without consulting Mumm, issued an order that the crops should be sown, and totally ignoring the Rada's land redistribution law he added that land that the peasants could not cultivate on their own should be sowed by the landlords, and that he who sowed the land should reap the crop.[5] The Rada decided to defy this order so as to win some support among the people, and on 13 April it told the peasants to disobey.

Whereas Groener believed in coercion, such as the Eichhorn order, as the only alternative to 'plunder and robbery', Mumm banked on what he called the 'Russian method': extensive bribery for which purposes the treasury gave him several million marks.[6] By the end of April the OHL had lost patience with the Rada government, and Groener was given permission to get rid of it. Ludendorff wrote: 'Your position is a little tricky, but I think that with powerful pressure the Rada can be persuaded or removed, and then you can get down to business. Russians still want to feel the knout. So get to work, you can be certain of my support.'[7]

Groener got down to work at once. The day after the receipt of Ludendorff's letter he met General Paul Skoropadsky to discuss the terms under which the Germans would support a new government under his leadership.[8] This professional soldier with his fervent anti-socialist beliefs and the conservative attitudes of a great landowner and tsarist officer seemed an ideal choice for the Germans. He agreed that the Rada would have to be dismissed, that private property in land should be restored, and that the state should cease to interfere with the free workings of the capitalist economy. Wide legal powers were to be given to the German army, including the right to requisition, and all his cabinet members would have to be approved by the generals. He also agreed to negotiate a new economic treaty with Germany which would be disastrous to the Ukrainians. Skoropadsky was prepared to accept these harsh terms because, as he put it: 'It is better to sell cheaply to the Germans than to give everything away free to a lot of landless peasants.'[9] Once more the fear of bolshevism proved effective in finding nationalist support for German imperialist ambitions.

While Groener was negotiating with Skoropadsky an event occured which provided an excellent excuse for overthrowing the Rada. A pro-German banker by the name of Dobri, who was a well-known and outspoken opponent of the Rada, was kidnapped by a pro-Rada group, the 'Committee to Save the Ukraine'. Eichhorn responded to Premier Holubovich's assurance that the government knew nothing of the kidnapping by declaring a state of martial law in the Ukraine.[10] Howls of protest came from the Rada, and heady speeches against German imperialism and Prussian militarism. Such conduct was altogether too much for Eichorn and Groener. On 28 April a detachment of troops was sent to the Rada chamber, members were ordered to put up their hands, and all ministers were placed under arrest. Eichhorn then had the nerve to send Holubovich a letter of apology for the behaviour of the military commandment of Kiev, no doubt so as to strengthen his position against possible attacks from the German foreign office.

On the following day the League of Landowners held its convention in the circus at Kiev. There were rousing calls for a dictatorship. Skoropadsky then appeared and the assembly bestowed upon him the ancient title of Hetman. The meeting was held under the close supervision of the German army, all other political meetings being banned. Skoropadsky was appointed by the six thousand delegates of an extreme right-wing party, their meeting staged by the German army. It was hardly a democratic mandate, and in order to give it a slightly more official character he was anointed that evening by the archbishop in Saint Sophia.[11]

In Berlin reactions to these events in the Ukraine were mixed. The foreign office was delighted to see the end of a government which it was convinced was communist, but it was less enthusiastic about the way it was done.[12] Hertling was also upset about the political meddling by the army, and insisted that Mumm should be given greater powers to control them. Eichhorn found a useful scapegoat in the commandant of Kiev, who was dismissed from his post.[13] On 4 May Eichhorn sent a telegram to the OHL complaining about the total inability of the chancellor to understand the nature of the situation in the Ukraine, and insisting that only strict military measures were of any use. 'There is only one good side to the situation in the Ukraine: a firm hand by the military works wonders; there is only one diplomatic method that works: the use of money.'[14] Ludendorff was delighted with this telegram, and forwarded it to the chancellor with a covering note expressing his full agreement. He then telegraphed to Groener congratulating the army in the Ukraine for acting in what he termed the best interests of the Reich, and for standing up manfully to the pin pricks of the government in Berlin.[15]

The army had succeeded in overthrowing the Rada and replacing it with a regime which seemed likely to be cooperative, they had warded off the attacks of the civilians in Berlin, and by maintaining a state of martial law Mumm and the foreign office had no more say in the formulation of policy in the Ukraine. Yet they were failing in the very objective for which they had come to the Ukrasne. The food and materials collected from the Ukraine did not come anywhere near the amounts stipulated in the economic agreements with the Ukrainian government, and were a bitter disappointment to the Germans. Although the Donets basin was now in German hands it was necessary to send 80,000 tons of coal each month to the Ukraine from Germany in order to keep the railways in operation.[16] The situation was so bad that the government seriously considered reinforcing the army in the Ukraine in order to extract more from the country, an argument which greatly strengthened the OHL's argument that German policy in the Ukraine should be regarded as a purely military concern.

It proved almost impossible to extract more from the Ukraine. There had been a bad harvest in 1917 and the 1918 harvest had yet to be reaped. The workers and the peasants were determined in their opposition to the German army, which in turn acted with great brutality. The price of manufactured goods had increased to twenty-four times the 1912 level. Coal production in the Donets was down from fifteen million tons in the first half of 1917 to just over five million tons in the corresponding period in 1918. High unemployment hit the urban proletariat, and the inability of the Germans to meet their obligations to supply manufactured goods and machinery to compensate for the foodstuffs taken, meant that the peasants were fobbed off with a worthless currency. Thus Eichhorn's vision that the Ukrainians would realise the considerable economic advantages of close cooperation with Germany, and would contrast their internal stability with the chaos and confusion of revolutionary Russia, and his dream of the Ukraine as the bridge linking the Reich with India was a hopeless illusion.[17]

Eichhorn was also determined to give support to the various anti-bolshevik groups working in the Ukraine. The OHL was also prepared to consider even the most scatterbrained attempts to overthrow the bolsheviks. Eichhorn was particularly impressed with the Cadet leader, Miliukov, but the OHL was prepared to agree with the foreign office that as he was well known for his sympathies for the Entente he was hardly suitable as an ally, and in any case he had little popular support.[18] The OHL therefore ordered Eichhorn to have nothing further to do with the Cadets. It proved far more difficult, however, to end the association between the OHL and Krasnov's cossacks. The army had begun its association with Krasnov shortly after the occupation of the Don basin by the German army. Kühlmann strongly objected to support for a movement which threatened to overthrow the bolsheviks and replace them with a monarchist but anti-German government. He managed to reach an agreement with Ludendorff that a liaison officer could be sent to the cossacks provided that he remained in civilian clothes, and an assurance that the OHL would not send any arms or munitions to Krasnov's army. The OHL simply ignored this agreement and delivered 11,000 rifles, 46 guns, 88 machine guns, 100,000 rounds of artillery munition and over one million rounds for the rifles, all between May and the end of June.[19]

The OHL's plan was now for a 'south-eastern alliance', in which the Ukrainians and the cossacks would join together under German control to form an anti-communist and pro-German state from Kiev to the Caucasus. Fifteen million roubles were given to Eichhorn to apply the 'Russian method' on Krasnov. At the crown council at Spa on 2 July 1918 Ludendorff argued that without massive bribes Krasnov might well combine with the Czechoslovaks who were fighting in the area around Tsaritsin (Stalingrad) and become as pro-Entente as the Czechs. Rosenberg summed up the foreign office's objections to support for Krasnov, but as soon as Ludendorff insisted that Germany needed the Don area and particularly Baku for essential military purposes, he made the extraordinary suggestion that the 'military measures which are deemed essential should be carried out behind the backs of the political leadership'.[20]

A few days after the Spa meeting it became clear that Ludendorff's attempt to win the cossacks away from the Czechs was unlikely to succeed. Krasnov informed the Germans that he would join the Czechs and march against Moscow. Even so it was not until there had been a fierce exchange of letters and a threat from Hertling that he would resign that Hindenburg agreed that he would no longer support the cossacks, at least until after the supplementary treaty to Brest Litovsk had been signed. As Bussche from the foreign office pointed out, at least the bolsheviks had signed the treaty of Brest Litovsk which formed the basis of German policy in Russia, whereas Krasnov for all his noble anti-bolshevik sentiments was an even more dubious partner.

The hatred shown towards the German army in the Ukraine was heightened by the murder of Eichhorn on 30 July. The murder was organised by the social revolutionaries, and planned by Irene Kakhovskaia, Gregory Smoliansky and Boris Donskoi. Donskoi assassinated Eichhorn and his adjutant with a bomb, made no attempt to escape and was shortly afterwards hanged. The deed was part of the social revolutionaries' determined efforts to force the bolsheviks into a more active anti-German policy, and to strengthen anti-German sentiments in the Ukraine.[21] The bolsheviks quite openly expressed their approval of the deed in their press, for they had every desire to see anti-German and anti-imperialist sentiments strengthened in the Ukraine, and knew that this was one steps towards the eventual unification of the Ukraine with Russia.

The murder of Eichhorn was only the most dramatic of these events. In March the workers of Nikolaev revolted, and the brutal repression of the movement merely helped to trigger off uprisings elsewhere. In July the Ukrainian railway workers went on strike, thus hindering the flow of food and goods to the Central Powers.[22]

Shortages combined with mounting labour militancy meant that the amount of food obtained by the Germans in the Ukraine was about equal to the amount consumed by the more than half a million troops stationed in the country.[23] The question thus became all the more pressing whether in fact these troops would not be better employed fighting on the western front. From about the middle of August the OHL began to have serious reservations about leaving the troops in the Ukraine, but Ludendorff was unwilling to awake from his dream of a German imperium in the east. As late as October he was still insisting to the chancellor, Prince Max of Baden, that the Ukraine expedition had kept the bolsheviks in check, and had provided valuable raw materials, but when pressed he was forced to admit that the army was so demoralised that it was unlikely to be of much use on the western front.[24] As is so often the case with armies of occupation that hold down a people, and that force upon them a government they do not wish to accept, the army was ultimately defeated by erosion from within. In the case of the German army in the Ukraine, morale was so low that some officers, ultimately even General Hoffmann and Ludendorff, felt that the army had become so influenced by bolshevism that if it were brought back to Germany it would spread the ideas of the Soviet revolution. It seemed that the army would have to remain in the Ukraine in order to save Germany from the revolution it might bring with it on its return home. Such was the superbly ironic end to the Ukrainian expedition.

German ambitions in the east were by no means limited to the Ukraine. The rapid German advance in the spring of 1918 brought the riches of the Caucasus within the grasp of the Germans. On 12 April the *Kriegsamt* informed the foreign office that members of the *Gelsenkirchener Bergwerks Aktiengesellschaft* and the *Kaukasische Grubenverein* were to be sent to Batum and Poti by torpedo boat to look for manganese, and that this expedition was essential to the German war effort as supplies of manganese had run out.[25] It was not only manganese that excited the appetite of German economic interests, led and organised by Helfferich, but also oil, ores, cotton and wool.

In the meantime, amid the chaos and confusion of post-revolutionary Russia a 'Trans-Caucasian Republic' had been formed, a federation of Georgia, Armenia and Azerbaijan. The Turks lay claim to part of this area, for they desired to win back the districts they had lost in 1878, and initially the Turks were supported in their claim by the OHL. In the middle of March negotiations began at Trapezunt between the Turks and the representatives of the Trans-Caucasian Republic. These talks led nowhere, and on 14 April the Turks declared war.

The Azerbaijani, most of whom were Muslims, were pro-Turk. The Armenians were massacred by the Turks with their traditional brutality. The Georgians were thus the key to the situation in the area. On 15 April the Turks occupied Georgia's only port, Batum, which was of critical strategic importance, controlling the routes to the near east and Persia, and acting as the bridgehead to central Asia. The foreign office was highly alarmed at this Turkish advance, and was concerned that this Turkish interest in the Caucasus might mean a slackening off of operations against the British, and even the possibility of a separate peace between Turkey and Britain.[26] The OHL shared much of the foreign office's concern. Initially they had encouraged the eastward movement of the Turks in order that they should not press their demands on Rumania, but now they too were worried that this economically and strategically valuable area might fall into Turkish hands. Hindenburg and Ludendorff therefore proposed that Germany should mediate between the Turks and the Georgians during the peace negotiations in the Caucasus.

The German delegate to the peace talks at Batum, for reasons that are obscure, was not a diplomat but the military plenipotentiary in Pera, von Lossow — a Bavarian who was later to play an important role in the Hitler *putsch* of 1923. Lossow was instructed to secure the economic interests of Germany in the area, and to make certain that the Turks respected the treaty of Brest Litovsk. The Turks were furious that the Germans had even sent a delegation to Batum, and after one session they broke off discussions and continued their advance. This marked the end of the short-lived Trans-Caucasian Republic.

Ludendorff did not support Lossow's diplomatic initiatives, and was particularly critical of his idea of giving part of Trans-Caucasia to Persia, a notion which to Ludendorff amounted to giving territory to England. His scheme was to head the Turks off in the direction of Teheran so that they would not penetrate too deeply into Trans-Caucasia. He was particularly concerned that the Georgians, 'our friends and a Christian people', should not become prey to the Turks, and that above all the Turks should not control the vital railway from Baku to Batum. Hertling was horrified at the thought of Ludendorff further extending the war in the Orient, to which Ludendorff had the incredible reply that it did not matter where the troops fought, it was all the same war against the same enemy. But he did reassure the chancellor that he did not intend to engage more troops in the east, at least not for the time being.[27]

For once it seemed that the OHL was trying to put the brakes on the ambitions of heavy industry. Writing to the foreign office in May, Ludendorff said: 'I am afraid that we want too much and will end up with nothing.'[27] At the beginning of June Lossow returned to Berlin full of indignation at the way he had been treated by the Turks, and enthusiastic about the tremendous economic potential of the region.[28] His reports seem to have had an effect on the OHL, which now began to abandon its cautiously pro-Turkish policy, and became increasingly sympathetic to the views of heavy industry and those who demanded direct annexation. Ludendorff told Seeckt that if the Turks did not stop their treaty violations Germany would cease to give her any aid and assistance. Hindenburg telegraphed to Enver Pasha demanding that Turkish troops be pulled back from the Trans-Caucasus, adding: 'I must particularly insist that with respect to the enormous economic importance of the oil fields of Baku, any disturbance of the inhabitants of the Baku district by Turkish troops or Turkish-Tartar irregulars must cease.'[29]

Georgia was now the key to the OHL's eastern policy. Georgia had declared its independence, and the plenipotentiary of the new government was asking for close association with Germany. The OHL thus intended to exploit the resources of Georgia and to train a Georgian army which would eventually fight alongside the German army to overthrow the Bolshevik regime. The Trans-Caucasus, with its largely non-Slav population, would then form the basis of German power and influence in the region, and an effective counterbalance to a united Russia and Ukraine. The OHL was still somewhat restrained in its policies, and would not dare to agree to the request of the Kalmyk leader, Tundutov, to send troops to Tsaritsin.[30]

It seemed that the OHL had abandoned its ambitious schemes for the Ukraine and had taken up the even more utopian notion of an alliance between Germany and the Trans-Caucasian provinces, with Georgia as the Finland of the south-east.[31] By now the OHL were prepared to ignore the wishes and the objections of the Turks. Ludendorff told the foreign office that it was about time that the foreign office stopped worrying about what the Turks thought about everything, and began to take notice of the exigencies of the military situation.[32] Enver Pasha reacted to the increasingly bullying attitude of the OHL by threatening to resign. This brought even Ludendorff to his senses, for the thought that the pro-German Enver Pasha might go opened up the even more serious possibility that Turkey might change over to the side of the Entente — a possibility that was widely discussed in Constantinople at the time.[33]

The reports from the OHL's representative in Georgia, Kress von Kressenstein, were hardly encouraging either to the foreign office with its plans for the economic exploitation of the Caucasus or to the OHL with their concern for using Georgia as a reservoir of manpower. Kress found that there were not enough trained men in the area to defend Georgia against the reds, and far from seeing Georgia as a source of manpower, he was obliged to ask the OHL for troops to make the German presence felt, and to discourage the rapacity of the Turks. Shipments of grain from the Ukraine had to be sent to feed a starving population, and oil had to be sent to provide fuel in Georgia. Even if Germany had been able to exploit the Baku oil it was discovered that the transport facilities were inadequate. Thus Georgia, far from being a rich source of men and raw materials, proved to be a drain on both.

The question of the Baku oil was still open. Joffe informed the German government that if the oil wells of Baku were to fall into the hands of the Turkish army, which was led in part by German officers, the wells would be blown up. The Soviet government saw the only hope of keeping some control over the oil wells was to come to an agreement with the Germans, so that Germany could restrain the Turks. The OHL ordered Enver Pasha to stop his advance, Hindenburg threatened to withdraw all German officers from the Turkish high command, and Seeckt said he would resign, but the Turks still advanced. It was their defeat outside Baku that saved the oil wells, not the activities of the OHL.

The bolshevik hold on Baku was short lived. At the end of July the Baku Soviet was overthrown by social revolutionary and menshevik elements. They invited the British to occupy the town, and a small force under General Dunsterville stayed in Baku until the middle of September.[34] The OHL proposed a joint German and Turkish attack on the town, but Hintze knew that the Soviet government would not tolerate a further Turkish advance. The Germans did not have enough troops in the area, and the Turks advanced in spite of German and Soviet protests. On 14 September they took the town. By now relations between the Germans and the Turks were at their most strained. To counterbalance the Turkish presence in Baku the German navy even planned to send dismantled submarines and motor torpedo boats by rail from Batum to Baku, reassemble them in the shipyards of Baku, and establish naval supremacy in the Caspian. These plans were discussed as late as early October 1918.[35] The collapse of Bulgaria brought a rapid end to the dreams of both Turkey and Germany. On

5 October the Turks formally agreed to vacate the Caucasus, and the Germans undertook to guarantee that the area was indeed evacuated.

The German advance into the Ukraine which led on to the Caucasus was also to lead to an attack on the Crimea. Although this was another clear breach of the treaty of Brest Litovsk, Ludendorff was quick to answer all objections by saying that the Russian navy had taken part in attacks on the German positions in Nikolayev and Kherson, and as these attacks were clearly breaches of the treaty, Germany had every reason to wipe out the 'pirates' nest' of Sebastopol.[36] The OHL would not listen to the objections of the foreign office to its plans for the Crimea which it saw as further proof of the vacillating policy of the 'ink-pot men'. On 17 April Ludendorff wrote:

> It is desirable that the Crimea declares itself independent and separate from Greater Russia by an open demand and with a request for the protection of the German army. Whether this is based on a monarchy or a republic is of little importance and must be settled according to existing conditions.[37]

To *Oberost* he wrote that Germany must ensure that a 'branch office of the Moscow soviet government' was not established on the southern border of the Ukraine. Summing up his policy towards the Crimea he wrote: 'Economically the same guide lines for the exploitation of the Crimea apply as for the Ukraine. Particular attention and protection should be given to German agricultural settlements.'[38]

The OHL's scheme was for an 'independent' Tartar republic which would be under German 'protection'. At *Oberost* Hoffmann was already talking of the Crimea as the 'German riviera', an expression which caused some alarm in diplomatic circles in Berlin.[39] At Spa on 13 May Ludendorff argued that Germany had to clear the Black Sea of enemy ships, and for this purpose it was necessary to occupy the Crimean ports, and added with amazing insolence that 'when the time comes we shall ask the foreign office, as we always do, what attitude we should take in the Crimea'. Neither Kühlmann nor Hertling raised any serious objections to the invasion of the Crimea, so that the OHL triumphed yet again.[40]

Ludendorff's further schemes for the Crimea involved allowing the Ukraine to annex the Crimea, an idea which was supported by Kühlmann.[41] Encouraged by this response from Kühlmann, Ludendorff began to think of the formation of a new state of 'Crimea-Tauria', which would consist of a collection of German colonies in southern

Russia joined in a federal association with the Ukraine. Mumm, Kühlmann and the foreign office all objected that this would drive the Ukraine back into the arms of Russia, and Ludendorff was obliged to retreat from this extreme position.[42]

Under the protection of the German army a government had been formed under General Sulkiewicz in the Crimea, and Ludendorff urged the chancellor to cooperate closely with him.[43] Kühlmann and Hertling knew that there would be no chance of the Russians signing the supplementary treaty to Brest Litovsk if the German government recognised Sulkiewicz, and thus refused to accept Ludendorff's arguments that without recognition the Sulkiewicz government would fall and the Crimea would become socialist, or be annexed by either Turkey or Russia.[44] Thus it was the supplementary treaty that spelt an end to Ludendorff's more excessive plans, at least in the Crimea. The dream of the 'German Riviera' providing troops for the army, and standing as an outpost of the German Empire, was shattered.

The ostensible reason for the German invasion of the Crimea was the activity of the Russian fleet in the Black Sea, the Sulkiewicz government providing the conventional cry for help somewhat later, in fact after the Crimea had been invaded. As early as March 1918 Ludendorff had been thinking of seizing at least part of the Black Sea fleet and giving it to Turkey, thus making Turkey the most powerful naval power in the area. Holtzendorff agreed with the scheme, but wanting to show a little more respect for the treaty of Brest Litovsk he suggested that the ships should be purchased rather than simply stolen.[45] Impatient with the legal arguments of the foreign office, and Holtzendorff's prevaricating attitude, Ludendorff then suggested that:

Ships which have arrived in Ukrainian harbours and which have not been involved in fights against us are to be given to the Ukraine. All other ships are to be regarded as enemy ships, for parts of the fleet have recently been involved in frequent attacks on water and on land.[46]

The ships had fired on German positions, therefore they could be seized as booty.

On 13 May a conference was held in Berlin with representatives from the OHL, the naval staff and the foreign office to discuss the question of the Black Sea fleet.[47] The naval staff sided with the foreign office which admitted that Germany had no right to the fleet, but wished to use it as a bargaining counter in negotiations with the Soviet government to win further economic concessions. A hideous compromise was reached whereby those states which had separated from Russia and which bordered the Black Sea were to be given some of the Russian ships, but were to compensate Germany for this act of friendship by allowing the German navy to use some of these ships for the duration of the war.

Ludendorff was furious with the naval staff for what he considered to be an act of disloyalty, and almost a breach of military discipline, since the operation against the Black Sea fleet was under the overall command of the OHL.[48] The future of the fleet also became yet another point of discord between Germany's allies. Djemal Pasha, the naval minister and commander of the Turkish troops in Syria was said to be threatening to resign if Turkey was not given the fleet. The Bulgarians violently opposed the suggestion that the Turks should be further strengthened. The Ukrainians felt that the fleet was rightfully their property. The German navy knew that they did not have enough men to man the ships, so had little use for them. Ludendorff would accept none of these arguments. He was still determined that Germany should control the fleet, but was prepared to give the Ukraine, Turkey and Bulgaria a few ships in return for giving up those territorial demands which the OHL was not prepared to accept.

Most of the fleet left Sebastopol at the end of April in the face of the German advance and sailed east to Novorossiysk. The Soviet government agreed to send the fleet back to Sebastopol provided that the Germans halted their advance in southern Russia and in Finland, and did not occupy Sebastopol. The foreign office, anxious to halt the OHL's advance, agreed, but Ludendorff objected strongly, demanding the return of the fleet within six days. Discussions dragged on until 11 June when the Russians landed a force of some 10,000 men at Taganrog. Although these troops seemed to be acting on their own initiative, and were easily defeated by the Württemberg *Landwehr* from Rostow, the foreign office was now prepared to accept the OHL's demand that unless the ships were returned to Sebastopol by 15 June the army would advance to Novorossiysk.[49] The Soviet government, understandably suspicious of German motives, ordered the fleet to be sunk. Some, but not all of the ships were sunk on the night of 17-18 June.

Frustrated in his plans for the Black Sea fleet, Ludendorff was now determined to get rid of Holtzendorff. A report on conditions in the Crimea from Vice-Admiral Hopman, which had been shown to the Kaiser without Ludendorff's knowledge made Ludendorff so angry that he demanded that Hopman be posted or he would resign. Holtzendorff complained to the Kaiser of Ludendorff's megalomania, and made it clear that he would not even consider posting Hopman. Yet in spite of this stand Holtzendorff, who was sick at the time, was in no mood for yet another fight with the OHL. He complained to Hindenburg that he had not even been invited to the crown council at Spa, and continued by criticising Ludendorff. Hindenburg gave his full support to Ludendorff, and Holtzendorff in desperation handed in his resignation to the Kaiser. Ludendorff had won a further victory over a tiresome rival.[50]

Meanwhile discussions continued between the foreign office and Joffe on the future of the Black Sea fleet. Hintze was determined to secure use of the ships, but he did not wish to compromise the chances of successful negotiations over the supplementary treaty for the sake of a fleet whose military value was hardly likely to be decisive. He succeeded in obtaining Soviet approval for use of the fleet for 'peaceful means', but it could also be used for military purposes if there was a question of the 'necessity of war'. At the beginning of September a few of the ships were manned by German sailors accompanied by a Soviet commissar. The war ended before they were put to any use.

Thus the Black Sea fleet had been of no use whatever to the Germans; it only served to worsen relations between Germany and her allies and between the foreign office and the OHL, and served to strain still further German-Soviet relations. Most of the fleet ended up in the hands of the Allies under the terms of the armistice, and part of it was used by the counter-revolutionary forces of Denikin and later Wrangel, and was then taken by the French to the north African port of Bizerta where it slowly rusted.[51]

NOTES

1. John S. Reshetar, *The Ukrainian Revolution 1917-1920. A Study in Nationalism*, Princeton 1952, p. 114. Reshetar's book is an invaluable source of information on developments within the Ukraine at this time. Peter Borowsky, *Deutsche Ukrainepolitik 1918*, Lubeck and Hamburg 1970, Historische Studien Heft 416 is an excellent study, particularly for Germany's economic aims in the Ukraine.
2. Reshetar, *Ukrainian Revolution*, p. 117.
3. For a detailed account of the military operations in the Ukraine see *Der Weltkrieg 1914-1918*, Band 13.
4. Baumgart, *Deutsche Ostpolitik*, p. 124, quoting I.I. Minc and R. Ejdeman, *Krakh Germanskoi Okkupatsii Na Ukraine*, Moscow 1936. Vol. I of this work was published in Strasburg in 1937 as *Die deutsche Occupation in der Ukraine*.

Geheimdokumente. Vol. II is in Russian only and can only be found in Moscow.

5. Reshetar, *The Ukrainian Revolution*, p. 123, quoting Minc and Ejdeman, p. 91.
6. Bundesarchiv Militärarchiv Freiburg, Nachlass Groener N46/17. PA Bonn AA Ukraine 1, Band 9.
7. Groener, *Lebenserinnerungen*, p. 399.
8. *Ibid.*, p. 398. Groener dates this meeting as 26 April, but all the other sources agree on 24 April. See Hans Beyer, 'Die Mittelmächte und die Ukraine 1918', *Jahrbuch für Geschichte Ost Europas*, Beiheft 2, Munich 1956, p. 40, whose argument that the OHL had nothing to do with Skoropadsky's *coup d'état* is impossible to accept; also Reshetar, *The Ukrainian Revolution*, p. 125.
9. *Deutschland im ersten Weltkrieg*, Vol. 3, p. 217.
10. Reshetar, *The Ukrainian Revolution*, p. 128.
11. *Ibid.*, p. 130.
12. PA Bonn AA Gr. HQ Russland 13, Band 12.
13. Baumgart, *Deutsche Ostpolitik*, p. 130, insists that the commandant acted on his own initiative but gives no evidence for this. It is true that Groener regarded his actions as 'regrettable', and Mumm called him a 'bull in a china shop' *(Quadratochs im Porzellanladen).* The idea that an officer would arrest members of a theoretically friendly government without the approval of his superiors is a trifle fanciful – the more so since both Groener and Eichhorn were determined to replace the Rada.
14. PA Bonn AA Ukraine, Band 10.
15. Bundesarchiv Militärarchiv Freiburg, Nachlass Groener N46/172.
16. Baumgart, *Deutsche Ostpolitik*, p. 132.
17. Bundesarchiv Militärarchiv Freiburg, Nachlass Groener N46/173 for Eichhorn memorandum 17-6-18.
18. Baumgart, *Deutsche Ostpolitik*, p. 139.
19. *Ibid.*, p. 141.
20. PA Bonn AA Weltkrieg 15 Geheim, Band 15. Bundesarchiv Militärarchiv Freiburg, Nachlass Groener N46/171 in a letter 16-7-18 stressed the great strategic importance of Tsaritsin, and felt that it was a great mistake that it had not been captured by the German troops.
21. See the account in Kakhovskaia, *Souvenirs d'une revolutionnaire*, Paris 1926, p. 63. The left social revolutionaries demanded the resumption of the war at the Fifth All Russian Council of Soviets in Moscow. E.H. Carr, *The Bolshevik Revolution*, Vol. I, p. 305.
22. Rosenfeld, *Sowjetrussland und Deutschland*, p. 87; *Deutschland im ersten Weltkrieg*, Band 3, p. 219.
23. There are no accurate figures available for the number of German troops in the Ukraine. The most plausible are in the account of General Kuhl in *Untersuchungsausschuss IV Reihe*, Band 3. The war minister said that 'the main reason why we went into the Ukraine was to get food supplies. If we now have to give that up because of the shortage of currency then we could have used our troops more usefully elsewhere.' The treasury constantly complained that the Ukraine policy was using up all the reserves of roubles. DZA Potsdam Stellvertreter des Reichskanzlers, Ukraine 13.
24. Matthias, Morsey, *Regierung Max von Baden*, pp. 115, 220.
25. PA Bonn AA Russland 97a, Band 12.
26. PA Bonn AA Russland 97a, Band 13.
27. PA Bonn AA Russland 97a, Band 12.
28. Baumgart, *Deutsche Ostpolitik*, p. 184.
29. PA Bonn AA Russland 97a, Band 16.
30. Bundesarchiv Militärarchiv Freiburg, Nachlass Groener N46/171.

31. PA Bonn AA Russland 97a, Band 17. Berckheim to foreign office 10-6-18. Ludendorff could claim to be acting in accordance with the Kaiser's wishes, for William had been carried away by Lossow's glowing account of the possibilities for Germany in Georgia. Baumgart, *Deutsche Ostpolitik*, p. 188.
32. PA Bonn AA Russland 97a, Band 17.
33. J. Pomiankowski, *Der Zusammenbruch des ottomanischen Reiches. Erinnerungen an die Turkei aus der Zeit des Weltkriegs*, Zurich 1928, p. 368.
34. Carr, *The Bolshevik Revolution*, Vol. I, p. 349; L.C. Dunsterville, *The Adventures of Dunsterforce*, London 1920.
35. Baumgart, *Deutsche Ostpolitik*, p. 204. Yet in his article 'Neue Quellen zur Beurteilung Ludendorffs. Der Konflikt mit dem Admiralstabschef über die deutsche Schwarzmeerpolitik im Sommer 1918', *Militärgeschichtliche Mitteilungen*, 1970 he claims that the naval staff was far more realistic than the OHL.
36. PA Bonn AA HQ 31e,f,g,h, Russland, Band 1. For developments in the Crimea see E. Kirimal, *Die Nationale Kampf der Krimtürken mit besonderer Berucksichtigung der Jahre 1917-1918*, Emsdetten 1952.
37. Bundesarchiv Militärarchiv Freiburg, Marineakten 69256: Schwarzes Meer, Band 1.
38. Bundesarchiv Militärarchiv Freiburg, Marineakten 75683 Krim, Band 1.
39. Baumgart, *Deutsche Ostpolitik*, p. 153. The 'German Riviera' was not just to be a playground, but was also intended to supply soldiers. For this reason the OHL decided not to allow Mennonites to settle in the area as they were pacifists.
40. Ritter, *Staatskunst und Kriegshandwerk*, Vol. 4, p. 347 argues that since Kühlmann got Ludendorff to state that 'our operations in Russia are now at an end', the state secretary had won a significant victory over the OHL. As the frontiers of 'Russia' were not yet settled this was an empty formula and qualified in any case by Ludendorff's remarks that German troops were being attacked by 'bolshevik bands and other Russian units'.
41. PA Bonn AA HQ 31 e,f,g,h, Russland, Band 1.
42. Fischer, *Griff nach der Weltmacht*, p. 743; Baumgart, *Deutsche Ostpolitik*, p. 154. Ludendorff's ideas are summed up in his letter to Bülow, the representative of the naval staff at headquarters on 4-6-18. The Germans in southern Russia were to concentrate in the Crimea which would then be in a federal union with the Ukraine. Germany would have 'economic advantages' and a naval base in Sebastopol. Bundesarchiv Militärarchiv Freiburg Marine Akten 69257 Schwarzes Meer, Band 2.
43. PA Bonn AA Gr. HQ 31e,f,g,y, Russland, Band 1.
44. *Ibid.*, Hertling to Berckheim 21-6-18, Ludendorff to chancellor 23-6-18, Kühlmann to Lersner 5-7-18, Ludendorff to Lersner for foreign office 16-7-18.
45. Bundesarchiv Militärarchiv Freiburg, Marine Akten 69256: Schwarzes Meer, Band 1.
46. *Ibid.*
47. PA Bonn AA Russland 72b, Band 31.
48. Bundesarchiv Militärarchiv Freiburg, Marine Akten 69257: Schwarzes Meer, Band 2.
49. Ritter, *Staatskunst und Kriegshandwerk*, Vol. 4, p. 352, without references claims that the foreign office was in favour of a 'compromise', the OHL for pressing on. However, from the documents – PA Bonn AA Deutschland 131, Band 40 – it seems that the foreign office was at the end of its patience after the Taganrog affair.
50. Baumgart, *Deutsche Ostpolitik*, p. 172.
51. *Ibid.*, p. 174.

THE HIGH COMMAND AND THE ARMISTICE

By the middle of July 1918 an increasing number of officers in the OHL were convinced that the war could no longer be won. This insight into the reality of the military situation was made all the more alarming by the attitude of Ludendorff, who seemed to refuse to accept this bitter truth, and who in a critical period of the war, suffered from a severe psychological crisis which made him unequal to the enormous tasks required of him. Disenchantment with Ludendorff grew among the more perceptive officers, with the result that the OHL became seriously divided, and Ludendorff's position, which depended so much on military success, was steadily eroded, not only by the politicians who were anxious to seize the opportunity to reassert the primacy of the political over the military, but also from within the ranks of the demigods of the supreme command.

It seems likely that it was General Fritz von Lossberg who was the first to be seriously concerned about Ludendorff's military ability.[1] Lossberg, an outstanding tactician and specialist with a mobile approach to defence, was attached to the OHL after the French and American breakthrough at Villiers-Cotterêts which had resulted in the penetration of the German lines for up to four miles, threatened the entire German position on the Marne, and meant that the area would have to be evacuated.[2] Lossberg arrived at headquarters shortly after this defeat on 18 July and was shocked to find Ludendorff highly nervous and all too willing to place the blame for this setback quite unjustifiably on the shoulders of Colonel Wetzell, the chief of the operations division of the OHL, and also on the German 7th army which, Ludendorff insisted, had failed miserably. Lossberg argued that the German army should be withdrawn to the Siegfried line, thus abandoning the gains made in the March offensive, but shortening the German lines. Ludendorff felt that although this might be a sound move militarily, it would have a disastrous effect on morale at home and give the Entente unnecessary encouragement. Lossberg replied that if this action was necessary from a military point of view it should be carried out, whereupon Ludendorff rather dramatically threatened to resign. Lossberg was now convinced that Ludendorff was no longer master of the situation, and had made a serious strategic mistake in refusing to withdraw.

He was not alone in his assessment of Ludendorff. On 30 July

Ludendorff discussed the military situation with Hintze and painted a ridiculously optimistic picture of the German position. On the following day Bartenwerffer complained to Merz about what he called 'this shocking state of affairs', and both men agreed that it was Ludendorff's overwhelming vanity which stopped him from putting the state secretary fully in the picture.[3]

Other officers at the OHL, although they were not yet openly critical of Ludendorff, were becoming highly alarmed about the military situation and could not share his nervous optimism or Hindenburg's confidence. Major Neimann circulated a memorandum among the senior officers of the OHL on 20 July which urged that all Germany's military power should be concentrated on trying to bring about negotiations for a satisfactory peace settlement which would have to be based on a complete reconsideration of foreign policy. Niemann felt that it was still possible for Germany to gain much from the war – his thinking ran along lines similar to that of liberal imperialists such as Friedrich Naumann – but he insisted that if negotiations were not set in motion at once then Germany could well lose everything.[4] Even Colonel Bauer was impressed by Niemann's arguments, although they must at first have seemed dangerously liberal to him, and he agreed that it might indeed be possible to come to some form of compromise with the western powers by restoring the autonomy of Belgium and abandoning demands for reparations. But Bauer was in fact talking a quite different language from Niemann, for he went on to say that there could be no question of abandoning Alsace and Lorraine, and Germany would have to claim Longwy and Briey.[5] Significant in Bauer's comments is the fact that he had made a slight step backwards from his usual extremist position. His grave concern for Germany's overall position is reflected in the memorandum he wrote in July 1918 calling for draconian measures at home to step up the war effort.[6] Yet even this slight retreat was enough to give Bauer the reputation of being a pessimist.[7]

The OHL had repeatedly tried to get rid of the auxiliary labour law and to regiment the labour force, and these efforts had been renewed after the wave of strikes in January 1918. In a lengthy memorandum to the chancellor on 18 June Hindenburg argued that wages were so high that there was no longer any incentive to work, labour leaders and workers worked as slowly as possible so as to avoid being sent to the front, for once workers came into the army they were no longer under union control and were thus lost to the labour movement.[8] Hindenburg demanded that all workers should be placed under military control, wages and profits should be controlled by the state, and the armaments factories, some of which were already thinking in terms of peacetime production, would have to be placed under military supervision.

These arguments were rejected by the chancellor and the war minister, and the OHL's statistics were challenged.[9] German manpower resources were so strained that even if the OHL's plan was put into operation it would have had little impact. Thus they were unable to make the changes in the law which they demanded. As the military situation grew steadily worse there was little that they could do except make wild demands and look around for scapegoats for the failure of a system which they had done so much to create. The OHL drew a caricature of the German worker at home living a life of luxury and idle opulence, in contrast to the brave men at the front sacrificing their lives for their country for little recompense. On 2 July Ludendorff asked that wages should be reduced so as to bring them in line with the soldier's pay. He refused to accept the minister of the interior's argument that such a course of action would lead to a dangerous radicalisation of the workers.[10] For Bauer the responsibility for setbacks in the war was placed firmly on the home front. He wrote: 'We shall win the war when the home front stops attacking us from behind.'[11] The stab in the back legend was already firmly established. The inability of the OHL to overcome the fact that Germany could never match the economic resources of the Entente was thus not explained by the objective fact of the impossibility of the German undertaking, but by a dangerous ideological obfuscation that was to seriously divide the Weimar republic, and equate liberal democracy with treason and defeat.

At first Ludendorff was prepared to listen to some of the arguments put forward by Niemann and Bauer, but he very quickly became more optimistic. The Entente had not been able to follow up the success of Villers-Cotterêts with a further significant breakthrough. The army had made orderly withdrawals to less exposed positions, and there was no question of the line breaking. Ludendorff now began to think of a fresh offensive, and objected to any further withdrawals. His mood of confidence seemed to be fully restored, but the fact that he was able to be so confident when the situation was still highly critical was indication not only to Merz and Bartenwerffer, but also to Hintze, that he no longer had the ability to make a realistic appraisal of the total situation. It was at this point that the Entente forced a major break in the German lines on the Somme, and in the face of a massive attack by tank units the German army lost its nerves and fled in panic. This was the *dies ater* of the German army, 8 August 1918.

This second setback within a few days proved to be too much for Ludendorff. He had been suffering from a severe depression for some days, and was now in a state of extreme nervous agitation and was no longer able to think clearly or to give decisive commands. The Bavarian military plenipotentiary complained that Ludendorff was suffering from a severe 'nervous tension' and was constantly making ill-considered decisions and interfering with the commands of the army groups with disastrous results.[12] The soldiers at the front were consequently becoming increasingly critical of the OHL. His collapse on 8 August was noted at the time by many of his close associates, and was seen as the culmination of his depressed mood since Villers-Cotterêts.[13]

Ludendorff placed the blame for the demoralisation on the 2nd army rather than on the total situation which showed the steadily increasing military superiority of the Entente forces, even though there was some justification for his concern. The 2nd army was an experienced and well-rested force, and yet it had been over-run without offering the kind of resistance that would have been expected. The very high number of prisoners of war taken indicated a demoralisation of the troops. Even worse was the news that a guards division had jeered at a division of Württembergers that was about to launch a counterattack with calls such as 'strike breakers' and 'prolongers of the war'.[14]

The Kaiser told Ludendorff that too much was being expected of the troops, and although Ludendorff refused to accept this argument, the Kaiser informed him that the army had now reached the limits of its defensive ability and that the war would have to be ended. He ordered a crown council to meet on 14 August where Hindenburg, Ludendorff, Hertling, Hintze and the crown prince would discuss the measures needed to be taken.[15]

In the course of preliminary discussions between Hintze and Ludendorff the state secretary was told that the Entente could not be defeated by offensive means as Ludendorff had claimed was possible as late as the middle of July. Ludendorff said that the strategy of the Central Powers would have to be changed to a defensive stance which would wear down the enemy to such a degree that they would eventually have to sue for peace.[16]

Hintze used these remarks as the basis for his presentation to the crown council the following day. He painted a gloomy picture of Germany's predicament. The Entente countries with their undoubted superiority in men and material were confident that time was on their side, and that eventually they were bound to win. This view was shared by many of the neutral powers. Austria-Hungary was clearly on the verge of collapse, and unlikely to be able to continue the war into the new year. Bulgaria made constantly increasing demands for subsidies and materials, and her army was no longer effective. Turkey was putting all her efforts into a 'war of murder and plunder' in the Caucasus, and was more of a hindrance than a help to German troops in the area. He closed his remarks by saying that Hindenburg had pointed out that the army would have to go over to a strategic defensive and by this means try to break the will of the Entente to continue the war, and added: 'the political leadership would give way to the ideas of the greatest general that had emerged in the course of the war.'[17]

Although Hintze had accurately reported Hindenburg's and Ludendorff's thinking, it now appeared that the OHL believed that if only the German army could hold the line in the west the difficulties which England and France were experiencing would become so severe that they would be forced to ask for peace. They had thus regained much of their old confidence, and Hintze found himself embarrassingly isolated. German policy was now virtually paralysed. The OHL and its supporters still lived in the dream world of an annexationist peace, but the essential precondition for the realisation of such plans did not exist. Germany could not defeat the Entente. Yet on the other hand the state secretary was not willing to draw the necessary conclusions from the situation which he grasped better than any of the others at the crown council. If Germany could not win the war then the extensive war aims would have to be abandoned in favour of new, more sober assessments of the possibility of bringing the war to a close under terms that would not be too damaging to Germany. Hintze, faced with the opposition of the OHL whom he still admired, and whose lead he had agreed to follow, was not prepared to take on this necessary, but highly unpopular task.

Ludendorff's optimism at the crown council did not last long, and he once more fell into a deep nervous depression. At the instigation of Colonel Bauer, Colonel Heye was brought to the OHL in order to relieve him of much of the burden of work which was proving too much for one man. Some officers felt that Bauer's move was pointless, for Heye was considered too young to be able to be really independent from Ludendorff.[18] But they were soon proved wrong. Heye quickly became one of the most influential officers in the OHL, and a leader of the opposition group to Ludendorff's leadership in the critical weeks that were to lead to the armistice offer and Ludendorff's resignation. Ludendorff accepted Heye's appointment because the other candidates, which included Lossberg, Seeckt and Schulenburg, were not acceptable to him. At the beginning of September Heye took over Wetzell's position as chief of the operations division, a change which was significant in that Heye was regarded as a 'pessimist', whereas Wetzell was still an 'optimist'.[18]

Even the optimistic Wetzell was beginning to have serious doubts about Ludendorff, and bitterly resented the accusations that he was largely to blame for the failures on the western front. On 1 September Ludendorff told some of his closest associates in the OHL that it was impossible for him to put the foreign office fully in the picture, and he had been obliged to withhold information from Hintze, because otherwise they were liable to get exceedingly anxious. Wetzell and von Bockelberg were both horrified to hear Ludendorff talking in these terms and decided to try to reduce Ludendorff's influence which they were convinced was exceedingly harmful. They agreed that the Kaiser had no real idea of what was going on, and therefore their only hope seemed to be to persuade Hindenburg to take a more critical attitude towards Ludendorff.[19] Wetzell continued to complain that Ludendorff was refusing to make decisions and was constantly prevaricating, but he was dismissed before his grand scheme could mature.[20]

The damage, as far as Ludendorff's position was concerned, had already been done. Wetzell, and those officers who agreed with him, managed to arrange a meeting between Ludendorff and a psychologist from the imperial headquarters in Spa, Dr Hochheimer. Hochheimer diagnosed overwork and suggested to Ludendorff that he relax more, sleep longer, and take more exercise. Much to everyone's surprise, Ludendorff accepted these suggestions without protest.[21] Some of the prescriptions of the learned doctor were more humorous. Ludendorff was *ordered* to take special pleasure in the roses in the villa where he stayed in Spa, and was instructed to sing German folksongs on waking in the morning.[22]

The full details of the divisions, rivalries and alliances within the OHL in August and September 1918 will probably never be fully clarified. The documentation is scanty, and the official documents of the OHL were destroyed in 1945 during an Allied raid on Potsdam. However, from the surviving documentation, an outline of the situation can be discerned. One group, which included Heye, Stülpnagel, Merz, Bockelberg, Brinckmann, Posek and the later chancellor, Schleicher, realised that a drastic change in policy was needed and that this would only be possible if Ludendorff's powers were greatly reduced. Others, like Haeften, although often inconsistent, usually supported Ludendorff and insisted that a demand for an armistice should not come from the

OHL, as this would be tantamount to an admission that all was
lost, which would in turn destroy the morale of the army. The third
group is more difficult to perceive clearly. It was headed by Colonel
Bauer, with the support of General Bartenwerffer. Bauer's position
was never clearly articulated. He realised that Ludendorff, like
Falkenhayn before him, no longer had that essential ingredient of
successful military leadership – 'fortune' – on which Frederick the
Great had placed so much emphasis. He also knew that Ludendorff
was no longer in a fit mental and physical state to play such an
important role in the affairs of the OHL. Bauer, who had always
stood for the most extreme war aims and for draconian political
measures, including a full-scale military dictatorship under the OHL,
now felt that Ludendorff had become weak-kneed and feeble
and should therefore be removed and replaced by a more energetic
man, preferably Schulenburg. Always an ambitious man, Bauer did
not wish to associate any longer with a man who was clearly on the
way out, but he also distrusted most of the younger officers who
saw a closer cooperation with the majority parties in the Reichstag
and the beginning of armistice negotiations before the army was
completely defeated as the only viable alternative policy.[23]

Bauer and Bartenwerffer were thus in a curious position during
these important weeks, and the fact that they were unable to play
any decisive role made it possible for the younger officers in the OHL
to seize the initiative and to force the issue of the armistice.
Indeed Bauer helped this group enormously by securing the
appointment of Heye and of Stülpnagel, both of whom were to play
important roles in setting the armistice procedures in motion. Thus
during these critical weeks, Ludendorff no longer could count on the
support of the demigods of the OHL, and when even Hindenburg
withdrew his support his fate was sealed.

By the last week of September it was clear to the more perceptive
officers at the OHL that the war not only could not be won, it had
actually been lost. If it was indeed a case of defeat rather than
stalemate then armistice talks should begin at once to avoid the
collapse of the army and the very real danger of revolution at home.
Ludendorff refused to accept this view, partly because he knew that
such an admission would mean the end of the unique position of the
OHL in German society. On 24 September Ludendorff discussed the
military situation with Groener, and gave an encouraging account of
developments. Heye contradicted him, saying that the situation was
exceedingly dangerous. Groener disregarded Heye's warnings, for he had

heard much about the new operations chief's pessimism.[24] On the following day Ludendorff issued an order to all army groups that there would be no retreat, and that the decisive battle would be fought from existing positions. Heye did not give up. He discontinued the order and told Ludendorff that he should go immediately to Berlin, tell the Kaiser and Hintze how critical the military situation was, and ask for the opening of armistice discussions.[25] Stülpnagel also urged Ludendorff to go to Berlin.[26]

Later that day Ludendorff told the surgeon general *(Generalstabsarzt der Armee),* Dr Schjerning, that the outbreak of Spanish flu in the French army was his 'last chance'. Schjerning was deeply shocked by this remark and at once reported it to Heye and to Merz von Quirnheim, another of the section chiefs who was in opposition to Ludendorff. Heye then called a meeting for the following morning to discuss the question in greater detail.[27] The atmosphere was tense. Heye and Stülpnagel were frustrated that they had been unable to persuade Ludendorff to go to Berlin. During the night the news that the Bulgarians were asking for an armistice had reached headquarters. It was then agreed that as Ludendorff would not go to Berlin, Hintze should be asked to come to Spa. Lersner was asked to join the meeting, and he agreed to tell Hintze that the military situation was hopeless and that he should come to Spa at once. Lersner then telephoned Berlin, without Ludendorff's knowledge, and relayed the message.[28]

At midday Heye told Ludendorff that Hintze had been invited to come to Spa. Much to Heye's relief Ludendorff raised no objections. The news from the east, combined with the fact that the allies were pressing hard on the western front at Cambrai and Ypres, in the Champagne and on the Meuse, had undermined his confidence. Heye and his supporters then turned their attention to Hindenburg to try to persuade him that an armistice was essential.

It was not until 6 p.m. on 28 September that Ludendorff first spoke to Hindenburg about an armistice. When he told Hindenburg that an armistice was needed the field marshal replied that he had been on the point of telling Ludendorff the same. However, neither would admit that Germany had been defeated, and they were still full of illusions. They knew that Germany would have to abandon the occupied areas in the west as an essential precondition for an armistice, but they had no intention of abandoning their positions in the east, and hoped that they would be able to use the Entente's fear of bolshevism as a screen for German territorial ambitions there. They agreed that

Germany needed a breathing space to gather her strength for the resumption of the war.[29]

Hintze, who discussed the armistice question with Hindenburg and Ludendorff at Spa on 29 September, had decided even before he heard from Lersner on 26 September that the war was lost and that an armistice was essential. He relied less and less on Ludendorff's judgement, particularly after the middle of July when Ludendorff had told him that Germany would be able to defeat the Entente 'finally and decisively'. After August such notions were hopelessly unrealistic, and Hintze relied increasingly on other sources of information, direct from the front. From these he was convinced that the military situation was so grave on both fronts that an armistice was essential. He was painfully aware that an armistice would place an almost intolerable strain on German society and that a revolution was distinctly possible. The question for Hintze was therefore one of 'dictatorship or revolution'. A dictator was doomed to fail because he would preside over a German defeat. The second alternative was therefore the most likely outcome of the crisis, but it could either be a revolution 'from below' or a revolution 'from above'.[30] The Hintze-Action, or the 'revolution from above', was thus carefully planned in the foreign office before Hintze left for Spa.[31]

The principal idea of the 'revolution from above' was that in order for peace negotiations to begin, a government would have to be formed on a broad national basis. Hertling would have to resign, and the new chancellor work closely with the Reichstag majority. Peace negotiations would begin on the basis of the fourteen points of President Wilson. Hertling had no idea of Hintze's plot against him, and at first decided not to go to Spa with the state secretary, but on 28 September the OHL's representative, Colonel von Winterfeldt told him that the OHL had decided that the government would either have to be changed, or placed on a broader footing. He therefore decided to travel immediately to Spa.[32]

Hindenburg, Ludendorff, Heye and Hintze met at the Hotel Britannique in Spa at 10 a.m. on 29 September.[33] Ludendorff replied to Hintze's gloomy picture of the military situation by saying that an armistice would have to be signed immediately, a reply which shocked even the pessimist Hintze who had imagined that the armistice could be postponed for some time to come. Ludendorff agreed with Hintze's plans for a 'revolution from above' saying that as many people as possible should be made responsible for the way the war was to be ended. At this point Hindenburg interjected that Germany

should try to annex Longwy and Briey, but Ludendorff quickly
pointed out that time had now run out, and Germany would have to
renounce annexations in the west.

Now that there was general agreement between Hintze and the OHL,
they went together to see the Kaiser. The Kaiser agreed to the
proposals for bourgeois democratic reforms which would include a
government with members from the SPD and the liberal parties.
He said that President Wilson should be asked to act as an intermediary
for the peace negotiations, and that the Hintze-Action should begin
at once.

Poor old Hertling did not arrive at Spa until after all these discussions
which had sealed his fate. Hertling had always objected strongly to the
parliamentarisation of German politics, and was overwhelmed by the
news that Germany was on the verge of collapse. His resignation was
immediately accepted, but his plea that the Kaiser should wait at least
a fortnight to see if there was any improvement in the military situation
was ignored, for Hindenburg and Ludendorff had insisted that the
armistice would have to be signed as soon as possible.[34]

On the morning of 30 September Ludendorff called the military
plenipotentiaries together and told them that the military situation
was so grave that the OHL had decided to seek an armistice. A new
government was to be formed in Berlin, and this government would
choose the time when the armistice offer was to be made.[35]   The fact
that Hindenburg and Ludendorff had decided to end the war was
common knowledge among the officers at headquarters, but it was
not until 9 a.m. on 1 October that Ludendorff addressed the section
chiefs of the OHL.[36] He appeared pale and agonised, but to Thaer, a
senior officer at the OHL, he was: 'a truly beautiful German hero.
I had to think of Siegfried with the mortal wound in his back from
Hagen's spear.' The Hagen who had stabbed Ludendorff in the back
was the Spartacus group and other socialists who had infected the
troops with pernicious ideas so that they were no longer reliable.
Ludendorff told the section chiefs that although the socialists were
responsible for the defeat of the army they would have to be brought
into the government. Of the SPD he said:

> I have asked His Majesty to bring those people into the
> government who are largely responsible that things have
> turned out as they have. We shall therefore see these
> gentlemen enter the ministries, and they must now make the
> peace which has to be made. They must now eat the soup

which they have served us!

Ludendorff was now beginning to panic, and he demanded an immediate despatch of the peace offer, even before the new government was formed.[37] He then agreed to wait for twenty-four hours provided that he got a guarantee that Prince Max of Baden would be able to form the new government immediately, otherwise he would insist on sending a note to the Entente governments that evening. Whilst Ludendorff was continually pressing for an immediate commencement of armistice negotiations, he was also beginning to look around for a scapegoat. The OHL concocted the ingenious theory that the foreign office was responsible for the collapse of Bulgaria in that it had not secured the removal of the American chargé d'affaires from Sofia. The collapse on the western front was now blamed on the war ministry for not applying the auxiliary labour law with sufficient energy so that not enough men were made available to the army.[38]

Prince Max arrived in Berlin at 4 a.m. on 1 October. He spoke half an hour later with the OHL's representative, Haeften, who told him that his superiors wanted an immediate armistice. Prince Max was adamant that an immediate commencement of armistice negotiations would have disastrous political consequences, and he urged Haeften to do his best to persuade Ludendorff to wait for at least a fortnight so that the new chancellor could 'prepare the political ground at home and abroad'. Haeften was unmoved by these arguments, and continued to insist that the army needed a breathing space immediately. Prince Max also found no support from Hintze who said that as the decision had been made on 29 September the armistice note should be sent at once. Haeften called Ludendorff from Berlin at midnight, and tried to persuade him to postpone the armistice negotiations, but Ludendorff refused saying that the army needed the respite, and that the army would surely give him the chance to recover strength and fight on. Coupled with this extraordinary wishful thinking was a growing confidence among some officers at the OHL, and the Bavarian plenipotentiary reported that many officers seemed almost unaware that the front might break at any moment.[39]

Hindenburg arrived in Berlin on 2 October and had his first conference with Prince Max that afternoon.[40] Hindenburg would not listen to Prince Max's request for a delay, and said that a fresh attack was expected within a week, and he could not guarantee that it would not lead to a catastrophe. At an impromptu crown council that evening Prince Max found that all the members of the retiring government supported Hindenburg, except Solf, and the Kaiser remarked that it was not his job to make life difficult for the high command.

Prince Max met Hindenburg again the following morning at 9 a.m. and made one last attempt to win him over. He told the field marshal that an immediate armistice offer would be tantamount to an admission of defeat, but he concluded by saying that he was prepared to send a note to the western powers if the OHL would state in writing that the military situation was such that a delay could not be tolerated.

Hindenburg wrote this note immediately after conferring with Ludendorff by telephone.[41] It was cunningly phrased: although the OHL requested that armistice negotiations should begin at once as there was no possibility of the German army winning the war, Hindenburg insisted that the army was able to stand and fend off the attacks of the Entente. The armistice request was thus couched in humanitarian terms, and there was nothing in the note of the panic striken tone of Ludendorff's initial demand for an armistice. An immediate armistice was desirable because 'every day means that thousands of brave soldiers will lose their lives'. Haeften was quite right to note in his diary that Hindenburg was less insistent on an immediate armistice than was Ludendorff.[42]

This reply was a trifle confusing to Prince Max, but it gave him some hope that a delay might indeed be possible. Prior to a second conference with Hindenburg that day he sent him a questionnaire which in essence asked the OHL how long the army would be able to hold out, and whether they were aware that an immediate armistice would mean that Germany would probably lose Alsace-Lorraine and the Polish parts of the Reich. The OHL's reply was that the army could probably hold out until next spring, and it agreed that 'small, French-speaking parts of Alsace-Lorraine might possibly be ceded', but was quite categorical in asserting that there could be no question of any German territory being abandoned in the east.[43] Prince Max saw this as a step back: there was little in the reply that could justify sending the note within the next few hours, so he looked forward to the next meeting with Hindenburg in a confident mood.

At first it seemed that Hindenburg was prepared to accept Prince Max's arguments in favour of delay, but pushed by Hintze he said that it should be sent immediately. As a last hope Prince Max asked Haeften to call Ludendorff to propose that Germany should make a peace offer rather than a request for an armistice. Haeften tried his best to persuade Ludendorff to accept this compromise, but Ludendorff insisted that the army needed a respite.[44]

Later that evening Prince Max met leading government officials to discuss the wording of the note to President Wilson that he felt could no longer be postponed. In the early hours of the morning the note was sent to the German envoy in Bern to forward to Wilson via the Swiss government. It called for an immediate conclusion of an armistice on land, by sea and in the air.[45]

The appeal for an armistice came not from the OHL, but in a document signed by the new chancellor and supported by his cabinet. The role of the OHL in demanding the armistice was carefully concealed from the public. From the very beginning the OHL had realised that the blame for the armistice could be placed on the shoulders of the Reichstag majority, and therefore the whole process of democratisation could be discredited. This view was clearly shared by Prince Max himself, who did not want the right wing to be represented in his government on the grounds that he would not be able to negotiate a peace if well-known annexationists were in his cabinet, and would not then be able to call on the nation to take part in a war of national defence should this be necessary.[46] Thus he rejected the idea of a national coalition government, even though the conservative leader Westarp was prepared to enter his government. At the OHL many officers were already scheming to turn Germany's defeat into a defeat of bourgeois democracy. The Bavarian military plenipotentiary reported:

> On the domestic political situation one often hears the opinion expressed that it is a good thing that the left-wing parties will have to incur the odium for the peace. The storm of indignation of the people will fall on them. One hopes that then one can get back into the saddle and continue to govern according to the old recipe.[47]

President Wilson's reply to the note arrived on 9 October. The wording of the note showed Wilson's willingness to begin negotiations, and in Prince Max's own words 'seemed to justify the optimists'.[48] Two days before Wilson's reply was known, Walter Rathenau had written an article in the *Vossische Zeitung* entitled 'a black day' which had been most favourably received in chauvinist circles. Rathenau's argument was that the government had lost its nerve, and should therefore be replaced by men who were equal to this moment of crisis. If Wilson's reply was not entirely satisfactory Germany should declare an all out effort for national defence with a *levée en masse* in the best traditions of the French revolution.[49]

The more perspicacious realised the absurdity of the scheme. The country was utterly exhausted after four years of war, and there could be no question of a *levée en masse* without there first being a political revolution which the proponents of the scheme abhorred. Nevertheless Prince Max was nervous that the OHL might get carried away with Rathenau's rhetoric, and might also reject Wilson's demands that the German army retreat to within the borders of Germany and accept the fourteen points. The chancellor was delighted to find Ludendorff seemingly in good health and in a conciliatory mood when they met on 9 October. He rejected the *levée en masse*, for he knew full well that it would lead to a total disruption of industrial production. He was now cautiously optimistic about the overall military situation, but he did not contradict Heye when he said that it would be little short of a desperate gamble if the OHL were not to ask for an immediate opening of negotiations for an armistice. Ludendorff told Prince Max that the occupied territories in the west could be evacuated if sufficient time was available, but he insisted that Metz would have to be held for 'reasons of military honour'.[50]

When the right wing parties heard that the OHL was about to abandon the gains in the west there was a storm of protest, and demands that the opinions of other generals be solicited.[51] Ludendorff had thus lost the unconditional support of the political right. Bauer was busy at work in Berlin telling heads of government departments that Ludendorff's health was broken, and articles critical of him were beginning to appear in the newspapers in spite of the censorship.[52] Colonel Bauer told Haeften that since Ludendorff had had a nervous breakdown in August it was essential that he be removed from his position in the OHL, and urged Haeften to persuade Prince Max to dismiss Ludendorff. Haeften refused, but Bauer renewed his efforts to persuade the politicians to secure the removal of Ludendorff who was now seen to be a 'pessimist'.[53]

Hindenburg and Ludendorff knew of the plot against Ludendorff, but they knew nothing of the important role played by Bauer. Hindenburg announced that he would resign if Ludendorff were dismissed, and he objected strongly to the fact that General Hoffmann had been called to Berlin to discuss political matters without the OHL

being informed.[54] Prince Max replied that he regarded Ludendorff
as 'irreplaceable', and that Hoffmann had merely come to discuss the
situation in Lithuania.[55] The chancellor was now beginning to support
Ludendorff against his critics on the right, while at the same time
Ludendorff, aware of the criticisms levelled against him, began to shift
his position by arguing that withdrawal in the west would cause great
damage to property, and therefore could be used as a bargaining
counter with the Entente.[56]

Wilson's second note arrive in Berlin in the early morning of
16 October.[57] It was far firmer in tone than the first note,
denouncing the 'illegal and inhuman' practices of the armed forces
of Germany, calling for an end to submarine warfare, of destruction
of property in Flanders and France, and for further changes in the
government. This reply greatly strengthened the hand of those who
were calling for a *levée en masse*, and Ludendorff began to think
of moving all the troops in the east to the western front and of a
'fight to the bitter end', ideas which moderate politicians like
Solf thought were 'extremely dangerous'.[58]

On the following day Ludendorff arrived in Berlin. He told
Prince Max that there was no danger of a military collapse and said
that if the government continued to consult with other generals
behind the back of the OHL, both he and Hindenburg would resign.
Discussing the resignation threat with his colleagues, Prince Max
shrewdly pointed out that Hindenburg was unlikely to identify
so completely with Ludendorff, and Roedern suggested that the
Kaiser should persuade Hindenburg to stay on, even if Ludendorff
were to resign. It was agreed not to consult other generals until the
OHL said that the front could no longer be held.[59]

Later that day Ludendorff attended a meeting of the war
cabinet and said that the Entente was incapable of forcing a decisive
breakthrough. He did not go so far as to argue that the armistice
negotiations should be broken off, as the extreme right was
clamouring, but he had moved a considerable distance from his
original position that an immediate armistice was essential at all
costs. Speaking privately to the chancellor after the meeting he said
that he felt that Germany could get better peace terms the next year,
and that he could look on the rupture of negotiations with Wilson
with equanimity.[60]

Prince Max did not believe that the military situation had changed
in any significant way, and there were those, like Solf, who argued
that other army leaders should be questioned, even if there was a risk

that Hindenburg and Ludendorff would resign.[61] Indeed among the politicians there was an increasingly marked feeling that Ludendorff's resignation was desirable. Prince Max and his government realised that submarine warfare would have to be abandoned if negotiations with Wilson were to continue. Ludendorff would only agree to abandon submarine warfare if there was a guarantee that Germany would not have to sign a 'dishonourable peace'.[62] When Prince Max refused to accept this view the OHL supported the navy's suggestion that only the sinking of passenger vessels should stop. Hindenburg then told the chancellor that Germany should fight to the last man for its honour, and to abandon the submarine war without any compensatory advantages would amount to capitulation and extinction without having used the very last ounce of strength.[63]

It needed the threat of resignation by Prince Max to convince the Kaiser that the submarine war would have to end.[64] Haeften, knowing full well what the answer would be, refused to relay this message to Hindenburg. Scheüch made a valiant attempt, but to no avail.[65] It was Haeften who offered a way out by suggesting that as the OHL had no political responsibility it did not have to agree with the reply to Wilson.[66] The chancellor's secretary, Kurt Hahn, imagined that the government had won a significant victory over the OHL when Hindenburg and Ludendorff agreed to the Haeften memorandum, and Erzberger and Scheidemann shared this view.[67] In fact the OHL's agreement was based on the desire not to be directly associated with the negotiations with Wilson and therefore with the eventual armistice. Hindenburg and Ludendorff could thus absolve themselves from any blame for ending the unrestricted submarine war, or for the political changes at home, and could hope to retain the support of their extremist admirers.

Wilson's reply on 23 October made it quite plain that Haeften's hope for a breathing space for the German army was illusory. Wilson said that he could not consider an armistice that did not make a resumption of hostilities by Germany impossible. As soon as Haeften knew the details of the Wilson note, and had heard Noske's cry for the resignation of the Kaiser, he went to the chancellor to argue that Wilson's terms were too humiliating, and that the war should be continued to the bitter end.[68] Haeften then called Ludendorff and asked him to come with Hindenburg to Berlin. At a meeting at the foreign office that day Haeften pleaded for a rejection of Wilson's note and for a continuation of the war. Major Kruger from the information section of the OHL mistook this outburst for official government policy, and forwarded it as such to Ludendorff. On the basis of this information Hindenburg issued an order to all army commanders saying that the conditions laid down by Wilson in his third note were unacceptable to the German army, and that the battle would have to be continued with all possible determination. At headquarters Hindenburg gathered his officers around him, drew his sword and shouted 'Long live His Majesty, our King, Emperor and Master!' Heye wrote: 'None of us doubted that the Kaiser, the chancellor and the cabinet would reject Wilson's note.'[69] But it was also clear to many, both at the OHL and at Berlin, that Haeften's intrigues and Ludendorff's impulsiveness would lead to a major crisis, or as Thaer put it in his diary, 'a big stink'.

When Prince Max heard that Hindenburg and Ludendorff had left Spa for Berlin he immediately drafted a letter to the Kaiser offering his resignation if Ludendorff were not dismissed, but also asking that everything possible should be done to make sure that Hindenburg remained in office.[70] Secure in the knowledge that the majority of the cabinet supported the idea of continuing the negotiations and of consulting other army leaders, Prince Max awaited the arrival of Hindenburg and Ludendorff, whom Lersner had described as 'wild'. Lersner added that the majority of the troops at the front would welcome a change in the OHL as they had lost confidence in its leadership, and as the military situation was indeed critical.[71]

Hindenburg and Ludendorff were met at the station in Berlin at 3 p.m. by Haeften who urged them to offer their resignations if the Wilson note was not rejected.[72] They went directly to see the Kaiser who made it clear that he sided with the government, and anxious to get rid of them referred the generals to the chancellor. Prince Max, however, was in bed with influenza and told them to meet vice-chancellor Payer that evening at 9 o'clock.

The confrontation between Ludendorff and Payer was dramatic. Hindenburg, Ludendorff, Haeften, Winterfeldt, Scheer and Levetzow had planned to win Payer over to their side. Ludendorff presented their case. Wilson's conditions were incompatible with the national and military honour of Germany and could not be accepted. The western front could hold out through the winter. Payer would not accept this argument, for he believed that there was no fight left at home or at the front, and he knew from Lersner and from Prince Rupprecht of Bavaria that the OHL's views no longer commanded automatic respect from the army commanders in the field. Ludendorff's dramatic appeals to the honour of the army did not impress him. 'I know nothing of soldier's honour, I am a burgher and civilian pure and simple. I can only see the starving people.' To which Ludendorff replied:

> In that case, Your Excellency, I cast the whole disgrace of the Fatherland in the teeth of you and your colleagues. And let me give you one warning: if you let things continue as they are, within a few weeks you will have bolshevism in the army and at home, then you can think of me.

Ludendorff then broke off the meeting abruptly, and shortly, afterwards told Heye that Germany was lost.[73]

At 10 a.m. the following morning Haeften told Ludendorff that the chancellor had written to the Kaiser saying that either Ludendorff should be dismissed or he would resign. Ludendorff was highly alarmed at this news, for in a fit of rage after his interview with Payer he had written yet another letter of resignation to the Kaiser. It was thus that Ludendorff went off the Schloss Bellevue in a state of considerable nervous agitation, for he now knew that his career hung in the balance.[74]

The audience was extremely stormy. The Kaiser accused Ludendorff of having first demanded an armistice and then four weeks later asking that the negotiations be broken off and the war continued. Even more serious, an order to this effect had been issued without the chancellor being informed. Ludendorff counterattacked, using such language that the Kaiser had to remind him that he was addressing his King and Emperor. The Kaiser accepted Ludendorff's offer of resignation, and Ludendorff refused the suggestion that he should take over command of any army group. Although Hindenburg had remained silent, even though Ludendorff had offered to resign twice, he now offered his resignation. The Kaiser ordered him to remain in office, and the field marshal bowed in acquiesence whereupon Ludendorff stormed out of the room. Hindenburg remained for a few moments with the Kaiser, whilst Ludendorff waited in the corridor anticipating the news that he too had resigned. When he heard that Hindenburg had agreed to stay in office he accused him of treachery, and refused to travel in the same car back to the general staff building. He went back to Spa in an ordinary express train.

Ludendorff had perhaps some reason for complaining to Haeften that Hindenburg had left him in the lurch, for they were jointly responsible for all the actions to which the Kaiser objected, and

Hindenburg had not spoken up in defence of the policies of the OHL.[75]
In many ways the interview is an excellent example of the differences
between these two men whose names are so closely linked.
Hindenburg the somewhat unimaginative, monarchical, traditionalist,
soldierly man whose burning ambition was concealed behind a quiet,
strong, aristocratic exterior, and Ludendorff the bourgeois man of
action, the blatantly political general, who had none of Hindenburg's
respect for the office and station of the Kaiser and whose style was
more brutal, less restrained by tradition. If Ludendorff was bitter
towards Hindenburg, Hindenburg was deeply shocked by the way
Ludendorff had behaved.

In government circles there was open rejoicing that Ludendorff
had gone. The right wing press described Ludendorff as a brilliant
general who had been 'hesitant and unclear' in his political judgements.
Here Bauer had done his work well. The papers of the majority parties
felt that he had brought about his own fall by his excessive ambition
and authoritarianism.[76] The political effects were also encouraging.
Rosen reported from The Hague that this striking reduction in the
power of the OHL was judged so significant that the Kaiser's
abdication might well be avoided.[77] Further reports also indicated
that Ludendorff's resignation would make the negotiations with the
Entente much more fruitful. But however hopeful these signs might
have been there were also obvious indications that Germany had little
strength left, and that defeat, humiliation, and most ominous of all,
revolution were just around the corner. Hindenburg now had second
thoughts about Ludendorff's departure, mainly because he realised
that the absolute supremacy of the OHL had been successfully
challenged. He and his disgruntled entourage began, as the
euphemism went, to become concerned about the future of the army.[78]

With the dismissal of Ludendorff the OHL lost much of its authority.
Further reforms reduced the Kaiser's power of command and placed
the army under greater political control, a move which filled many
officers with alarm. Great was the despondency of the OHL. Some
still hoped for a *levée en masse* and filled their heads with ideas of a
repeat performance of 1813, others had equally romantic visions of
a *Götterdämmerung* where Germany would be destroyed, but her
honour would be saved.

Such pictures of an army betrayed by the home front which was
no longer worthy of the destiny of a great nation was a gross
distortion of reality. Reports from the front clearly indicated that the
army was demoralised, and that the Kaiser and the OHL were no

longer respected. Films of the Kaiser and Hindenburg were booed by
troops at the front. Discipline was breaking down, and in some units
mutiny had broken out. Revolution at home seemed such a distinct
possibility that an increasing number of influential people, even those
on the extreme right, were now urging an immediate peace. On
30 October leading representatives of German finance capital, led by
representatives of the Deutsche Bank, met at the Hotel Adlon in
Berlin and issued a statement welcoming Prince Max's political reforms
and calling for an immediate peace. It took the OHL some time to
accept the logic of this position, for it was still over-optimistic about the
attitude and fighting ability of the army.

On 1 November the Prussian minister of the interior, Drews, went
to Spa and suggested to the Kaiser that he abdicate. William II replied:

> My duty as supreme warlord forbids me to leave the army in the
> lurch. The army is engaged in a heroic battle with the enemy. It is
> held firmly together by the person of the supreme warlord. If he
> goes, the army will fall apart and the enemy will pour into the
> homeland without meeting any resistance.

Hindenburg supported the Kaiser, adding that if he abdicated half the
army would return home as a 'marauding band'. Groener placed the
entire blame for the situation on the civilians:

> The army stands splendidly; the poison comes from home. The
> present government is responsible that all authority is attacked
> in the press and at meetings without being stopped or controlled,
> this is shown in the development of the Kaiser question, the
> question of abdication must be withdrawn from public
> discussion by government action.

Drews dryly replied to this outburst that it was the OHL's demand
for an armistice that had precipitated the parliamentarisation of the
government.

Groener, who had replaced Ludendorff, seemed to share his
predecessor's unrealistic attitude, but gradually his grasp of the true
dimensions of the crisis became clearer. As late as 6 November the
OHL issued an order saying that there was no 'Kaiser question', but
by that time even Groener realised that the Kaiser would have to
abdicate if peace were to come soon and if revolution were to be
avoided. This placed the OHL in a difficult dilemma. On the one hand

the unique constitutional position of the army rested to a considerable extent on the close connection between the officer corps and the Kaiser as supreme warlord, and if the Kaiser were to resign the danger of the army's control by the Reichstag majority would become very real. On the other hand the OHL had come to the conclusion that the Kaiser would have to go so that the army could be brought home as quickly as possible, and a revolution could then be crushed. Groener, Heye and Stülpnagel suggested to the Kaiser that the best way out of this dilemma would be for him to find a hero's death at the front in a carefully staged suicide mission against enemy lines. At first this theatrical gesture appealed to the Kaiser's taste for the dramatic, but then, rather understandably, he began to have second thoughts. He preferred the idea of returning home at the head of his army to crush the rebellion and restore the authority of the crown.

By 8 November Groener realised that such ideas were hopelessly unrealistic, and for him the only question that now mattered was to preserve the authority, prestige and power of the officer corps and the general staff. Heye collected information from the front which showed clearly that the army would not be prepared to follow the Kaiser in a struggle against the revolution, nor would it be prepared to join in a crusade against the bolsheviks. It was exhausted, and would fight no longer. Thus if the army was to remain intact the Kaiser would have to go. Hindenburg did not have the courage to tell the Kaiser this bitter truth, and preferred to hide behind Groener so as not to incur the odium of his King and Emperor. Groener had no such scruples. He went to the Kaiser to say the fateful words 'the army no longer stands behind Your Majesty'. Within a few hours the Kaiser was on his way to Holland and exile.

Groener thus showed himself in these crucial days to be the most far-sighted of the officers at the OHL. By riding the political storm rather than making a heroic and futile last stand on the western front or precipitating a bloody civil war, he was able to a remarkable degree to preserve the unity of the officer corps and the discipline of the returning army. Thus the officer corps was able to withstand all attempts at democratisation, and was to become an anti-republican and reactionary force. The influence of the army was not broken even in defeat and political upheaval, and by severing its traditional links with the monarchy at that critical juncture the army did not go the same way as the Hohenzollern dynasty, but remained a powerful and profoundly harmful force in German society.

268   *The Silent Dictatorship*

NOTES

1. Siegfried A. Kaehler, *Zur Beurteilung Ludendorffs im Sommer 1918,* Nachrichten der Wissenschaften in Göttingen I. philologisch-historische Klasse Nr. 1, Jahrgang 1953, p. 5. This section is based largely on F. von Lossberg, *Meine Tätigkeit im Weltkriege 1914-1918,* Berlin 1939.
2. Lossberg was sent as an observer to AOK 7 by the OHL from 19 July to 26 July; he was then posted as staff chief to the *Heeresgruppe* Boehn.
3. Bundesarchiv Militärarchiv Freiburg, Nachlass Groener N46/63, Tagebuch Generals von Mertz 31-7-18.
4. *Untersuchungsausschuss IV Reihe,* Band 2, p. 214. See also Joachim Petzold, 'Die Entscheilung vom 29 September 1918', *Zeitschrift für Militärgeschichte,* Heft 5, 1965.
6. Bundesarchiv Koblenz, Nachlass Bauer, Band 2. Evidence in Bauer's papers and in the Nachlass Berg makes it clear that the memorandum was written at the end of July.
7. Bauer, *Der Grosse Krieg in Feld und Heimat,* p. 225.
8. Bundesarchiv Koblenz, Nachlass Bauer, Band 11; DZA Potsdam Reichskanzlei, Allgemeines 2398/11; PA Bonn AA Weltkrieg Geheim, Band 40; Ludendorff, *Urkunden der OHL,* p. 107.
9. DZA Potsdam Reichskanzlei, Allgemeines 2398/11; Ludendorff, *Urkunden der OHL,* p. 110.
11. *Ibid.*
12. Bayerisches Hauptstaatsarchiv Abteilung IV Kriegsarchiv M. Kr. 1832, Bevollmächt. im Gr. HQ 1918, 8-8-18.
13. The declaration of 16 August 1919 reprinted in Ludendorff, *Urkunden der OHL,* p. 526 and signed by Mertz, Thaer and others is, as Kaehler correctly points out, highly ambiguous and in no way corresponds to the ample evidence at the time, supplied by Mertz among others, that Ludendorff did suffer from some form of collapse. The declaration of 1919 said that Ludendorff did not suffer a nervous breakdown in the summer of 1918. This may be true in the strictly medical sense of the term 'nervous breakdown', as far as it is possible to make an exact clinical definition of such a condition.
14. Bundesarchiv Militärarchiv Freiburg, Nachlass Haeften N35/5, *Erinnerungen.*
15. Niemann, *Kaiser und Revolution,* p. 44. A more extensive version is contained in the copy of *Der Tag,* number 185, May 1922.
16. *Amtliche Urkunden zur Vorgeschichte des Waffenstillstandes 1918,* 2 Auflage, Berlin 1924, p. 7.
17. *Ibid.,* p. 3.
18. Albrecht von Thaer, *Generalstabsdienst an der Front und in der OHL, Aus Briefen und Tagebuchaufzeichnungen 1915-1919,* Hrsg. von Siegfried A. Kaehler (Abhandlungen der Akademie der Wissenschaften in Göttingen. Phil. Hist. Klasse 3, Folge Nr. 40), Göttingen 1958.
19. Bundesarchiv Militärarchiv Freiburg, Nachlass Groener N46/63, Tagebuch Generals von Mertz, 1-9-18.
20. *Ibid.,* 4-8-16.
21. Siegfried A. Kaehler, *Zur Beurteilung Ludendorffs,* p. 21.
22. Bundesarchiv Militärarchiv Freiburg, Nachlass Heye, N18/5, *Lebenserinnerungen,* p. 72.
23. Bundesarchiv Koblenz, Nachlass Bauer, Band 21. Bauer argued now that Germany did not need Belgium as 'there are already enough unreliable people in the German Reich', and England would never agree to the German annexation of the Flanders coast. If the Entente would not accept these terms then Germany would have to continue the war, and thus

a really 'firm hand' was needed at home. At the same time Bauer was trying to remove all the blame from the OHL (letter to Fleischer 3-9-18 in Nachlass, Band 13) by saying that as the OHL had no influence on domestic politics and could not influence morale in any way it could not be held responsible for the parlous state of affairs. Bauer still held Bethmann largely responsible, and felt that the Pan Germans were the only hope for the country. Petzold, 'Die Entscheidung vom 29 September 1918', points out the similarities between the attitude of the opposition group within the OHL and the 20 July 1944 plotters. Even some of the names are the same — Mertz, Haeften, Harbou and Stülpnagel — although they were members of the next generation.

24. Bundesarchiv Militärarchiv Freiburg, Nachlass Haeften N35/4, diary entry 24-9-1918.
25. Wolfgang Foerster, *Der Feldherr Ludendorff im Unglück,* Wiesbaden 1952, p. 85.
26. Bundesarchiv Militärarchiv Freiburg, Nachlass Stülpnagel N5/27.
27. Bundesarchiv Militärarchiv Frieburg, Nachlass Haeften N35/4, diary entry 25-9-18.
28. *Ibid.,* 26-9-18.
29. *Ibid.,* 28-9-18.
30. PA Bonn AA Weltkrieg 23 Geheim, Band 32.
31. *Amtliche Urkunden,* p. 47.
32. Siegfried A. Kaehler, *Vier quellenkritische Untersuchungen zum Kriegsende 1918,* Nachrichten der Akademie der Wissenschaftern Göttingen 1960, Nr. 8, p. 433. Bundesarchiv Koblenz, Nachlass Bauer, Band 23.
33. *Untersuchungsausschuss IV Reihe,* Band 2, pp. 260, 386.
34. PA Bonn AA Weltkrieg 23 Geheim, Band 32.
35. *Amtliche Urkunden,* pp. 52, 59.
36. PA Bonn AA, Weltkrieg 23 Geheim, Band 32. *Amtliche Urkunden,* p. 61.
37. *Amtliche Urkunden,* pp. 60, 62. Ludendorff, *Urkunden der OHL,* p. 529. Prince Max von Baden, *Memoirs,* London 1928, Vol. 2, p. 4.
38. Bayerisches Hauptstaatsarchiv Abteilung IV, Kriegsarchiv M. Kr. 1832. Report of the military plenipotentiary 1-10-18. Attempts by men like Bussche to claim that the OHL did not say that there was an imminent danger of the front collapsing is of course ridiculous. See Ludendorff, *Urkunden der OHL,* p. 529.
39. Bayerisches Hauptstaatsarchiv Abteilung IV, Kriegsarchiv M. Kr. 1832. Military plenipotentiary's report 2-10-18.
40. Prince Max von Baden, *Memoirs,* Vol. 2, p. 14.
41. *Amtliche Urkunden,* p. 73.
42. Bundesarchiv Militärarchiv Freiburg, Nachlass Haeften N35/3.
43. Ludendorff, *Urkunden der OHL,* p. 540.
44. Prince Max von Baden, *Memoirs,* Vol. 2, p. 21.
45. *Amtliche Urkunden,* p. 74.
46. Prince Max von Baden, *Memoirs,* Vol. 2, p. 14.
47. Bayerisches Hauptstaatsarchiv Abteilung IV Kriegsarchiv, M. Kr. 1832. Bavarian military plenipotentiary's report 7-10-18.
48. Prince Max von Baden, *Memoirs,* Vol. 2, p. 65.
49. *Ibid.,* p. 55 for a reprint of the article.
50. *Ibid.,* p. 66.
51. *Ibid.,* p. 71.
52. For rumours of Ludendorff's impending resignation see press conference 4-10-18 in Deist, *Militär und Innenpolitik,* Vol. 11, p. 1300.
53. Bundesarchiv Militärarchiv Freiburg, Nachlass Haeften N35/3, diary

entry 8-10-18.
54. *Ibid.*, 12-10-18.
55. DZA Potsdam, Reichskanzlei, Verkehr des Reichskanzlers mit den Gr. HQ 2403/6.
56. PA Bonn AA Weltkrieg 23 Geheim, Band 22. Berckheim to foreign office 12-10-18.
57. Ludendorff, *Urkunden der OHL*, p. 109.
58. *Ibid.*, p. 123.
59. DZA Potsdam, Reichskanzlei, Beschlüsse des Kriegsrats 2462/1.
60. Prince Max von Baden, *Memoirs*, Vol. 2, p. 102.
61. *Amtliche Urkunden*, p. 162. Scheüch replied to Solf's letter saying that the army commanders should not be questioned without the knowledge of Hindenburg and Ludendorff. Bundesarchiv Militärarchiv Freiburg, Nachlass Haeften N35/3, diary entry 20-10-18.
62. *Ibid.*, 19-10-18.
63. Ludendorff, *Urkunden der OHL*, p. 166.
64. Prince Max von Baden, *Memoirs*, Vol. 2, p. 153.
65. Bundesarchiv Militärarchiv Freiburg, Nachlass Haeften N35/3, diary entries 19-10-18 and 20-10-18.
66. *Amtliche Urkunden*, p. 172.
67. Prince Max von Baden, *Memoirs*, Vol. 2, p. 163.
68. *Ibid.*, appendix VI, p. 385. Bundesarchiv Militärarchiv Freiburg, Nachlass Haeften N35/7, 24-10-18.
69. Bundesarchiv Militärarchiv Freiburg, Nachlass Heye N18/4. According to Thaer, *Generalstabsdienst*, 25-10-18 the order to the army commanders was sent off by Ludendorff without Hindenburg's knowledge.
70. Prince Max von Baden, *Memoirs*, Vol. 2, p. 195.
71. Ludendorff, *Urkunden der OHL*, p. 199.
72. Bundesarchiv Militärarchiv Freiburg, Nachlass Haeften N35/7, 25-10-18.
73. Bundesarchiv Militärarchiv Freiburg, Nachlass Heye N18/5, p. 115.
74. *Ibid.* The role of Colonel Niemann in the affair is a little obscure. According to his own account *(Revolution von Oben*, p. 183) he proposed a compromise to the Kaiser, whereby Ludendorff would give his word not to meddle in politics and the chancellor would then be able to remain. Heye, however, insists that it was Niemann who persuaded the Kaiser to drop Ludendorff on the morning of 26 October. Judging by the Kaiser's attitude at the audience Heye's version seems the most plausible.
75. PA Bonn AA Weltkrieg 23 Geheim, Band 27. Lersner to foreign office 26-10-18.
76. Bundesarchiv Militärarchiv Freiburg, Nachlass Groener N46/156, 'Die deutsche Presse zum Rücktritt des Generals Ludendorff'.
77. PA Bonn AA Weltkrieg 23 Geheim, Band 27. Rosen to foreign office 26-10-18.
78. PA Bonn AA Weltkrieg 23 Geheim, Band 41. Hintze to foreign office 28-10-18.

CONCLUSION

The politics of the OHL under Hindenburg and Ludendorff were a mixture of the two most significant forms of domination in the Second Reich: militarism and bonapartism. This mixture was hybrid and contradictory, for the militarist tradition was in many ways different from bonapartism, and both forms were seriously modified by the exigencies of the World War. Militarism had been traditionally elitist, and indeed the desire to preserve a homogeneous, ultra-conservative and largely aristocratic officer corps had resulted in the army being seriously short of officers at the outbreak of the war, and the size of the army being too small for the needs of the only war plan, the Schlieffen plan. Thus the rabble rousing, pseudo-democratic and quasi-plebiscitary dimension of bonapartism was quite alien to the traditions of the German officer corps. But the war had to be fought against a numerically vastly superior enemy, and the officer corps therefore had to be expanded drastically. 'Undesirable elements' — the commercial middle class, democrats and Jews — had to be admitted to the officer corps; but this in turn did not lead to a democratisation of the officer corps, but rather it became somewhat more receptive to bonapartist notions. The traditional politics of the officer corps, based largely on anti-modernist agrarian conservatism had, even in the prewar years, been changing under the stress of economic change and social pressure, and there was in some circles a growing awareness of the need for mass popular support. The paramilitary, youth and veterans' organisations of the army which were to become so large and powerful were thus to the officer corps what the *Bund der Landwirte* was to the Junkers, and their ideologies have many common features. Both the officer corps and the Junkers were losing something of the political aloofness of their class and were looking for mass support. This certainly did not imply that their politics were becoming in any sense more democratic, but rather that they were attempting to conceal social antagonisms behind a mythical community *(Gemeinschaft)*, and were trying to convince as many people as possible that the particular class interests of this elite group were identical with the true interests of the nation.

The ideology of the officer corps was thus in the course of a

271

modification that was bringing it closer to bonapartism, and this process was greatly hastened by the structural weaknesses of the imperial constitution. The failure of the Kaiser to play the constitutional role that was designed for him strengthened the position of the OHL against the civilian government, and thus made possible the 'dictatorship of the OHL'. There were those, led by Colonel Bauer, and supported by the 'Adlon group', who hoped for an open dictatorship of the army and an elimination of the Reichstag, but this ultimate form of military dictatorship was too radical a break with the traditions, however fraudulent, of an 'unpolitical' officer corps. Moreover an open dictatorship had considerable disadvantages, as Hindenburg and Ludendorff knew full well, and Bauer in his more sober moments agreed. A civilian chancellor was a very useful 'lightning conductor' for the OHL. He could be made responsible for the failures and the shortcomings of policies over which the OHL had managed to gain ultimate control. In this situation it is hardly surprising that the OHL did not wish to appear openly to bear the responsibility for political decisions that might well prove to be ill-considered. The army could seem to be engaged in purely military affairs, offering their humble advice to the chancellor and the Kaiser, and remaining aloof from the sordid day-to-day quarrels of the politicians. The OHL's campaign against Bethmann Hollweg served a double purpose. The chancellor was sacrificed as a scapegoat for the shortcomings of German policy, the demand for his resignation transcending momentarily political divisions and antagonisms; and the authority of the OHL was greatly enhanced by the chancellor's defeat. Thus paradoxically the more the OHL was able to hide behind the figure of the chancellor, the greater became its power and strength. Such was the nature of the 'silent dictatorship'.

A further significant similarity between the militarism of the OHL and bonapartism was its distinct plebiscitary element. Hindenburg and Ludendorff both insisted on numerous occasions that they stood in some almost mystical way outside the constitution, and incorporated the will of the people. The officer corps had traditionally considered itself to be in a sense outside the constitution, owing direct allegiance to the Kaiser as commander-in-chief. Oldenburg Januschau's famous remark before the war that the Kaiser should be able at any time to send a lieutenant and ten men to close down the Reichstag was a somewhat drastic formulation of this widely held attitude. But it was one thing to claim to stand outside the constitution, which seemed to the conservatives to be little more than

an unfortunate and misguided pact between Bismarck and the
bourgeoisie to keep the latter happy, and quite another to claim to
incorporate the will of the people. William II realised clearly that
this claim to embody the general will of the German people in a
moment of national crisis meant the end of the traditional
Prussian monarchy, and Bethmann was deeply concerned that the
Kaiser had alienated too many of his rights, particularly in the U-boat
crisis. Neither could have realised that it meant quite literally the
end of the monarchy, nor could they have foreseen how helpless the
crown was to become during the last two years of the war. By contrast
the figure of Hindenburg, with clever propaganda manipulations,
and by the fact that he incorporated the hopes and aspirations of so
many Germans, had taken on mythical proportions. By some curious
workings of social psychology it seems that Hindenburg and
Ludendorff appeared more infallible and invincible the more it became
apparent that Germany's military position was precarious in the extreme.
Similarly the demands of the OHL became all the more excessive as
the possibility of achieving them became increasingly doubtful.

The law on the state of siege, which the OHL had managed to
impose against the wishes of the chancellor, was the legal basis of the
military dictatorship in domestic politics. Here again the position
of the army was contradictory. On the one hand the law gave the
deputy commanding generals virtually dictatorial power within
their areas of command, but on the other hand there was a lack of
coordination and central control, and a breakdown of legal norms. The
significant degree of independence enjoyed by the deputy commanding
generals is however a poor argument to use to assert that there was
no such thing as a dictatorship of the OHL. The deputy
commanding generals followed the guidelines established by
Hindenburg and Ludendorff, and there is no instance of a confrontation
between the deputy commanding generals and the OHL. Nor does the
fact that not all of the wishes of the OHL were immediately carried
out negate the fact of a dictatorship. By such a strict definition Hitler,
for example, could not be considered a dictator. The OHL under
Hindenburg and Ludendorff greatly strengthened its authority over
the commanding generals. It was in matters of censorship that the
deputy commanding generals had the greatest autonomy, but under
Hindenburg and Ludendorff the OHL played a far more active role in
censorship, and thus exercised a far closer control over the deputy
commanding generals. This tendency to control the deputy
commanding generals was clearly seen in the 'patriotic instruction'

which forced them to follow the guidelines of the OHL.

Censorship was a powerful political weapon in the hands of the OHL. Originally military control over censorship was designed to ensure that information that might be of military value to the enemy was not printed. The OHL extended the concept of the 'purely military' to include almost all aspects of political life. Thus censorship was aimed against the left on the grounds that their activity was contrary to the concept of the *Burgfrieden* and was harmful to the military effort. Similarly in November 1916 Ludendorff was to ensure that the debate on war aims could be conducted without censorship, arguing that promises of annexations were good for military morale. The removal of the censorship restrictions meant that the way was open for flagrant attacks on Bethmann Hollweg that were sanctioned and encouraged by the OHL. Similarly 'patriotic instruction' was used as a forum for right wing extremist criticism of the chancellor. The authority of the OHL could remain undiminished, in spite of setbacks at the front, because reports of the true gravity of the military situation were carefully edited by Haeften, so that an unjustified optimism could prevail, and also by the fact that any criticism of the OHL, however mild, was instantly censored as detrimental to the war effort, and even treasonable.

Just as the OHL preferred to use its political power hiding behind the figure of the chancellor, so they also hoped that the responsibility for censorship would be assumed by the civilians, and that the unpopularity of the censorship methods could then be laid at their door. The civilians were well aware of this stratagem, and as a result there was a considerable degree of confusion over censorship matters, and an effective propaganda ministry was never established. As in so many other matters, the OHL was to hand over responsibility for censorship to the civilians at the very end of the war, and profess total innocence for the failure of their past policies.

In economic affairs the OHL triumphed with the auxiliary labour law. Acting in the interests of heavy industry, the OHL secured a high degree of control over German labour, hastening the tendency towards the monopolisation and cartelisation of industry, and was able to gain a considerable degree of control over the workings of the economy. The goals of the Hindenburg programme were hopelessly unrealistic – a 100 per cent increase in the production of ammunition, and a three fold increase in the production of artillery and machine guns could not possibly be achieved within the short space of time allowed – and the shortcomings and failures of the auxiliary labour law were blamed on the civilians. In their attempts to get the law abrogated and to use more force against the working class the OHL met the limits of their power. Such a move would only have been possible if there had been an open dictatorship of the army, and this Hindenburg and Ludendorff wished to avoid. By insisting that the Reichstag should pass the auxiliary labour law the OHL ensured that the Reichstag could be made responsible for its shortcomings. Once again the 'lightning conductor' principle worked admirably.

The struggle for the auxiliary labour law enabled the OHL to win at least a partial victory over the war ministry, and this marked a further chapter in the history of the struggle between the general staff and the war ministry. Bethmann was able to stop the OHL destroying the war ministry entirely by raising genuine constitutional objections to such a move, but the creation of a *Kriegsamt* eclipsed much of the power of the ministry. But General Groener of the *Kriegsamt* soon fell foul of the OHL and the captains of heavy industry. He was dismissed not so much because he was thinking of cutting back the industrialists' profits, but rather because he was regarded as being too soft on labour, in spite of the fact that he had earned the hatred of the active sectors of the working class by his hostile attitude to the labour movement. The fact that the auxiliary labour law had failed to achieve its aims did not lead to a serious analysis of the economic situation, but rather was the occasion for wild accusations against the leaders of the unions and the SPD. This frustrated rage against the civilians did much to prepare the ground for the *Dolchstoss* legend which was to play such a fateful role in the politics of the Weimar republic.

The OHL did not have unchallenged and complete authority in domestic politics, but its influence was nevertheless preponderant. They were able to secure the dismissal of, amongst others, the war minister, Wild; the chancellor, Bethmann Hollweg; the chief of the naval staff, Holtzendorff; the chief of the civil cabinet, Valentini; and the foreign secretary, Kühlmann. Even the dismissal of Michaelis and the appointment of Hertling, in which the Reichstag majority played a crucial role, was carried out in consultation with the OHL, and Hertling was supported by them. The OHL may not always have secured the appointment of their favourite candidates, but they made sure that the men that were selected were likely to be subservient to their wishes. Similarly although the OHL was extremely bitter that it had not been consulted by the Kaiser or the government about the Easter message, they were able to secure a total victory over the

civilians on the suffrage issue. By reserving the right to decide when
the military situation would allow for suffrage reform the OHL could
hold the Prussian *Landtag* at gun point.

In foreign policy the OHL also managed to secure most of their
aims. In the struggle with the general governor, Bissing, they were
victorious on the issue of the deportation of Belgian workers. Their
persistent demands for the domination of Belgium made any peace
initiative with the allies impossible. On the issue of unrestricted
submarine warfare the OHL was able to outmanoeuvre the
government by insisting that it was a purely military question, and the
Kaiser was forced to alienate more of his sovereign rights. In Poland the
OHL demanded the declaration of an 'independent' Poland and the
formation of a Polish army. When this policy backfired it was blamed
on the civilians, just as they blamed the failure of their own auxiliary
labour law on the government and the Reichstag. Their Polish policy
was in turn part of their policy towards Austria-Hungary, and here
again the OHL triumphed over the civilians. Once again they looked
towards a 'purely military' solution of the Austrian problem —
Anschluss with Germany, by force if necessary, and the creation of a
new complex of client states in the Balkans. The Baltic was a
particular area of interest to Hindenburg and Ludendorff since their
days at *Oberost.* Here again they were able to override most of the
objections of the foreign office, and backed by a powerful alliance
of Baltic barons, agrarians and Pan Germans they were able to counter
the objections of those who, like Kühlmann, urged a more cautious
and flexible policy in the Baltic. Here the OHL incorporated two
powerful motivating forces in German policy: imperialist ambitions
towards the east, and anti-bolshevism, the new and intensified form of
the anti-Russian dimension of Bismarck's bonapartism. This policy was
to reach a climax during the negotiations over the treaty of Brest
Litovsk, when the OHL's repetoire of threatened resignations, 'purely
military' arguments, and extremist demands were used to the full. This
policy was continued in the Ukraine, against the objections of the
foreign office, and led to the support offered to Krasnov's cossacks in
spite of the fact that the OHL had finally to admit that Krasnov was
indeed pro-Entente. Although the German position on the western front
steadily deteriorated, the OHL relentlessly pursued its policy of
conquest, plunder and colonisation in the east: in the Caucasus, the
Crimea, the Black Sea and in the expedition against Finland. The
foreign office at times urged restraint, but in almost every instance the
OHL was triumphant. In the moment of defeat, when the OHL's powers

had been significantly reduced by the establishment of a parliamentary regime under Prince Max of Baden, they were able to avoid responsibility for the defeat of the German army, and to appear as unvanquished but betrayed. Even when it was crushed the army still embodied the hopes and aspirations of powerful sections of society who were unwilling and unable to accept the reality of the situation, and who still harboured dreams which were soon to become the substance of fascism.

Between the OHL and the civilian government there was a broad similarity of aims, but a fierce disagreement over tactics. It would be mistaken to assume that because of these differences there were two fundamentally opposing concepts of politics and society looked in battle: the realistic, restrained, fundamentally decent politicians against the fanatic, extremist and wicked militarists. Both sides were determined that Germany should end the war as a world power, and that significant additions should be made to German territory — war aims that have been analysed in scrupulous detail by Fritz Fischer. The fierce debate between the two sides was over how much should be seized, and whether it should be taken directly or indirectly. In almost every instance the OHL demanded the most extensive war aims, which were to be achieved by direct annexation. They had little patience with the complex economic treaties that would reduce states to total subservience, and preferred a more straightforward approach of outright annexation, usually in the form of personal union with the crown of Prussia. If it would be a mistake to lay too much stress on the differences between the OHL and the government, and almost as fallacious to ignore them altogether, even more serious would be to look at the politics of Hindenburg and Ludendorff in terms of their personalities. Such crude personalism, which unfortunately pervades much of the writing on the First World War, totally ignores the fact that Hindenburg and Ludendorff could never have established the powerful position which they enjoyed were it not for the fact that they embodied the aspirations of significant sectors of society. These can easily be identified as the heavy industrialists, the agrarians, and their political organisations: the Pan Germans and the *Vaterlandspartei*. The propaganda efforts of the OHL were used to gain wide popular support, giving to the regime its distinct bonapartist flavour.

It is precisely this feature which allows for a historical aetiology of the 'Silent Dictatorship'. It stands halfway between the bonapartism of Bismarck and the fascist dictatorship of Hitler.

Similarities between the aims of the OHLand the fascists are so obvious that it is pointless to list them, and the development of a pre-fascist ideology is equally clear. But similarity of aims should not be confused with the forms of domination. Here the OHL exercised a certain degree of restraint in the outward forms, and the similarity is here more with Bismarck's Germany than the Third Reich. That the politics of the OHL were cruder and more excessive than those of Bismarck is explained by the fact that the social, economic and structural problems facing German society had become more acute, and their solution impossible without fundamental reform. In turn the fact that the army was able to resist this reform, and discredit the democratic forces as cowards and traitors meant that the contradictions within German society were to become even more intense. The palliative measures used to preserve the position of the ruling class taken in 1933 were to be of such unprecedented brutality, and the contradictions between the aims of the regime and the means of achieving them were to become so severe that many members of the officer corps were forced into opposition. To some this served to preserve the honour of the officer corps, but other more far-sighted men realised that the problem lay much deeper. It was not enough for the politicians to control the military and ensure a strict definition of the 'purely military'; the politicians themselves had to be subject to democratic control, and the society they represented had to be a democratic society. The problem of militarism is thus not merely a problem of the military: it is a problem of society as a whole.

BIBLIOGRAPHY

1. Unpublished Sources

Politisches Archiv des Auswärtigen Amts, Bonn, Akten der Politischen Abteilung

Gr. Hauptquartier 9 England Band 1.

        9y Estland und Livland Band 2.

        23 Oesterreich-Ungarn Band 5 und 6.

        25 Personalangelegenheiten Band 2.

        26a Polen.

        28 Presse Band 1 und 2.

        31a Russland Band 1, 2, 3, 4 und 5.

        31e, f, g, h, Russland Band 1.

        36 Finnland A-Z 10 Band 1, 2, 3, 3 Teil 2, und 4.

        37 Sozialisten Band 1.

        41 Finnland A-Z 10a Band 1.

        42 Finnland A-Z 1a und 10a Band 1.

        42 U-Bootkrieg Band 3.

        232 Kriegsziele 16a Band 1.

        235 Kronprinz Nr. 16a.

        237 Personalien Nr 25 Band 1.

        247 Reichskanzler 29 Band 1.

        248 Reichskanzler 29 Band 2.

Weltkrieg 15 Band 2, 23 und 28.

Weltkrieg 20b (Die Zukunft der besetzten Gebiete: Frankreich)

Weltkrieg Geheim Band 30, 31, 32, 33, 34, 35, 36, 37, 38, 39, 40, 41.

Weltkrieg 2 Geheim Band 55 und 63.

Weltkrieg 15 Geheim Band 2, 2a, 3, 4, 5, 6.

Weltkrieg 20a Geheim Band 2.

Weltkrieg 20c Geheim Band 22.

Weltkrieg 23 Geheim Band 14, 15, 18, 19, 20, 21, 22, 23, 24, 25, 26, 27, 28, 29, 32.

Weltkrieg 10 Geheim Finanzielle Massnahmen Band 8, 9 und 10.

Weltkrieg 2 Ganz Geheim Band 1.

Russland 63 Band 7, 17, 18, 20, 21.

Russland 63 Nr. 1 Band 8 und 9.

Russland 97a Band 12, 13 (Russisch-Asien), 14, 16, 17 (Russisch-Asien).

Deutschland 107 Band 1 und 2.
Deutschland 129 Band 5.
Oesterreich 95 Band 4, 5, 7.
Rumänien Politisches Nr. 1 Band 9.

Deutsches Zentralarchiv Abteilung 1, Potsdam

Reichskanzlei: Allgemeines 2398/6, 2398/7, 2398/8, 2398/9, 2398/10.
    2398/11, 2398/12, 2398/13.
Reichskanzlei: Reichskanzler und Gr. Hauptquartier: 2403/5.
Reichskanzlei: Kurland und Litauen: 2404, 2405, 2406.
Reichskanzlei: Finnland: 2406/4.
Reichskanzlei: Verschiedenes: 2402/3, 2402/4, 2402/5, 2402/6,
    2402/7, 2403, 2403/1.
Reichskanzlei: England: 2404/12, 2407, 2408, 2409, 2409/1, 2409/2,
    2409/3.
Reichskanzlei: Notständen: 2427/1, 2428, 2429, 2430, 2431, 2432,
    2433, 2434, 2435.
Reichskanzlei: Presse: 2437/11, 2438, 2439, 2439/1.
Reichskanzlei: Rumänien: 2458/3.
Reichskanzlei: Beschwerden über die Führung der Friedensverhandlungen
    in Bukarest: 2458/4.
Reichskanzlei: Beschlüsse des Kriegsrats 2462/1.
Reichskanzlei: Vorschläge pp zu Friedensverhandlungen: 2444/7, 2446,
    2447, 2447/1, 2447/2.
Reichskanzlei: Verkehr des Reichskanzlers mit den Gr. Hauptquartier:
    2403/6.
Alldeutsche Verband: Ludendorff 1916-1924: 460/2.
Vertreter des Reichskanzlers bei der OHL: 1, 7, 15, 25, 27, 30, 31, 38.
Stellvertreter des Reichskanzlers: Ukraine: 13.
Stellvertreter des Reichskanzlers: 48, 53, 67(Juden), 72(Weltkrieg),
    73 (Weltkrieg), 111 (Presse).
Reichsamt des Innern: Kriegszustand: 12217, 12255, 12260.
Reichsamt des Innern: Presse: 12271, 12272, 12273.
Reichsamt des Innern: Deutsch-Polnisch Militärkonvention: 19683.
Reichsamt des Innern: Das Polnische Heer: 19831.
Reichsamt des Innern: Die Stimmung im Lande 12476, 12475.
Reichsamt des Innern: Presse und Nachrichtenwesen: 12271, 12289.
Reichsamt des Innern: Das Stickstoffhandelsmonopol: 7309.

Deutsches Zentralarchiv Abteilung II, Merseburg

Zivilkabinett 2.2.1. Nr. 32450, 32450, 32404, 32411.

Rep 90a Preussisches Staatsministerium Abteilung III 2b Nr. 6.
Band 165, 166 und 167.
Rep 92 Nachlass Valentini.
Rep 92 Nachlass Kapp.

Bundesarchiv Koblenz

Justizministerium P135/1751, P135/6356, P135/1831, P135/10974,
P135/10973.
Nachlass Mentzel.
Nachlass Bauer.
Nachlass Heinrichs.
Nachlass Schwertfeger.
Nachless Bülow.
Nachlass Hertling.
Nachlass Berg.

Heeresarchiv Stuttgart

Persönliche Angelegenheiten des Württembergischen Kriegsminister:
Band 86, 87, 114.
Württembergisches Kriegsministerium Kriegsarchiv:
Band 1104 (Zensurbestimmungen der Presse)
Band 1105 (Zensurvorstösse der Württ. sozialdemokratischen
Tageszeitung 'Der Beobachter' während des Weltkriegs)
Band 1109 (Revolutionäre Vorboten im Weltkrieg 1916/18)
Band 1036 (Oeffentliche Klagen über Missbräuche im Heere 1918)
Band 1081 (Reichskanzler von Bethmann Hollweg, politische
Umsturzversuche)
Band 1082 (Die politische Haltung der deutschen Arbeiterschaft
während des Weltkrieges)
Band 1083
Band 1084 (Volksaufkläurung während des Weltkrieges)
Band 1071.
Württembergisches Kriegsministerium: Württ. Bevollmächtigte in Berlin:
Band 34.
Kriegsministerium Abteilung für allgemeine Armee- und für persönliche
Angelegenheiten: 1047, 1217, 1272, 1273, 1727, 1729, 10001.
Nachlass Marchtaler.

Hauptstaatsarchiv Stuttgart

Königliches Ministerium der auswärtigen Angelegenheiten. Krieg IV
2a (Friedensschluss)

Krieg IV. 1.
Kreig IV. 2.
E 74 I. Berliner Gesandtschaft. Krieg 1914-18. Politische Berichte
   Nr. 167. 168.
E 74 170 (Vaterländische Hilfsdienste)
E 75 487 Württembergische Gesandtschaft München
E 75 488 Würtembergische Gesandtschaft München

Staatsarchiv Ludwigsburg

Akten des Königlichen Staatsministeriums: Massnahmen des Württ.
Zivilverwaltung E 130. v Xa 31.
V 4/1 Band IV.

Bundesarchiv Militärarchiv Freiburg

Nachlass Heye.
Nachlass von Haeften.
Nachlass Wild von Hohenborn.
Nachlass Mertz von Quirnheim.
Nachlass Groener.
Marine Akten: 69211: Friede Band 1.
            69212: Friede Band 2.
            69213: Friede Band 3.
            69256: Schwarzes Meer Band 1.
            69257: Schwarzes Meer Band 2.
            69258: Schwarzes Meer Band 3.
            69259: Schwarzes Meer Band 4.
            69260: Schwarzes Meer Band 5.
            94801: Verkehr mit dem Kriegspresseamt Band 1.
            94802: Verkehr mit dem Kriegspresseamt Band 2.
            75659: Aaland.
            75660: Ostsee-Finnland Band 1.
            75710: Finnland 1.
            75686: Marineabkommen mit Ukraine Band 1.
            75683: Krim: Band 1.
            75684: Kiew: Band 1.
            69240: Russland Band 1.
            69241: Russland Band 2.
            69242: Russland Band 3.
            69243: Nordische Staaten Band 1.
            69244: Nordische Staaten Band 2.
            69245: Nordische Staaten Band 3.

25-16-3: Wirtschaftliches Band 3.
25-16-4: Wirtschaftliches Band 4.
25-16-5: Wirtschaftliches Band 5.

Bayerisches Hauptstaatsarchiv Abteilung IV Kriegsarchiv

M. Kr. 1830 Berichte des Militärischen Bevollmächtigten im Grossen Hauptquartier 1916 IIIa XV 39.

M. Kr. 1831 ditto 1917.

M. Kr. 1832 ditto 1918.

M. Kr. 41 Berichte des Bayr. Mil. Bevollmächtigten und Bevollmächtigten zum Bundesrat 1911-1917.

2. Published Sources

Scherer, A., Grunewald, J., *L'allemagne et les problemes de la paix pendant la premiere guerre mondiale,* 2 Vols., (Paris, 1962-6).

Huber, E.R., *Dokumente zur Deutschen Verfassungsgeschichte,* Band 2, (Stuttgart, 1964).

Matthias, E., Morsey, R., *Der Interfraktionelle Ausschuss,* 2 Vols., (Düsseldorf, 1959).

—————— *Die Regierung des Prinzen Max von Baden,* (Düsseldorf, 1962).

Institut für Marxismus-Leninismus Beim ZK der SED, *Dokumente und Materialien zur Geschichte der deutschen Arbeiterbewegung,* Reihe II, Band 1 und 2, (Berlin, 1957-8).

Stern, Leo, (Ed) *Archivalische Forschungen zur Geschichte der deutschen Arbeiterbewegung,* Band 4/II bis IV, (Berlin, 1959).

Spartakusbriefe, (Berlin, 1958).

Das Werk des Untersuchungsausschusses der Verfassungsgebenden Deutschen Nationalversammlung und des Deutschen Reichstages.
IV Reihe:
Die Ursachen des Deutschen Zusammenbruches. Band 1 – 12, (Berlin, 1919-29).

Baumgart, W., Repgen, K., *Brest-Litovsk,* (Göttingen, 1969).

Ludendorff, E., *Urkunden der Obersten Heeresleitung über ihrer Tätigkeit 1916/18,* (Berlin, 1920).

Minc, I.I., Ejdemann, R., *Die deutsche Okkupation der Ukraine, Geheimdokumente,* (Strasburg, 1937).

Deist, Wilhelm, *Militär und Innenpolitik,* 2 Vols., (Düsseldorf, 1970).

Zeman, Z.A., *Germany and the Revolution in Russia 1915-1918,* (London, 1950).

Ministerium für auswärtige angelegenheiten der UdSSR und Ministerium
für auswärtige angelegenheiten der DDR, *Deutsch-Sowjetische
Beziehungen von den Verhandlungen in Brest-Litovsk bis zum
Abschluss des Rapallovertrages,* Band 1, (Berlin, 1967).
Amtliche Urkunden zur Vorgeschichte des Waffenstillstandes 1918,
(Berlin, 1967).
*Verhandlungen des Reichstags. XIII. Legislaturperiode. II. Session.
Stenographische Berichte,* (Berlin, 1914-18)
Michaelis, Herbert, Schraepler, Ernst, *Ursachen und Folgen. Vom
deutschen Zusammenbruch 1918 und 1945 bis zum staatlichen
Neuordnung Deutschlands in der Gegenwart,* Band 1-3, (Berlin, 1958).

3. Memoirs, Diaries etc.

Bauer, Max, *Der Grosse Krieg in Feld und Heimat. Erinnerungen und
Betrachtungen,* (Tübingen, 1921).
Bethmann Hollweg, Th. von. *Betrachtungen zum Weltkriege,* 2 Vols.,
(Berlin, 1919, 1922).
————— *Kriegsreden,* hrsg. von F. Thimme, (Stuttgart, 1919).
Braun, Magnus Freiherr von, *Von Ostpreussen bis Texas. Erlehnisse
und Zeitgeschichtliche Betrachtungen eines Ostdeutschen,*
(Stollhamm, 1955).
Cramon, A. von, *Unser österreich-ungarischer Bundesgenosse im
Weltkriege,* (Berlin, 1920).
Czernin, Ottokar, *Im Weltkriege,* (Berlin, Vienna, 1919).
David, Eduard, *Das Kriegstagebuch des Reichstagsabgeordneten
Eduard David 1914-1918,* hrsg. von E. Matthias and S. Miller,
(Dusseldorf, 1966).
Dunsterville, L.C., *The Adventures of Dunsterforce,* (London, 1920).
Eisenhart Rothe, Ernst von, *Im Banne der Persönlichkeit. Aus den
Lebenserinnerungen des Generals der Infanterie Ernst von Eisenhart
Rothe,* (Berlin, 1931).
Erzberger, Matthias, *Erlebnisse im Weltkrieg,* (Stuttgart, 1920).
Falkenhayn, Erich von, *Die Oberste Heeresleitung 1914-1916 in
ihren wichtigsten Entscheidungen,* (Berlin, 1920).
Goltz, Rüdiger Graf von der, *Meine Sendung in Finnland und im
Baltikum,* (Leipzig, 1920).
Groener, Wilhelm, *Lebenserinnerungen. Jugend, Generalstab, Weltkrieg,*
hrsg. von Friedrich Freiherr von Gaertringen, (Göttingen, 1957).
Haussmann, Conrad, *Schlaglichter. Reichtagsbriefe und Aufzeichnungen,*
hrsg. von U. Zeller, (Frankfurt, 1924).

Helfferich, Karl, *Der Weltkrieg,* (Karlsruhe, 1919).

Hertling, K. Graf von, *Ein Jahr in der Reichskanzlei. Erinnerungen and die Kanzlerschaft meines Vaters,* (Freiburg im Breisgau, 1919)

Hindenburg, Generalfeldmarschall Paul von, *Aus meinem Leben,* (Leipzig, 1927).

Hoffmann, Max, *Die Aufzeichnungen des Generalmajors Max Hoffmann,* hrsg. von Karl Friedrich Nowak, 2 Vols., (Berlin, 1929).

Hutten-Czapski, Bogdan Graf, *Sechzig Jahre Gesellschaft und Politik.* Band 2, (Berlin, 1936).

Kakhovskaia, *Souvenirs d'une revolutionnaire,* (Paris, 1926).

Kühlmann, Richard von, *Erinnerungen,* (Heidelberg, 1948).

Lancken Wakenitz, O. Freiherr von der, *Meine 30 Dienstjahre 1888-1918,* (Potsdam, 1931).

Lossberg, F. von, *Meine Tätigkeit im Weltkrieg 1914-1918,* (Berlin, 1939).

Ludendorff, Erich, *Meine Kriegserinnerungen,* (Berlin, 1919).

Mannerheim, G., *Erinnerungen,* (Zurich, 1952).

Max von Baden, Prinz, *Erinnerungen und Dokumente,* (Berlin, 1927).

Merton, Richard, *Erinnernswertes aus meinem Leben,* (Frankfurt, 1955).

Michaelis, Georg, *Für Staat und Volk,* (Berlin, 1922).

Moltke, H. von, *Erinnerungen, Briefe, Dokumente 1877-1916,* hrsg. von E. von Moltke, (Stuttgart, 1922).

Müller, Georg Alexander von, *Regierte der Kaiser? Kriegstagebücher Aufzeichnungen und Briefe des Chefs des Marine-Kabinetts Admiral Georg von Müller 1914-1918,* hrsg. Walter Görlitz, (Göttingen, 1959).

Nadolny, Rudolf, *Mein Beitrag,* (Wiesbaden, 1955).

Nicolai, Walter, *Nachrichtendienst, Presse und Volksstimmung im Weltkrieg,* (Berlin, 1920).

Payer, Friedrich von, *Von Bethmann Hollweg bis Ebert. Erinnerungen und Bilder,* (Frankfurt, 1923).

Rathenau, Walter, *Politische Briefe,* (Dresden, 1929).

Rupprecht von Bayern, Kronprinz, *Mein Kriegstagebuch,* hrsg. von Eugen Frauenholz, 3 Vols., (Berlin, 1929).

Scheidemann, Philipp, *Der Zusammenbruch,* (Berlin, 1921).

—————— *Memoiren eines Sozialdemokraten,* 2 Vols., (Dresden, 1928).

Seeckt, Hans von, *Aus meinem Leben 1866 bis 1917,* hrsg. von Fr. von Rabenau, (Leipzig, 1938).

Stein, Dr von, *Erlebnisse und Betrachtungen aus der Zeit des Weltkrieges,* (Leipzig, 1919).

Stürgkh, Josef Graf, *Im deutschen Grossen Hauptquartier,* (Leipzig, 1921).

Thaer, Albrecht von, *Generalstabsdienst and der Front und in der OHL.*

Aus Briefen und Tagebuchaufzeichnungen 1915-1919, hrsg. von Siegfried A. Kaehler, (Göttingen, 1958).

Tirpitz, A. von, *Erinnerungen,* (Leipzig, 1919).

Valentini, Rudolf von, *Kaiser und Kabinettschef. Nach eigenen Aufzeichnungen und dem Briefwechsel des wirklichen Geheimen Rats Rudolf von Valentini dargestellt von Bernhard Schwertfeger,* (Oldenburg, 1931).

Westarp, Kuno Graf von, *Konservative Politik im Letzten Jahzehnt des Kaiserreiches,* Band 2, (Berlin, 1935).

Wilhelm, Kronprinz, *Erinnerungen,* hrsg, von K. Rosner, (Stuttgart, 1922).

Wrisberg, Ernst von, *Erinnerungen an die Kriegsjahre im Königlich Preussischen Kriegsministerium,* Band 1-3, (Leipzig, 1921-2).

4. Secondary Sources

Adler, G., *Die imperialistische Sozialpolitik,* (Tübingen, 1897).

Anderson, P.R., *The Background of Anti-English Feeling in Germany 1890-1902,* (Washington, 1939).

Armeson, R.B., *Total Warfare and Compulsory Labour. A Study of the Military-Industrial Complex in Germany during World War I,* (The Hague, 1964).

Barnett, Correlli, *The Swordbearers: Studies in Supreme Command in the First World War,* (London, 1963).

Basler, W., *Deutschlands Annexionspolitik in Polen und im Baltikum 1914-1918,* (Berlin, 1962).

——————'Die Politik des deutschen Imperialismus gegenüber Litauen 1914-1918', *Jahrbuch für die Geschichte der UdSSR und der Volksdemokratischen Länder Europas,* Band 4, 1960.

Baumgart, W., *Deutsche Ostpolitik 1918,* (Munich, 1966).

——————'Ludendorff und das auswärtige Amt, zur Besetzung der Krim 1918', *Jahrbuch für die Geschichte Osteuropas,* 14, 1966.

——————'Neue Quellen zur Beurteilung Ludendorffs. Der Konflikt mit dem Admiralstabschef über die deutsche Schwarzmeerpolitik im Sommer 1918', *Militärgeschichtliche Mitteilungen,* 1970.

Bechtel, H., *Wirtschaftsgeschichte Deutschlands,* (Munich, 1956).

Benaerts, P., *Les origines de la grande industrie allemande,* (Paris, 1933).

Berghahn, Volker, *Der Tirpitz-Plan. Genesis und Verfall einen innenpolitischen Krisenstrategie unter Wilhelm II,* (Düsseldorf, 1971).

——————'Zu den Zielen des deutschen Flottenbaus unter Wilhelm II',

Historische Zeitschrift, Band 210, 1970.

Bergsträsser, L., *Die preussische Wahlrechtsfrage im Kriege und die Entstehung der Osterbotschaft 1917*, (Tübingen, 1924).

Beyer, Hans, 'Die Mittelmächte und die Ukraine 1918' *Jahrbuch für die Geschichte Ost Europas*, Beiheft 2, Munich, 1956.

Birnbaum, K.E., *Peace Moves and U-Boat Warfare, A Study of Imperial Germany's Policy Towards the United States April 18, 1916 – January 9, 1917*, (Stockholm, 1958).

Boldt, H., *Rechtsstaat und Ausnahmezustand*, (Berlin, 1967).

Born, K.E., 'Die soziale und wirtschaftliche Strukturwandel Deutschlands am Ende des 19. Jahrhunderts', *Vierteljahrsschrift für Sozial- und Wirtschaftsgeschichte*, Band 50, 1963.

Borowsky, Peter, *Deutsche Ukrainepolitik 1918*, (Lübeck and Hamburg, 1970).

Böhme, H., *Deutschlands Weg zur Grossmacht*, (Cologne, 1966).

——————— *Prolegomena zu einer Sozial- und Wirtschaftsgeschichte Deutschlands in 19. und 20. Jahrhundert*, (Frankfurt, 1968).

Bloch, Ernst, 'Der Faschismus als Erscheinungsform der Ungleichzeitigkeit', in *Erbschaft dieser Zeit*, (Frankfurt, 1962).

Blücher, W. von, *Deutschlands Weg nach Rapallo*, (Wiesbaden, 1951).

Breucker, W., *Die Tragik Ludendorffs*, (Oldenburg, 1953).

Bub, Gertraude, *Der deutsche Film im Weltkrieg*, (Berlin, 1938).

Bunyan, J., Fisher, H.H., *The Bolshevik Revolution 1917-1918*, (New York, 1961).

Carr, E.H., *The Bolshevik Revolution, 1917-1923*, 3 Vols., (London, 1951-3).

Colliander, B., *Die Beziehungen zwischen Litauen und Deutschland während der Okkupation 1915-1918*, Akademische Abhandlung, (Abo, 1935).

Conze, W., *Polnische Nation und deutsche Politik im ersten Weltkrieg*, (Cologne, Graz, 1958).

Craig, Gordon, 'The World War I Alliance of the Central Powers in Retrospect: The Military Cohesion of the Alliance', *Journal of Modern History*, 37, 1965.

——————— 'Military Diplomats in the Prussian and German Service: The Attachés 1816-1914', *Political Science Quarterly*, 64, 1949.

——————— *The Politics of the Prussian Army 1640-1945*, (Oxford, 1955).

Cron, H., *Die Organisation des deutschen Heeres im Weltkrieg*, (Berlin, 1923).

Crone, Wilhelm, *Achtung! Hier Grosses Hauptquartier*, (Lübeck, 1934).

288   *The Silent Dictatorship*

Deist, Wilhelm, 'Zur Institution des Militärbefehlshabers und
   Obermilitärbefehlshabers im Ersten Weltkrieg', *Jahrbuch für die
   Geschichte Mittel- und Ostdeutschlands,* Band 13/14, Berlin, 1965.
Deuerlein, E., 'Zur Friedensaktion Benedikts XV', *Stimmen der Zeit,*
   80, 1954-5.
Deutschland im Ersten Weltkrieg, 3 Vols., (Berlin, 1968-9).
Dorpalen, Andreas, 'Empress Auguste Victoria and the Fall of the
   German Empire', *American Historical Review,* 1952.
Edwards, Marvin I., *Stresemann and the Greater Germany,* (New York,
   1963).
Engelberg, E., 'Zur Entstehung und historischen Stellung des
   preussisch-deutschen Bonapartismus', *Beiträge zum neuen
   Geschichtsbild,* hrsg. von F. Klein und J. Streisand, (Berlin, 1956).
Epstein, Klaus, *Matthias Erzberger and the Dilemma of German
   Democracy,* (Princeton, 1959).
————'The Development of German-Austrian War Aims in the
   Spring of 1917', *Journal of Central European Affairs,* Vol. XVII,
   April 1957.
Feldman, G.D., *Army, Industry and Labor in Germany, 1914-1918,*
   (Princeton, 1966).
Festinger, Leon, *A Theory of Cognitive Dissonance,* (New York, 1957).
Fischer, Fritz, *Griff nach der Weltmacht,* (Düsseldorf, 1961).
———— *Krieg der Illusionen,* (Düsseldorf, 1969).
Foerster, W., *Der Feldherr Ludendorff in Ungluck. Eine Studie über
   seine seelische Haltung in der Endphase des Ersten Weltkrieges,*
   (Wiesbaden, 1952).
Fricke, Dieter, 'Der Reichsverband gegen die Sozialdemokratie',
   Zeitschrift für Geschichtswissenschaft, Heft 7, 1959.
Galos, A., Gentzen, F.H., Jakobczyk, W., *Die Hakatisten. Der
   deutsche Ostmarkenverein 1894-1934,* (Berlin, 1966).
Gatzke, H.W., *Germany's Drive to the West. A Study in Germany's
   Western War Aims During the First World War,* (Baltimore, 1950).
———— 'Zu den deutsch-russischen Beziehungen im Sommer 1918'
   Vierteljahrshefte für Zeitgeschichte, Heft 3, 1955.
Geiss, I., *Der polnische Grenzstreifen 1914-1918,* (Lübeck and
   Hamburg, 1960).
Gerschenkron, H., *Bread and Democracy in Germany,* (Berkeley, 1943).
Giese, Hans-Joachim, *Die Film Wochenschau im Dienste der Politik,*
   (Dresden, 1940).
Gollwitzer, H., 'Der Cäsarismus Napoleons III in Widerhall der
   öffentlichen Meinung Deutschlands', *Historische Zeitschrift,*

Band 173, 1952.

Gratz, G., Schüller, R., *Die äussere Wirtschaftspolitik Oesterreich-Ungarns,* (Vienna, 1925).

Gutsche, W., 'Bethmann Hollweg und die Politik der 'Neuorientierung'. Zur innenpolitischen Strategie und Taktik der deutschen Reichsregierung während des Ersten Weltkrieges', *Zeitschrift für Geschichtswissenschaft,* Heft 17, 1965.

Hahlweg, W., *Lenins Rückkehr nach Russland. Die deutschen Akten,* (Leiden, 1957).

——————'Lenins reise durch Deutschland', *Vierteljahrshefte für Zeitgeschichte,* Heft 5, 1957.

——————*Der Diktatfrieden von Brest-Litovsk 1918 und die bolschewistische Weltrevolution,* (Münster, 1960).

Hallgarten, G.W.P., *Imperialismus vor 1914,* 2 Vols., (Munich, 1963).

Hamerow, T.S., *Restoration, Revolution, Reaction, Economics and Politics in Germany,* (Princeton, 1958).

Hannula, J.O., *Finland's War of Independence,* (London, 1939).

Hardach, K.W., *Die Bedeutung wirtschaftlicher Faktoren bei der Wiedereinführung der Eisen- und Getreidezölle in Deutschland,* (Berlin, 1967).

Heffter, H., 'Bismarcks Sozialpolitik', *Archiv für Sozialforschung,* 3, 1963.

Hegemann, M., 'Der deutsch-rumänische Friedensvertrag im Mai 1918 – ein Vorstoss der imperialistischen Reaktion gegen die junge Sowjetmacht', *Zeitschrift für Geschichtswissenschaft,* Heft 5, 1957.

Henning, Heinz, *Die Situation der deutschen Kriegswirtschaft im Sommer 1918 und ihre Beurteilung durch Heeresleitung, Reichsführung und Bevölkerung,* phil. Diss., (Hamburg, 1957).

Herzfeld, Hans, *Die deutsche Sozialdemokratie und die Auflösung der nationalen Einheitsfront im Weltkrieg,* (Leipzig, 1928).

——————*Der Erste Weltkrieg,* (Munich, 1968).

Hiden, J.W., 'The Baltic Germans and German Policy towards Latvia after 1918', *Historical Journal,* Vol. XIII, 1970, No. 2.

Hoffmann, W.G., 'The Take-off in Germany', in *The Economics of Take-off into Sustained Growth,* ed. W.W. Rostow, (London, 1963).

——————*Das Wachstum der deutschen Wirtschaft seit der Mitte des 19. Jahrhunderts,* (Heidelberg, 1965).

Horkheimer, Max, 'Die Juden und Europa', *Zeitschrift für Sozialforschung,* Jahrgang 8, 1939, Heft 1 und 2.

Horn, Allistair, *The Price of Glory, Verdun 1916,* (London, 1962).

Horneffer, Ernst, *Soldaten-Erziehung. Eine Ergänzung zum allgemeine Wehrpflicht,* (Munich, 1918).

Hubatsch, Walter, 'Grosses Hauptquartier 1914-1918. Zur Geschichte einer deutschen Führungseinrichtung', *Ostdeutsche Wissenschaft*, Band 5, Munich, 1959.

———'Finnland in der deutschen Ostseepolitik 1917/18', *Jahrbuch des ostdeutschen Kulturrats*, Munich 1955.

Jaeger, H., *Unternehmer in der deutschen Politik (1890-1914)*, (Bonn, 1967).

Janssen, K-H., *Der Kanzler und der General. Die Führungskrise um Bethmann Hollweg und Falkenhayn*, (Göttingen, 1966).

———'Der Wechsel in der OHL 1916', *Vierteljahreshefte für Zeitgeschichte*, Heft 7, 1959.

———*Macht und Verblendung, Kriegszielpolitik der Bundesstaaten 1914/1918*, (Göttingen, 1963).

Jutikkala, Eino, Pirinen, Kauka, *Geschichte Finnlands*, (Stuttgart, 1964)

Kaeble, H., *Industrielle Interessenpolitik in der wilhelminischen Gesellschaft*, (Berlin, 1967).

Kaehler, S.A., *Zur Beurteilung Ludendorffs im Sommer 1918*, Studien zur deutschen Geschichte des 19. und 20. Jahrhunderts, (Göttingen, 1961).

——— *Vier quellenkritische Untersuchungen zum Kriegsende 1918*, Nachrichten der Akademie der Wissenschaften, (Göttingen, 1960).

Kehr, Eckart, *Primat der Innenpolitik*, hrsg. von H.-U. Wehler, (Berlin, 1965).

——— *Schlachtflottenbau und Parteipolitik 1894-1901*, (Berlin, 1931).

Kennan, George F., *Soviet-American Relations 1917-1920. Russia Leaves the War*, (Princeton, 1956).

Kirimal, E., *Die nationale Kampf der Krimtürken mit besondere Berucksichtigung der Jahre 1917-1918*, (Emsdetten, 1952).

Kitchen, Martin, *The German Officer Corps 1890-1914*, (Oxford, 1968).

——— 'August Thalheimer's Theory of Fascism', *Journal of the History of Ideas*, 1972.

Klein, Fritz (Ed), *Politik im Krieg 1914-1918. Studien zur Politik der herrschenden Klassen im Ersten Weltkrieg*, (Berlin, 1964).

Knesebeck, L., *Die Wahrheit über den Propagandafeldzug und Deutschlands Zusammenbruch. Der Kampf um die Publizistik im Weltkriege*, (Munich, 1927).

Komarnicki, T., *The Rebirth of the Polish Republic. A Study in the Diplomatic History of Europe 1914-1920*, (London, 1957).

Koschnitzke, R., *Die Innenpolitik des Reichskanzlers Bethmann Hollweg in Weltkrieg*, Diss. phil. (Kiel, 1952).

Koszyk, K., *Pressepolitik im Ersten Weltkrieg*, (Düsseldorf, 1968).

Kruck, A., *Geschichte des Alldeutschen Verbandes 1890-1939*, (Wiesbaden, 1954).

Kuczynski, J., *Die Geschichte der Lage der Arbeiter unter dem Kapitalismus*, Band 4 (Berlin, 1967), Band 5 (Berlin, 1966).

——————— 'Die Barbarei', *Zeitschrift für Geschichtswissenschaft*, Heft 7, 1961.

Kühnl, R., *Die nationalsozialistische Linke*, (Meisenheim, 1966).

Leberke, Botho, *Die wirtschaftlichen Ursachen des amerikanischen Kriegsantritts 1917*, (Berlin, 1940).

Lenin, V.I., *Selected Works*, (Moscow, 1970).

Lewerenz, L., *Die deutsche Politik im Baltikum 1914-1918*, Diss. phil., (Hamburg, 1958).

Linde, Gerd, *Die deutsche Politik in Litauen im Ersten Weltkrieg*, (Wiesbaden, 1965).

Ludendorff, E., *Der Totale Krieg*, (Berlin, 1935).

——————— *Kriegführung und Politik*, (Berlin, 1922).

Lütge, L., 'Die Grundprinzipien der Bismarckschen Sozialpolitik', *Jahrbücher für Nationalökonomie und Statistik*, 134, 1931.

Manes, A., 'Arbeiterversicherung in Deutschland', *Handwörterbuch für Staatswissenschaften*, Band 1.

Mann, Bernhard, *Die baltischen Länder in der deutschen Kriegspublizistik 1914/18*, (Tübingen, 1965).

Marwick, Arthur, *The Deluge*, (New York, 1970).

Marx-Engels, *Werke*, (Berlin, 1957).

Massing, P.W., *Vorgeschichte des politischen Antisemitismus*, (Frankfurt, 1959).

May, E.R., *The World War and American Isolation 1914-17*, (Cambridge, Mass., 1959).

Meinecke, F., *Kühlmann und die päpstliche Friedensaktion von 1917*, (Berlin, 1928).

Meyer, H.C., *Mitteleuropa in German Thought and Action 1815-1945*, (The Hague, 1955).

Michaelis, W., 'Der Reichskanzler Michaelis und die päpstliche Friedensaktion 1917', *Geschichte in Wissenschaft und Unterricht*, Heft 7, 1956.

——————— 'Der Reichskanzler Michaelis und die päpstliche Friedensaktion 1917. Neue Dokumente', *Geschichte in Wissenschaft und Unterricht*, 12, 1961.

——————— 'Zum Problem des Königstodes am Ende der Hohehzollern-monarchie', *Geschichte in Wissenschaft und Unterricht,* 1962.

Michelson, Andreas, *Der U-Bootkrieg 1914-1918,* (Leipzig, 1925).

Mockelmann, Jürgen, *Das Deutschlandbild in den USA 1914 bis 1918 und die Kriegszielpolitik Wilsons,* phil. Diss. (Hamburg, 1964).

Moser, Otto von, *Die obersten Gewalten im Weltkrieg,* (Stuttgart, 1931).

Müffelmann, Leo, *Die Wirtschaftliche Verbände,* (Leipzig, 1912).

Mühlmann, C., *Oberste Heeresleitung und Balken im Weltkrieg 1914-1918,* (Berlin, 1942).

Niemann, A., *Kaiser und Heer. Das Wesen der Kommandogewalt und ihre Ausübung durch Kaiser Wilhelm II,* (Berlin, 1929).

——————— *Kaiser und Revolution. Die entscheidenden Ereignisse im Grossen Hauptquartier im Herbst 1918,* (Berlin, 1922).

Nitzsche, M., *Die handelspolitische Reaktion in Deutschland,* (Stuttgart, 1905).

Noske, G., *Von Kiel bis Kapp. Zur Geschichte der deutschen Revolution,* (Berlin, 1920).

Nussbaum, H., *Unternehmer gegen Monopole,* (Berlin, 1966).

Passelecq, F., *Déportations et travail forcé des ouvriers et de la population civile de la Belgique occupée,* (Paris, New Haven, 1928).

Patemann, R., *Der Kampf um die preussische Wahlrechtsreform im Ersten Weltkrieg,* (Düsseldorf, 1964).

Petzold, J., 'Ludendorff oder Kühlmann? Die Meinungsvershiedenheiten zwischen OHL und Reichsregierung zur Zeit der Friedensverhandlungen in Brest-Litovsk', *Zeitschrift für Geschichtswissenschaft,* Heft 12, 1964.

———————'Die Entscheidung von 29 September 1918', *Zeitschrift für Militärgeschichte,* 1965.

Pirenne, H., *La Belgique et la guerre mondiale,* (Paris, 1928).

Pohle, H.-J., *Agrarische Interessenpolitik und preussischer Konservatismus im wilhelminischen Reich,* (Hanover, 1966).

Pomiankowski, J., *Der Zusammenbruch des ottomanischen Reiches. Erinnerungen an die Turkei aus der Zeit des Weltkrieges,* (Zurich, 1968).

Räikkonen, Erkki, *Svinhufvud baut Finnland,* (Munich, 1936).

Reichsarchiv, *Der Weltkrieg 1914-1918,* (Berlin, 1929).

Rein, A., *Die Revolution in der Politik Bismarcks,* (Göttingen, 1957).

Reshetar, J.S., *The Ukrainian Revolution, 1917-1920,* (Princeton, 1952).

Ritter, Gerhard, *Staatskunst und Kriegshandwerk,* Band 3 (Munich, 1964), Band 4 (Munich, 1968).

Röhl, J.C.G., *Germany without Bismarck,* (London, 1967).

——————— 'Staatsstreich oder Staatsstreichbereitschaft?',
Historische Zeitschrift, Band 209, 1969.

Roth, Paul, *Die Entstehung des polnischen Staates,* (Berlin, 1926).

Rosenberg, Hans, *Grosse Depression der Bismarckzeit,* (Berlin, 1967).
——————— *Probleme der deutschen Sozialgeschichte,* (Frankfurt, 1969).

Rosenfeld, Günter, *Sowjetrussland und Deutschland 1917-1922,*
(Berlin, 1960).

Rothfels, Hans, 'Bismarck's Social Policy and the Problems of State
Socialism in Germany', *Sociological Review,* 30, 1938.

Sauer, Wolfgang, 'Das Problem des deutschen Nationalstaates',
Politische Vierteljahrsschrift, Band 3, 1962.

Saul, K., 'Der Deutsche Kriegerbund. Zur innenpolitischen Funktion
eines nationalen Verbandes im kaiserlichen Deutschland',
Militärgeschichtliche Mitteilungen, Heft 2, 1969.

Saul, S.B., *The Myth of the Great Depression 1873-1896,* (London, 1969).

Scharlau, W.B., Zeman, Z.A., *Freibeuter der Revolution. Parvus
Helphand,* (Cologne, 1964).

Schellenberg, Johanna, 'Die Herausbildung der Militärdiktatur in den
ersten Jahren des Krieges', in *Politik in Krieg 1914-1918,*
(Berlin, 1964).

Schöne, Siegfried, *Von der Reichskanzlei zum Bundeskanzleramt,*
(Berlin, 1968).

Schmidt-Reichberg, W., Matuschka, E. Graf von, *Handbuch der
deutschen Militärgeschichte,* Band 3, (Frankfurt, 1967).

Schröter, A., *Krieg-Staat-Monopol 1914-1918. Die Zusammenhänge
von imperialistischer Kriegswirtschaft Militarisierung der Volks-
wirtschaft und Staatsmonopolistischem Kapitalismus in
Deutschland während des Ersten Weltkrieges,* (Berlin, 1965).

Schweke, Hans-Jürgen, *U-Bootkrieg und Friedenspolitik,* phil. Diss.,
(Heidelberg, 1952).

Schybergson, M.G., *Politische Geschichte Finnlands 1809-1919,*
(Gotha, Stuttgart, 1925).

Sichler, R., Tiburtius, J., *Die Arbeiterfrage, eine Kernfrage des
Weltkrieges,* (Berlin, 1925).

Skalweit, A., *Die deutsche Kriegsernährungswirtschaft,* (Berlin, 1927).

Smith, C.Jay, *Finland and the Russian Revolution 1917-1922,*
(Athens, Georgia, 1958).

Spindler, A., *Wie es zu dem Entschluss zum uneingeschränkten U-Boot-
Krieg 1917 gekommen ist,* (Göttingen, 1961).

Steglich, W., *Die Friedenspolitik der Mittelmächte 1917/18.*
Band 1, (Wiesbaden, 1964).

Stegmann, Dirk, *Die Erben Bismarcks,* (Cologne, 1970).

Stern, Fritz, *Bethmann Hollweg und der Krieg. Die Grenzen der Verantwortung,* (Tübingen, 1968).

Stupperich, Robert, 'Siedlungspläne im Gebiet des Oberbefehlshabers Ost', *Jomsburg* 5, 1941.

Thieme, H., *Nationalliberalismus in der Krise. Die nationalliberalen Fraktion des preussischen Abgeordnetenhauses 1914/1918,* (Boppard, 1963).

Thimme, Annelise, *Flucht in den Mythos. Die Deutschnationale Volkspartei und die Niederlage von 1918,* (Göttingen, 1969).

Tuchmann, B.W., *The Zimmermann Telegram,* (London, 1959).

Umbreit, P., *Die deutschen Gewerkschaften im Kriege,* (Stuttgart, 1928).

——————— 'Gemeinsame Arbeit der Behörden und der Gewerkschaften', *Sozialistische Monatshefte,* 26, 1916.

Varain, H.J., *Freie Gewerkschaften, Sozialdemokratie und Staat. Die Politik der Generalkommission unter der Führung Carl Legiens (1890-1928),* (Düsseldorf, 1958).

Vogel, W., *Bismarcks Arbeiterversicherung,* (Braunschweig, 1951).

Volkmann, E.O., *Der Marxismus und das deutsche Heer im Weltkrieg,* (Berlin, 1925).

Waschnek, E., *Weltkrieg und Propaganda,* (Berlin, 1936).

Weber, H., *Ludendorff und die Monopole,* (Berlin, 1966).

Wehler, H.-U., *Bismarck und der Imperialismus,* (Cologne, 1969).

Wendt, Hermann, *Verdun 1916. Die angriffe Falkenhayns im Maasgebiet mit Richtung auf Verdun,* (Berlin, 1936).

Wertheimer, M.S., *The Pan-German League 1890-1914,* (New York, 1924).

Westarp, Kuno Graf von, *Das Ende der Monarchie am 9 November 1918,* (Berlin, 1952).

Wheeler-Bennett, J., *Hindenburg, the Wooden Titan,* (London, 1936).

——————— *Brest-Litovsk, the Forgotten Peace, March 1918,* (London, 1938).

Winkler, Erwin, *Die Bewegung der Berliner Revolutionären Obleute in Ersten Weltkrieg,* phil. Diss., (Berlin, 1964).

Zechlin, E., *Die deutsche Politik und die Juden im Ersten Weltkrieg* (Göttingen, 1968).

——————— *Staatsstreichpläne Bismarcks und Wilhelms II 1890-1894,* (Stuttgart, 1929).

Zeman, Z.A., *The Break-up of the Habsburg Empire. A Study in National and Social Revolution,* (London, 1961).

Zorn, W., 'Wirtschafts- und sozialgeschichtliche Zusammenhänge der deutschen Reichsgründungszeit 1850-1879', *Historische Zeitschrift*, Band 197, 1963.

Zwehl, H. von, *Erich von Falkenhayn General der Infanterie. Eine biographische Studie*, (Dresden, 1926).

INDEX